Student Workbook

# Exploring Economics

## THIRD EDITION

**Robert L. Sexton**

Pepperdine University

Prepared by

**Stephen L. Jackstadt**

University of Alaska, Anchorage

**Lee Huskey**

University of Alaska, Anchorage

THOMSON

SOUTH-WESTERN

Australia · Canada · Mexico · Singapore · Spain · United Kingdom · United States

**THOMSON**

**SOUTH-WESTERN**

**Student Workbook to accompany Exploring Macroeconomics, 3e**

Robert L. Sexton

**VP/Editorial Director:**
Jack W. Calhoun

**VP/Editor-in-Chief:**
Michael P. Roche

**Publisher of Economics:**
Michael B. Mercier

**Acquisitions Editor:**
Michael Worls

**Developmental Editor:**
Andrew McGuire

**Executive Marketing Manager:**
Lisa Lysne

**Senior Production Editor:**
Kara ZumBahlen

**Media Developmental Editor:**
Peggy Buskey

**Media Production Editor:**
Pam Wallace

**Manufacturing Coordinator:**
Sandee Milewski

**Printer:**
Darby Printing Company

**Senior Design Project Manager:**
Michelle Kunkler

For permission to use material from this
text or product, contact us by
Tel (800) 730-2214
Fax (800) 730-2215
http://www.thomsonrights.com

For more information
contact South-Western,
5191 Natorp Boulevard,
Mason, Ohio 45040.
Or you can visit our Internet site at:
http://www.swlearning.com

# Table of Contents

# CHAPTER 1
# THE ROLE AND METHOD OF ECONOMICS

## SECTION 1.1
## ECONOMICS: A BRIEF INTRODUCTION

### KEY POINTS

- Economics is a unique way of analyzing human behavior over a broad range of topics.

- **Economics** is the study of the allocation of limited resources to satisfy our unlimited wants.

- **Resources** are inputs that are used to produce goods and services.

- Our wants exceed what our resources can produce. This is what we call **scarcity.** Scarcity forces us to make choices on how to best use our limited resources.

- **The economic problem:** Scarcity forces us to choose and choices are costly because we must give up other opportunities that we value. This economizing problem is evident in every aspect of our lives.

- Economics concerns anything that is considered worthwhile to some human being. Virtually everything we decide to do, then, has an economic dimension.

- Living in a world of scarcity means facing trade-offs. It is important that we know what these trade-offs are so we can make better choices about the options available to us.

# Chapter 1: The Role and Method of Economics

## I     REVIEW

A student of economics learns that much of life involves making a __Choice__ between conflicting wants in a world of scarcity. Students develop an economic way of __thinking__ about their options, which is a valuable problem-solving tool.

_____ is defined as the study of the allocation of our __limited__ resources to satisfy our unlimited wants.

The factors like machinery, labor, water, and land that are used to make goods and services are called __resources__.

The problem of __scarcity__ results because our wants are greater than the goods and services our resources can produce.

We are forced to make __choices__ about the best use of our limited resources. The cost of choosing to use a resource one way is the lost __opportunity__ to use the resource in another way.

Making costly choices about the use of scarce resources is known as the __economic__ problem.

## II     TRUE/FALSE

_____1. The Mayor's Crime Commission has recommended increased spending on midnight basketball programs, which are intended to reduce the city's crime rate. The Crime Commission is making choices with regard to scarce resources.

_____2. Economic resources are only those things produced by nature.

_____3. We have to make choices about the use of resources because they are scarce.

_____4. Since a steel company owns its trucks, there is no cost involved when they are used to ship steel.

_____5. Economics is only useful for analyzing decisions about goods and services that are bought and sold in stores.

_____6. When you stay up late to watch the *David Letterman Show*, you have made an economic decision.

## III     MULTIPLE CHOICE

1. Which of the following is not an example of a resource?
   A) rubber trees
   B) paint sprayers
   C) toys
   D) hammers

2. What are the two parts of the economic problem?
   A) Economics explains many things, but some things it doesn't.
   B) Natural resources are scarce, but man-made resources aren't.
   C) Scarcity makes us choose, and choices are costly.
   D) We have unlimited wants and unlimited resources.

3. Which answer best describes why the choice of how much time to sleep is an economic problem?
   A) The amount of time you sleep determines the type of bed you buy and buying a bed is an economic decision.
   B) Time is a scarce resource and an hour of sleep costs since you have to give up other uses of time.
   C) If you sleep in a hotel, you must pay for the room.
   D) Sleep helps you become a more productive worker.

4. Which of the following does not involve a trade-off?
   A) deciding what to do on a Friday night
   B) choosing the best way to get to your best friend's house
   C) depositing your paycheck in the bank
   D) winning the lottery after you have purchased your ticket

## IV    APPLICATION AND DISCUSSION

1. In most countries the birth rate has fallen as incomes and the economic opportunities for women have increased. Use economics to explain this pattern.

2. Explain why each of the following is an economic problem.
   A) going on a date
   B) a basketball coach awards one of 10 available scholarships to a point guard
   C) the university's admission policy

3. Write your own definition of economics. What are the main elements of the definition?

# SECTION 1.2
# ECONOMICS AS A SCIENCE

## KEY POINTS

- Economics, like the other social sciences, is concerned with reaching generalizations about human behavior. It is the social science that studies the choices people make in a world of limited resources.

- Conventionally, we distinguish between two main branches of economics: macroeconomics and microeconomics.

- **Macroeconomics** is the study of the aggregate, or total, economy. It looks at economic problems as they influence the whole of society, including the topics of inflation, unemployment, business cycles, and economic growth.

- **Microeconomics** deals with the smaller units within the economy, attempting to understand the decision-making behavior of firms and households and their interaction in markets for particular goods or services.

# Chapter 1: The Role and Method of Economics

## I      REVIEW

Like other social sciences, the central concern of economics is _____ _____. It is the social science that studies people's _____.

Of the two main branches of economics, _____ examines the effects of human behavior on the total economy, while _____ deals with human behavior in smaller units like the household or the firm. Economic problems affecting the whole of society such as inflation and unemployment are topics of _____. Microeconomics examines the choice making behavior of firms and households and their interaction in _____.

## II      TRUE/FALSE

_____ 1. The various social sciences—psychology, sociology, anthropology, political science, and economics—examine special questions and very rarely overlap or complement each other.

_____ 2. When economists study the economics of the avocado industry they are doing microeconomics.

_____ 3. Since the two branches of economics, microeconomics and macroeconomics, deal with different levels of aggregation, they have nothing in common.

_____ 4. An economist forecasting the change in the general price level is doing microeconomics.

## III      MULTIPLE CHOICE

1.  Which of the following is not a social science?
    A)  Psychology
    B)  Sociology
    C)  Economics
    D)  Biology

2.  Which of the following is the best example of a microeconomics study?
    A)  a study of the determinants of the business cycle
    B)  a study of the relation between the price level and unemployment
    C)  a study of the factors that can lower a firm's production costs
    D)  a study of the factors that determine the rate of inflation

3.  Which of the following is *not* an example of the use of the problem solving perspective provided by economics?
    A)  An investor looks at the tax consequences of selling stocks to buy bonds, which he believes offer a better return.
    B)  A rancher recognizes that raising more cattle this year will damage his pasture and limit next year's herd size.
    C)  The Archer family takes its vacation at Lake Arrowhead this year because they have done this for as long as anyone can remember.
    D)  An economic student thinks about the other subjects that she should be studying before she decides to study economics tonight.

4. Economist Kenneth Boulding said that knowledge is always gained by the systematic loss of information and the elimination of the "great buzzing confusion of information" that the world provides. What did he mean?
   A) Economists can't understand how things work by concentrating on the particulars so we must generalize about human behavior.
   B) Economics can't do everything so it must only concentrate on certain aspects of society, like making money.
   C) Economics can't begin to explain the complex world so economists must concentrate on creating theories and not worry about the real world.
   D) Since there are so many countries in the world, economists must concentrate only on the particular country they know about, like the United States.

5. Which of the following is not a true statement?
   A) The study of unemployment is a topic of macroeconomics.
   B) The study of the effects of unemployment on the demand for fig bars is a topic of microeconomics.
   C) The study of health consequences of unemployment is a topic of social science.
   D) The study of a community's support of the unemployed is a topic of social science.

## IV    APPLICATION AND DISCUSSION

1. Identify which of the following headlines represents a microeconomic topic and which represents a macroeconomic topic.

| Topic | Microeconomics | Macroeconomics |
|---|---|---|
| A. "U.S. Unemployment Rate Reaches Historic Lows" | | |
| B. "General Motors Closes Auto Plant in St. Louis" | | |
| C. "OPEC Action Result in a General Increase in Prices" | | |
| D. "Companies Cut the Cost of Health Care for Employees" | | |
| E. "Lawmakers Worry about the Possibility of a US Recession" | | |
| F. "Colorado Rockies Make Outfielder Highest Paid Ballplayer" | | |

# SECTION 1.3
# ECONOMIC BEHAVIOR

## KEY POINTS

- Economists assume that individuals act as if they are motivated by self-interest and respond in predictable ways to changing circumstances.

- Most economists believe that it is rational for people to try and anticipate the possible consequences of their behavior before making a decision.

- Actions have consequences. Even inaction, which is a choice not to do something or not to make changes, has consequences.

## I    REVIEW

Economists assume that people act _____ _____ they were motivated by self-interest. Since people are also assumed to respond to changes in _predictable_ ways, self-interest is a good predictor of behavior.

Self-interest _motivates_ people to produce more and may also encourage _____. Pursuing self-interest is not the same as being _____.

Choices will have both positive and negative _consequences_. Economists believe that it is rational for people to _consider_ consequences of their actions before they make a decision.

## II    TRUE/FALSE

_____1. Economists believe that people who commit crimes are not considering the consequences.

_____2. Economists assume that we are motivated primarily by our concern for others.

_____3. Economists assume that a person who has decided to take up smoking after the reading the warning label is wrong.

_____4. Economists believe that not much of human behavior can be predicted by assuming that people pursue their own self-interest.

_____5. Economics cannot explain the actions of people who donate their time and money to helping others.

_____6. Friends describe Chandler as "clueless." Even Chandler recognizes that he always seems to do things without the slightest thought about the consequences. Economists would consider Chandler's behavior irrational.

## III    MULTIPLE CHOICE

1.  Which one of the following scientists observes how people will respond in predictable ways to changing incentives, especially changes in price and costs?
    A)  psychiatrist
    B)  journalist
    C)  biologist
    D)  economist

2.  Which of the following is not consistent with economists' assumption that individuals generally consider the consequences of their actions?
    A)  Robert, the father of two, smokes but takes out extra life insurance.
    B)  Marlene, a middle-aged accountant, saves regularly each month toward her retirement.
    C)  Mr. Haviland invites Tony and his bull, "Tornado" into his china shop.
    D)  Claudia decides to forego studying and settle for a "D" on her physics exam in order to see the Dave Matthews Band in concert the night before her midterm.

3.  Most economists assume that peoples' actions are
    A)  motivated by submerged emotional needs.
    B)  driven by magnetic forces generated by planetary movements.
    C)  undertaken in an attempt to improve the well-being of others.
    D)  motivated by self-interest.

4.  Suppose the general manager of the Kansas City Chiefs football team has negotiated a new contract with star quarterback, Bobby Thompson. The contract pays Bobby a bonus of $1,000 for every pass he completes during the season. Which of the following is most likely to describe Bobby's actions?
    A)  Bobby trains less in the off-season since he already has a contract.
    B)  Bobby will take risks during the season, throwing long passes that are less likely to be caught but more likely to result in touchdowns.
    C)  Bobby will run the ball more than last year.
    D)  Bobby will throw mostly short passes, which are most likely to be caught but less likely to result in touchdowns.

## IV    APPLICATION AND DISCUSSION

1.  Psychologist Kenneth Lux says that economists are wrong in assuming that people are motivated primarily by self-interest. Furthermore, he laments economists' success at selling this view of human behavior to politicians, business leaders, journalists, and people in general, since he believes that self-interest leads to social strife, pollution, and other ills. Lux says that the pursuit of self-interest encourages cheating. According to Lux, "from the standpoint of self-interest it would be irrational for someone not to cheat if they could be reasonably sure of getting away with it." (Kenneth Lux, *Adam Smith's Mistake*, Shambala Publications, 1990, p. 83.)

    What do you think? Are economists wrong to assume that self-interest is the motivation behind economic behavior? Do people other than economists agree with this view? Does self-interest lead to cheating?

# SECTION 1.4
# ECONOMIC THEORY

## KEY POINTS

- A **theory** is an established explanation that accounts for known facts or phenomena. Economic theories are statements or propositions about patterns of human behavior that are expected to take place under certain circumstances.

- Economic theories help us to sort out and understand the complexities of economic behavior. We expect a good theory to explain and predict well. A good economic theory, then, should help explain and predict human economic behavior.

- Economic theories must abstract from many of the particular details of situations to better focus on the behavior to be explained (like a road map). An economic theory provides a broad view, not a detailed examination, of human economic behavior.

- The beginning of any theory is a **hypothesis,** a testable proposition that makes some type of prediction about behavior in response to certain changed conditions. A hypothesis in economic theory is a testable prediction about how people will behave or react to a change in economic circumstances.

- **Empirical analysis**, the use of data to test hypotheses, is applied to determine whether or not a hypothesis fits well with the facts.

- Determining whether an economic hypothesis is acceptable is more difficult than is the case in the natural or physical sciences. The laboratory of economists is usually the real world, and economists cannot control all the variables that might influence human behavior.

- If an economic hypothesis is supported by the data, it can then be tentatively accepted as an economic theory.

## I    REVIEW

A _____ is an explanation that is supported by the facts of the real world. Economic theories are propositions used to _____ and _____ human behavior in different circumstances.

Economic theories cannot account for every event; to be useful theories must _____ or focus on only the essential factors.

A _____ is a prediction about how people will behave in certain economic circumstances and can be tested to see how well the prediction fits the _____.

Economists engage in _____ analysis to test hypotheses by seeing if they are consistent with the real world observations.

## II    TRUE/FALSE

_____1. We expect a good theory will describe everything about a particular economic behavior.

_____2. The statement "incentives matter" is an example of an economic theory.

_____3. A good hypothesis is "Living on Mars would increase the amount of coffee people drink."

_____4. A hypothesis is not the same as a theory.

_____5. Lee McKenzie has an idea that the natural tendency for stock prices is to rise. He promotes this hypothesis as "the Helium Market Strategy to Riches." As a hypothesis, this strategy offers a good way to make money in the stock market.

## III    MULTIPLE CHOICE

1.  What is the difference between a hypothesis and a theory?
    A)  A hypothesis is the prediction made using a theory.
    B)  A hypothesis has not been tested, but empirical analysis has shown that a theory is supported by the facts.
    C)  A hypothesis makes a prediction about human behavior but a theory does not makes a prediction.
    D)  A hypothesis abstracts from reality while a theory describes reality.

2.  In her new book "Women Play the Infield but Men are from Leftfield," Marion Knott presents the proposition that women and men react in different but predictable ways in sports and recreation. How can we decide whether her proposition is a good theory?
    A)  The theory is a good one if Marion sells a lot of books.
    B)  The theory is a good one if many scientists agree with the proposition.
    C)  The theory is a good one if it explains and predicts well human behavior.
    D)  The theory is a good one since the publisher agreed to print it.

3.  William Hanks owns country music station, KQED, in Boise. He would like to predict how changes in the community and in his radio format would affect KQED's share of the Boise radio market. Which of the following do you think is important for a theory that would help Hanks predict his share of the radio audience?
    A)  The theory includes a log of every song the station has played for the last ten years.
    B)  The theory describes the number and type of cars and car radios everyone in Boise owns.
    C)  The theory includes predictions by the fortuneteller, Madam Ouzinke.
    D)  The theory isolates only the most important factors Hanks thinks affect his audience share.

4.  An economist has been asked to explain why coffee bean production has declined in Brazil during the 1990s. Which of the following would not be an important step in the development of a theory of coffee bean production?
    A)  Develop a hypothesis, such as producers reduce coffee production when the price falls.
    B)  Do empirical analysis and see whether coffee production has fallen when prices have fallen in the past.
    C)  Go "back to the drawing board" and develop a new hypothesis if this one does not fit the facts.
    D)  Drink only three cups of coffee a day when he conducts the study.

## IV    APPLICATION AND DISCUSSION

1.  In the United States, the average woman's annual earnings is less than 75 percent of the average man's earnings. Develop a hypothesis that would help to explain this fact.

2.  The Environmental Protection Agency asks you to help them understand the causes of urban pollution. Air pollution problems are worse the higher the Air Quality Index. You develop the following two hypotheses.

    Hypothesis I: Air pollution will be a greater problem the higher the average temperature in the urban area.

Hypothesis II: Air pollution will be a greater problem, the greater the population of the urban area.

Test each hypothesis with the facts given below. Which hypothesis fits the facts better? Have you developed a theory?

| Metropolitan Statistical Area | Days with Polluted Air* | Average Maximum Temperature | Population (thousands) |
|---|---|---|---|
| Cincinnati, OH | 30 | 64 | 1,979 |
| El Paso, TX | 13 | 77.1 | 680 |
| Milwaukee, WI | 12 | 55.9 | 1,690 |
| Atlanta, GA | 24 | 72.0 | 4,112 |
| Philadelphia, PA | 33 | 63.2 | 5,101 |
| Albany, NY | 8 | 57.6 | 876 |
| San Diego, CA | 20 | 70.8 | 2,814 |
| Los Angeles, CA | 80 | 70.6 | 9,519 |

*Air Quality Index greater than 100 (2002)

**Source:** U.S. Dept. of Commerce, Bureau of Census, 2002 Statistical Abstract of the United States, Tables Nos. 30, and 363; U.S. EPA, Airtrends Report, 2002, EPA.Gov/airtrends/Factbook.

# SECTION 1.5
# PROBLEMS TO AVOID IN SCIENTIFIC THINKING

## KEY POINTS

- Virtually all theories in economics are expressed using a *ceteris paribus* ("let everything else be equal" or "holding everything else constant") assumption. In trying to assess the effect of one variable on another, we must isolate their relationship from other events that might also influence the situation that the theory is trying to explain or predict.

- Without a theory of causation, no scientist could sort out and understand the enormous complexity that occurs in the real world. But one must always be careful not to confuse **correlation** with **causation**. The fact that two sets of phenomena are related does not necessarily mean that one caused the other to occur.

- One must be careful with problems associated with aggregation, particularly the **fallacy of composition.** That is, even if something is true for an individual, it is not necessarily true for many individuals as a group.

## I      REVIEW

The Latin expression for "let everything else be equal" is _____ _____.

Without a theory of _____, scientists cannot understand the complexity that occurs in the real world.

In seeking to find causes for events, people sometimes mistake _____ for causation.

If someone observes that new car sales and auto accidents rise at the same time and concludes that new car sales cause auto accidents, they are mistaking _____ for causation.

When someone assumes that what is true of an individual is also true of a group, they are committing the fallacy of

_____.

## II    TRUE/FALSE

_____1. The Latin term *ceteris paribus* means "the bus stops here."

_____2. Scientists studying the relationship between two variables try to hold other variables constant.

_____3. If two phenomena occur together one must be the cause of the other.

_____4. The fallacy of composition is committed when someone believes that what is true for an individual is also true of the individuals in a group.

## III    MULTIPLE CHOICE

1.  A scientist trying to test a theory about the relationship between peoples' consumption of alcohol and their longevity would want to hold all of the following variables constant except
    A)  the number of cigarettes that people in the experimental group smoke.
    B)  the amount of alcohol that people in the experimental group consume.
    C)  past histories of heart and lung disease among people in the experimental group.
    D)  the amount of animal fat that people in the experimental group consume each day.

2.  Five-year-old Dimitri observes that people who play basketball are taller than normal and tells his mom that he's going to play basketball because it will make him tall. Dimitri is
    A)  committing the fallacy of composition.
    B)  violating the *ceteris paribus* assumption.
    C)  mistaking correlation for causation.
    D)  confusing the direction of causation.

3.  Many people have heard that the stock market rises when a team from the National Football Conference (NFC) wins the Super Bowl and falls when a team from the American Football Conference (AFC) is victorious. If Veronica concludes that there is a causal relationship between which team wins the Super Bowl and the direction of stock prices, she is probably
    A)  confusing correlation with causation.
    B)  violating the *ceteris paribus* assumption.
    C)  committing the fallacy of composition.
    D)  confusing the direction of causality, since everyone knows that stock market prices determine which team wins the Super Bowl.

4. "When one major league baseball team spends more money acquiring better players it is better off, but if all other teams do the same thing in order to compete, none of them is better off." This statement demonstrates
   A) the confusion of association with causation.
   B) the *ceteris paribus* assumption.
   C) the problem associated with the misspecification of the direction of causality.
   D) the fallacy of composition.

## IV    APPLICATION AND DISCUSSION

1. In the 1940s, Dr. Melvin Page, a Florida dentist and head of the Biochemical Research Foundation, conducted a national campaign to stop people other than infants from drinking milk. According to Page, milk was a dangerous food and a leading cause of cancer. He pointed to the fact that more people died of cancer in Wisconsin, the nation's leading milk producer, than any other state as proof of his claim. (Cited in Martin Gardner, *Fads & Fallacies in the Name of Science*, Dover Publications, 1957, pp. 222–223.)

   From what you know about scientific thinking, the importance of *ceteris paribus,* and the danger of mistaking association for causation, how would you evaluate Dr. Page's claim?

# SECTION 1.6
# POSITIVE AND NORMATIVE ANALYSIS

## KEY POINTS

- In the role of scientist, an economist tries to objectively observe patterns of behavior without reference to the appropriateness or inappropriateness of that behavior. This objective, value-free approach utilizing the scientific method is called **positive analysis.**

- In positive analysis, we want to know the impact of Variable A on Variable B. A positive statement does not have to be a true statement, but it does have to be a testable statement.

- A good economist/scientist strives to be as fair and objective as possible in evaluating evidence and in stating conclusions based on the evidence.

- Opinions expressed about the desirability of various actions are called **normative analysis.** Normative statements, such as incomes should be more equally distributed, involve judgments about what should be or what ought to happen. Normative statements are subjective, non-testable statements.

- It is important to distinguish between positive and normative analysis because many controversies in economics revolve around policy considerations that contain both.

- Disagreement is common in most disciplines. The majority of disagreements in economics stem from normative issues as differences in values or policy beliefs result in conflict.

- Economists may disagree as to the validity of a given economic theory for the policy in question because the empirical evidence appears somewhat conflicting.

- Most economists agree on a wide range of issues, including the effects of rent control, import tariffs, export restrictions, the use of wage and price controls to curb inflation, and the minimum wage. Often, economists argue that if market forces are allowed to work freely, economic analysis can predict certain phenomena with a high degree of success.

## I      REVIEW

When economists study human behavior, they emphasize how people behave, not how they should behave. This objective approach is called _____ analysis.

When economists comment on the desirability of particular actions they are making _____ statements. Normative statements involve judgements about what _____ ought _____ to happen.

It is especially important to be able to _____ distinguish _____ between normative and positive analysis when policy considerations contain both. The majority of _____ disagreements _____ among economists involve normative issues.

A second important reason economists disagree is disagreement on the _____ validity _____ of the economic _____ theories _____ in a particular policy application.

## II      TRUE/FALSE

_____1. The following statement is a normative statement: If the tax on cigarettes is increased, people will smoke fewer cigarettes.

_____2. When economists make normative statements they are stating their opinions.

_____3. Since economics is a science, economists never disagree.

_____4. We would expect more agreement among economists with the statement, "Raising the fine the library charges for overdue books will reduce the number of overdue books" than we would expect to find with the statement, "We don't want to discourage the use of the library with fines on overdue books because people ought to read more."

_____5. If an economics professor presents her opinions about policy issues in class, she is still teaching economics.

## III    MULTIPLE CHOICE

1.  In the recent congressional debate about agricultural price supports, senators, congress women and men, and experts made the following four statements. Which of these statements is a normative statement?
    A)  Price supports are important because America should preserve the small family farm.
    B)  Without price supports the price of wheat and corn will fall by over twenty percent.
    C)  The decline in commodity prices caused by the removal of price supports will result in fewer, larger farms.
    D)  The decline in commodity prices caused by the removal of price supports will reduce the number of tractors sold in the United States.

2.  Your mother tells you, "Watching ten hours of TV a day will make you stupid." Why is this a positive statement?
    A)  She says it with a positive tone in her voice.
    B)  It is a proposition that can be tested.
    C)  She really means that she doesn't think you should watch so much TV.
    D)  Your father agrees with her.

3.  Economists sometimes run for public office. Why is it important to be able to distinguish their positive from their normative statements about economic policy?
    A)  Economists are always making assumptions and policy should not be based on assumptions.
    B)  We really don't have to worry, since trained economists never make normative statements.
    C)  Their positive statements will help us predict the consequences of a particular policy while their normative statements will only tell us their opinions.
    D)  Their positive statements help us understand the good results of a policy change and their normative statements help us understand the negative results.

4.  Which of the following is *not* a reason the textbook gives for disagreement among economists over policy issues?
    A)  differences in values, opinions, and beliefs among economists
    B)  some economists value freedom while others value fairness
    C)  conflicting empirical evidence supporting various theories
    D)  economists, like most people, just like to argue with their friends

## IV    APPLICATION AND DISCUSSION

1.  In the debate about clean air standards we have often heard the statement, "A nation as rich as the United States should have no pollution." Why is this a normative statement? Would it help you make a decision on the national air quality standards? Describe two positive statements that might be useful in determining the air quality standards.

Questions

1.  Mr. Lowell has a theory. What is it?
2.  What information do you think Mr. Lowell used to develop his theory?

# CHAPTER 2
# THE ECONOMIC WAY OF THINKING

# SECTION 2.1
# IDEA 1: SCARCITY

## KEY POINTS

- Most of economics is knowing certain principles well and when and how to apply them.

- Economics is primarily concerned with **scarcity**—how well we satisfy our unlimited wants in a world of limited resources. People are not able to fulfill all of their wants—material desires and nonmaterial desires. As long as human wants exceed available resources, scarcity will exist.

- The scarce resources that are used in the production of goods and services can be grouped into four categories: **labor, land, capital,** and **entrepreneurship**.

- **Labor** is the total of both physical and mental effort expended by people in the production of goods and services.

- **Land** is the natural resources used in the production of goods and services.

- **Capital** are goods that are used to produce other goods. It also includes **human capital**, the productive knowledge and skill people receive from education and on-the-job training.

- **Entrepreneurship** is the process of combining the labor, land, and capital together to produce goods and services. The entrepreneur is the one who makes the tough and risky decisions about what to produce and how to produce it. Entrepreneurs are always looking for new ways to improve production techniques or to create new products. They are lured by the chance to make a profit.

- We are all entrepreneurs when we try new products or when we find better ways to manage our households or our study time.

- **Goods** are those items that we value or desire. They can be **tangible goods**, which are physical, or **intangible goods**, which are not. **Services** are the intangible acts for which people are willing to pay.

- All goods and services, whether they are tangible or intangible, are produced from scarce resources and can be subjected to economic analysis.

- The scarce goods that are created from scarce resources are called **economic goods.** If there are not enough economic goods for all of us, we will have to compete for those scarce goods. That is, scarcity ultimately leads to competition for the available goods and services.

- We all want more tangible and intangible goods and services. In economics, we assume that more goods lead to greater satisfaction, or utility.

- However, because we assume that people want more goods, it does not mean that economics also presumes that people are selfish and greedy. People are willing to give up their money and time for what they believe to be important causes, revealing that charitable endeavors are desirable goods. Many desires, like building new friendships or helping charities, can hardly be defined as selfish, yet these are desires that many people share. "Self-interest" is not the same as "selfishness" or "greed."

- We all face scarcity because we cannot have all of the goods and services that we desire. However, because we all have different wants and desires, scarcity affects everyone differently.

- Even the richest person must live with scarcity and must, at some point, choose one want or desire over another. As we get more affluent, we learn of new luxuries to provide us with satisfaction. Wealth creates a new set of wants to be satisfied.

- There is no evidence that people would not find a valuable use for additional income, no matter how rich they become. Even the wealthy individual who decides to donate all of her money to charity faces the constraints of scarcity. If she had greater resources, she could do still more for others.

- Scarcity never has and never will be eradicated. The same creativity that permits new methods to produce goods and services in greater quantities also reveals new wants. It is very possible that our wants grow as fast, if not faster, than our ability to meet those wants, so we still feel scarcity as much or more than we did before.

## I     REVIEW

_____ is the problem that exists because we have limited resources and unlimited wants for goods and services.

The physical and mental labor expended by people in the production of goods and services is called
_____.

Natural resources like trees, water, and minerals that are used in production are classified as _____ resources.

Resources like tools, office buildings, and factories are called _____ goods, while people who make the risky decisions about what goods to produce and how to produce them are called _____.

Items that we value or desire are called _____, while tangible acts for which people are willing to pay are called _____.

Because no one can have all the goods and services they _____, everyone, even the very rich, faces the common problem of scarcity.

Over time resources available to individuals and societies may increase but scarcity will not be eliminated because wants also _____ *increase* _____.

## II    TRUE/FALSE

_____1. The per capita U.S. standard of living has more than tripled since the end of the Great Depression of the 1930s. This represents a dramatic increase in the resources available to the U.S. economy and implies that scarcity is no longer a problem in the United States.

_____2. While scarcity is a problem for the average college student, it is not a problem for a rich person like Donald Trump.

_____3. The world has seen technology solve problems of hunger and sickness, but technology will never solve the problem of scarcity.

_____4. Harriet, the wealthy heiress, decides to simplify her life and give all of her millions to charity. She faces no scarcity problem.

## III    MULTIPLE CHOICE

1.  Which of the following is a true statement about scarcity?
    A)  Bill Gates is so rich that he does not face the problem of scarcity.
    B)  Mother Teresa had modest wants, so she did not face the problem of scarcity.
    C)  The U.S. president is so powerful that he does not face the problem of scarcity.
    D)  Scarcity is a universal problem faced by the humble, the rich, and the powerful.

2.  Invention and innovation are examples of creativity that allows the production of greater quantities of goods and services. Why doesn't this creativity reduce or eliminate the problem of scarcity?
    A)  Invention and innovation aren't important in the modern world.
    B)  Invention and innovation don't increase resources; they simply allow us to use our fixed resources differently.
    C)  Invention and innovation often reveal new wants.
    D)  Invention and innovation use up resources.

3.  The introduction of the passenger jet reduced travel time, thereby allowing us to produce more goods and services with our resources. Which of the following is an example of an increase in wants caused by this innovation?
    A)  increased desire for tourist travel
    B)  increased desire for auto travel
    C)  increased desire for road maintenance
    D)  increased desire for color TVs

4.  Which of the following is the best example of the inability of increasing riches to eliminate the problem of scarcity?
    A)  Studies show that as societies get richer they spend more on cleaning up pollution and preserving the natural environment.
    B)  Studies show people are happiest with less.
    C)  Studies show that taking increased doses of vitamin C will produce a rosy outlook on life.
    D)  Studies show that there are more natural resources than we know about.

5. Which of the following is *not* a tangible good?
   A) an automobile
   B) a bouquet of flowers
   C) a haircut
   D) a bag of potato chips

## IV    APPLICATION AND DISCUSSION

1. Explain the difference between poverty and scarcity.

2. The automotive revolution after World War II reduced the time involved for travel and shipping goods. This innovation allowed the U.S. economy to produce more goods and services since it freed resources involved in transportation for other uses. The transportation revolution also increased wants. Identify two ways the car and truck revealed new wants.

# SECTION 2.2
# IDEA 2: OPPORTUNITY COST

## KEY POINTS

- If we had unlimited resources, and thus an ability to produce all of the goods and services anyone wanted, we would not have to choose among those wants.

- The essence of economics is to fully understand the implications that scarcity has for wise decision making, suggesting another way to define economics: *Economics is the study of the choices we make among our many wants and desires.*

- We are all faced with the fact of scarcity and, as a consequence, we must make choices. Because none of us can afford to buy everything we want, each time we do decide to buy one good or service, we reduce our ability to buy other things we would also like to have.

- People must choose. The cost of a choice is the values that must be forgone. The highest or best forgone opportunity resulting from a decision is called the **opportunity cost.**

- *"To choose is to lose."* To get more of anything that is desirable, you must accept less of something else that you also value.

- Opportunity cost illustrations: The opportunity cost of going to college must include the opportunity cost of your time; the opportunity cost of rearing a child includes the opportunity cost of the time spent in child rearing that could be used pursuing a career or volunteering at a local mission.

- *"There's no such thing as a free lunch."* A lunch may be free to you (i.e., subsidized), but it is not free from society's perspective because some of society's scarce resources that could have been used to produce something else of value will have been used in the preparation of the lunch.

# Chapter 2: The Economic Way of Thinking

## I      REVIEW

Economics is the study of the _____choice_____ we make among our unlimited wants and desires and our _____limited_____ resources.

The highest, or best, forgone opportunity resulting from a decision is called the _____opportunity_____ cost of that decision. The expression "There's no such thing as a free _____lunch_____," is often used to express the relationship between scarcity and opportunity cost.

## II     TRUE/FALSE

_____ 1. Since resources are limited while human wants are unlimited, people must choose among alternatives.

_____ 2. If Corrine gives up a job at which she earns $20,000 a year in order to go to college, her forgone income is part of the opportunity cost of going to college.

_____ 3. The opportunity cost of an action is always measured in monetary terms.

_____ 4. Since students at public elementary and secondary schools don't pay tuition, their education is free.

_____ 5. The price of a steak dinner can be exactly the same for two people, but the cost can be greater for one than for the other.

## III     MULTIPLE CHOICE

1. Economics is the study of
   A) the allocation of scarce resources to satisfy our unlimited wants.
   B) how social values mold human behavior.
   C) how the actions of profit-making businesses affect the natural environment.
   D) how political parties compete with one another for votes.

2. Opportunity cost is the
   A) money a business makes by taking advantage of a business opportunity.
   B) value of the best foregone opportunity resulting from a decision.
   C) cost an individual incurs by not taking advantage of an opportunity.
   D) price an individual pays for making a mistake.

3. The opportunity cost of training for a marathon is
   A) the money it costs to enter the twenty-six-mile race.
   B) the cost of all the equipment, like shoes, shorts, and sweatpants, that are required to train for a marathon.
   C) the value of all the other activities a person gives up in order to train, plus any cash outlays for shoes and other necessary equipment.
   D) zero, since training for a marathon is an optional activity that a person chooses over other alternative activities.

4. Which of the following is an expression that economists often use to express the relationship between scarcity and opportunity costs?
   A) "Nothing ventured, nothing gained."
   B) "Here today, gone tomorrow."
   C) "What's sauce for the goose is sauce for the gander."
   D) "There's no such thing as a free lunch."

## IV APPLICATION AND DISCUSSION

1. The price of a one-way bus trip from Los Angeles to New York City is $150.00. Sarah, a school teacher, pays the same price in February (during the school year) as in July (during her vacation), so the cost is the same in February as in July. Do you agree?

2. Whenever St. Louis Cardinal's slugger Mark McGwire hits a home run into the upper deck at Busch Stadium, McDonald's gives anyone with a ticket to that day's game a free Big Mac. If holders of ticket stubs have to stand in line for ten minutes, is the Big Mac really "free?"

# SECTION 2.3
# IDEA 3: MARGINAL THINKING

## KEY POINTS

- Most choices involve how much of something to do rather than whether or not to do something at all.

- Economists emphasize **marginal thinking** because the focus is on additional, or marginal, choices. Marginal choices involve the effects of adding or subtracting from the current situation.

- **The rule of rational choice** is that in trying to make themselves better off, people alter their behavior if the expected marginal benefits to them from doing so outweigh the expected marginal costs they will bear.

- In an uncertain world, the actual result of changing behavior may not always make people better off. However, as a matter of rationality, people are assumed to engage only in behavior that they think ahead of time will make them better off. That is, individuals will only pursue an activity if expected marginal benefits are greater than expected marginal costs [or $E(MB) > E(MC)$].

- We can use the concept of marginal thinking to evaluate pollution levels. We have to weigh the expected marginal benefits of a cleaner environment against the expected marginal costs of a cleaner environment. Zero pollution levels would be far too costly in terms of what we would have to give up.

- Just as we can have optimal (or best) levels of pollution that are greater than zero, the same marginal thinking can be used to analyze crime and safety issues. What would it cost society to have zero crime? In fact, it would probably be impossible to eliminate crime. Regarding safety, the issue is not safe versus unsafe products, but rather how much safety do consumers want.

# Chapter 2: The Economic Way of Thinking

## I    REVIEW

People rarely make "all or nothing" choices. Most choices involve changes from the status quo or _____ changes.

The positive results of these additional changes are called marginal _____ and the negative results are marginal _____.

When people make choices for which the expected marginal benefits exceed the marginal costs of the change, they are following the rule of _____ choice.

The benefits and costs of many choices occur in the future. We can't know future outcomes for certain because the world is _____. When people make choices, they can only compare what they think is likely to happen, so they compare the _____ marginal benefits and costs.

## II    TRUE/FALSE

_____ 1. I am making a marginal choice when I decide that over my lifetime I will go to Tuscaloosa, Alabama, only twenty-seven times.

_____ 2. If as a nation we decide to reduce the level of water pollution by five percent because the added benefits to health and recreation from the cleaner water are greater than the added costs of the clean up, we are following the rule of rational choice.

_____ 3. When the city of Plattsburgh, Pennsylvania, decides to double the number of police patrols in neighborhoods, they hope to decrease crime by raising its expected cost.

_____ 4. Henry Thoreau was right when he said, "There can never be too much wilderness."

## III    MULTIPLE CHOICE

1.  Which of the following would most likely result in an increase in the time you spend studying for your next economics test?
    A)  The test is only one percent of your total grade.
    B)  The test is the day after the Academy Awards and you are a movie fan.
    C)  Your score on this exam will determine whether you pass the course.
    D)  You have a 2.5 Grade Point Average after two semesters in school.

2.  Which of the following is *not* an example of using marginal thinking?
    A)  the decision to eat one more potato chip
    B)  the decision to decrease the Air Force by five thousand people
    C)  the decision to extend your Hawaiian vacation a few extra days
    D)  the decision to become a vegetarian

3. Which of the following are likely to increase the number of times your friend jaywalks?
   A) an increase in the commission she is paid selling subscriptions door-to-door
   B) an increase in the number of police walking patrols in her neighborhood
   C) a change in the law that makes jaywalking a capital offense
   D) an increase in the amount of fast traffic in her neighborhood

4. Bill is thinking about expected marginal benefits and costs of traveling to Hawaii. Many things that affect his benefits and costs are uncertain. Which of the following is certain?
   A) the weather in Hawaii
   B) the fun loving nature of the people in his hotel
   C) the price of his airline ticket which is $512.34
   D) his health during the trip

5. If we use marginal thinking and the rule of rational choice, we should undertake a reduction in the level of air pollution
   A) any time we have the opportunity.
   B) whenever the health of the population can be improved by doing so.
   C) only when the expected marginal costs of cleaner air exceed the expected marginal benefits.
   D) only when the expected marginal benefits of cleaner air exceed the expected marginal costs.

## IV    APPLICATION AND DISCUSSION

1. Should you go to the movies this Friday? List the factors that affect the possible benefits and costs of this decision. Explain where uncertainty affects the benefits and costs.

2. Explain why following the rule of rational choice makes a person better off.

# SECTION 2.4
# IDEA 4: INCENTIVES MATTER

## KEY POINTS

- In acting rationally, people respond to incentives. That is, they react to changes in expected marginal benefits and expected marginal costs. In fact, much of human behavior can be explained and predicted as a response to incentives.

- For most policy purposes, the primary concern is what causes the level of some activity to change. If the benefits of some activity rise and/or if the costs fall, economists expect the amount of that activity to rise. Likewise, if the benefits of some activity fall and/or if the costs rise, economists expect the amount of that activity to fall.

- Almost all of economics can be reduced to incentive [E($MB$) versus E($MC$)] stories, where consumers and producers are driven by incentives that affect expected benefits and costs.

- **Positive incentives** are those that either increase benefits or reduce costs and thus result in an increase in the level of the related activity or behavior. **Negative incentives**, on the other hand, either reduce benefits or increase costs, resulting in a decrease in the level of the related activity or behavior.

# Chapter 2: The Economic Way of Thinking

- Human behavior is shaped and influenced in predictable ways by changes in economic incentives, and economists use this information to predict what will happen when the benefits and costs of any choice are changed.

- Incentives examples: Would birth rates fall if the income tax deduction for dependents were removed? Would a death sentence for drug traffickers reduce drug trafficking? Would stricter penalties deter cheating? Would stricter drunk-driving laws reduce drunk driving?

## I    REVIEW

According to economists, rational people react to changes in expected marginal ____costs____ and expected marginal _____. If a rational person engages in criminal activity, the perceived benefits of criminal activity must be greater than the perceived ____costs____.

Economists expect that harsher penalties for criminal activity will ____reduce____ the amount of crime.

Positive incentives are things that either ____increase____ benefits or reduce costs.

Negative incentives are things that ____reduce____ benefits or increase costs.

Because economists believe that people respond to incentives, they would predict that couples would choose to have ____fewer____ children if the government imposed a tax on each baby born.

Economists would predict a(n) ____decrease____ in the amount of cheating that takes place in schools if penalties or cheating were harsher.

## II    TRUE/FALSE

____T____1. Economists believe that people alter their behavior in response to changes in incentives.

____F____2. Economists believe that people engage in criminal activity primarily because they are genetically predisposed to do so.

____F____3. A tax on bicycle ownership is an example of a positive incentive.

____F____4. An income tax deduction for each child a family has is an example of a negative incentive.

____T____5. Economists believe that the amount of drug trafficking in Singapore is affected by the fact that drug traffickers can receive the death penalty.

____F____6. The odds that an American high school student will be caught if she cheats on her schoolwork are very high.

____T____7. Because Norway has lower legal blood alcohol limits for drivers than the United States, we would expect lower average blood alchohol levels for Norwegian drivers.

## III    MULTIPLE CHOICE

1. Which of the following is consistent with the notion that rational people respond to incentives?
   A) The crime rate remains unchanged in spite of the imposition of tougher jail sentences on all types of crime.
   B) Drug trafficking continues to plague Singapore even after passage of a law mandating the death penalty for such activity.
   C) More generous unemployment benefits result in people remaining unemployed for longer periods of time.
   D) The birth rate falls after Congress enacts a law that provides generous income tax deductions for dependent children.

2. Which of the following is an example of a positive incentive?
   A) A father says he will ground his son if his son flunks high school physics.
   B) The police in your town give a speeding ticket to anyone who drives over 25 miles per hour.
   C) Your calculus teacher says she will give a free laptop computer to each student who scores over 90 percent on the midterm exam.
   D) Your piano teacher raps you on the knuckles every time you hit a wrong note.

3. Which of the following is an example of a negative incentive?
   A) The Cincinnati Reds give Ken Griffey, Jr. $10,000 for every home run he hits.
   B) The Philadelphia 76'ers fine Allen Iverson $10,000 every time he is late for practice.
   C) The Washington Mystics give Chamique Holdsclaw $10,000 each time she scores over 30 points in a game.
   D) Jive Records gives 'NSYNC an extra $800,000 for each week any of their songs is number one on the Billboard charts.

4. Which of the following is most likely to provide teenagers with an incentive not to smoke?
   A) A public service TV ad features actor Jack Nicholson telling kids to abstain from cigarettes.
   B) A law prohibits cigarette smoking in old peoples' homes.
   C) Steven Spielberg convinces his fellow movie directors to stop making movies that glamorize smoking.
   D) A $2.00 per pack tax on cigarettes is levied.

## IV    APPLICATION AND DISCUSSION

1. Modern medicine has made organ transplants a common occurrence, yet the number of organs that people want far exceeds the available supply. According to CNN ten people die each day because of a lack of transplantable organs like kidneys and livers. Some economists have recommended that an organ market be established through which doctors and others could pay people for the right to use their organs when they die. The law currently forbids the sale of organs.

   What do you think of such a proposal? What kind of incentives would an organ market provide for people to allow others to use their organs? What would happen to the supply of organs if, instead of relying on donated kidneys, livers, and retinas, doctors and hospitals could bid for them? What drawbacks would a free market in organs have? Have you made arrangements to leave your organs to your local organ bank? Would you do so if you could receive $50,000 for them?

S E C T I O N   2 . 5

# Idea 5: Specialization and Trade

## KEY POINTS

- People **specialize** by concentrating their energies on the activity to which they are best suited. As a result, they incur lower opportunity costs. This allows them to make the best use of (and thus gain the most benefit from) their limited resources.

- If a person, a region, or a country can produce a good or service at a lower opportunity cost than others, we say that they have a **comparative advantage** in the production of that good or service. They can gain by specializing in the production of the good in which they have a comparative advantage.

- We all specialize to some extent and rely on others to produce most of the goods and services we want. The income earned for that work can then be used to buy goods and services from others who specialize in the production of those goods and services.

- The primary advantages of specialization are that employees acquire greater skill from repetition, they avoid wasted time in shifting from one task to another, and they do the types of work for which they are best suited.

- Trade, or voluntary trade, directly increases wealth by making both parties better off (or they wouldn't trade). It is the prospect of wealth-increasing exchange that leads to productive specialization. Trade increases wealth by allowing a person, a region, or a nation to specialize in those products that it produces better and to trade for the products that others produce better, i.e., U.S. wheat and Brazilian coffee.

## I     REVIEW

When people _Specialize_, they dedicate their resources to one primary activity.

Specialization allows people to make the most out of their limited resources by lowering the _opportunity_ _cost_ of producing goods and services. When a person, region, or country can produce a good at a lower opportunity cost, they have a _comparative advantage_ in the production of it.

When we specialize, we rely on others to produce most of the goods and services we consume, so _trade_ is important for specialization to succeed.

Trade allows people, regions, and countries to increase their _wealth_ by concentrating on the production of goods and services at which they are relatively better.

## II     TRUE/FALSE

_F_ 1. If compared to Europe the United States has a comparative advantage in the production of computers, it has higher opportunity costs.

_F_ 2. Stan put himself through medical school by painting houses. Since he is very fast and very good at painting, he should always paint his own house.

_F_ 3. While countries specialize and trade, people within a country don't specialize.

___T___ 4. In a large business, specialization is possible with both labor and capital equipment.

___T___ 5. The growing importance of international trade for the U.S. economy is a good thing.

___F___ 6. It is possible to grow coffee in the United States, so we should create a U.S. coffee industry and no longer import coffee from Brazil.

## III    MULTIPLE CHOICE

1.  The Butcher, the Baker, and the Candlestick Maker were discussing their career choices. Which reason best illustrates the principle of comparative advantage?
    A)  The Butcher said her father made the choice for her.
    B)  The Baker said he was baking because he wanted to learn all aspects of the restaurant business.
    C)  The Candlestick Maker said she could make more producing candles than in the other two trades.
    D)  They all said they would rather play third base for the St. Louis Cardinals.

2.  Axel is one of the best car mechanics in Greerfield. Axel used to brag he was the best grass cutter in Greerfield. Why doesn't Axel cut his own grass?
    A)  Axel can't fix the motor on his lawn mower.
    B)  In the time it takes to cut his lawn, Axel can make more working on cars than it costs him to have his lawn mowed.
    C)  Axel has developed a grass allergy and he is thinking about cementing over his lawn.
    D)  Axel knows he has a comparative advantage in yard work.

3.  As Bev's Paint Company grows, Bev is able to add more employees and make their jobs more specialized. Which of the following is *not* a benefit Bev might expect from putting her workers in more specialized jobs?
    A)  Workers will get better at their jobs through repetition.
    B)  Workers will be able to choose jobs for which they are best suited.
    C)  Workers waste less time shifting from one job to another.
    D)  Workers will learn all parts of Bev's production process.

4.  The North American Free Trade Agreement (NAFTA) has increased trade between Canada, Mexico, and the United States by lowering trade barriers. Why would we expect this agreement to also increase the wealth and prosperity of the three countries?
    A)  Trade allows countries to specialize and concentrate production where they have the lowest opportunity cost.
    B)  The United States cannot produce many of the things they produce in Canada and Mexico.
    C)  Mexican wages and U.S. wages will rise to the higher levels of Canadian workers.
    D)  Increased trade will mean increased tax revenues in all countries.

5.  Prior to the U.S. Civil War, the regions of the United States specialized. The North specialized in manufactured goods, the West in food production, and the South in cotton. Which of the following is a true statement about the early U.S. regional economies?
    A)  It took more labor, fertilizer, and other inputs to grow food in the South than in the West.
    B)  The West had a comparative advantage in manufactured goods.
    C)  The South had no comparative advantage.
    D)  The opportunity cost of growing food in the South was higher than in the West.

6.  Sergei makes millions of dollars a year playing hockey for the Anaheim Mighty Ducks. Sergei is also the best tailor in his hometown, Petropoligrad, Russia. Why doesn't Sergei make his own clothes?
    A) He has already made all of the clothes he will need for a few years.
    B) The opportunity cost of making clothes is his time, which is valuable because it takes away from his hockey career.
    C) Sergei just can't find the material he likes in the United States.
    D) Sergei has a comparative advantage in sewing.

## IV    APPLICATION AND DISCUSSION

1.  Identify the good or service in which your community or region of the country specializes.

2.  Throughout history many countries have chosen the path of autarky, choosing to not trade with other countries. Explain why this path would make a country poorer.

3.  Farmer Fran can grow soybeans and corn. She can grow 50 bushels of soybeans or 100 bushels of corn on an acre of her land for the same cost. The price of soybeans is $1.50 per bushel and the price of corn is $.60. Show the benefits to Fran of specialization. What should she specialize in?

# SECTION 2.6
# IDEA 6: MARKET PRICES COORDINATE ECONOMIC ACTIVITY

## KEY POINTS

- In a market economy, private individuals and firms own most of the resources. Well-defined **property rights** encourage investment, innovation, exchange, conservation and economic growth.

- The market system provides a way for suppliers and consumers to allocate scarce resources through their actions and inaction in the marketplace. Buyers and sellers indicate their wants through their actions and inaction in the marketplace, and it is this collective "voice" that determines how resources are allocated.

- Market prices serve as the language of the market system. They communicate crucial information to both consumers and suppliers. These prices communicate information about the relative availability of products to consumers, and they provide suppliers with critical information about the relative value that consumers place on those products. This communication results in a shifting of resources from those uses that are less valued to those that are more valued.

- The basis of a market economy is voluntary exchange and the price system that guides people's choices and produces solutions to the questions of what goods to produce and how to produce those goods and distribute them.

- Government **price controls** sometimes force prices above or below what they would be in a market economy, short-circuiting the market's information transmission function. They effectively strip the market price of its meaning for both consumers and suppliers, such as is the case with agricultural price supports and the minimum wage.

- The market mechanism is a simple but effective and efficient general means of allocating resources among alternative uses. But **market failure** can lead the economy to fail to allocate resources efficiently as in the case of pollution and scientific research. When the economy produces too little or too much of something, the government can improve society's well-being by intervening.

- Sometimes the market economy does not always communicate honestly and accurately. Some firms may have market power to distort prices in their favor and, without adequate information, unscrupulous producers may be able to misrepresent their products to the disadvantage of the unwary. These situations may also lead to government intervention.

- There is sometimes a painful trade-off between how much an economy can produce efficiently and how that output is distributed—the degree of equality. There is no guarantee that the market economy will provide everyone with adequate amounts of food, shelter, and health care. That is, not only does the market determine what goods are going to be produced and in what quantities, it also determines the distribution of output among members of society. This equity argument can generate some sharp disagreements, as what seems "fair" to one person may seem highly "unfair" to someone else.

## I    REVIEW

In a market economy most of the resources are owned by _private_ individuals and firms.

The _market_ system provides a way for millions of producers and consumers to allocate _scarce_ resources. Individuals indicate their wants and desires through their _____ and inaction in the marketplace. Market _prices_ serve as the language of the market.

Market prices communicate important _information_ to buyers and sellers. This communication results in a shifting of resources from uses that are less valued to those that are _more_ valued.

Government policies that set prices above or below what they would be in a free market are called price _controls_ .

When the market mechanism fails to allocate resources efficiently it is called market _failure_ . For example, lack of competition in a market can lead to _higher_ prices and _reduced_ product quality.

A question of special concern is whether or not the market economy provides a _fair_ distribution of income.

## II    TRUE/FALSE

_F_ 1. In a market economy the government owns most of the resources.

_F_ 2. People may not be perfect, but one thing they don't do is fight over scarce resources.

_T_ 3. Currently, the predominant form of allocating goods in most countries is the market system.

_F_ 4. Prices give information to buyers about the value other people place on goods, but sellers have no way of getting that information.

_F_ 5. Government price controls make communication of information between buyers and sellers more efficient.

_T_ 6. Minimum wage laws increase unemployment among unskilled teenagers.

___T___ 7. Market failure occurs when the economy fails to allocate resources efficiently on its own.

## III   MULTIPLE CHOICE

1. The textbook uses _____ to describe the role that market prices play in the economy.
   A) sports
   B) music
   C) violence
   D) language

2. Since prices communicate information about the relative availability of products, an increase in the price of oranges tells consumers and producers that
   A) oranges are more abundant than ever.
   B) consumers are buying fewer than ever.
   C) oranges have become more scarce.
   D) consumers are buying fewer oranges relative to the amount that is being produced than before.

3. Using the metaphor of market prices as the language of the market, price controls would be akin to
   A) lying.
   B) telling a joke.
   C) confessing.
   D) yelling.

4. Mrs. Fields owns a grocery store and hires Alex and Todd part time to sweep up, open boxes, and wash windows. How would a $1.00 per hour increase in the minimum wage affect the behavior of Mrs. Fields, Alex, and Todd?
   A) Alex and Todd would offer to work more and Mrs. Fields would gladly increase their hours.
   B) Mrs. Fields would ask Alex and Todd to work more hours, but they would quit.
   C) Alex and Todd would ask to work more hours, but Mrs. Fields would want to offer them fewer hours.
   D) Mrs. Fields would cut Alex and Todd's hours and they would rejoice.

5. Which of the following is a symptom of market failure?
   A) cutthroat competition
   B) falling prices
   C) scarcity of resources
   D) air pollution

## IV   APPLICATION AND DISCUSSION

1. People communicate with each other in the market through the effect their decisions to buy or sell have on prices. Indicate how each of the following would affect prices by putting a check in the appropriate space.

   A) People who see an energetic and loveable Jack Russell Terrier in a popular TV series want Jack Russell Terriers as pets.
      Price of Jack Russell Terriers ___X___ Rises ___ Falls

   B) Aging retirees flock to Tampa, Florida, to live.
      Price of housing in Tampa ___X___ Rises ___ Falls

C) Weather-related crop failures in Colombia and Costa Rica reduce coffee supplies.
Price of Coffee        X Rises ___ Falls

D) Sugar cane fields in Hawaii and Louisiana are replaced with housing.
Price of sugar        X Rises ___ Falls

E) More and more students graduate from U.S. medical schools.
Wages of U.S. doctors        ___ Rises X Falls

F) Americans are driving more and they are driving bigger, gas-guzzling cars like sports utility vehicles.
Price of gasoline        X Rises _____ Falls

2. As the textbook says, prices communicate information about the relative value of resources. Which of the following would cause the value and, hence, the price of potatoes to rise?
A) Fungus infestation wipes out half the Idaho potato crop.
B) The price of potato chips rises.
C) Scientists find that eating potato chips makes you better looking.
D) The prices of wheat, rice, and other potato substitutes fall dramatically.

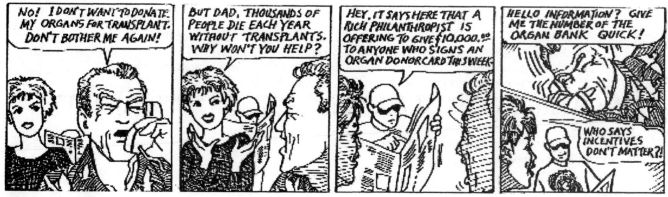

THE LOWELLS

## Questions

1. What incentives do people have to donate their organs to others?

2. How did Mr. Lowell's incentives change?

3. Changes in incentives lead to changes in human behavior. Can you think of three other examples of this principle?

# CHAPTER 3
# SCARCITY, TRADE-OFFS, AND ECONOMIC GROWTH

# SECTION 3.1
# THE THREE ECONOMIC QUESTIONS EVERY SOCIETY FACES

## KEY POINTS

- Because of scarcity, certain economic questions must be answered, regardless of the level of affluence of the society or its political structure: (1) What is to be produced? (2) How are these goods to be produced? (3) For whom are the goods produced?

- In market-oriented economies, people "vote" on economic affairs with their dollars. **Consumer sovereignty** describes how individual consumers in market economies determine what and how much is to be produced (or not produced).

- Economies are organized in different ways to answer the question of what is to be produced.

- A **command economy** relies on central planning, where decisions about what to produce and how many to produce are largely determined by a government official associated with the central planning organization.

- A **market economy**, on the other hand, largely relies on a **decentralized decision-making process** in which literally millions of individual producers and consumers of goods and services determine what goods, and how many of them, will be produced.

- Most countries, including the United States, have a **mixed economy** in which the government and private sector determine the allocation of resources.

# Chapter 3: Scarcity, Trade-Offs, and Economic Growth

- All economies, regardless of political structure, must decide between several possible ways to produce the goods and services that they want. When digging a ditch, a contractor must decide between many workers using their hands, a few workers with shovels, or one person with a backhoe. A decision must be made as to which method is appropriate. The best method is the least-cost method.

- The best or "optimal" form of production will vary from one economy to the next. Why? Each nation tends to use the production processes that conserve its relatively scarce (and thus relatively more expensive) resources and use more of its relatively abundant resources. **Labor-intensive** methods will be used where capital is relatively scarce and **capital-intensive** methods will be used where labor is relatively scarce.

- In every society, some mechanism must exist to determine how goods and services are to be distributed among the population. (Who gets what?) The question of distribution is an issue that always arouses strong emotional responses.

- In a market economy, with private ownership and control of the means of production, the amount of output one is able to obtain depends on one's income, which in turn, depends on the quantity and quality of the scarce resources the individual controls.

## I    REVIEW

Scarcity forces all societies from the richest to the poorest to answer three fundamental questions:
1) _____what_____ do we produce?
2) _____how_____ do we produce these goods and services?
3) For _____whom_____ do we produce the goods and services?

In market economies, individuals control the production decisions by "voting" with their _____dollars_____ for the goods and services they want. This consumer control is called consumer _____sovereignty_____.

Societies organize in two major ways to answer these economic questions. Economies are called _____command_____ economies when government officials make decisions in a highly centralized system.

When many individual producers and consumers make economic decisions in a decentralized manner the economy is a _____market_____ economy.

Since there are several ways to produce any good or service, all economies must decide _____how_____ to produce the goods and services they want. If an economy uses lots of labor to produce goods and services, economists would say production is _____labor_____ intensive.

Countries tend to use production processes that conserve its relatively _____scarce_____ resources and use more of their relatively _____abundant_____ resources.

"Who gets what?" is an economic question that _____scarcity_____ forces all societies to answer. This question is about the _____distribution_____ of output.

In a market economy, the amount of output any one person can secure depends on their _____income_____, which depends on the amount and quality of scarce _____resources_____ they control.

## II    TRUE/FALSE

_F_ 1. Decisions about what to produce are difficult because it's hard to know what people want.

_F_ 2. Even in market economies the decisions about what goods and services to provide are made by a few industrialists and corporate executives.

_T___ 3. Production methods in high-wage countries likes the United States tend to be more capital intensive than in low-wage countries like Mexico.

_F___ 4. Once a society has chosen what to produce there are no more economic decisions to be made.

_F___ 5. The basketball star LeBron James consumes more goods and services than the average college student does because he is taller and taller people need more.

## III     MULTIPLE CHOICE

1.   The last two decades have witnessed the transition from command toward market economies in many countries around the world. Which of the following changes would we expect to see in the countries making this shift?
   A) More decisions are being made by individual producers and consumers and fewer made by central planning organizations.
   B) Fewer decisions are being made by individual producers and consumers and more made by central planning organizations.
   C) The importance of government begins increasing in the economy.
   D) More decisions are being made using government sovereignty and fewer made using consumer sovereignty.

2.   Barry Henley is running for the Senate on the "Consumer is King" platform. Barry says that as a senator he will stop companies from producing goods consumers don't want and force them to produce those goods that will improve consumers' lives. Barry has a list of the products he will promote. What is wrong with Barry's platform?
   A) Barry is forgetting that in a market economy consumers already do this.
   B) Barry's list of products is too short.
   C) Barry's list should include some goods that let people have a good time.
   D) Barry is forgetting that the government already takes care of this.

3.   Which of the following is an example of a capital resource?
   A) an unskilled worker
   B) a large coal deposit
   C) a fishing boat
   D) a yellow-fin tuna

4.   Which of the following best illustrates how economists view the problem of how to produce goods and services?
   A) "A bird in the hand is worth two in the bush."
   B) "There is more than one way to brew green tea."
   C) "Once burned, twice shy."
   D) "What's sauce for the goose is sauce for the gander."

5.   In the United States, who has the greatest claim on the economy's output?
   A) the thirty homeless families with a combined yearly income of $90,000
   B) the thirty college students with a combined yearly income of $600,000
   C) the thirty school teachers with a combined yearly income of $900,000
   D) the thirty-year-old ballplayer with a yearly income of $1,000,000

## IV    APPLICATION AND DISCUSSION

1.  Recently the American Film Institute selected *Citizen Kane* as the best movie of all time. *Citizen Kane* is a fictional psychological biography of one of the most powerful newspaper publishers in history, William Randolph Hearst. *Titanic,* an epic romance about the sinking of the Titanic, has made the most money of any film in history. Unlike *Titanic, Citizen Kane* was not a box office success. Do you think Hollywood will make more movies like *Titanic* or like *Citizen Kane?* Why?

2.  As women's wages and employment opportunities have expanded over the past 50 years, Americans have purchased more and more labor-saving home appliances like automatic washers and dryers, dishwashers, and microwave ovens.

    Do you think these phenomena are related? Could higher wages and better job opportunities lead to a more capital-intensive way of performing household chores? Explain.

# SECTION 3.2
# THE CIRCULAR FLOW MODEL

## KEY POINTS

- **Product markets** are the markets for consumer goods and services. Households are buyers and firms are seller.

- **Factor markets** are markets where households sell their resources to firms. Firms are the buyers and households are sellers.

- Firms receive payments from households for the purchase of goods and services in the product market.

- Households receive payments from firms as compensation for the resources needed to produce goods and services.

- The **circular flow model** illustrates the interaction between households and firms where income flows from firms to households and spending flows from households to firms.

## I    REVIEW

Households make payments to firms for goods and services in the ~~product~~ market. ~~money~~ flows to the firms in exchange for the goods and services that flow to households.

Firms buy ~~inputs~~ from households in the factor market. Firms use households' labor, land, capital, and entrepreneurship to produce ~~goods~~ and ~~service~~

Money flows from the firms to the households as ~~compensation~~ for the use of these inputs. The households receive payments in the form of ~~wages, rent, interest,~~ and ~~profit~~

The simple ~~circular~~ flow model illustrates the continuous flow of payments, income, inputs, and goods and services between households and firms. This model shows how product and factor markets are ~~interrelated~~

## II    TRUE/FALSE

~~T~~ 1. In the simple circular flow model money moves in the same direction as the flow of goods and services.

_____ 2. Resources like labor, land, and capital are purchased in factor markets.

_____ 3. Payments for resources in the factor markets create the income of households.

## III MULTIPLE CHOICE

1. According to the circular flow model of an economy, the money firms pay households for inputs:
   A) leaves the economy as soon as it is paid.
   B) is used by the households to buy the goods and services produced by the firms.
   C) is less than the amount of money paid to the firms for goods and services.
   D) is mostly saved and not used in the economy.

2. Which of the following is a true statement about what occurs in the product market?
   A) Inputs are purchased by households in this market.
   B) Household consumption spending becomes revenue for firms.
   C) Capital, labor and land are turned into consumer products.
   D) Goods and services are exchanged for inputs.

3. Which of the following is not a type of payment found in the factor market?
   A) Wage
   B) Interest
   C) Retail price
   D) Profit

## IV. APPLICATION AND DISCUSSION

Identify the appropriate market where each of the following transactions takes place by placing an X in the appropriate box.

| Transaction | Factor Market | Product Market |
|---|---|---|
| Billy buys a sofa from Home Time Furniture for his new home. | | X |
| Home Time Furniture pays its manager her weekly salary. | X | |
| The manager buys dinner at Billy's Café. | | X |
| After he pays all of his employees their wages and pays his other bills, the owner of Billy's Café takes his profit. | X | |

SECTION 3.3

# THE PRODUCTION POSSIBILITIES CURVE

## KEY POINTS

- The economic concepts of scarcity, choice, and trade-offs can be illustrated by the use of a **production possibilities curve**, which represents the potential total output combinations of any two goods for an economy. That is, it illustrates an economy's potential for allocating its limited resources for producing various combinations of goods in a given time period.

- On a production possibilities curve, we assume that the economy has a given quantity and quality of resources and technology available to use for production.

- The economy cannot produce beyond the levels indicated by the production possibilities curve during a given time period because there are not enough resources to produce that output. However, it is possible to operate inside the production possibilities curve.

- If an economy is operating inside its production possibilities curve, it is not at full capacity and is operating inefficiently. The economy is not getting the most it can from its scarce resources; as a result, actual output is less than potential output.

- Most modern economies have resources that are idle, at least for some period of time. If those resources were not idle, people would have more scarce goods and services available for their use.

- Unemployed resources create a serious problem, not just for labor, but for all resources entering into production. All resources must be used effectively for efficient production.

- Underutilized resources or those not being put to their best uses are illustrated by output combinations inside the production possibilities curve. By putting unemployed resources to work or by putting already employed resources to better uses, we could expand output.

- **Efficiency** requires society to use its resources to the fullest extent—getting the most we can out of our scarce resources.

- If resources are being used efficiently, that is at a point along a production possibilities curve, the cost for more of one good or service is the sacrifice of another good or service.

- The production possibilities curve is not a straight line. It is concave from below (that is, bowed outward from the origin), reflecting **increasing opportunity costs** of producing additional amounts of a good.

- The basic reason for increasing opportunity cost is that some resources and skills cannot be easily adapted from their current uses to alternative uses. Easily adaptable resources are soon exhausted and resources and workers that are less well-suited or appropriate (those with a relatively greater opportunity cost) must then be employed to increase output further.

## I    REVIEW

The problem of making choices regarding what to produce and in what quantities can be illustrated with a
_____production_____ possibilities curve.

Most economies have resources that are _____idle_____ for at least some period of time.

Efficiency requires society to use its resources to the fullest extent and get the _____greatest_____ output from its scarce resources.

# Chapter 3: Scarcity, Trade-Offs, and Economic Growth

If an economy is operating at a point off and below its production possibilities curve, it means that resources are not being utilized ___efficiently___ .

When a production possibilities curve is bowed outward from the origin it is because of the law of _increasing opportunity_ cost.

---

## II TRUE/FALSE

___F___ 1. The production possibilities curve represents the various amounts of a good a country can produce using different amounts of labor and capital.

___T___ 2. A production possibilities curve might be used to represent the total output combinations of rice and soybeans in South Korea.

___T___ 3. Increasing opportunity cost occurs because some productive resources cannot be easily adapted from production of one good or service, like farming, to another, like manufacturing.

___F___ 4. Idle factories represent unemployed land resources.

___T___ 5. If an economy has lots of unemployed workers and idle factories, it is not operating efficiently.

---

## III MULTIPLE CHOICE

1. In Exhibit 1, South Korea's production possibilities curve for rice and soybeans is shown. Point A represents total output of
   A) 500 million bushels of rice and 350 million bushels of soybeans.
   B) 850 million bushels of rice.
   C) 350 million bushels of rice and 500 million bushels of corn.
   D) 800 million bushels of soybeans.

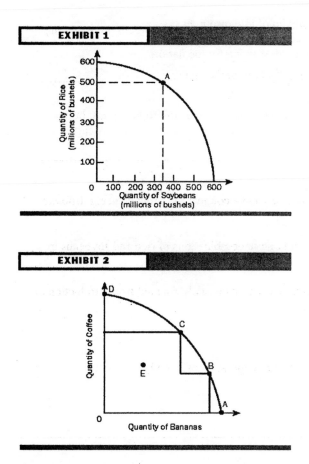

**EXHIBIT 1**

**EXHIBIT 2**

Refer to Exhibit 2, which represents Costa Rica's production possibilities for coffee and bananas, to answer questions 2, 3, and 4 below.

2.  If Costa Rica produces no coffee and devotes all of its resources to growing bananas, it will be operating at point
    A)  A.
    B)  B.
    C)  D.
    D)  E.

3.  If Costa Rica's economy is not operating efficiently, it will be at point
    A)  A.
    B)  C.
    C)  D.
    D)  E.

4.  As Costa Rica moves from point A to point D on its production possibilities curve, the opportunity cost of producing coffee, in terms of bananas
    A)  does not change.
    B)  decreases.
    C)  increases.
    D)  increases to point C, then decreases to point E.

5.  What is the main reason economists are concerned about the problem of idle resources?
    A)  Government benefits paid to unemployed workers put stress on the federal budget.
    B)  Unemployed resources mean less production and lower standard of living for the nation.
    C)  High rates of crime are correlated with high rates of unemployment.
    D)  We want to avoid high rates of inflation that are caused by idle resources.

6.  Exhibit 3 represents the production possibilities for a country that can use its resources to produce guns, butter, or a combination of both. Which of the following concepts is *not* illustrated by this production possibilities curve?
    A)  scarcity
    B)  opportunity cost
    C)  increasing opportunity cost
    D)  economic growth

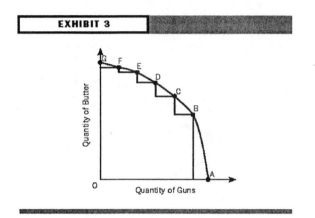

EXHIBIT 3

## IV    APPLICATION AND DISCUSSION

1.  During wartime, countries shift production from civilian goods, like automobiles and clothing, to military goods, like tanks and military uniforms. When the United States entered World War I in April 1917, for example, the federal government created the War Industries Board and charged it with determining production priorities and converting plants to meet war needs. In the following year, automobile production fell 43 percent as output of military vehicles soared. When the war ended, 19 months later, in November 1918, the government cancelled $2.5 billion in military contracts and the nation resumed normal production. Assuming that in 1917 the United States was at point A on the production possibilities curves shown in Exhibit 4, show what happened between April 1917 and November 1918. Show what happened once the war ended.

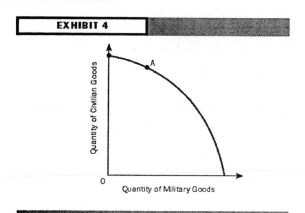

**EXHIBIT 4**

2. In Exhibit 5, read the examples of idle or unemployed resources and indicate which resource, Capital, Labor, or Land, is involved by putting a check (☐) in the appropriate column.

**EXHIBIT 5**

| | Unemployed Capital | Unemployed Labor | Unemployed Land |
|---|---|---|---|
| A) During the 1981–1982 recession, unemployment reached a post–World War II high of 9.7 percent of the labor force. Over 10 million workers were unemployed and output of goods and services fell 2.1 percent. | _____ | _____ | _____ |
| B) During the same recession, the capacity utilization rate, which shows the percentage of factory capacity being used in production, fell from 81 percent in 1981 to 75 percent in 1982. | _____ | _____ | _____ |
| C) Between 1929 and 1933, during the Great Depression, unemployment soared to 25 percent of the labor force. Output of goods and services fell by 30 percent. | _____ | _____ | _____ |
| D) In the mid-1990s, millions of acres of farm land in countries that used to be part of the Soviet Union lay fallow because no one knew who owned them and therefore no one had any incentive to farm them. | _____ | _____ | _____ |

3. Is it possible for a country to have unemployed or idle entrepreneurs? In his book *A Bend in the River,* Nobel prize winner V. S. Naipaul describes an underdeveloped country in which the government's constantly changing tax policies and vague laws regarding ownership of property cause entrepreneurs to become demoralized and unresponsive to economic opportunities.

Is this actually a case of idle or unemployed entrepreneurs? How can tax laws and rules governing property affect entrepreneurs willingness to start new businesses or improve existing enterprises?

SECTION 3.4

# ECONOMIC GROWTH AND THE PRODUCTION POSSIBILITIES CURVE

## KEY POINTS

- Some nations have been able to rapidly expand their output of goods and services over time, while others have been unable to increase their standard of living at all.

- Investing in capital goods will increase the future production capacity of the economy, so an economy that invests more now (consumes less now) will be able to produce, and therefore consume, more in the future.

- An economy can grow with qualitative or quantitative changes in the factors of production—land, labor, capital, and entrepreneurship. Advancements in technology, improvements in labor productivity, or new natural resource finds could all lead to outward shifts of the production possibilities curve.

- Economic growth means an outward shift in the production possibilities curve. With growth comes the possibility to have more of both goods than were previously available.

- It is important to remember that increases in a society's output do not make scarcity disappear. Even when output has grown more rapidly than population, so that people are made better off, they still face trade-offs. At any point along the production possibilities curve, in order to get more of one thing, you must give up something else.

- The production possibilities curve can be used to illustrate the economic concepts of scarcity, choice, opportunity costs, efficiency, and economic growth. Scarcity is represented by the fact that resource combinations outside the production possibility curve are unattainable. Choice is the fact that one must choose among the alternative bundles available along the production possibilities curve. Opportunity costs are how much of one good you give up to get another unit of the second good as you move along the production possibilities curve. Efficiency would mean being on the production possibilities curve rather than inside it. And economic growth is represented by shifting out the production possibilities curve.

## I     REVIEW

A country's economic growth depends on the _Sacrifices_ made today. To grow we have to give up _____ goods and produce more _capital_ goods.

An increase in an economy's capital stock will allow it to increase its future _productive_ capacity and consume more in the future. The effect of the increase in a country's capital stock is represented by a(n) _outward_ shift in its production possibilities curve.

Investment can be more than building new physical capital stock. Upgrading the _skills_ and _knowledge_ of a country's workforce has a similar effect on economic growth.

While today's sacrifices allow a country to produce more in the future, growth will not eliminate _scarcity_ . Even with more resources, countries must still make _choices_ among the ways these resources will be used.

## II     TRUE/FALSE

# Chapter 3: Scarcity, Trade-Offs, and Economic Growth

_____ 1. Economic growth just happens. For any country, growth is determined by factors like climate, which it cannot influence.

_____ 2. B. G. Song wants to be President of Discovakia. He campaigns on the theme "Economic Growth is Always Good." A country will always be better off pursuing economic growth.

_____ 3. The best economic growth strategy a country can pursue is to produce the most consumer goods it can to keep its workers happy and productive.

_____ 4. Economic growth is represented by a shift to the right in the production possibilities curve.

_____ 5. Economic growth will eventually eliminate the problem of scarcity.

## III    MULTIPLE CHOICE

1.  Which of the following is not an example of an investment in human capital?
    A)  Bulgaria builds more classrooms to educate more children.
    B)  Uganda increases healthcare spending to reduce the incidence of AIDS.
    C)  Chile invests in facilities and equipment to start a salmon industry.
    D)  The United States creates a new program to train workers who lost their jobs because of foreign competition.

2.  A new economic consulting firm, Growfast Consultants, promotes sacrifice-free economic growth. If they do truly offer growth without sacrifices, their program must include which of the following elements?
    A)  reducing consumption today to increase future consumption
    B)  receiving gifts of capital from other countries
    C)  reducing food production to increase the production of hydroelectric dams
    D)  increasing current consumption and reducing the capital goods produced

3.  Consider the production possibilities curve in Exhibit 6. Which of the following movements is _not_ economic growth?
    A)  from A to C
    B)  from C to D
    C)  from C to B
    D)  from B to D

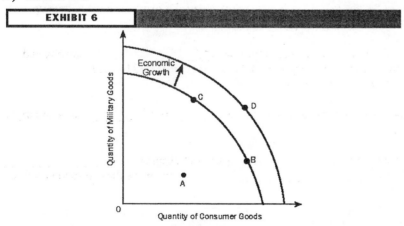

EXHIBIT 6

## IV    APPLICATION AND DISCUSSION

43

# Chapter 3: Scarcity, Trade-Offs, and Economic Growth

1. Why one nation experiences economic growth and another doesn't is a question that has intrigued economists since Adam Smith wrote *An Inquiry into the Nature and Causes of the Wealth of Nations* in 1776. Explain why each of the following would limit economic growth.

   A) The politically connected elite secure a large share of a country's output and put the proceeds in Swiss banks.

   B) A country has a very low output per person.

   C) The national philosophy is live for the moment and forget about tomorrow.

   D) The government closes all of the schools so more people will be available for work.

   E) The country fears military invasion and spends half of its income on military goods.

Questions

1. If you drew Julie Lowell's production possibilities curve, what would you put on each axis?

2. Why isn't Julie *on* her production possibilities curve?

# CHAPTER 4
# SUPPLY AND DEMAND

# SECTION 4.1
# MARKETS

## KEY POINTS

- A market is the process of buyers and sellers exchanging goods services.

- The conditions under which exchange occurs between buyers and sellers can vary incredibly, and these varying conditions make it difficult to precisely define a market.

- Goods being priced and traded at various locations by various kinds of buyers and sellers further compound the problem of defining a market. Some markets are local but numerous, others are global.

- The important point about a market is not what it looks like, but what it does—it facilitates trade.

- Buyers, as a group, determine the demand side of the market, whether it is consumers purchasing goods or firms purchasing inputs. Sellers, as a group, determine the supply side of the market, whether it is firms selling their goods or resource owners selling their inputs.

# Chapter 4: Supply and Demand

## I     REVIEW

A _____ is the process of buyers and sellers exchanging goods.

The term "market" is hard to define because an incredible variety of _____ arrangements exist in the world.

For some goods, like housing and cement, markets are numerous but _____ limited. For other goods, like gold and automobiles, markets are _____.

The _____ determine the demand side of the market, while _____ determine the supply side.

A _____ market is one characterized by lots of buyers and sellers and in which no single buyer or seller can influence the market price.

## II     TRUE/FALSE

_____1. A bookstore is an example of a market.

_____2. A doctor's office is an example of a market.

_____3. A market is always a place.

_____4. Baseball fans determine the supply side of the market for baseball.

## III     MULTIPLE CHOICE

1. Which of the following is *not* an example of a market?
   A)  a drugstore
   B)  the New York Stock Exchange
   C)  a factory
   D)  a barbershop

2. *Ceteris paribus,* when transportation costs are high relative to the selling price, markets are _____ and
   _____.
   A)  numerous; geographically isolated
   B)  numerous; concentrated in a few areas
   C)  few; geographically isolated
   D)  few; concentrated in a few areas

3. The market for automobiles is
   A)  local.
   B)  national.
   C)  global.
   D)  intergalactic.

## IV     APPLICATION AND DISCUSSION

1. Is the market for laptop computers local, national, or global?

# SECTION 4.2
# DEMAND

## KEY POINTS

- According to the law of demand, the quantity of a good or service demanded varies inversely with its price, ceteris paribus. More directly, other things equal, when the price of a good or service falls, the quantity demanded increases.

- The law of demand reflects the fact that the price of a good reflects the sacrifice a buyer must make to buy it. A higher price implies a greater sacrifice or opportunity cost. Other things equal, people would want less of a good or service as the necessary sacrifice increases.

- One reason for the inverse relationship between price and quantity demanded is diminishing marginal utility. Since people derive less satisfaction from successive units of the things they consume, they will buy additional units only if the price is reduced.

- Another reason for the inverse relationship between price and quantity demanded is the substitution effect. At higher prices, buyers have an incentive to substitute other goods for the good that now has a higher relative price.

- An individual demand schedule reveals the different amounts of a particular good a person would be willing and able to buy at various possible prices in a particular time interval, other things equal.

- An individual demand curve for a particular good illustrates the same information as the individual demand schedule. It reveals the relationship between the price and the quantity demanded, showing that when the price is higher, the quantity demanded is lower.

- Economists usually speak of the demand curve in terms of large groups of people. The horizontal summing of the demand curves of many individuals is called the market demand curve for a product. It reflects the fact that the total quantity purchased in the market at a price is the sum of the quantities purchased by each demander.

- The market demand curve shows the amounts that all the buyers in the market would be willing to buy at various prices.

- The relative price of a good is its price relative to (or in terms of) other goods. In a world where virtually all prices are changing, relative prices are crucial to economic decisions because changing relative prices alters the trade-offs decision makers face among various goods and services.

- The money price of a good can be higher than in the past and yet have a lower relative price than in the past. (For example: gasoline prices are higher than in the past in money terms, yet they are cheaper relative to other goods and services than they have been in the past.)

## I     REVIEW

According to the law of demand, other things being equal, the quantity of a good or service demanded goes up when its price goes _____. The primary reason for the inverse relationship between price and quantity demanded is the _____ effect.

# Chapter 4: Supply and Demand

A(n) _____ demand curve is a graphical representation of the relationship between the price of a good and the _____ demanded. The horizontal summing of the demand curves of all the buyers in the market is called the _____ demand curve.

## II    TRUE/FALSE

_____1. According to the law of demand, the quantity of a good that people will buy rises as the price of that item rises.

_____2. If the price of bananas falls, we would expect banana consumption to go up.

_____3. The concept of demand is really just an imaginary notion based on what people might want but really can't afford.

_____4. Economists believe that the concept of need is extremely powerful in helping them understand human behavior.

_____5. An individual's demand schedule shows the amount of a good that a person would like to buy whether or not he or she can afford it.

_____6. An individual's demand curve is a graphical representation of that person's demand schedule.

_____7. A market demand curve is constructed by the horizontal summing of many individuals' demand curves.

## III    MULTIPLE CHOICE

1.  The law of demand says that
    A)  as the price of a good rises, people will buy more of it.
    B)  as the price of a good rises, people will buy less of it.
    C)  as the price of a good falls, people will buy less of it.
    D)  demand is related to human needs and has nothing to do with price.

2.  According to the law of demand, the relationship between the price of a good and the quantity purchased is a(n) _____ relationship.
    A)  positive
    B)  unnatural
    C)  inverse
    D)  legal

3.  If Nike were to reduce the price of Air Jordan basketball shoes, what do you predict would happen to the quantity of shoes people will want to buy?
    A)  It would stay the same because everyone likes Air Jordans.
    B)  It would fall because no one likes cheap shoes.
    C)  It would increase because price and quantity are inversely related.
    D)  There would never be a reason to reduce the price of Air Jordans.

4.  When discussing the law of demand, what do we mean when we say *ceteris paribus?*
    A)  It is a Latin term that means the other non-price factors that affect the amount we consume do not change.
    B)  It is a Latin term that means "gnarly dude."
    C)  It is a Latin term that means there is an inverse relationship.
    D)  It is a Latin term that means goods are for sale.

5. An individual's demand curve for a good
   A) shows the amounts of a good that person will buy at various prices.
   B) indicates the market price of an individual good.
   C) is determined by the cost of producing an individual good.
   D) reveals the amounts of a good an individual needs to survive.

6. A market demand curve is
   A) a graphical represenation of the actual demand for markets.
   B) a line that shows the positive relationship between the price of a product and the amount people will buy.
   C) the result of the horizontal summing of many individual demand curves.
   D) a line that shows the amount of a good that will be produced in a given market in a given period of time.

7. A demand curve slopes
   A) up and to the right.
   B) up and to the left.
   C) down and to the left.
   D) down and to the right.

## IV    APPLICATION AND DISCUSSION

1. Sid moves from New York City, where he lived in a small condominium, to rural Minnesota, where he buys a big house on five acres of land. Using the law of demand, what do you think is true of land prices in New York relative to those in rural Minnesota?

2. Shown below is Hillary's demand schedule for Cherry Blossom Makeup. Plot Hillary's demand curve on the first graph below.

| Price (dollars per ounce) | Quantity Demanded (ounces per week) |
|---|---|
| $15 | 5 oz. |
| 12 | 10 |
| 9 | 15 |
| 6 | 20 |
| 3 | 25 |

3. Below are Cherry Blossom Makeup demand schedules for Hillary's friends, Barbara and Nancy. If Hillary, Barbara, and Nancy constitute the whole market for Cherry Blossom Makeup, complete the market demand schedule and draw the market demand curve on the second graph below.

| Price (dollars per ounce) | Quantity Demanded (ounces per week) | | | |
|---|---|---|---|---|
| | Hillary | Barbara | Nancy | Market |
| $15 | 5 | 0 | 15 | |
| 12 | 10 | 5 | 20 | |
| 9 | 15 | 10 | 25 | |
| 6 | 20 | 15 | 30 | |
| 3 | 25 | 20 | 35 | |

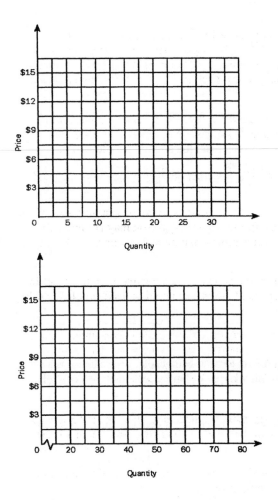

# SECTION 4.3

# SHIFTS IN THE DEMAND CURVE

## KEY POINTS

- Consumers are influenced by the prices of goods when they make their purchasing decisions. At lower prices, people prefer to buy more of a good than at higher prices, holding other factors constant, primarily because many goods are substitutes for one another.

- A change in a good's price leads to a change in quantity demanded, illustrated by moving along a given **demand** curve. A change in a good's price does not change its demand.

- A change in demand, illustrated by a shift in the entire demand curve, is caused by changes in any of the other five factors (besides the good's own price) that would affect how much of the good is purchased: the prices of closely related goods, the incomes of demanders, the number of demanders, the tastes of demanders, and the expectations of demanders. An increase in demand is represented by a rightward shift in the demand curve; a decrease in demand is represented by a leftward shift in the demand curve.

- The *ceteris paribus* assumption (holding constant the shifters of the demand curve as the price of the good itself changes) allows us to isolate the effect of the price of a good on the quantity of that good demanded from other possible determinants.

- The major variables that shift the demand curve are: the prices of closely related goods; income; number of buyers; tastes of buyers; expectations of buyers.

- Two goods are called substitutes if an increase (a decrease) in the price of one causes a decrease (an increase) in the demand for the other good. Because personal tastes differ, what are substitutes for one person may not be so for another person. Further, some substitutes are better than others (i.e., butter and margarine; economics textbooks and T-shirts).

- Two goods are complements if an increase (a decrease) in the price of one good causes a decrease (an increase) in the demand for the other good. Complements are goods that "go together," often consumed or used simultaneously, i.e., skis and bindings; hot dogs and mustard).

- Generally the consumption of goods and services is positively related to the income available to consumers. As individuals receive more income, they tend to increase their purchases of most goods and services. Other things equal, an increase in income usually leads to an increase in demand for goods (rightward shift), and decreasing income usually leads to a decrease in the demand for goods (leftward shift). Such goods are called normal goods, i.e., CDs, movie tickets).

- Some goods exist for which rising (falling) income leads to reduced (increased) demand. These are called inferior goods, which tend to be lower-quality substitutes for more preferred, higher-quality goods, i.e., thrift shop clothes, store-brand products, bus rides).

- The demand for a good or service will vary with the size of the potential consumer population. An increase in the potential consumer population will increase (shift right) the demand for a good or service.

- Changes in fashions, fads, advertising, etc. can change tastes or preferences. An increase in tastes or preferences for a good or service will increase (shift right) the demand for a good or service.

- While changes in preferences lead to shifts in demand, much of the predictive power of economic theory stems from the assumption that tastes are relatively stable over a substantial period of time (because we cannot precisely and accurately measure taste changes).

- Sometimes the demand for a good or service in a given time period will dramatically increase or decrease because consumers expect the good to change in price or availability at some future date. An increase in the expected future price of a good or a decrease in its expected future availability will increase (shift right) the current demand for it; a decrease in the expected future price of a good or an increase in its expected future availability will decrease (shift left) the current demand for it. However, what is important in terms of demand is what people expected to happen, rather than what actually happened.

- Changes in demand versus changes in quantity demanded revisited: If the price of a good changes, we say this leads to a change in quantity demanded. If one of the five other factors influencing consumer behavior changes, we say there is a change in demand.

## I      REVIEW

A change in a good's price leads to a change in _____ demanded, while a change in one of the _____ of demand will lead to a shift in the entire demand curve.

# Chapter 4: Supply and Demand

Determinants of demand are called demand _____ and they lead to a change in _____. Some possible demand shifters are: the prices of closely _____ goods; income; number of _____; _____ of buyers; and _____ of buyers.

Two goods are substitutes if an increase in the price of one good causes an _____ in the demand for the other. Two goods are complements if an increase in the price of one good causes a _____ in the demand for the other.

As their incomes rise, consumers generally buy _____ of most goods. When higher income leads to an increase in demand for a good, the good is called a _____ good. If higher income leads to a reduction in demand for a good, it is called _____ good.

The vital statistics of the potential consumer population, including size, income, and age characteristics, are referred to as the _____ of a product.

When demand changes with changes in fashion, the cause of the change is referred to as a change in _____.

_____ about the future, such as fear of shortages or concern over future price rises, may affect consumer _____.

If the price of a good changes, it leads to a change in quantity _____, but if one of the other factors influencing consumer behavior changes, it leads to a change in _____.

## II     TRUE/FALSE

_____1. A change in a good's price will lead to a change in demand for that good.

_____2. *Ceteris paribus,* a fall in the price of a good will result in a decrease in demand for its substitutes.

_____3. A fall in the price of CDs will result in a reduction in the demand for tapes.

_____4. An increase in the price of a complementary good will increase the demand for the product in question.

_____5. If the price of tennis racquets falls, the demand for tennis balls is likely to increase.

_____6. If watermelons and mangos are normal goods, demand for them will fall as consumers' incomes rise.

_____7. If duct tape is an inferior good, demand for it will fall as consumers' incomes rise.

_____8. As the U.S. population becomes older on average, we are likely to see an increase in the demand for items like playpens and stuffed animals.

## III     MULTIPLE CHOICE

1. The difference between a change in quantity demanded and a change in demand is that
   A) a change in quantity demanded is caused by a change in a good's price, while a change in demand is caused by a change in a variable such as income, tastes, or expectations.

B) a change in demand is caused by a change in a good's price, while a change in quantity demanded is caused by a change in a variable such as income, tastes, or expectations.

C) a change in quantity demanded is a change in the amount people actually buy, while a change in demand is a change in the amount they want to buy.

D) This is a trick question. A change in demand and a change in quantity demanded are the same thing!

2. Which of the following will not cause a change in the demand for a product?
A) a change in consumers' income
B) a change in consumers' tastes
C) a change in the price of the product
D) a change in the price of a substitute for the product

3. News that eating jelly beans makes you better looking will likely cause
A) the demand curve for jelly beans to shift to the left.
B) the demand curve for jelly beans to shift to the right.
C) a decrease in the quantity of jelly beans demanded.
D) a decrease in the quantity of jelly beans supplied.

4. If an increase in consumers' incomes causes a decrease in the demand for video rentals, then video rentals are
A) a luxury.
B) a normal good.
C) a necessity.
D) an inferior good.

5. Suppose the demand for fish tacos increases as the result of an increase in consumers' incomes. Fish tacos must be
A) a luxury.
B) a normal good.
C) an inferior good.
D) an incredible good.

6. Which of the following is most likely to cause an increase in the demand for disposable diapers?
A) a decrease in peoples' incomes
B) a decrease in the price of cloth diapers
C) an increase in the number of newborn babies
D) a decrease in the price of disposable diapers

7. If fewer people get tattoos as a result of an increase in tattoo prices, then there has been
A) an increase in the demand for tattoos.
B) a decrease in the demand for tattoos.
C) an increase in the quantity of tattoos demanded.
D) a decrease in the quantity of tattoos demanded.

8. In the three months before a new $1 per pack cigarette tax took effect in Alaska, smokers in the 49th state bought 175 million more cigarettes than they had during the same period a year earlier. This represents an increase
A) in the quantity of cigarettes demanded due to an increase in price.
B) in demand caused by a change in consumers' expectations about the future.
C) in demand due to a change in consumers' tastes.
D) in demand due to a change in the number of demanders.

## IV    DISCUSSION AND APPLICATION

1. On the graphs below, show the effects of each of the following on the demand for hamburger in Hilo, Hawaii. Identify the responsible determinant of demand in the space provided.

# Chapter 4: Supply and Demand

A.   The price of chicken falls.

    Determinant: _____

B.   The price of hamburger buns doubles.

    Determinant: _____

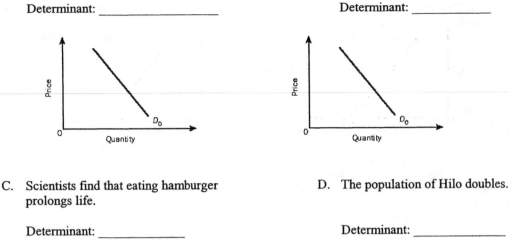

C.   Scientists find that eating hamburger
    prolongs life.

    Determinant: _____

D.   The population of Hilo doubles.

    Determinant: _____

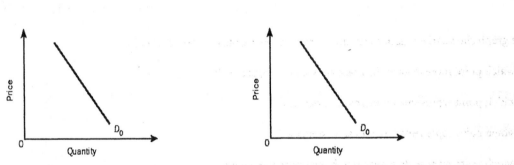

2.   On the graphs below, show the effects of each of the following on the demand for Chevrolets in the United States.

    A. The price of Fords plummets.

    Determinant: _____

B.   Consumers believe that the price of Chevrolets will
    rise next year.

    Determinant: _____

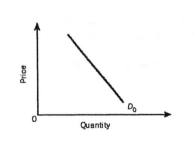

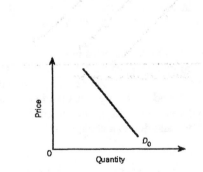

C. The incomes of Americans rise.

    Determinant: _____

D.   The price of gasoline falls dramatically.

    Determinant: _____

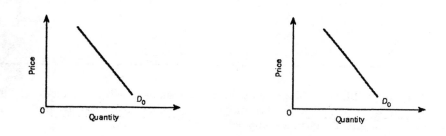

3.  The graph shows three market demand curves for cantaloupe. Starting at point A,

    A. which point represents an increase in quantity demanded?

    B. which point represents an increase in demand?

    C. which point represents a decrease in demand?

    D. which point represents a decrease in quantity demanded?

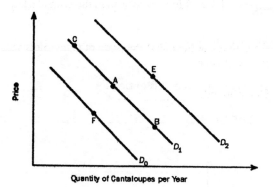

# SECTION 4.4
# SUPPLY

## KEY POINTS

- The law of supply states that, other things equal, the quantity supplied will vary directly with the price of the good. According to the law of supply, the higher the price of the good, the greater the quantity supplied, and the lower the price of the good, the smaller the quantity supplied.

- The quantity supplied is positively related to the price because firms supplying goods and services want to increase their profits, and the higher the price per unit, the greater the profitability generated by supplying more of that good or service. Also, if costs are rising for producers as they produce more units, they must receive a higher price to compensate them for their higher costs.

- An individual supply schedule reveals the different amounts of a product a person would be willing to produce and sell at various possible prices in a particular time interval, other things equal. An individual supply curve illustrates that information graphically.

- The individual supply curve is upward sloping. At higher prices, it will be more attractive to increase production. Existing firms will produce more at higher prices than at lower price in a particular time interval, other things equal.

- The market supply curve for a product is the horizontal summation of the supply curves for individual firms. It reflects the fact that the total quantity sold in the market at a price is the sum of the quantities sold by each supplier.

## I      REVIEW

The answer to the questions, "What do we produce and in what quantities?" depends on the interaction of both _____ and _____.

The law of supply states that, other things being equal, quantity supplied varies _____ with price.

A producer requires a higher price to produce additional units of the good because of the law of _____ opportunity costs.

The individual supply curve is _____ sloping as you move from left to right.

Adding the amount each individual producer would supply at each price will give us the _____ supply curve.

## II      TRUE/FALSE

_____1. Once we know the demand for a product we can predict how much will be produced.

_____2. A direct relationship between two variables means they move in opposite directions.

_____3. Without a change in technology or input prices, the opportunity costs of production increase as more is produced.

_____4. Individual supply curves usually slope upward and to the right.

_____5. *Ceteris paribus,* a change in a good's price will result in a change in the quantity supplied of the good.

## III   MULTIPLE CHOICE

1. In a market economy, the amount of a good that is produced is decided by the interaction of
   A) buyers and sellers.
   B) all consumers.
   C) producers and input suppliers.
   D) all producers.

2. According to the law of supply, when the price of a good increases, we would predict that
   A) more will be consumed.
   B) less will be produced.
   C) more will be produced.
   D) less will be consumed.

3. When the price people are willing to pay for oil decreases, what would we predict would happen to the amount of oil produced in any oil field?
   A) It would decline.
   B) It would stay the same.
   C) It would increase.
   D) It would fluctuate up and down.

4. To produce more wheat, Farmer Jones has to use fields that are on a mountain slope, where it costs $500 more to grow each ton of wheat. Farmer Jones would only produce from these fields when
   A) the price of wheat increases.
   B) the price of wheat decreases.
   C) the cost of wheat increases.
   D) the cost of wheat decreases.

5. When we add up all of the individual firm supply curves, what do we have?
   A) nothing important
   B) the market supply curve
   C) the individual supply curve
   D) the amount produced

## IV   APPLICATION AND DISCUSSION

1. Felix is a wheat farmer who has two fields he can use to grow wheat. The first field is right next to his house and the topsoil is rich and thick. The second field is 10 miles away in the mountains and the soil is rocky. On which field do you think the opportunity cost of producing wheat is the highest? Why?

2. At current wheat prices, Felix just produces from the field next to his house because the market price for wheat is just high enough to cover his costs of production including a reasonable profit. What would have to happen to the market price of wheat for Felix to have the incentive to produce from the second field?

3.   Below is the supply schedule for Rolling Rock Oil Co. Plot Rolling Rock's supply curve on the first graph below.

| Price | Quantity Supplied |
|---|---|
| (dollars per barrel) | (barrels per month) |
| $ 5 | 10,000 |
| 10 | 15,000 |
| 15 | 20,000 |
| 20 | 25,000 |
| 25 | 30,000 |

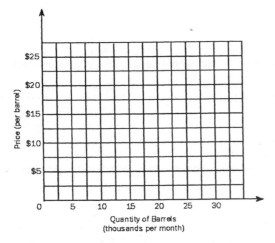

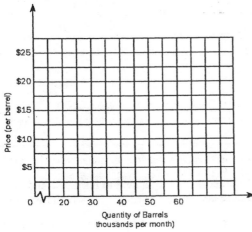

4.   Below are the supply schedules for Rolling Rock and two other petroleum companies, Armadillo Oil and Pecos Petroleum. Assuming these three companies make up the entire supply side of the oil market, complete the market supply schedule and draw the market supply curve on the second graph above.

| Price | Quantity Supplied (barrels per month) | | | |
|---|---|---|---|---|
| (DOLLARS PER BARREL) | ROLLING ROCK | ARMADILLO | PECOS | MARKET |
| $ 5 | 10,000 | 8,000 | 2,000 | _____ |
| 10 | 15,000 | 10,000 | 5,000 | _____ |

| 15 | 20,000 | 12,000 | 8,000 | _____ |
| 20 | 25,000 | 14,000 | 11,000 | _____ |
| 25 | 30,000 | 16,000 | 14,000 | _____ |

S E C T I O N   4 . 5

# SHIFTS IN THE SUPPLY CURVE

## KEY POINTS

- Changes in the price of a good lead to changes in quantity supplied, which are shown as movements along a given supply curve. Changes in supply occur for other reasons than changes in the price of the product itself. A change in any other factor that can affect supplier behavior results in a shift of the entire supply curve. These factors include: supplier input prices; the price of related goods, expectations; number of suppliers; and technology, regulation, taxes, subsidies and weather. An increase in supply shifts the supply curve to the right; a decrease in supply shifts the supply curve to the left.

- Higher input prices increase the cost of production, reducing the per-unit profit potential at existing prices, causing the supply of a good to decline. Lower input prices decrease the cost of production, which increases the per-unit profit potential at existing prices. This, in turn, causes the supply of a good to increase.

- The supply of a good can be influenced by the price of related goods. Firms producing a product can sometimes use their resources to produce alternative goods. Suppose a farmer's land can be used to grow either barley or cotton. If the farmer is currently growing barley and the price of barley falls, then this provides an incentive for the farmer to shift acreage out of barley and into cotton. Thus a decrease in the price of barley will increase the supply of cotton.

- If producers expect a higher price in the future, they will supply less now, preferring to wait and sell when their goods will be more valuable. If producers expect a lower price for their products in the future, they will supply more today, rather than waiting to sell when their goods will be worth less.

- Since the market supply curve is the horizontal summation of the individual supply curves, an increase in the number of suppliers will increase market supply. A decrease in the number of suppliers will decrease market supply.

- Technological progress can lower the cost of production and increase supply.

- Supply may also change because of changes in the legal and regulatory environment in which firms operate, such as safety and pollution regulations, minimum wages, taxes, etc. If these changes increase costs, they will decrease supply. If they decrease costs, they will increase supply. An increase in costly government regulations, taxes or adverse production conditions will increase the cost of production, decreasing supply. Subsidies, the opposite of a tax can lower the cost of production and shift the supply curve to the right. In addition, weather can affect the supply of certain commodities.

- If the price of a good changes, it leads to a change in its quantity supplied, but not its supply. If one of the other factors influences sellers' behavior, it leads to a change in supply.

# Chapter 4: Supply and Demand

I        REVIEW

When other factors remain the same, price change results in a movement along the supply curve; this is called a change in _____ supplied. When the other important factors that affect supplier behavior change, the entire supply curve shifts; this is called a change in _____.

Labor, materials, and energy are examples of supplier _____. Higher input prices increase the _____ of production and shift the supply curve to the left. Lower input prices _____ the costs of production and shift the supply curve to the _____.

When two goods can be produced using the same resources they are called _____ in production. Producers tend to substitute the production of _____ profitable goods for that of _____ profitable goods.

If suppliers expect the price of a good will be higher in the future, they will sell _____ now so that they will have _____ to sell in the future. If they expect prices to fall in the future they will supply _____ now rather than wait for their goods to be worth less.

An increase in the number of suppliers leads to an _____ in supply, while a decrease in the number of suppliers will lead to a _____ in supply.

Improvements in _____ lead to lower costs and increase in supply.

Government regulations that increase production costs cause _____ in the supply of goods.

Weather can also affect the supply of certain goods, especially _____ products.

If the price of a good changes it will lead to a change in the _____ supplied. If one of the determinants of supply, such as supplier input prices or technology, changes, it will lead to a change in _____ and to a shift in the _____ curve.

II        TRUE/FALSE

_____1. *Ceteris paribus,* if the price of timber increases, we would expect an increase in the supply of lumber.

_____2. When the price of cotton falls, the supply of barley, which can be grown using the same land, will increase.

_____3. Midge sells Persian carpets in the United States. If she expects the price of these carpets will rise next year, she will increase this year's supply and sell more now rather than waiting to sell her stock next year.

_____4. An increase in the number of suppliers selling a product will result in a decrease in the supply of the product.

_____5. Improving technology in an industry usually lowers the cost of producing the product and results in a leftward shift in the supply curve.

_____6. Government can decrease the supply of a product by imposing taxes or regulations that increase the cost of production.

# Chapter 4: Supply and Demand

1. John and Kate decide that coffee would be a good business to be in, so they form J & K Coffee Co. What will happen to the market supply of coffee as a result?
   A) It will decrease.
   B) It won't change.
   C) It will increase.
   D) It only changes the price.

2. The difference between a change in quantity supplied and a change in supply is that a change in
   A) the quantity supplied is caused by a change in a good's price, while a change in supply is caused by a change in a variable such as input prices, prices of related goods, expectations, or taxes.
   B) supply is caused by a change in a good's price, while a change in the quantity supplied is caused by a change in a variable such as input prices, prices of related goods, expectations, or taxes.
   C) the quantity supplied is a change in the amount people want to sell. A change in supply is a change in the amount they actually sell.
   D) supply and a change in the quantity supplied are the same thing.

3. Which of the following will *not* cause a change in the supply of a product?
   A) a change in the price of suppliers' inputs
   B) a change in the price of related products
   C) a change in the price of the product
   D) a change in the expected future price of the product

4. El Niño has caused both drought and flood-producing rains in various wheat-growing regions. What would be the likely affect of El Niño on the wheat market?
   A) an increase in supply
   B) a decrease in supply
   C) El Niño will not affect supply.
   D) a decrease in demand

5. Which of the following actions of government would not result in a decrease in the supply of fast-food meals?
   A) an increase in the minimum wage that raises the wages of most workers in the fast-food industry
   B) increased health standards governing fast-food kitchens
   C) decreased property taxes on fast-food outlets
   D) worker safety regulations requiring that lettuce be chopped with a dull knife

6. Pan Am Airlines went bankrupt in 1998 and left the airline industry. What was the likely effect of this change on the airline market?
   A) an increase in supply
   B) a decrease in supply
   C) no change in supply
   D) an increase in demand

7. Steel producers offer to sell sheet steel to U.S. auto producers for a lower price than in the past. With all other factors remaining constant, what would you expect to happen in the auto market?
   A) an increase in supply
   B) a decrease in supply
   C) no change in supply
   D) an increase in demand

# Chapter 4: Supply and Demand

**IV      APPLICATION AND DISCUSSION**

1.  On the following graphs show the effects of each of the following on the supply of salsa in the United States. Identify the responsible determinant of supply in the space provided.

    A.  Tomato prices skyrocket!

        Determinant: _____

    B.  Congress places a 26 percent tax on salsa.

        Determinant: _____

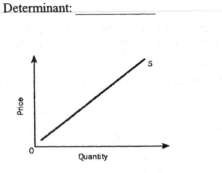

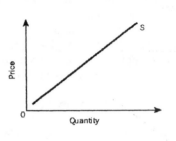

    C.  Ed Scissorhands introduces a new, faster vegetable chopper.

        Determinant: _____

    D.  Elton John, Madonna, and Paul Newman each introduce a new brand of salsa.

        Determinant: _____

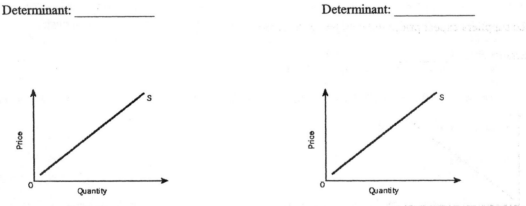

2.  On the graphs below, show the effects of each of the following on the supply of coffee worldwide. Identify the responsible determinant of supply in the space provided.

    A.  Freezing temperatures wipe out half of Brazil's coffee crop.

        Determinant: _____

    B.  Wages of coffee workers in Latin America rise as unionization efforts succeed.

        Determinant: _____

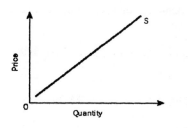

C. Indonesia offers big subsidies to its coffee producers.

Determinant: _____

D. Genetic engineering produces a super coffee bean that grows faster and needs less care.

Determinant: _____

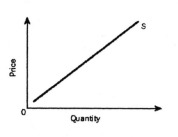

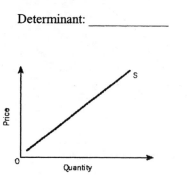

E. Coffee suppliers expect prices to be higher in the future.

Determinant: _____

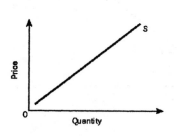

3. Below are three market supply curves for cantaloupe. Compared to point A, which point represents

   A) an increase in quantity supplied?

   B) an increase in supply?

   C) a decrease in quantity supplied?

   D) a decrease in supply?

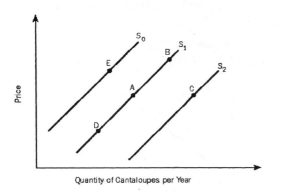

# CHAPTER 5
# BRINGING SUPPLY AND DEMAND TOGETHER

SECTION 5.1 MARKET EQUILIBRIUM PRICE AND QUANTITY

SECTION 5.2 CHANGES IN EQUILIBRIUM PRICE AND QUANTITY

SECTION 5.3 PRICE CONTROLS

# SECTION 5.1
# MARKET EQUILIBRIUM PRICE AND QUANTITY

## KEY POINTS

- The price at the intersection of the market demand curve and the market supply curve is called the equilibrium price and the quantity is called the equilibrium quantity.

- At the equilibrium market price, the amount that buyers are willing and able to buy is exactly equal to the amount that sellers are willing and able to produce. If the price is set above or below the equilibrium price, there will be shortages or surpluses. However, the actions of many buyers and sellers will move the price back to the equilibrium level.

- At the equilibrium price, both buyers and sellers are able to carry out their purchase and sales plans. However, at any other price, either suppliers or demanders would be unable to trade as much as they would like.

- At a price greater than the equilibrium price, a surplus, or excess quantity supplied, would exist. Sellers would be willing to sell more than demanders would be willing to buy. Frustrated suppliers would cut their price and cut back on production, and consumers would buy more, eliminating the unsold surplus and returning the market to equilibrium.

- At a price less than the equilibrium price, a shortage, or excess quantity demanded, would exist. Buyers would be willing to buy more than sellers would be willing to sell. Frustrated buyers would compete for the existing supply, causing the price to rise, which would make producers willing to increase the quantity supplied and decrease the quantity demanded, eliminating the shortage, and returning the market to equilibrium.

# Chapter 5: Bringing Supply and Demand Together

## I    REVIEW

The price at the intersection of the market demand curve and the market supply curve is called the _____ **price.**

If the price of a good or service is below the equilibrium price, a _____ **will result.**

If the price is above equilibrium, a _____ will result.

If there is a shortage of a good, the price of that good will _____. **If there is a surplus of a good, the price will** _____.

## II    TRUE/FALSE

_____1. The actual price of a good or service is identical to the equilibrium price.

_____2. If the market for bing cherries is in equilibrium, the quantity of bing cherries demanded will be equal to the quantity of bing cherries supplied.

_____3. A shortage of housing in Columbus, Ohio, will cause the price of housing there to rise.

_____4. Surpluses are the result of too much demand and too little supply.

_____5. As people leave Forlorn, Saskatchewan, the resulting surplus of housing will put upward pressure on housing prices.

## III    MULTIPLE CHOICE

Refer to Exhibit 1, the hypothetical monthly demand and supply schedules for cans of macadamia nuts in Kapaa, Hawaii, in order to answer questions 1, 2, and 3.

EXHIBIT 1

| Price | Quantity Demanded | Quantity Supplied |
|---|---|---|
| $6 | 700 cans | 100 cans |
| 7 | 600 | 200 |
| 8 | 500 | 300 |
| 9 | 400 | 400 |
| 10 | 300 | 500 |

1.  The equilibrium price of macadamia nuts in Kapaa is
    A)  $6.00.
    B)  $7.50.
    C)  $8.00.
    D)  $9.00.

2.  At a price of $7.00 per can, there is a
    A)  shortage of 300 cans.
    B)  #shortage of 400 cans.
    C)  market equilibrium.
    D)  surplus of 400 cans.

3.  At a price of $10.00, there is a
    A)  shortage of 200 cans.
    B)  surplus of 200 cans.
    C)  market equilibrium.
    D)  surplus of 400 cans.

Refer to Exhibit 2, the hypothetical demand and supply curves for donuts in Chicken, Alaska, to answer questions 4, 5, and 6.

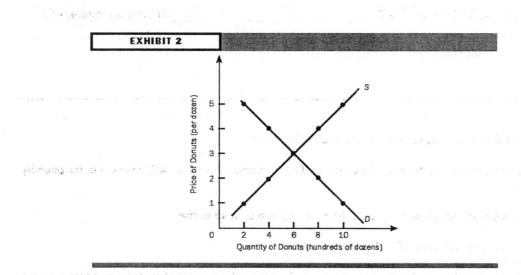

4.  At a price of $5.00 per dozen,
    A)  a surplus of donuts will exist.
    B)  a shortage of donuts will exist.
    C)  the market will be in equilibrium.
    D)  This is a trick question because no one would pay $5.00 for a dozen donuts in Chicken.

5.  At a price of $3.00,
    A)  a surplus of donuts will exist.
    B)  a shortage of donuts will exist.
    C)  the market will be in equilibrium.
    D)  Both (A) and (B) are co#rrect.

6.  If the price of donuts in Chicken was $2.00 per dozen,
    A)  quantity demanded would be less than quantity supplied and prices would rise.
    B)  quantity demanded would be less than quantity supplied and prices would fall.
    C)  quantity demanded would be greater than quantity supplied and prices would rise.
    D)  quantity demanded would equal quantity supplied and prices would remain constant.

## IV    APPLICATION AND DISCUSSION

When asked about the reason for a lifeguard shortage that threatened to keep one-third of the city's beaches closed for the summer, the Deputy Parks Commissioner of New York responded that "Kids seem to want to do work that's more in tune with a career. Maybe they prefer carpal tunnel syndrome to sunburn." (*Newsweek*, July 6, 1998)

As someone who knows about the causes of shortages, what do you think is causing the shortage? What would you advise the Deputy Parks Commissioner to do in order to alleviate the shortage?

SECTION 5.2

# CHANGES IN EQUILIBRIUM PRICE AND QUANTITY

## KEY POINTS

- As discussed earlier, demand curves shift when any of the other factors that affect buyers' behavior change (but not the price of the good itself), and supply curves shift when any of the other factors that affect sellers' behavior change (but not the price of the good itself). These changes (shifts) in the demand and supply curves will lead to changes in the equilibrium price and equilibrium quantity.

- An increase in demand results in a greater equilibrium price and a greater equilibrium quantity. Conversely, a decrease in demand results in a lower equilibrium price and a lower equilibrium quantity.

- A decrease in supply results in a higher equilibrium price and a lower equilibrium quantity. Conversely, an increase in supply results in a lower equilibrium price and a higher equilibrium quantity.

- Very often, supply and demand will both shift in the same time period. That is, supply and demand will shift simultaneously.

- When supply and demand move at the same time, we can predict the change in one variable (price or quantity), but we are unable to predict the direction of effect on the other variable. This change in the second variable, then, is said to be indeterminate because it cannot be determined without additional information about the relative changes in supply and demand.

- We can predict what will happen to equilibrium prices and equilibrium quantities in situations where both supply and demand change by breaking them down into their individual effects, then putting together the price and quantity effects that each of the shifts would have separately.

- An increase in supply decreases the equilibrium price and increases the equilibrium quantity. A decrease in demand decreases both the equilibrium price and quantity. Taken together, they will decrease the equilibrium price, but result in an indeterminate change in the equilibrium quantity. The change in quantity will depend on the relative changes in supply and demand. If the decrease in demand is greater than the increase in supply, the equilibrium quantity will decrease. If the increase in supply is greater than the decrease in demand, the equilibrium quantity will increase.

- An increase in demand increases the equilibrium price and equilibrium quantity. An increase in supply decreases the equilibrium price and increases the equilibrium quantity. Together, they increase the equilibrium quantity, but the change in equilibrium price depends on the relative sizes of the demand and supply shifts. If supply shifted more than demand, the equilibrium price would drop.

- The eight possible changes in demand and/or supply are presented, along with the resulting changes in equilibrium price and equilibrium quantity.

## I   REVIEW

A shift in either the supply or demand curves for a good will result in a change in both its _____
price and quantity.

An increase in the demand for a good or service is represented by a shift of the demand curve to the _____
and results in an _____ in the equilibrium price and quantity.

If the supply curve does not change, an increase in demand causes a _____ along
the supply curve and an increase in the _____ of the good supplied.

A(n) _____ in the supply of a good or service is represented by a shift in the supply curve
to the left. If demand does not change, the decrease in supply will cause a decrease #in the quantity _____
of the good and an _____ in the equilibrium price.

If supply increases at the same time that demand decreases, equilibrium price will _____ while the change in quantity will be _____.

If both supply and demand increase, the equilibrium quantity will _____, while the change in equilibrium price will be _____.

An increase in either demand or supply is shown by shifting the curve to the _____. A decrease in either demand or supply is shown by shifting the curve to the _____.

## II    TRUE/FALSE

_____1. If the bing cherry market is in equilibrium at a price of $1 per quart, an increase in the demand for bing cherries will cause a shortage at the existing price.

_____2. Unless there are other changes, when there is a decrease in the price of compact disc players, the equilibrium price of compact discs will also fall.

_____3. While the demand for chicken has not changed, the price of chicken has risen because of an increase in the number of farmers producing chicken.

_____4. At a given equilibrium price, a surplus can be created by either an increase in supply or a decrease in demand.

_____5. Doctors announce that eating chocolate reduces a person's cholesterol, a major cause of heart disease. Barring other changes, the quantity of chocolate consumed will increase.

_____6. If the demand for apples increases at the same time supply of apples falls, the price of apples will tend to fall.

_____7. If the population of Fallbrook, Ohio, decreases dramatically while contractors are busy building more houses, the price of housing in Fallbrook will tend to decrease.

_____8. When both the supply and demand curves shift at the same time, we can determine the direction of both equilibrium price and quantity.

## III    MULTIPLE CHOICE

1.  Troy Oz, the movie star, is a trendsetter. His promotion of ostrich steaks changes peoples' ta#stes and increases the demand for ostrich meat. What would be the expected effect of this change in the ostrich meat market?
    A)  A shortage will occur at the original price, resulting in an increase in the price and the quantity produced.
    B)  A shortage will occur at the original price, resulting in a decrease in the price and the quantity produced.
    C)  A surplus will occur at the original price, resulting in an increase in the price and a decrease in the quantity produced.
    D)  A surplus will occur at the original price, resulting in a decrease in the price and an increase in the quantity produced.

2.  What will happen in the market for Broadway shows after unions win a 14 percent wage increase for actors and stage crews?
    A)  Ticket prices will rise and the number of shows will increase.
    B)  Ticket prices will rise and the number of shows will decline.
    C)  Ticket prices will fall and the number of shows will decline.
    D)  Ticket prices will fall and the number of shows will increase.

3. How do chicken farmers react to the news of medical research findings that eating chicken makes a person smarter?
   A) They increase the supply of chickens.
   B) They increase the quantity of chickens supplied.
   C) They decrease the supply of chickens.
   D) They decrease the quantity of chickens they supply.

4. Geneticists have discovered a way to increase the average weight of beef cattle by 20 pounds using no more feed than is used today. What effect will this technological improvement have on the beef market?
   A) The price per pound of beef will fall and the quantity consumed will increase.
   B) The price per pound of beef will fall and the quantity consumed will decrease.
   C) The price per pound of beef will rise and the quantity consumed will increase.
   D) The price per pound of beef will rise and the quantity consumed will decrease.

5. The gasoline market is in equilibrium at a price of $1.19 per gallon. Which of the following will not be a result of an increase in the dem##and for gasoline?
   A) A shortage will occur at a price of $1.19.
   B) The new equilibrium price will be more than $1.19.
   C) The gasoline supply curve will shift to the right.
   D) There will be an increase in the quantity of gasoline supplied.

6. Hurricane Andrew caused over $15 billion in damage when it swept through southern Florida in 1992. One result was an increased local demand for plywood to replace broken windows. At the pre-hurricane equilibrium price of plywood, we woul#d expect to see
   A) a surplus caused by excess supply.
   B) a shortage caused by excess demand.
   C) the quantity demand equal to the quantity supplied.
   D) an increase in the supply of plywood.

7. Which of the following could be responsible for an increase in the price of wheat?
   A) an increase in the supply of wheat
   B) an increase in the demand for wheat
   C) a decrease in the demand for wheat
   D) a simultaneous increase in supply and decrease in demand for wheat

8. Nora is delighted to see that the price of her favorite food, artichokes, has fallen. Which of the following could be responsible?
   A) an increase in the demand for artichokes
   B) a decrease in the supply of artichokes
   C) a simultaneous increase in demand and decrease in supply of artichokes
   D) a simultaneous decrease in demand and increase in supply

9. When the demand and the supply of oranges increase at the same time, we can safely predict that
   A) the price of oranges will fall.
   B) the price of oranges will rise.
   C) the quantity of oranges bought and sold will fall.
   D) the quantity of oranges bought and s#old will rise.

10. If the price of cellular telephones went down after simultaneous increases in the supply and demand for cellular telephones, we know that
    A) the supply curve for cellular phones shifted more than the demand curve.
    B) the demand curve for cellular phones shifted more than the supply curve.
    C) the supply and demand curves shifted by the same amount.
    D) the supply and demand curves actually shifted leftward.

## IV    APPLICATION AND DISCUSSION

1.  Show the effects of the changes listed below on the relevant supply and demand curves. Label the new equilibrium price, $P_1$, and the new equilibrium quantity, $Q_1$.

   A)   An increase in the price of hot dogs on the hamburger market.

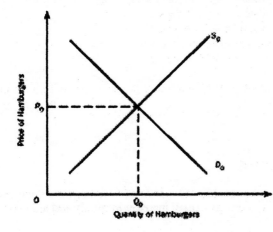

   B)   A decrease in the number of taxicab companies in New York City on cab trips.

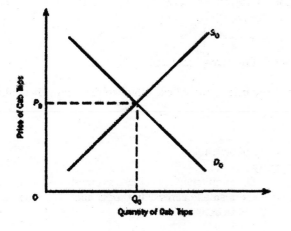

# Chapter 5: Bringing Supply and Demand Together

C) El Niño rain storms destroys the broccoli crop in two California counties.

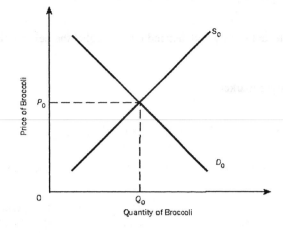

2. Use the supply and demand curves below to show:

A. simultaneous increases in supply and demand, with a large increase in supply and a small increase in demand.

B. simultaneous increases in supply and demand with a small increase in supply and a large increase in demand.

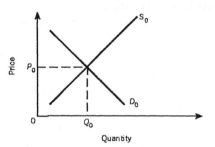

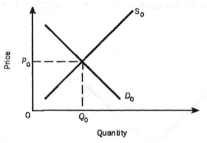

C. simultaneous decreases in supply and demand, with a large decrease in supply and a small decrease in demand

D. simultaneous decrease in supply and demand, with a small decrease in supply and a large decrease in demand

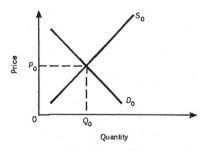

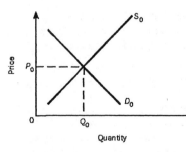

# SECTION 5.3
# PRICE CONTROLS

## KEY POINTS

- While non-equilibrium prices can crop up in the private sector, reflecting uncertainty, they seldom last for long. Governments, however, often impose non-equilibrium prices for significant time periods.

- Price controls involve the use of the power of the state to establish prices different from the equilibrium prices that would otherwise prevail.

- The motivations for price controls vary with the market under consideration. A price ceiling, or maximum price, is often set for goods deemed "important," like housing. A price floor, or minimum price, may be set on wages because wages are the primary source of income for most people.

- Price ceiling example: rent control. Under rent control the price (or rent) of an apartment is held below market rental rates over the tenure of an occupant. When an occupant moves out, the owner can usually, but not always, raise the rent to a near-market level for the next occupant.

- Some results of rent controls:

  Because living in rent-controlled apartments is a good deal, one which would be lost by moving, tenants are very reluctant to move and give up their governmentally granted right to a below-market-rent apartment.

  Because the rents received by landlords are constrained at below market levels, the rate of return on housing investments falls compared to that on other forms of real estate not subject to rent controls, reducing the incentives to construct new rental housing. Where rent controls are truly effective, there is generally little new construction going on and a shortage of apartments persists and grows over time.

  Since landlords are limited in what rent they can charge, there is little incentive to improve or upgrade rental apartments in order to get more rent. In fact, there is some incentive to avoid routine maintenance, thereby lowering the cost of apartment ownership to a figure approximating the controlled rental price.

  Rent controls promote housing discrimination. With rent controls, there are likely to be many families wanting to rent a controlled apartment, some desirable and some undesirable, as seen by the landlord, because the rent is at a below-equilibrium price. The landlord can indulge in his "taste" for discrimination in favor of "desirable" renters without any additional financial loss beyond that required by the controls.

- Price floor example: the minimum wage. Since 1938, the federal government has, by legislation, made it illegal to pay most workers an amount below a legislated minimum wage (price for labor services).

- Some results of the minimum wage:

  Because it would produce willing workers who will be unable to find jobs, an increase in the minimum wage would create additional unemployment for low skill workers.

  The unemployment impact of the minimum wage falls mainly on the least-experienced, least-skilled persons, often teenagers and minorities, holding the lowest paying jobs. They lose their jobs or are unable to get them in the first place and suffer a decline in earnings, not a gain.

  Those who continue to hold jobs with the same hours and working conditions after the minimum wage is increased gain substantially, and therefore are supporters of efforts to increase the minimum wage.

- The analysis does not "prove" minimum wages are "bad." There is an empirical question of how much unemployment is caused by minimum wages, and some might believe that the cost of unemployment resulting from a minimum wage is a reasonable price to pay for assuring that those with jobs get a decent wage. But it does impose a cost, and it falls not only on unskilled workers and employers, but also on consumers of products that were made more costly by the minimum wage.

# Chapter 5: Bringing Supply and Demand Together

- When markets are altered for policy reasons, it is wise to remember that the actual results of actions are not always as intended, as we have seen in the cases of rent control and the minimum wage. We must always look for unintended consequences, the secondary effects of an action that may occur along with the intended effects. The unintended effects may sometimes completely undermine the intended effects.

## I    REVIEW

Price controls involve the use of government power to impose _____ prices.

A maximum price imposed by government is called a _____ price. A minimum price is called a price _____.

Rent controls are laws that# set rental prices _____ the equilibrium price. Rent controls have several effects. First, people living in rent-controlled apartments are _____ to move; second, the incentive to build new rental housing is _____; third, the stock of rental housing tends to _____ over time; and fourth, rent control promotes _____ against people that landlords deem undesirable.

Minimum-wage laws set wages for unskilled workers _____ the equilibrium wage. Minimum wage laws result in a(n) _____ in the quantity of labor demanded and a(n) _____ in the quantity of labor supplied. Minimum wage laws may also result in a _____ of fringe benefits to employees.

## II    TRUE/FALSE

_____1. The main purpose of government price controls is to keep prices at equilibrium levels.

_____2. Price "ceilings" get their name from the fact that they are set above equilibrium.

_____3. Price "floors" get their name from the fact that they represent a "floor" below which the legal price cannot fall.

_____4. The rent control law in Berkeley, California, is an example of a price ceiling.

_____5. Price floors cause surpluses.

## III    MULTIPLE CHOICE

Please refer to Exhibit 1  to answer questions 1, 2, and 3.

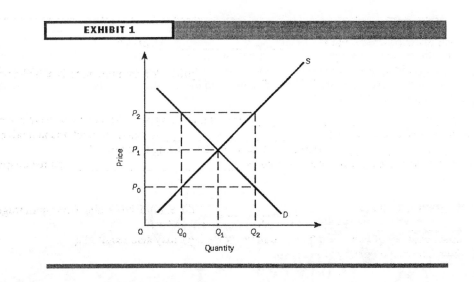

1.  In the market shown in Exhibit 1, the equilibrium price is
    A)  $P_2$.
    B)  $P_1$.
    C)  $P_0$.
    D)  not shown.

2.  If the government establishes a price ceiling at $P_0$ in the market shown in Exhibit 1, the result will be
    A)  a surplus in the amount $Q_2 - Q_0$.
    B)  a shortage in the amount $Q_1 - Q_0$.
    C)  a shortage in the amount $Q_2 - Q_0$.
    D)  market equilibrium at $Q_1$.

3.  If the government establishes a price floor at $P_2$, the result will be
    A)  a surplus in the amount $Q_2 - Q_0$.
    B)  a shortage in the amount $Q_2 - Q_0$.
    C)  a shortage in the amount $Q_0 - Q_1$.
    D)  market equilibrium at $Q_2$.

4.  Which of the following is *not* an effect of rent controls?
    A)  reduced incentives to build new rental housing
    B)  reduced incentives for landlords to keep rental units in good repair
    C)  discrimination against people# deemed undesirable on the part of landlords
    D)  increased turnover as tenants move more frequently from one rental unit to another

5. Which of the following is not likely to be an effect of an increase in the federal minimum wage?
   A) an increase in the quantity of low-skilled labor supplied
   B) a decrease in the quantity of low-skilled labor demanded
   C) a decrease in teenage unemployment
   D) an increase in teenage unemployment

## IV    APPLICATION AND DISCUSSION

Giving in to pressure from voters who charge that local theater owners are gouging their customers with ticket prices as high as $10.00 per movie, the city council of a Midwestern city imposes a price ceiling of $2.00 on all movies. What effect is this likely to have on the market for movies in this particular city? What will happen to the quantity of tickets demanded? What will happen to the quantity supplied? Who gains? Who loses?

**Questions**

1. When the price was $3.00, was there a surplus or a shortage of autographs?

2. What happened to the quantity of autographs demanded when the price rose to $10.00?

# CHAPTER 6
# ELASTICITIES

SECTION 6.1 PRICE ELASTICITY OF DEMAND

SECTION 6.2 TOTAL REVENUE AND PRICE ELASTICITY OF DEMAND

SECTION 6.3 PRICE ELASTICITY OF SUPPLY

SECTION 6.4 OTHER TYPES OF ELASTICITIES

SECTION 6.1

# PRICE ELASTICITY OF DEMAND

## KEY POINTS

- The law of demand establishes that quantity demanded changes inversely with changes in price, *ceteris paribus*. But how much does quantity demanded change? This is very important to understand for many economic issues. This is what the **price elasticity of demand** is designed to answer.

- The price elasticity of demand measures how responsive consumer behavior (quantity demanded) is to an incentive (price) change.

  The price elasticity of demand is defined as the percentage change in quantity demanded divided by the percentage change in price.

  Price elasticity of demand ($E_D$) = $\dfrac{\text{Percentage change in quantity demanded}}{\text{Percentage change in price}}$

- Following the law of demand, there is an inverse relationship between price and quantity demanded. For this reason, in theory price elasticity of demand is always negative. In practice, however, this quantity is always expressed in absolute value terms or as a positive number for simplicity.

- The percentage changes in the elasticity of demand formula are measured using the average price and average quantity, so that we do not get different values for the elasticity of demand depending on whether we moved up or down the demand curve. We are actually calculating the midpoint elasticity.

# Chapter 6: Elasticities

- The basic intuition behind elasticities is straightforward if you use an analogy to a rubber band. If the quantity demanded (or length) is very responsive to even a small change in price (or pressure), we call it elastic. If even a huge change in price (or pressure) results in only a small change in quantity demanded (or length), then demand is said to be inelastic.

- A demand curve or a portion of a demand curve can be relatively elastic, unit elastic, or relatively inelastic.

- A segment of a demand curve is **elastic** ($E_D > 1$) if the percentage change in quantity demanded is greater than the percentage change in price that caused it (a perfectly elastic demand curve is the limiting case).

- A segment of a demand curve is **inelastic** ($E_D < 1$) if the percentage change in quantity demanded is less than the percentage change in price that caused it (a perfectly elastic demand curve is the limiting case).

- A segment of a demand curve is **unit elastic** ($E_D = 1$) if the percentage change in quantity demanded equals the percentage change in the price that caused it.

- At a given point, quantity demanded is much more responsive to a given change in price on a flatter, more elastic demand curve. Therefore, when a demand curve is relatively steep, *ceteris paribus,* its price elasticity of demand is relatively low (more inelastic), and when the demand curve is relatively flat, its price elasticity of demand is relatively high (more elastic).

- For the most part, the price elasticity of demand depends on the availability of close substitutes, the proportion of income spent on the good, and the amount of time people have to adapt to a price change.

- Goods with close substitutes tend to have more elastic demands, while goods without close substitutes tend to have less elastic demand. For example, the elasticity of demand for a Ford, Toyota, or a Honda is more elastic than the demand for a car because there are more and better substitutes for a certain type of car than for a car itself. The fewer close substitutes, the less elastic the demand curve, such as insulin for diabetics, heroin for an addict, and emergency medical care.

- The smaller the proportion of income spent on a good, the lower its elasticity of demand. If the amount spent on a good relative to income is small (such as salt), then the impact of a change in its price on one's budget will also be small. As a result, consumers will respond less to price changes for these goods than for similar percentage changes in large-ticket items (such as textbooks), where a price change could have a potentially large impact on the consumer's budget.

- The more time that people have to adapt to a new price change, the greater the elasticity of demand. The more time that passes, the more time consumers have to find or develop suitable substitutes and to plan and implement changes in their patterns of consumption. Hence, the short-run demand curve is generally less elastic than the long-run demand curve.

## I    REVIEW

The price elasticity of demand measures the _____ of quantity demanded to changes in the price.

Price elasticity of demand is defined as the _____ change in quantity demanded divided by the _____ change in price.

Demand is _____ when the quantity demanded is very responsive to changes in price. In this case the price elasticity is _____ than one and the percentage change in quantity is _____ than the percentage change in price.

When demand is inelastic, the price elasticity is _____ than one and the quantity demanded is _____ very responsive to price changes.

If the demand is perfectly _____, consumers will buy the same amount regardless of the price.

# Chapter 6: Elasticities

Demand for a good will be more elastic the greater is the number of close _____ available for the good. Elasticity of demand will also be greater for goods that take up a _____ proportion of a household's budget.

The price elasticity of demand will be greater the _____ the time period consumers have to adjust to price changes.

## II     TRUE/FALSE

_____1. The price elasticity of demand equals the change in quantity demanded divided by the change in price.

_____2. The widespread availability of e-mail has increased the elasticity of demand for the service of the U.S. Postal Service.

_____3. Tim and Becky Tew have a business that organizes tours to exotic locations. They know that after raising their prices by ten percent, the quantity of tours they sell will fall by six percent. The demand for their services is inelastic.

_____4. Since auto wax is a product used to maintain a car, the elasticity of demand for auto wax is similar to the elasticity of demand for cars.

## III     MULTIPLE CHOICE

1. Marge and Al Costa own a steel mill and know that a seven percent increase in the price of the steel they sell will result in a twenty percent reduction in the quantity of steel they sell. The demand curve facing their firm is
   A) elastic.
   B) inelastic.
   C) unit elastic.
   D) unit inelastic.

2. The Up and Down Garage Door Co. knows that a five percent increase in the price they charge for doors results in a fifteen percent decrease in the number of doors they sell. What is the elasticity of demand facing the Up and Down Company?
   A) 0.05
   B) 0.33
   C) 3.0
   D) 0.15

3. In America's War on Drugs, dramatic increases in the price of heroin have had little effect on the use of the drug by heroin users. The demand for heroin among users is
   A) elastic.
   B) inelastic.
   C) unit elastic.
   D) unit inelastic.

4. The demand for petroleum products over a year is more elastic than the demand over a month. What will be the difference in the response in each of these time periods to a twenty-percent increase in price?
   A) The percentage change in quantity demanded will be greater over the year than over a month.
   B) The percentage change in quantity demanded will be less over the year than over a month.
   C) The percentage change in quantity demanded will be the same over the year than over a month.
   D) The percentage change in quantity demanded over the year will be in the opposite direction of the change over the month.

## IV    APPLICATION AND DISCUSSION

Complete the following table by circling the good that you think has a relatively *more* price elastic demand and then identify the most likely reason by putting a check in the appropriate box.

| | More Substitutes | Greater Share of Budget | More Time |
|---|---|---|---|
| 1. Cars or Chevrolets | ☐ | ☐ | ☐ |
| 2. Salt or Housing | ☐ | ☐ | ☐ |
| 3. New York Mets or Cleveland Indians | ☐ | ☐ | ☐ |
| 4. Natural Gas this month or over the year | ☐ | ☐ | ☐ |

# SECTION 6.2
# TOTAL REVENUE AND PRICE ELASTICITY OF DEMAND

## KEY POINTS

- When demand is relatively price elastic ($E_D > 1$), **total revenues** will rise as the price declines because the percentage increase in the quantity demanded is greater than the percentage reduction in price. If the price rises and the quantity demanded falls, then total revenue falls because the percentage decrease in the quantity demanded is greater than the percentage increase in price.

- When demand is relatively price inelastic ($E_D < 1$), total revenues will fall as the price declines because the percentage increase in the quantity demanded is less than the percentage reduction in price. If the price rises and the quantity demanded falls, then total revenue rises because the percentage decrease in the quantity demanded is less than the percentage increase in price.

- A straight-line demand curve (having a constant slope) will change price elasticity continuously as you move up or down it. When the price falls on the upper half of the demand curve, there is a negative relationship between price and total revenue, so demand is relatively price elastic. When the price falls on the lower half of the demand curve, there is a positive relationship between price and total revenue, so demand is relatively price inelastic.

## I    REVIEW

Total revenue is equal to the price of a good times the _____ of the good sold.

If the demand for a good is elastic, total revenues will _____ as price declines. On the other hand, if the demand for a good is inelastic, total revenues will _____ as the price declines.

If the demand for wheat is inelastic, farmers as a group will become _____ off as a result of a reduction in the supply of wheat.

The steeper one demand curve is relative to another, the more _____ it is relative to the other, although the elasticity of demand _____ along a linear demand curve.

# Chapter 6: Elasticities

As you move along a linear demand curve from a high price to a low price, the demand changes from relatively
_____ at high prices to relatively _____ at low prices.

## II    TRUE/FALSE

_____1. If Guillermo sells 100 dozen donuts at $3.60 per dozen, the total revenue he receives is $360.00

_____2. If Guillermo increases the price of his donuts and the total revenue he receives goes down, the demand for donuts is elastic.

_____3. When the demand for a good is relatively elastic, price and total revenue vary in the same direction.

## III    MULTIPLE CHOICE

1.  When the demand for a good is relatively *elastic,* total revenues will rise as the price declines because the
    A)   percentage increase in the quantity demanded is greater than the percentage decrease in price.
    B)   percentage increase in quantity demanded is less than the percentage decrease in price.
    C)   quantity demanded remains the same as price decreases.
    D)   decline in price is offset by a decline in quantity demanded.

2.  If the demand for a good is relatively *inelastic,* total revenues will rise as price rises because the
    A)   percentage increase in price is offset exactly by the percentage decrease in quantity demanded.
    B)   increase in price is accompanied by an equal increase in quantity demanded.
    C)   percentage increase in price is greater than the percentage decrease in quantity demanded.
    D)   percentage increase in price is less than the percentage decrease in quantity demanded.

Use the weekly demand schedule for Sunshine Video Rentals in Cloverdale, Minnesota, shown in Exhibit 1 to answer questions 3 and 4.

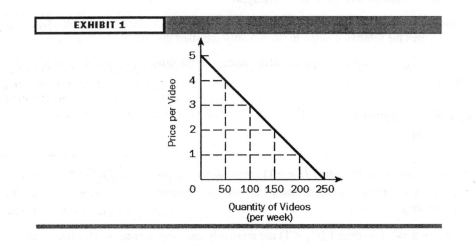

**EXHIBIT 1**

3.  When Sunshine Video Rentals lowers their rental price from $4 to $3, total revenue
    A)   goes from $200 per week to $300 per week.
    B)   goes up from $250 per week to $400 per week.
    C)   goes down from $300 per week to $200 per week.
    D)   remains the same.

4. Between a price of $2 and a price of $1, demand is
   A) elastic.
   B) inelastic.
   C) unitary elastic.
   D) multielastic.

## IV    APPLICATION AND DISCUSSION

1. The Cowtown Hotel is the only first-class hotel in Fort Worth. The hotel owners were concerned by an increase in the hotel's vacancy rates. Wayne Bruce, the manager of the hotel, hired Lastic and Associates, an economics consulting group, to offer advice about improving the hotel's profitability. Dr. Lastic suggested they could increase this year's revenue by raising prices.

   "What's going on?" thought Wayne. He asked Dr. Lastic, "Won't raising prices reduce the quantity of hotel rooms demanded and increase vacancies?"

   What was Lastic's reply? Explain why Lastic would suggest increasing prices.

SECTION 6.3

# PRICE ELASTICITY OF SUPPLY

## KEY POINTS

- According to the law of supply, there is a positive relationship between price and quantity supplied, *ceteris paribus*. But by how much does quantity supplied change as price changes?

- The **price elasticity of supply** measures how responsive the quantity sellers are willing to sell is to changes in the price. In other words, it measures the relative change in the quantity supplied that results from a change in price.

- The price elasticity of supply ($E_S$) is defined as the percentage change in the quantity supplied divided by the percentage change in price.

  $E_S =$ Percentage change in quantity supplied
  
     Percentage change in price

- Goods with a supply elasticity that is greater than 1 ($E_S > 1$) are relatively elastic in supply. With that, a 1 percent change in price will result in a greater than 1 percent change in quantity supplied. (The extreme case is perfectly elastic supply, where $E_S =$ infinity.)

- Goods with a supply elasticity that is less than 1 ($E_S < 1$) are relatively inelastic in supply. This means that a 1 percent change in the price of these goods will induce a proportionately smaller change in the quantity supplied. (The extreme case is perfectly inelastic supply, where $E_S = 0$.)

- Time is usually critical in supply elasticities because it is more costly for producers to bring forth and release resources in shorter periods of time. Hence, supply tends to be more elastic in the long run than the short run.

# Chapter 6: Elasticities

- The relative elasticity of supply and demand determines the distribution of the tax burden for a good. If demand has a lower elasticity than supply in the relevant tax region, the largest portion of the tax is paid by the consumer. However, if demand is relatively more elastic than supply in the relevant tax region, the largest portion of the tax is paid by the producer. In general, the tax burden falls on the side of the market that is less elastic, which has nothing to do with who actually pays the tax at the time of the purchase.

## I    REVIEW

The price elasticity of _____ is defined as the percentage change in the quantity supplied divided by the percentage change in the price. It measures how _____ the quantity sellers are willing to sell is to changes in price.

When supply is perfectly _____, a change in the price will not change the amount supplied. When supply is perfectly _____, no goods will be sold below a certain price, but at higher prices, as much as buyers want will be supplied.

Supply is more elastic in the _____ run than in the _____ run.

The relative supply and demand elasticities determine the _____ of the burden of a tax imposed on a good or service. If the demand is relatively _____ elastic than supply, the producer pays the greater proportion of the tax. If demand is relatively _____ elastic than supply, the consumer pays the greater proportion of the tax.

## II    TRUE/FALSE

_____ 1. While the price elasticity of demand increases with time, the price elasticity of supply for all goods and services is constant over time.

_____ 2. If the supply elasticity of electricity in California is less than the supply elasticity in New York, the prices in California must be higher.

_____ 3. If the supply of corn is perfectly inelastic, there is no price increase that will result in an increase in the quantity supplied.

## III    MULTIPLE CHOICE

1. An increase in the price elasticity of the supply of cement since 2001 means that a given percentage increase in the price of cement will result in
   A) a smaller percentage increase in the quantity of cement supplied than prior to 2001.
   B) a larger percentage increase in the quantity of cement supplied than prior to 2001.
   C) a smaller percentage increase in the quantity of cement demanded than prior to 2001.
   D) a larger percentage decrease in the quantity of cement supplied than prior to 2001.

2. When the supply of a good is perfectly inelastic, an increase in the price will result in
   A) an increase in the quantity of the good supplied.
   B) a decrease in the quantity of the good supplied.
   C) no change in the quantity of the good supplied.
   D) an increase in the quantity of the good demanded.

3. Past studies have shown that a 10 percent increase in the price of men's shoes results in a 23 percent increase in the quantity producers will supply. What is the price elasticity of supply in this case?
   A) 23.0
   B) 2.30
   C) 0.43
   D) 0.23

4. Suppose that government programs to discourage smoking, like ad campaigns and warning labels, have the effect of changing elasticity of demand for smoking from inelastic to elastic. How will this change the distribution of the burden of the cigarette sales tax?
   A) Smokers' share of the burden will increase.
   B) Producers' share of the burden will increase.
   C) The share of the burden will not change.
   D) The share of the burden will increase for both consumers and producers.

## IV    APPLICATION AND DISCUSSION

Mayor George Henry has a problem. He doesn't want to anger voters by taxing them because he wants to be reelected, but the town of Gapville needs more revenue for its schools. He has a choice between taxing tickets to professional basketball games or food.

If the demand for food is relatively inelastic while the supply is relatively elastic, and if the demand for professional basketball games is relatively elastic while the supply is relatively inelastic, in which case would the tax burden fall primarily on consumers? In which case would the tax burden fall primarily on producers?

# SECTION 6.4
# OTHER TYPES OF ELASTICITIES

## KEY POINTS

- The **cross price elasticity of demand** measures both the direction and magnitude of the impact that a price change for one good will have on the quantity of another good demanded at a given price.

- The cross price elasticity of demand is defined as the percentage change in quantity demanded of one good at a given price divided by the percentage change in price of another good.

Cross price elasticity of demand = $\dfrac{\text{Percentage change in quantity demanded of one good at a given price}}{\text{Percentage change in price}}$

- If the cross price elasticity of demand between two goods is positive, they are substitutes because the price of one good and the demand for the other move in the same direction. If the cross price elasticity of demand between two goods is negative, they are complements because the price of one good and the demand for the other move in opposite directions.

- The **income elasticity of demand** is a measure of the relationship between a relative change in income and the consequent relative change in quantity demanded, *ceteris paribus*. The income elasticity of demand coefficient not only expresses the degree of the connection between the two variables, but it also indicates whether the good in question is normal or inferior.

- The income elasticity of demand is defined as the percentage change in quantity demanded at a given price divided by the percentage change in income.

Income elasticity of demand = $\dfrac{\text{Percentage change in quantity demanded at a given price}}{\text{Percentage change in income}}$

- If the income elasticity is positive, then the good in question is a normal good because the change in income and the change in quantity demanded move in the same direction. If the income elasticity is negative, then the good in question in an inferior good because the change in income and the change in quantity demanded move in opposite directions.

## I    REVIEW

The cross elasticity of demand measures the effect on the quantity demanded of one good of a change in the price of _____ good. It is equal to the percentage change in the quantity demanded of one good at a given _____ divided by the percentage change in the price of a second good.

The _____ as well as the magnitude of the change is measured by the cross elasticity.

In general, a positive cross elasticity means the two goods are _____ and a negative cross price elasticity means the two goods are _____ .

An elasticity that measures the percentage change in the quantity demanded of a good, *ceteris paribus,* given a 1-percent change in income is called the _____ elasticity of demand.

The good is a normal good when demand and income move in the _____ direction and it will have a positive income elasticity. If the income elasticity of demand is negative, the good is an _____ good.

## II    TRUE/FALSE

_____1. The cross elasticity of demand of cars made by Ford and Toyota is negative.

_____2. If bus travel in the United States is an inferior good, a five percent increase in per capita incomes will result in an increased number of bus trips per person in the United States.

_____3. Last year the consumption of melons increased by about four percent. While prices and many other factors affecting melon consumption remained the same, per capita income increased by about four percent. The income elasticity of melon demand is four.

_____4. The income elasticity of food is less than 1, so as a country's income grows it will spend a decreasing share of its national income on food products.

## III    MULTIPLE CHOICE

1.  A study commissioned by the Santa Fe Zephyrs baseball team found that, *ceteris paribus*, when incomes in Santa Fe increased by 40 percent, ticket sales went up by 20 percent. What is the income elasticity of demand for Zephyrs tickets?
    A)  20
    B)  40
    C)  2.0
    D)  0.5

2.  If the cross elasticity of demand between football ticket prices and baseball ticket sales was negative, football and baseball games are
    A)  substitutes.
    B)  complements.
    C)  inferior.
    D)  superior.

3.  A study of the housing market in Anchorage, Alaska, found the income elasticity of demand for mobile homes was negative. This shows that mobile homes in Anchorage are
    A)  substitute goods.
    B)  complementary goods.
    C)  inferior goods.
    D)  normal goods.

4.  Which of the following identifies a pair of goods that are substitutes?
    A)  Food and water: the income elasticity of food is less than the income elasticity of water.
    B)  Frozen food and gasoline: the cross price elasticity of demand is greater than zero.
    C)  Lawn mowers and electric saws: the price elasticity of demand for mowers is less than the elasticity of saws.
    D)  Cigarettes and coffee: the cross price elasticity of demand is negative.

## IV    APPLICATION AND DISCUSSION

You have the following observations on U.S. intercity rail travel:

Between 1990 and 1993 rail travel increased from 17.5 passenger miles per person to 19 passenger miles per person. At the same time neither per mile railroad price or incomes changed but the per mile price of intercity airline travel increased by 7.5 percent.

Between 1995 and 1998 per capita incomes rose by approximately 13 percent while the price of travel by rail and plane stayed constant. Intercity rail travel was 20 passenger miles per person in 1995 and 19.5 in 1998.

Assuming the demand for travel didn't change between these periods:

1.  Calculate the income elasticity of demand for intercity rail travel.

2.  Calculate the cross price elasticity of demand for intercity rail travel.

3.  What type of good is intercity rail travel?

## Questions

1. Why did Mr. Lowell choose chicken rather than steak for his barbecue?

2. In the comic strip, the price of chicken has fallen. Cite two things that could have made the price of chicken fall.

# CHAPTER 7
# MARKET EFFICIENCY AND WELFARE

SECTION 7.1 CONSUMER SURPLUS AND PRODUCER SURPLUS

SECTION 7.2 THE WELFARE EFFECTS OF TAXES AND SUBSIDIES

# SECTION 7.1
# CONSUMER SURPLUS AND PRODUCER SURPLUS

## KEY POINTS

- What a consumer actually pays for a good is usually less than what she is willing to pay. The monetary difference between what the consumer is willing to pay and what the consumer actually pays is called **consumer surplus.**

- Consumer surplus is shown graphically as the area under the demand curve (willingness to pay for the units consumed) and above the market price (what must be paid for those units).

- If the consumer is a buyer of several units of a good, the earlier units will have greater marginal value and therefore create more consumer surplus because marginal willingness to pay falls as greater quantities are consumed in any period.

- An increase in supply will lower the price and increase your consumer surplus for each of the units you were already consuming, and will also increase consumer surplus from increased purchases at the lower price. Conversely, a decrease in supply will increase the price and lower the amount of consumer surplus.

- **Producer surplus** is the difference between what a producer is paid for a good and the seller's cost for producing each unit of the good. Because some units can be produced at a cost that is lower than the market price, the seller receives a surplus, or net benefit, from producing those units.

- Producer surplus for a particular unit is the difference between the market price and the seller's cost of producing that unit. Total producer surplus is shown graphically as the area under the market price (what was paid for those units) and above the supply curve (the total cost, or sum of marginal costs, of producing those units).

- A higher market price due to an increase in demand will increase total producer surplus. Part of the added surplus is due to a higher price for the quantity already being produced, and part is due to the expansion of output made profitable by the higher price.

# Chapter 7: Market Efficiency and Welfare

- With the tools of consumer and producer surplus, we can better analyze the total gains from exchange. The demand curve represents a collection of maximum prices that consumers are willing and able to pay for additional quantities of a good or service, while the supply curve represents a collection of minimum prices that suppliers require to be willing to supply additional quantities of that good or service.

- At the market equilibrium, consumers receive consumer surplus and producers receive producer surplus. Both consumers and producers benefit from trading every unit up to the market equilibrium output. Buyers purchase each good, except for the very last unit, for less than the maximum amount that they would have been willing to pay; sellers receive more than the minimum amount they would have been willing to accept to supply the good.

- Once the equilibrium output is reached at the equilibrium price, all of the mutually beneficial trade opportunities between the suppliers and the demanders will have taken place, and the sum of consumer and producer surplus is maximized.

- The **total welfare gain** to the economy from trade in a good is the sum of the consumer and producer surplus created. Consumers benefit from additional amounts of consumer surplus and producers benefit from additional amounts of producer surplus.

- A deadweight loss is the net loss of total surplus that results from the misallocation of resources.


## I        REVIEW

The difference between what a consumer *actually* pays for a good and what they are *willing* to pay is called consumer

_____.

A consumer's willingness to pay _____ for each additional unit of the good he consumes. Earlier units purchased add _____ to consumer surplus for later ones.

When price falls consumer surplus increases because you buy _____ of the good and because you get _____ consumer surplus from those units you would have purchased at the original price.

As the price of a product falls, the consumer surplus derived from consumption of the product _____.

The difference between the price a seller is paid for a good and her cost of providing it is _____ surplus.

The welfare gain from trade of a product equals the _____ of the consumer surplus and the producer surplus created by each unit traded. Both buyer and seller are _____ from each of the units traded than they would have been without trade.

Once the equilibrium output is reached, all _____ _____ trade opportunities between suppliers and demanders will have taken place.

A deadweight loss is a reduction in total surplus that results from the _____ of resources.


## II        TRUE/FALSE

_____1. In an efficient market, the prices that consumers pay for goods and services are equal to the value that they derive from those goods and services.

_____2. If Choon would be willing to pay $30 to attend a Dodger game but actually pays $20, he receives a consumer surplus of $10.

_____3. During the winter of 2000–2001, regulations prevented California electric utilities from raising the price per kilowatt hour they charged customers. When the cost of producing electricity rose, the utilities' producer surplus declined.

## III    MULTIPLE CHOICE

1.  When Roy buys one more apple because of a decrease in the price of apples, the marginal willingness to pay for the extra apple is
    A)  greater than that of previous apples and his consumer surplus goes up.
    B)  less than that of previous apples but his consumer surplus is larger.
    C)  less than that of previous apples and his consumer surplus goes down.
    D)  the same as that of previous apples and there is no change in his consumer surplus.

To answer questions 2 and 3 please refer to Exhibit 2.

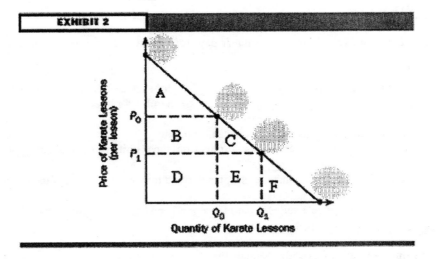

2.  Carmine thinks he should be more assertive and believes that karate lessons would help. If the price of each karate lesson is $P_0$, his consumer surplus is equal to the area
    A)  a + b + c + d + e + f
    B)  d + e + f
    C)  a
    D)  b + c + d + e

3.  If the price falls from $P_0$ to $P_1$, the change in Carmine's consumer surplus is equal to the area
    A)  a + b + c
    B)  b + c
    C)  d + e
    D)  c + e + f

4.  The group, Doctors of Optometry Protest Exchange in Sunglasses, wants to stop international trade in sunglasses. These D.O.P.E.S. argue that because producing countries earn a producer surplus, free, unregulated trade is bad because producers are exploiting consumers. What do the D.O.P.E.S. ignore about trade?

A) Consumers will be better off as long as the consumer surplus is greater than the producer surplus.
B) Consumers will be better off as long as the consumer surplus plus the producer surplus is greater than one.
C) Consumers will be better off as long as the consumer surplus is greater than zero.
D) Consumers will be better off as long as the producer surplus is less than zero.

## IV    APPLICATION AND DISCUSSION

Steve loves potato chips. His weekly demand curve is shown in Exhibit 3.

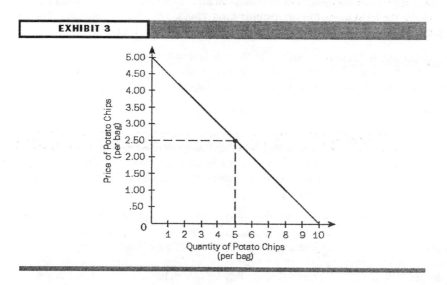

EXHIBIT 3

A) How much is Steve willing to pay for one bag of potato chips?

B) How much is Steve willing to pay for a second bag of potato chips?

C) If the actual market price of potato chips is $2.50, and Steve buys five bags as shown, what is the value of his consumer surplus?

D) What is Steve's total willingness to pay when he buys five bags?

SECTION 7.2
# THE WELFARE EFFECTS OF TAXES AND SUBSIDIES

## KEY POINTS

- We can use consumer and producer surplus to measure the welfare effects of various government programs, such as taxes, subsidies, and price controls.

# Chapter 7: Market Efficiency and Welfare

- **Welfare effects** refer to the gains and losses associated with government intervention.

- After a tax is imposed, consumers pay a higher price and lose the corresponding amount of consumer surplus as a result. Producers receive a lower price after tax and lose the corresponding amount of producer surplus as a result. The government gains the amount of the tax revenue generated, which is transferred to others in society.

- The deadweight loss of a tax occurs because the tax reduces the quantity exchanged below the original output level, reducing the size of the total surplus realized from trade. The tax distorts market incentives: the price to buyers is higher than before the tax, so they consume less, and the price to sellers is lower than before the tax, so they produce less. This leads to deadweight loss, or market inefficiencies—the waste associated with not producing the efficient output.

- The size of the deadweight loss from a tax, as well as how the burdens are shared between buyers and sellers, depends on the elasticities of supply and demand. Other things equal, the less elastic the demand curve, the smaller the deadweight loss. Similarly, the less elastic the supply curve, the smaller the deadweight loss. The more elastic the curves the greater the change in output and the larger the deadweight loss.

- Elasticity differences can help us understand tax policy. Those goods that are heavily taxed often have a relatively inelastic demand curve in the short run. This means that the burden falls mainly on the buyer. It also means that the deadweight loss to society is smaller than if the demand curve was more elastic.

- A government subsidy also produces a deadweight loss. This welfare loss results from production that is greater than competitive equilibrium.

- We can see the welfare effects of a price ceiling by observing the change in consumer and producer surplus from the implementation of the price ceiling. Consumers can now buy at a lower price, but cannot buy as much as before (since suppliers will not supply as much). Producers lose producer surplus from the lower imposed ceiling price. The net loss is a deadweight loss triangle.

- We can also use consumer and producer surplus to see the welfare effects of a price floor, where the government buys up the surplus. Consumers lose consumer surplus due to the higher price floor, and must also pay taxes to pay for the buying and storing of the unsold (to consumers) output. Producers gain producer surplus from the higher prices and greater output (since the government buys up what is not sold on the market). On net, there is a deadweight loss from the price floor because consumers are buying less than the market equilibrium output and producers are producing more.

## I    REVIEW

The efficient output occurs at the market-clearing price, which is where the sum of consumer and producer surplus is _____. Economists refer to the gains and losses associated with government intervention in the economy as _____ effects.

The net loss in consumer and producer surplus from government intervention in the economy is called a _____ loss. This loss results because government intervention distorts market _____, like price.

Taxes result in consumers buying _____ because they pay a higher price and suppliers selling less because they receive a _____ price. The net loss results because the _____ output is not produced.

The size of the deadweight loss from a tax on a good depends on the _____ of supply and demand.

The deadweight loss from a price ceiling results from production that is _____ than the efficient output. The loss from a price floor results from consumers buying _____ than the efficient output and producers producing _____.

## II    TRUE/FALSE

_____1. While deadweight loss from a tax is smaller the less elastic the demand for a product, it is greater the less elastic the supply.

_____2. If the governor of the Misty Isles imposes a $75 tax on tourists coming for day visits, only the tourists will suffer the deadweight loss.

_____3. Rent control is a price ceiling that imposes losses on consumers.

_____4. Economists don't worry much about the losses imposed by taxes because we are only losing deadweight.

## III    MULTIPLE CHOICE

1. In which of the following cases will there be no deadweight loss from a tax increase?
   A) The demand for the product is perfectly elastic.
   B) The demand for the product is perfectly inelastic.
   C) The demand for the product is more elastic than supply.
   D) The demand for the product is less elastic than supply.

2. Mayor Lexion needs to raise public revenues to balance the budget before this year's election. He doesn't want to impose much of a welfare loss on his community. Mayor Lexion should probably *not* tax which of the following goods?
   A) salt
   B) used cars
   C) cigarettes
   D) matches

3. When the government introduced agricultural price supports, it ususally also became the buyer of last resort, purchasing the surplus created by the price floor. Which of the following is *not* a likely outcome of a price support program for cheese?
   A) Consumer surplus declines because consumers pay a higher price and consume less.
   B) Consumers' tax bills go up as they pay to buy the surplus cheese surplused.
   C) Producer surplus declines because they receive less and produce more.
   D) Producers sell less to consumers and more to the government.

## IV    APPLICATION AND DISCUSSION

The 2000–2001 California energy crisis produced brownouts, utility company bankruptcies, and worries about high prices. The California electric power regulatory program imposed price ceilings on electricity sold to consumers. Exhibit 4 describes the California situation with $P_S$ as the price ceiling. Answer the following referring to this exhibit.

# Chapter 7: Market Efficiency and Welfare

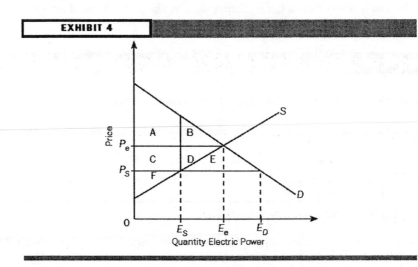

A) What was the loss imposed on consumers by this price ceiling?

B) What was the loss imposed on producers by this price ceiling?

C) What was the loss imposed on California by this price ceiling?

D) Use this exhibit to explain the brownouts in California.

E) What would have to be true for consumers to support market set prices? Use the exhibit to explain why there might not be support among consumers for raising prices.

# CHAPTER 8
# MARKET FAILURE AND PUBLIC CHOICE

## SECTION 8.1
# MARKET FAILURE AND EXTERNALITIES

### KEY POINTS

- Sometimes the market system fails to produce efficient outcomes because of a lack of competition or the side effects of what economists call **externalities**.

- An **externality** is said to occur whenever there are physical impacts (benefits or costs) of an activity on individuals not directly involved in the activity. If the impact on the outside party is negative, it is called a **negative externality**; if the impact is positive, it is called a **positive externality**.

- The classic example of a negative externality is the air used by a polluting factory. The polluted air "spills over" to outside parties. Such damages are real costs. Unlike the other resources the firm uses in production, no one owns the air, so the firm does not have to pay for its use.

- If a firm can avoid paying the cost it imposes on others—the external costs—it lowers its own costs of production, but not the true cost to society. As a result, it will tend to produce too much from society's standpoint, causing an efficiency loss due to an overallocation of scarce resources to the production of the good.

- The government can intervene in market decisions in an attempt to take account of negative externalities. It may do this by estimating the amount of those external costs and then taxing the manufacturer by that amount, forcing the manufacturer to bear the costs. If government could impose a pollution tax equal to the cost of the negative externality, then the firm would produce at a socially desired level of output. Tax revenues could be used to compensate those who had suffered damages from the pollution or in some other productive way.

- As an alternative to pollution taxes, the government might simply prohibit certain types of activities causing pollution, or might force firms to clean up their emissions.

- For some goods, the individual consumer does not receive all of the benefits. The benefits not received by the consumer are called positive externalities. (Examples include landscaping and education.)

- Because the decision makers involved ignore some of the real social benefits, the private market does not provide enough of goods that generate external benefits. This often results in the government subsidizing or producing many goods, such as subsidized education and "free" inoculations against communicable diseases.

- At the market equilibrium for goods providing external benefits, output is less than the efficient level because many people that benefit do not have to pay for those benefits. If we could add the benefits that are derived by nonpaying consumers, the demand curve would shift to the right, increasing output.

- Because producers are unable to collect payments from all of those that are benefiting from the good or service, the market has a tendency to underproduce goods with external benefits, causing an efficiency loss. A subsidy equal to external benefits would shift the demand curve to the right and result in an efficient level of output. The government could also use regulation in such situations.

- In either the case of external benefits or external costs, buyers and sellers are receiving the wrong signals: The apparent benefits or costs of some action differ from the true social benefits or costs.

- Sometimes externality problems can be handled by individuals without the intervention of government. People may decide to take steps to minimize their own negative externalities or to contribute to the production of goods with positive externalities. (Examples include choosing not to drive a gas guzzling car, or choosing to donate time or money to schools because of the positive externality associated with education.)

## I        REVIEW

When the costs or benefits of an activity impact people outside the market mechanism, economists say a(n) _____ exists.

If production or exchange harms outside parties, it is called a(n) _____ externality. If production or exchange benefits outside parties, it is called a(n) _____ externality.

Air pollution is an example of a(n) _____ externality.

If the education of a person benefits not only that person, but others as well, economists say that education generates _____ externalities.

When producers are unable to collect payments from all those who benefit from a good, the market has a tendency to produce too _____ of the good.

When producers shift the costs of producing a good onto others who are not involved in production or consumption of the good, the market tends to produce too _____ of the good.

## II       TRUE/FALSE

_____1. Litter is an example of a positive externality.

_____2. Economists believe that producers pollute because they are evil.

_____3. Cigarette smoke is an example of a negative externality.

_____4. The aroma from a neighbor's lilac bush is an example of a positive externality.

_____5. If fertilizer producers are able to shift some of their production costs onto outside parties, the actual output of fertilizer is likely to fall short of society's ideal.

_____6. When production of a good generates significant positive externalities, the government can improve economic efficiency by subsidizing it.


## III    MULTIPLE CHOICE

1. Mae likes to go to bed early while Vinnie, who lives in the apartment next door, likes to stay up late and play the drums. Vinnie is probably
   A) a thoughtful and considerate neighbor.
   B) providing Mae with a positive externality.
   C) inflicting a negative externality on Mae.
   D) "rocking" Mae to sleep.

2. In a market where firms are able to cut their private costs by shifting costs onto others, which of the following will *not* be found?
   A) Negative externalities will occur.
   B) Output of the good being produced will be too low.
   C) The prices of products produced by the firms will be too low.
   D) Inefficiencies will occur.

3. If Carl spends thousands of dollars beautifying his front yard, he is probably
   A) inflicting a negative externality on his neighbors.
   B) providing his neighbors with a positive externality.
   C) reducing the value of his own home.
   D) reducing the value of his neighbors' homes.

4. Mayor Casterbridge believes that education benefits everyone and urges the City Council to provide the school district with more money. An economist would say that the Mayor believes that
   A) there are nontrivial external costs associated with education.
   B) there are positive external benefits associated with education.
   C) teachers are overpaid.
   D) teachers promote ideas that undermine family values.

5. To correct a negative externality like pollution, government may properly consider all but which of the following?
   A) impose special taxes on activities that cause pollution
   B) prohibit activities that cause pollution
   C) force polluting firms to clean up emissions
   D) provide special subsidies for activities that cause pollution

6. To promote activities that generate positive externalities like a healthier, more beautiful environment, government may properly consider all but which of the following?
   A) special taxes on the activities that generate positive externalities
   B) provide subsidies to producers who produce goods that provide positive externalities
   C) provide subsidies to consumers who consume goods that provide positive externalities
   D) pass laws that require people to consume goods that provide positive externalities like education and inoculations for communicable diseases


## IV    APPLICATION AND DISCUSSION

In the town of Appleton, where apple growing is the primary industry, Mayor Singleton has asked the City Council to provide parcels of free public land to beekeepers for the establishment of apiaries (places where honey bees are kept). From what you know about bees, externalities, and opportunity costs, evaluate the Mayor's proposal.

# SECTION 8.2
# PUBLIC GOODS

## KEY POINTS

- **Public goods** are another source of market failure. Unlike private goods, the consumption of public goods is neither **rival** nor **excludable**. (National defense and flood control are examples—all those affected benefit simultaneously and it is prohibitively costly to exclude anyone from consuming it.)

- Public goods and externalities can lead to the **free-rider problem**. It might well be advantageous from society's perspective to provide a public good, such as cleaner air, but people have little incentive to pay for the benefits they will receive because they know that they cannot be prevented from receiving the benefits.

- We are likely to get too little of public goods without some intervention. The fact that people who do not pay for public goods cannot be excluded from consuming them precludes charging consumers for benefits received, encouraging beneficiaries to act as free riders, so that some goods with benefits greater than costs will not be produced.

- Because non-payers cannot be excluded from enjoying the benefits of public goods the free-rider problem prevents the private market from supplying the efficient amount of public goods. The government may be able to overcome the free-rider problem by providing or financing the public good and imposing taxes to pay for it.

## I    REVIEW

A good that is yours and yours alone is called a _____ good. Goods that are both not rival and not excludable are called _____ goods.

Someone who receives benefits that they don't pay for is called a _____ rider.

Because non-payers can't be excluded from consumption and because of the free-rider problem, the market tends to produce too _____ public goods.

## I    TRUE/FALSE

_____1. National defense is an example of a public good.

_____2. A Ford Expedition is an example of a public good.

_____3. The difference between private and public goods is whether or not a private party or a public agency owns them.

_____4. Since the free market tends to overproduce public goods, governments often undertake policies to discourage their production.

## III    MULTIPLE CHOICE

1.  Leanne pays $5.00 to attend a Fourth of July fireworks display at Prospect Park, while Crystal watches the fireworks from the parking lot next to the park. Crystal is
    A) a free rider.
    B) a rivalrous consumer.
    C) an excludable consumer.
    D) unpatriotic.

2.  Talk radio programs like "Rush Limbaugh" and "Dr. Laura" are
    A) rival in consumption.
    B) not excludable.
    C) excludable.
    D) positive externalities.

3.  Public goods are
    A) cheap to produce, but expensive to buy.
    B) exclusive in consumption and rival in consumption.
    C) nonrival in consumption and nonexclusive.
    D) impossible for free riders to consume.

4.  Where a free-rider problem exists, goods tend to be
    A) underproduced and overconsumed.
    B) underconsumed and overproduced.
    C) high priced and available only to the rich.
    D) low priced and available only to the poor.

## IV    APPLICATION AND DISCUSSION

Review the list of goods below and determine whether they are private or public goods by indicating whether or not they are nonrival and/or nonexclusive. Remember public goods are both nonrival in consumption (one person's consumption doesn't diminish another's) and nonexclusive (you can't keep nonpayers out).

| Good | Nonrival Consumption | Nonexclusive | Private Good | Public Good |
|---|---|---|---|---|
| 1. Hot Dogs | ☐ | ☐ | ☐ | ☐ |
| 2. Cable TV | ☐ | ☐ | ☐ | ☐ |
| 3. Broadcast TV | ☐ | ☐ | ☐ | ☐ |
| 4. Automobiles | ☐ | ☐ | ☐ | ☐ |
| 5. National Defense | ☐ | ☐ | ☐ | ☐ |
| 6. Pollution Control | ☐ | ☐ | ☐ | ☐ |
| 7. Parking in a Parking Structure | ☐ | ☐ | ☐ | ☐ |

| | | | | |
|---|---|---|---|---|
| 8. A Sunset | ☐ | ☐ | ☐ | ☐ |
| 9. Admission to a Theme Park | ☐ | ☐ | ☐ | ☐ |

# SECTION 8.3

# IMPERFECT INFORMATION

## KEY POINTS

- Information can be treated like most other scarce goods: It is desirable and limited, and people are willing to pay a positive price to obtain it. Just as in any other cost–benefit evaluation, however, individuals will stop searching for information prior to making decisions when the cost of obtaining that additional information outweighs the benefit they expect to gain from it.

- When information costs to consumers are greater than the perceived benefits, consumers will make less informed decisions. As George Stigler pointed out, "It is perfectly rational for people to make 'poor' decisions if the cost of information necessary to make good decisions exceeds the benefits."

- Much legislation passed at the federal as well as the state and local levels in the past 50 years seems directed towards reducing information costs and keeping consumers from making dangerous or worthless purchases. (Examples include food inspection, occupational licensing, and requiring provision of certain information.)

- Few quarrel with the objective of reducing information costs to consumers and suppliers, which permits more intelligent market decisions and leads to greater satisfaction. However, there is opposition to certain types of governmental action in this area on the grounds that the costs of providing the information is too high, that the government is disseminating inaccurate or misleading information, or that special interest groups have managed to manipulate the regulation to their own advantage, which may not be in the public interest. (An example is occupational licensing laws, which supposedly protect misinformed consumers from getting shoddy services, but may also restrict competition, reducing the supply of workers providing these services, and leading to higher prices. FDA testing requirements are another example.)

- Government-provided information can be an efficient mechanism for reducing market failure from information costs. But excessive government information policies can actually worsen the allocation of resources when the information provided is costly, relatively useless, and/or creates other market imperfections, such as monopoly due to licensing.

- **Caveat Emptor**, or "let the buyer beware," is less comforting as products become more sophisticated and numerous and consumers have a more difficult time getting objective information to evaluate products. Information costs are very high. But product liability laws can make it unprofitable to sell shoddy merchandise, providing a substantial incentive to provide safe products independent of government regulations.

- **Asymmetric information** exists when the available information is initially distributed in favor of one party relative to another. Examples include sellers of defective used cars (lemons).

- If quality-detection costs are sufficiently high, high quality products will tend to be withdrawn from the market and the average quality will fall. The phenomenon where one party enters into an exchange with another who has more information is called **adverse selection**.

- In adverse selection situations, the least-cost solution would have the seller reveal his superior information to a potential buyer. The problem is that it's not individually rational for the seller to provide a truthful and complete disclosure, and this is known by a potential buyer. Only if the seller is punished for not truthfully revealing exchange-relevant information will a potential buyer perceive the sellers disclosure as truthful.

- The existence of asymmetric information gives rise to **signaling** behavior on the part of sellers, such as demonstrating the ability to complete a college degree. Signaling cuts employers' hiring costs.

- Another information problem associated with the insurance market is **moral hazard**. If an individual is insured against a cost, they have reduced incentives to take precautions against those costs, which can result in higher costs and therefore higher insurance rates. Moral hazard arises from the fact that it is costly for the insurer to monitor the behaviors of the insured party. Warranty agreements that limit the responsibility of the insurer in those situations are one method of controlling a user's potential abuse.

## I      REVIEW

Since information is scarce like other goods, people will stop searching for it when the _____ of obtaining additional information outweighs the _____ they expect to gain from it.

Government often acts to reduce _____ costs for consumers.

Occupational _____ laws are intended to insure consumers that certain standards will be met by providers of goods and services.

Occupational licensing laws often restrict the _____ of services and lead to _____ prices to consumers.

Governmental information policies can actually reduce efficiency when the costs of providing the information exceed the _____ of the information.

Asymmetric _____ exists when one party to a trade has better information than the other. In the used car market this may result in "_____ cars driving good cars from the market."

Obtaining a college degree may be considered a form of _____ behavior that indicates intelligence and perseverance.

_____ hazard is an information problem in the insurance market that results from the high cost of monitoring the insured. Insurance against risks changes a person's _____ to take precautions against risk.

## II      TRUE/FALSE

_____1. A rational person will get all the information she possibly can before making any decision.

_____2. Information supplied to consumers by the government helps them make better decisions.

_____3. Warning labels on cigarette packages are a form of information provided to consumers by government.

_____4. Climbers on North America's highest peak, Mt. McKinley take more risks because current National Park Service policy insures that they will be rescued if they get into trouble.

_____5. Signaling behavior on the part of job-seekers is futile because employers know it has nothing to do with real job performance or productivity.

## III    MULTIPLE CHOICE

1. The City Council of a northeastern city has recently voted to eliminate their requirement that taxis have special licenses in order to operate. Henceforth anyone with a valid driver's license can carry passengers for a fee. The likely effect of this program will be
   A)  higher cab fares.
   B)  fewer taxis.
   C)  higher cab fares and fewer taxis.
   D)  lower cab fares and more taxis.

2. Which of the following statements is false?
   A)  Information can be useful.
   B)  Gathering information is costly.
   C)  You can't have too much information.
   D)  Rational people will gather information as long as the marginal benefits of information are greater than the marginal costs.

3. Which of the following is *not* an objection to the provision of government information services?
   A)  The costs to government of providing some types of information is too high.
   B)  Government sometimes disseminates inaccurate information.
   C)  Government often provides consumers with valuable information about potentially dangerous products.
   D)  Special interest groups often manage to manipulate regulations to their own advantage.

4. Good apples cost more to produce than bad apples because good apples are harvested later and with more care. Consumers, however, can't tell the difference between the two before they bite into them. Why will the good apples be driven from the market?
   A)  Producers will always concentrate on the lowest cost goods and would never produce good apples.
   B)  Consumers don't know enough to identify a really good apple until after they've tasted it, and would prefer to pay less.
   C)  Consumers would not be willing to pay more than the cost of a bad apple for any apple, so good apples growers would lose money and leave the business.
   D)  Producers wouldn't sell bad apples unless consumers preferred them to good apples.

## IV    APPLICATION AND DISCUSSION

In order to get a license to practice in the United States, foreign-trained veterinarians must take an exam given by the American Veterinary Association. Only 48 people per year are allowed to take the exam, which is administered at only two universities. The fee for the exam, which must be booked at least 18 months in advance, was recently raised from $2,500 to $6,000. ("Checkbooks Ready?" *Wall Street Journal*, July 7, 1998, p. 1.)

What effects does this clinical competency exam have on the number of veterinarians practicing in the United States? Do you think it improves the quality of veterinary services?

# SECTION 8.4
# PUBLIC CHOICE

## KEY POINTS

- When the market fails, as in the externality or the public good case, it may be necessary for government to intervene and make public choices. However, just because markets have failed to generate efficient results doesn't necessarily mean that government can do a better job.

- **Public choice analysis** is the application of economic principles to politics. Public choice economists believe that government actions are an outgrowth of individual behavior. Specifically, they assume that the behavior of individuals in politics, like those in the marketplace, will be influenced by self-interest. Bureaucrats, politicians, and voters make choices that they believe will yield them expected marginal benefits that are greater than their expected marginal costs.

- There are differences between the private sector and the public sector in the "rules of the game." But the self-interest assumption is central to the analysis of behavior in both arenas.

- Scarcity and competition are present in the public sector, as well as in the private sector.

- In private markets, there is an **individual-consumption-payment link,** where the goods one gets reflects what one is willing to pay for. The link breaks down when goods are decided on by majority rule. If the majority decides that certain goods will be provided, people will have to purchase the goods through higher taxes, whether they value the goods or not.

- In a two-party political system successful candidates will seek to please **median voters**, those in the middle of the distribution of voter preferences.

- There are both costs and benefits to being politically informed.

- For most people, the costs of becoming politically informed are substantial, while the benefits are negligible. As a result, most people assume a state of **rational ignorance**.

- Individuals often come together with others that have similar political goals to form **special interest groups**. The activities of these groups are usually aimed at getting substantial benefits for a relatively few individuals while spreading the costs over such a large number of taxpayers that the amount any one person will have to pay is negligible.

## I    REVIEW

The application of economic principles to politics is called public _____ theory.

Economists assume that people are influenced by self-_____ in both the private and public arenas.

In the public sector the presence of _____ forces politicians and voters to make choices.

Unlike the private sector, choices made in the public sector by majority rule break the individual-consumption-_____ link. When the majority decides what to purchase, individuals pay for goods through higher _____, independent of the value they attach to the goods.

# Chapter 8: Market Failure and Public Choice

## II    TRUE/FALSE

_____1. Public choice theory is the study of how people make decisions in their private lives.

_____2. Public choice economists believe that politicians and voters are motivated primarily by their concern for the welfare of others.

_____3. Making efficient decisions in the public sector is more difficult than in the private sector because efficient public decisions would require information on the desires of all of the many people affected.

## III    MULTIPLE CHOICE

1. Public choice analysis of government behavior shares each of the following principles with economic analysis of market behavior *except* which one?
   A)  the assumption that people act out of self-interest
   B)  that scarcity is present in both the public and private sectors
   C)  the assumption that people in the private sector act out of self-interest while those in the public sector are motivated by concern for the good of all
   D)  the belief that competition is present in both the public and private sectors

2. Clinton's Supermarket has established a new policy. Consumers no longer shop for individual items, filling their grocery carts and paying for the total purchased. They are now assigned carts that are already filled and must pay the price assigned to the cart. This approach to shopping is inefficient because it
   A)  breaks the individual-consumption-payment link.
   B)  lowers the information costs involved in shopping.
   C)  causes more wear and tear on the carts since they are used more often.
   D)  saves consumers precious time spent shopping.

3. Most independent studies of sports facilities like major league ball parks have found that they
   A)  provide no significant economic benefits to the community.
   B)  actually reduce overall income in the community.
   C)  usually boost overall employment in the community.
   D)  are particularly good investments because they generate significant benefits without costing the community anything.

4. Surveys reveal that most citizens are not well-informed about political issues. According to public choice theory, this is due to the fact that
   A)  most TV and radio news shows are of poor quality.
   B)  most people tend to identify themselves as either Republicans or Democrats and mindlessly follow the recommendations of party leaders.
   C)  schools tend to do a poor job teaching students about political issues.
   D)  for most people, the costs of being politically informed exceed the benefits.

## IV    APPLICATION AND DISCUSSION

As you have learned, economists assume that individuals respond in predictable ways to incentives. Public choice theorists assume that this is true in both the private *and* public sectors. Examine the lists below and match each individual with the incentive to which they are likely to respond.

Individual

1) Grocery Shopper
2) U.S. Senator
3) Business Owner
4) U.S. Federal Agency Director
5) Factory Worker
6) Voter

Incentive

a) re-election
b) higher salary
c) low food prices
d) high profits
e) a bigger budget
f) more government services

Questions

1.  How do helmet laws affect the costs of motorcycle riding?

2.  How do they affect the benefits of motorcycle riding?

# CHAPTER 9
# MACROECONOMIC GOALS

# SECTION 9.1
# MACROECONOMIC GOALS

## KEY POINTS

- Nearly every society has been interested in three major macroeconomic goals: (1) maintaining unemployment at a low level, meaning that jobs are relatively plentiful and financial suffering from lack of work is relatively uncommon; (2) maintaining prices at a relatively stable level, so that consumers and producers can make better decisions; and (3) achieving a high rate of economic growth, meaning a growth in real, per-capita total output over time.

- In addition to these primary goals, concern has been expressed at various times and places about other economic issues, such as the "quality of life," reducing "bads" such as pollution, fairness in the distribution of income or wealth, or becoming self-sufficient in the production of certain goods or services.

- Individuals differ considerably in their evaluation of the relative importance of certain issues, or even whether certain "problems" are really problems after all. Economic growth, viewed positively by most people, is considered bad by some; while some people think the income distribution is just about right, others think it provides insufficient incomes to the poorer members of society. Still others think it involves an excessive confiscation of the income of the relatively rich and thereby reduces incentives to carry out productive income-producing activities.

# Chapter 9: Macroeconomic Goals

- Many economic problems—particularly those involving unemployment, price instability, and economic stagnation—are pressing concerns for the U.S. government. The concern over both unemployment and price instability led to the passage of the **Employment Act of 1946**, in which the United States committed itself to policies designed to reduce unemployment in a manner consistent with price stability.

## I      REVIEW

The three major macroeconomic goals of the United States are: (1) maintaining employment of human resources at relatively _____ levels; (2) maintaining prices at a relatively _____ level; and (3) achieving a _____ rate of economic growth.

Other economic goals that the United States has pursued include concern for the _____ of life, _____ in the distribution of income, and becoming self-_____ in the production of certain goods and services.

With the Employment Act of 1946, the U.S. government committed itself to reduce _____ in a manner consistent with price _____.

## II      TRUE/FALSE

_____1. When the United States implemented policies in the 1970s that reduced U.S. dependence on foreign oil, it was pursuing an important economic goal.

_____2. The macroeconomic goals of high employment, a stable price level, and high economic growth are shared by most societies.

## III      MULTIPLE CHOICE

1. If the president makes a speech in which he states that "inflation and deflation are scourges that must be avoided," he is expressing support for which of the following macroeconomic goals?
   A) a high level of employment
   B) a stable level of prices
   C) a high rate of economic growth
   D) becoming self-sufficient in the production of certain goods and services

2. In 1971, President Nixon ordered that all prices and wages be "frozen" at their current levels. Nixon was pursuing which of the following macroeconomic goals?
   A) a high level of employment
   B) a stable level of prices
   C) a high rate of economic growth
   D) clean air and water

## IV    APPLICATION AND DISCUSSION

| | EXHIBIT 1 | High Rate of Employment | Stable Level of Prices | High Economic Growth |
|---|---|---|---|---|
| A study of economics usually reveals that the best time to buy anything was last year.—Marty Allen | | ☐ | ☐ | ☐ |
| Inflation is the one form of taxation that can be imposed without legislation. —Milton Friedman | | ☐ | ☐ | ☐ |
| A lot of fellows nowadays have a B.A., M.D., and Ph.D. Unfortunately, they don't have a J.O.B.—Fats Domino | | ☐ | ☐ | ☐ |
| In practice, growth creates winners and losers. It spurs the expansion of some industries and regions—and the decline of others. It confers and revokes status. It undermines tradition. It empowers some nations and imperils others. It disrupts settled ways and compels people (and institutions) to alter comfortable habits. It generates insecurity.—Robert Samuelson, in The Good Life and Its Discontents | | ☐ | ☐ | ☐ |
| We should offer help and hope to those Americans temporarily left behind by the global marketplace or by the march of technology. That's why we have more than doubled funding for training dislocated workers since 1993—and if my new budget is adopted, we will triple funding.—President Bill Clinton in his 1998 State of the Union Address | | ☐ | ☐ | ☐ |

Read the quotations in Exhibit 1 and indicate which of the major macroeconomic goals they refer to by checking the appropriate box.

# SECTION 9.2
# EMPLOYMENT AND UNEMPLOYMENT

## KEY POINTS

- High rates of unemployment in a society can lead to increased tensions and despair. Society loses some potential output of goods when some of its productive resources—human or nonhuman—remain idle, and potential consumption is also reduced. Clearly, then, there is a loss in efficiency when people are willing to work but productive equipment remains idle. Hence, other things equal, relatively high rates of unemployment are almost universally viewed as bad.

- The unemployment rate is one measure of labor market conditions. The **unemployment rate** is the number of people officially unemployed divided by the labor force.

- Official unemployment measures those over the age of 16 who are available for employment, but are unable to obtain a job. The **labor force** is number of people over the age of 16 who are either employed or unemployed. The civilian labor force figure excludes those in the armed services, prison or mental hospitals, as well homemakers, retirees, and full-time students because they are not considered currently available for employment.

- By far the worst employment downturn in United States history was the Great Depression, which began in late 1929 and continued until 1941. Unemployment fell from only 3.2 percent of the labor force in 1929 to more than 20 percent in the early 1930s, and double-digit unemployment persisted through 1941. The debilitating impact of having millions of productive persons out of work led Americans (and persons in other countries too) to say "Never again." Some economists would argue that modern macroeconomics, with its emphasis on the determinants of unemployment and its elimination, truly began in the 1930s.

- Unemployment since 1960 has ranged from a low of 3.5 percent in 1969 to a high of 9.7 percent in 1982. Unemployment in the worst years is twice or more what it is in good years. Before 1960, variations tended to be even more pronounced.

- In periods of prolonged recession, some individuals feel that the chances of landing a job are so bleak that they quit looking. These "discouraged workers," who have not actively sought work for four weeks, are not counted as unemployed; instead they fall out of the labor force. Also, people looking for full-time work who grudgingly settle for a part-time job are counted as "fully" employed, yet they are only "partly" employed. However, at least partially balancing these two biases in government employment statistics is the number of people who are overemployed— that is, working overtime or extra jobs. Also, jobs in the underground economy are not reported at all. In addition, there may be many people who claim they are actually seeking work when, in fact, they may just be going through the motions so that they can continue to collect unemployment compensation or receive other government benefits.

- Unemployment usually varies greatly between different segments of the population and over time. Across sex and race, the unemployment rate among college graduates is significantly lower than for those without a high-school diploma or for those with some college education, but who have not completed a bachelor's degree. Unemployment tends to be greater among the very young, among blacks and other minorities, and among less-skilled workers. Adult female unemployment tends to be higher than adult male unemployment.

- Considering the great variations in unemployment for different groups in the population, we calculate separate unemployment rates for groups classified by sex, age, race, family status, and type of occupation.

- There are four main categories of unemployed workers: **job losers** (temporarily laid off or fired), **job leavers** (quit), **re-entrants** (worked before and now re-entering labor force), and **new entrants** (entering the labor force for first time—primarily teenagers).

- Job losers typically account for 50 to 60 percent of the unemployed, but sizeable fractions are also due to job leavers, new entrants, and re-entrants.

- While unemployment is painful, reducing unemployment is not costless. In the short run, a reduction in unemployment may come at the expense of a higher rate of inflation, especially if the economy is close to full capacity, where resources are almost fully employed. Also, trying to match employees with jobs quickly may lead to significant inefficiencies because of mismatches between the worker's skill level and the level of skill required for a job. The skills of the employee may be higher than that necessary for the job, resulting in **underemployment**.

- The duration of unemployment is equally as important as the amount of unemployment in determining its financial consequences. The duration of unemployment tends to be greater when the amount of unemployment is high, and smaller when the amount of unemployment is low. Unemployment of any duration, of course, means a potential loss of output that is permanent; it is not made up when unemployment starts falling again.

- The percentage of the population that is in the labor force is called the **labor force participation rate**. Since 1950 it has increased from 59.2 percent to 67.1 percent, mostly between 1970 and 1990. The increase can be attributed in large part to the entry of the baby boomers into the labor force and a 14.2 percentage point increase in women's labor force participation rate.

## I    REVIEW

High rates of _____ cause society to suffer losses in the potential output of goods and services because some of its productive resources are idle. High unemployment results in a loss of _____.

The _____ force is the number of people over the age of 16 who are willing and able to work. This includes people who are employed and _____.

The unemployment rate is the _____ of the labor force who are unable to find a job. To calculate the unemployment rate, we _____ the number of unemployed by the number of people in the labor force.

When people think the chances of finding a job are so bleak that they quit looking, they are called _____
workers. They are _____ counted as unemployed because they are not in the labor force.

The incidence of unemployment varies widely among the population. Unemployment rates are _____
than average for the very young, racial minorities, and less-skilled workers. Unemployment rates are also significantly
_____ for college educated people than for those without a high school diploma.

It is a common misconception that most of the unemployed have lost their jobs. In reality there are four categories of
unemployed workers: job _____, job _____, re-entrants, and
_____ entrants to the labor force.

Government policies to reduce unemployment may result in inflation and inefficiencies resulting from the
_____ of worker skills and job requirements. _____ occurs when the skills an
employee has are greater than those required by the job.

The duration of unemployment is as important as the amount of unemployment at any time. The duration of unemployment
tends to be _____ when the amount of unemployment is high.

## II    TRUE/FALSE

_____1. While the consequences of unemployment for individuals and families may be grave, society suffers no loss.

_____2. When unemployment is low, a greater proportion of the unemployed are likely to be job leavers.

_____3. The unemployed who are returning to the labor force or entering it for the first time are not included in the
unemployment rate.

## III    MULTIPLE CHOICE

1.  In Iuka, Mississippi, there are 500 people willing and able to work and only 250 of those people have jobs. The
    unemployment rate in Iuka is
    A) 200 percent.
    B) 250 people.
    C) 50 percent.
    D) 2.5 percent.

2.  Which of the following groups is most likely to have unemployment rates that are less than the national average?
    A) teenagers
    B) college graduates
    C) blacks
    D) high-school dropouts

3.  After looking for full-time work for ten weeks, Wendy finds a part-time job and the unemployment rate falls. How
    does the official unemployment rate understate the true degree of unemployment?
    A) It continues to treat Wendy as unemployed because she is only employed part time.
    B) It treats Wendy as a discouraged worker and drops her from the labor force.
    C) Since Wendy is overemployed, it counts her twice.
    D) Even though Wendy is working less than she wants to work, she is no longer considered unemployed.

## IV    APPLICATION AND DISCUSSION

1.  Find the appropriate unemployment rate for the sequence of events described below.

    A)  Potterville has a labor force of 10,000 people and 1,000 of them cannot find work. The unemployment rate is
    _____.

    B)  In Potterville, 500 of the unemployed become discouraged and stop looking for work. The unemployment rate is
    _____.

    C)  The Potterville government creates jobs for 250 of the discouraged workers. The unemployment rate is
    _____.

    D)  The Potterville Peanut Butter Company lays off 750 people. The unemployment rate is _____.

    E)  The Potterville Peanut Butter Company creates 250 new jobs for 250 high-school graduates who are entering the
    labor force. The unemployment rate is _____.

# SECTION 9.3
# TYPES OF UNEMPLOYMENT

## KEY POINTS

- There are numerous types of unemployment: frictional, structural, and cyclical.

- **Frictional unemployment** results from persons being temporarily between jobs; it is short term and results from the normal turnover in the labor market.

- Geographic and occupational mobility are considered good for the economy, generally leading human resources from activities of relatively low productivity or value to areas of higher productivity, increasing output in society as well as the wage income of the mover. Hence, frictional unemployment, while not good in itself, is a by-product of a healthy phenomenon, and because it is short-lived, is therefore not generally viewed as a serious problem. It is unusual for it to be much less than 2 percent of the labor force. It tends to be somewhat greater in periods of low unemployment, when job opportunities are plentiful.

- **Structural unemployment** reflects the existence of persons who lack the necessary skills for jobs that are available. Structural employment makes it wise to look at both unemployment and job vacancy statistics in assessing labor market conditions. Like frictional unemployment, it reflects the dynamic dimension of a changing economy. Over time, new jobs open up that require new skills, while old jobs that required different skills disappear. Many persons advocate
government-subsidized retraining programs as a means of reducing structural unemployment.

- The dimensions of structural unemployment are debatable, in part because of the difficulty in precisely defining the term in an operational sense. Structural unemployment varies considerably.

- To a considerable extent, one can view both frictional and structural unemployment as phenomena resulting from imperfections in the labor market. If individuals seeking jobs and employers seeking workers had better information about each other, the amount of frictional unemployment would be considerably lower. But because information and job searches are costly, the bringing of demanders and suppliers of labor services together does not occur instantaneously.

- In years of relatively high unemployment, cyclical unemployment may result from short-term cyclical fluctuations in the economy. During a recession, or whenever the unemployment rate is greater than the natural rate, there is **cyclical unemployment**.

- Given its volatility and dimensions, unemployment resulting from inadequate demand is viewed as especially correctable through government policies. Most attempts to solve the unemployment problem have placed an emphasis on increasing aggregate demand. Attempts to reduce frictional unemployment by providing better labor market information and to reduce structural unemployment through job retraining have also been made, but these efforts have received fewer resources and much less attention from policy makers.

- The median, or typical annual unemployment rate, has been at or slightly above 5 percent. Some economists call this the **natural rate of unemployment.** When unemployment rises well above 5 percent, we have abnormally high unemployment; when it falls below 5 percent, we have abnormally low unemployment. The natural rate of unemployment of approximately 5 percent roughly equals the sum of frictional and structural unemployment when they are at a maximum. Thus, one can view unemployment rates below the natural rate as reflecting the existence of a below average level of frictional and structural unemployment. When unemployment rises above the natural rate, however, it reflects the existence of cyclical unemployment.

- Today, economists, for the most part, have come to accept a current range somewhere between 4.5 and 5.5 percent for the natural rate of unemployment. The natural rate of unemployment may change over time as technological, demographic, institutional, and other conditions vary.

- When all of the economy's labor resources, and other resources like capital, are fully employed, the economy is said to be producing its potential level of output. That is, at the natural rate of unemployment, all resources are fully employed and the economy is producing its **potential output**.

- When the economy is experiencing cyclical unemployment, the unemployment rate is greater than the natural rate. The economy can also temporarily exceed potential output, as workers take on overtime or moonlight by taking on extra employment.

## I    REVIEW

Unemployment that results from persons being temporarily between jobs is called _frictional_ unemployment, while unemployment that reflects a mismatch between the skills that people have and the skills they need to find employment is called _structural_ employment.

Unemployment that results from insufficient overall demand for labor is called _cyclical_ unemployment.

Unemployment that occurs because certain types of jobs are seasonal in nature is called _seasonal_ unemployment.

Unemployment compensation _lowers_ the opportunity cost of being unemployed and _raises_ the unemployment rate.

New inventions generally _lower_ production costs, generate _higher_ incomes for producers, and _reduce_ prices for consumers.

Economists refer to the median or "typical" rate of unemployment as the _natural_ rate of unemployment.

## II    TRUE/FALSE

_T_ 1. Economists consider frictional unemployment to be the by-product of a healthy economy.

_F_ 2. Unemployment compensation generally helps to lower the unemployment rate.

F 3. The natural rate of unemployment has not changed since the 1960s.

## III    MULTIPLE CHOICE

1.  A ski instructor who becomes unemployed during the summer is
    A)  frictionally unemployed.
    B)  structurally unemployed.
    C)  cyclically unemployed.
    D)  seasonally unemployed.

2.  When an office worker loses her job because she lacks the computer skills her employer requires, she becomes
    A)  frictionally unemployed.
    B)  structurally unemployed.
    C)  cyclically unemployed.
    D)  seasonally unemployed.

3.  When unemployment rises above the natural rate, it reflects the existence of _____ unemployment.
    A)  frictional
    B)  structural
    C)  cyclical
    D)  seasonal

## IV    APPLICATION AND DISCUSSION

Throughout history, technological advances have resulted in the displacement of workers. Mechanical harvesters replaced workers with scythes, bulldozers replaced men with shovels, and machinery has replaced millions of factory workers. Yet the number of jobs available today in all industrial countries is far greater than it was a hundred years ago.  How is this possible? Why doesn't technological advance result in an overall reduction in the number of available jobs?

# SECTION 9.4
# REASONS FOR UNEMPLOYMENT

## KEY POINTS

- Obstacles in labor markets prevent wages from adjusting to bring into balance the quantity of labor supplied and the quantity of labor demanded. When wages are higher than the market equilibrium wage, the quantity of labor supplied is greater than the quantity of labor demanded, leading to unemployment.

- Economists have cited three reasons for the failure of wages to balance labor demand and labor supply—minimum wages, unions, and the efficiency wage theory. Each results in wage rates above their equilibrium level, decreasing employment and increasing unemployment.

- A **minimum wage** can set the wage for unskilled workers above the equilibrium level, leading to a surplus of unskilled workers and higher unemployment.

- Unions negotiate their wages and benefits through **collective bargaining.** If bargaining raises the union wage above the equilibrium level, the quantity of union labor supplied will exceed the quantity of union labor demanded, leading to higher unemployment.

- Union workers who keep their jobs are better off, but those who become unemployed either seek nonunion work or wait to be recalled in the union sector, which is the reason many economists believe there is a wage premium to union jobs over comparable nonunion jobs. This has led to the **insider-outsider hypothesis,** that those who keep the union wage above the equilibrium level—the insiders—have little or no concern for outsiders—nonmembers or previous members.

- In the **efficiency wage model,** employers pay their employees more than the equilibrium wage to be more efficient, believing that higher wages will lead to greater productivity by attracting the most productive workers, reducing job turnover, increasing worker morale, lowering hiring and training costs, reducing absenteeism, and reducing shirking. (Henry Ford's $5 a day wage is an example.) But because the wage is above the equilibrium level, the quantity of labor supplied exceeds the quantity of labor demanded, and greater amounts of unemployment result.

- Because of frictional unemployment, we would have some unemployment even if there were a balance between labor supply and labor demand, as workers and employers engage in a search for costly information about abilities, opportunities, compensation packages, tastes, and preferences. In a dynamic economy, jobs are constantly being destroyed and created. This leads to lots of temporary unemployment as workers search for the best job for their skills.

- Unemployment insurance is designed to offset the hardships of unemployment. Those who have worked a certain period of time and lost their job because the employer no longer needed their skill get compensation that is typically half salary for up to 26 weeks. However, it also leads to prolonged periods of job searching because it lowers the opportunity cost of being unemployed. It has been estimated that this may raise unemployment rates by as much as 1 percentage point. A longer search might mean a better match, but it comes at the expense of lost production and greater amounts of tax dollars.

- Although many believe technological advances displace workers, this is not necessarily the case. If new equipment is a substitute for labor (e.g., self-service beverage bars), then it might displace workers. However, new capital equipment means that new workers will be needed to manufacture and repair it, and it may generate a whole new growth industry that creates jobs. The key point is that new inventions are generally cost saving, and these cost savings will generally generate higher incomes for producers and lower prices and better products for consumers—benefits that will ultimately result in the growth of other industries. The problem is that it is easy to just see the initial effect (displaced workers) of technological advances, without recognizing the implications of that invention throughout the whole economy over time.

## I     REVIEW

When wages are above the equilibrium wage rate, the quantity of labor supplied is _greater_ than the quantity of labor demanded.

Economists have cited three reasons for the failure of wages to balance labor _demand_ and supply. They are (1) _minimum_ wages; (2) unions; and (3) _efficiency_ wages.

Unemployment insurance _lowers_ the opportunity cost of being unemployed and _raises_ the rate of unemployment.

New technologies usually _reduce_ production costs and generate _higher_ incomes for producers and result in _lower_ prices and better products for consumers.

## II    TRUE/FALSE

___F___ 1. The main effect of minimum wage laws is on the market for highly skilled workers.

___T___ 2. According to the "insider-outsider hypothesis," union members have little concern for nonmembers when engaged in collective bargaining with employers.

## III    MULTIPLE CHOICE

1. Which of the following is likely to occur following an increase in the minimum wage?
   A) an increase in the number of unskilled workers hired
   B) a decrease in the number of unskilled workers hired
   C) a decrease in the unemployment rate for teenagers
   D) an increase in the unemployment rate for highly skilled workers

2. According to the efficiency wage model, which of the following is *not* a reason that employers pay higher wages?
   A) Employers believe that higher wages reduce turnover.
   B) Employers believe that higher wages result in better worker morale.
   C) Employers believe that higher wages help attract the most productive employees.
   D) Employers believe that higher wages will increase training costs.

3. Economists believe that the introduction of new, labor-saving technology
   A) results in a steady increase in the unemployment rate.
   B) displaces workers in certain industries, but creates new jobs in others.
   C) actually lowers the profits of firms in the industry that adopts the new technology.
   D) results in higher prices for consumers.

## IV    APPLICATION AND DISCUSSION

In the United States, unemployed workers can typically receive about half of their former salary for a maximum of 26 weeks. What do you think would happen to the unemployment rate and the average duration of unemployment if the law were changed so that workers could get two-thirds of their former pay for a year? Explain.

# SECTION 9.5
# INFLATION

## KEY POINTS

- Just as full employment brings about economic security of one kind, an overall stable price level increases another form of security. **Inflation** is a continuing rise in the overall price level. **Deflation** is a falling overall price level. In both inflation and deflation, a country's currency unit changes in purchasing power. Without price stability, consumers and producers will experience more difficulty in coordinating their plans and decisions.

- In general, the only thing that can cause a sustained increase in the rate of inflation is a high rate of growth in money.

- Unanticipated and sharp price changes are almost universally considered to be a "bad" thing that needs to be remedied by some policy.

- The **Consumer Price Index** is the standard measure of inflation.

- Retirees on fixed pensions, creditors, and those whose incomes are tied to long-term contracts can be hurt by inflation because it erodes the purchasing power of money they receive. Debtors and those who can quickly raise the prices on their goods can gain from inflation.

- Wage earners sometimes lose from inflation because wages may rise at a slower rate than the price level.

- The uncertainty that inflation creates can also discourage investment and economic growth.

- Inflation brings about changes in real incomes, and these changes may be either desirable or undesirable. The redistributional impact of inflation is not the result of conscious public policy; it just happens.

- Inflation can raise one nation's price level relative to price levels in other countries, which can lead to difficulties in financing the purchase of foreign goods or to a decline in the value of the national currency relative to that of other countries. In its extreme form, inflation can lead to a complete erosion in faith in the value of money, as in Germany after both world wars, or hyperinflation, as in Argentina in the 1980s and Brazil in the 1990s.

- In periods of high and variable inflation, households and firms have a difficult time distinguishing changes in relative prices from changes in the general price level, distorting the information that flows from price signals. This undermines good decision making.

- Another cost of inflation is the cost that firms incur as a result of being forced to change their prices more often. These include **menu costs**—the costs of changing posted prices—and **shoe-leather costs**—the costs of checking on your assets. These costs are modest with low inflation rates, but can be quite large where inflation is substantial.

- The **real interest rate**—the increase in purchasing power per year—equals the **nominal interest rate**—the amount you have to pay in dollars and cents—minus the inflation rate.

- If people correctly anticipate inflation, they will behave in a manner that will largely protect them against loss. To protect themselves, creditors will demand a rate of interest that is large enough to compensate for the deteriorating value of the dollar.

- An interest rate is, in effect, the price that one pays for the use of funds. Like other prices, interest rates are determined by the interaction of demand and supply forces. The lower the interest rate (price), the greater the quantity of funds people will demand, *ceteris paribus*; the higher the interest rate (price), the greater the quantity of loanable funds supplied by individuals and institutions like banks, *ceteris paribus*. The equilibrium price, or interest rate, will be where the quantity demanded equals the quantity supplied.

- When people start expecting future inflation, creditors become less willing to lend funds at any given interest rate because they fear they will be repaid in dollars of lesser value than those they loaned. This is depicted by a leftward shift in the supply curve of loanable funds (a decrease in supply). Likewise, demanders of funds (borrowers) are more anxious to borrow because they think they will pay their loans back in dollars of lesser purchasing power than the dollars they borrowed. Thus, the demand for funds increases. Both the decrease in supply and the increase in demand push up the interest rate to a new, higher equilibrium level. Whether the equilibrium quantity of loanable funds will increase or decrease depends on the relative sizes of the shifts in the respective curves.

- Often lenders are able to anticipate inflation with reasonable accuracy. If the inflation rate is accurately anticipated, new creditors do not lose, nor do debtors gain, from inflation.

- Nominal interest rates and real interest rates do not always move together. For example, in periods of high unexpected inflation, the nominal interest rates can be very high while the real interest rates are low or even negative.

- Increasingly, groups (laborers, pensioners, etc.) try to protect themselves from inflation by using cost-of-living clauses in contracts. Personal income taxes are also now indexed for inflation. Some have argued that we should go one step further and index everything, meaning that all contractual arrangements would be adjusted frequently to take account of changing prices. Such an arrangement might reduce the impact of inflation, but it would also entail additional contracting costs (and not every good—notably currency—can be indexed).

# Chapter 9: Macroeconomic Goals

- Approaches to try to stop inflation include various policies relating to the amount of government spending, tax rates, or the amount of money created, as well as **wage and price controls**—legislation limiting wage and price increases.

## I    REVIEW

Most prices in the U.S. economy tend to _____rise_____ over time.

When the price level is rising, we have _____inflation_____. When the price level is _____falling_____, we have deflation. The standard measure of the price level in the United States is the Consumer Price _____Index_____.

Without price stability, it is difficult to _____coordinate_____ plans and decisions. Most people consider _____unanticipated_____ sharp price changes a bad thing.

Inflation _____lowers_____ the real incomes of people who live on fixed incomes such as retirees. Workers and suppliers who operate on _____long_____-term contracts that set prices will also see their real incomes decline as a result of inflation.

Creditors may be hurt by inflation because it reduces the real value of the _____Principal_____ loaned by the time it is paid back. _____Debtors_____ gain from inflation because the dollars they are paying back have less purchasing power.

Inflation imposes other costs on society. _____Menu_____ costs are the costs incurred when firms have to change posted prices frequently. _____Shoe_____-leather costs are the costs associated with managing your assets to minimize the loss from inflation.

The real interest rate is corrected for _____inflation_____. The nominal interest rate is the real interest rate plus the _____anticipated_____ rate of inflation. We can calculate actual real interest rates by _____subtracting_____ the inflation rate from the nominal interest rate.

Nominal interest rates are determined by the intersection of the _____demand_____ and _____supply_____ for loanable funds. Expected inflation will shift the demand curve for loanable funds to the _____right_____ and the supply curve to the _____left_____, which increases the _____nominal_____ interest rate.

If people correctly _____anticipate_____ inflation, they will behave in a way that will protect them from loss. When creditors expect inflation, they will be _____less_____ willing to lend funds at any given nominal interest rate, which results in nominal rates _____rising_____ to account for the effects of inflation. Groups, such as labor unions, may also use _____cost_____ of living clauses in contracts to protect themselves from inflation.

## II    TRUE/FALSE

_F_ 1. Price instability may be a fact for some economies, but this instability imposes no real costs.

_F_ 2. There is no way for wage earners to protect themselves from the effects of inflation.

_T_ 3. An increase in the real rate of interest will result in an increase in the nominal rate of interest even though there is no expected increase in the rate of inflation.

# Chapter 9: Macroeconomic Goals

## III    MULTIPLE CHOICE

1. In the nineteenth century, U.S. farmers were ordinarily debtors, since they had to borrow from banks to develop new farms and to buy inputs prior to each growing season. Why did farmers generally support public policies that were inflationary?
   A) Inflation meant the real value of the farmers' products would be greater.
   B) Inflation meant farmers would be repaying their loans with more valuable dollars.
   C) Inflation meant farmers would be repaying their loans with less valuable dollars.
   D) Inflation meant the nominal value of the farmers' products would be less.

2. Murray "the calculator" Miller is an economist who advises the local loan shark, Nathan Toledo. Murray anticipates a 10 percent rate of inflation. What advice would Murray give to Nathan?
   A) To protect himself from inflation, Nathan should raise the interest rate he charges by 10 percent.
   B) To protect himself from inflation, Nathan should lower the interest rate he charges by 10 percent.
   C) To protect himself from inflation, Nathan should not make loans when there is anticipated inflation.
   D) To protect himself from inflation, Nathan should increase the number of loans he makes at the current interest rate.

3. What will happen to the nominal interest rate when suppliers of loanable funds expect significant inflation but demanders anticipate deflation?
   A) Nominal interest rates will always rise.
   B) Nominal interest rates will always fall.
   C) Nominal interest rates will never change but real rates will fall.
   D) Nominal interest rates may either rise or fall or stay the same.

## IV    APPLICATION AND DISCUSSION

Suppose you are a banker who expects the rate of inflation to remain the same from year to year. In other words, if the rate of inflation in 2001 was 3 percent, you would expect the same rate of inflation in 2002. Assume the real rate of interest is zero. Fill in Exhibit 2 for a one-year loan of $1,000. In which of these historical periods would a banker be worse off making such a loan?

**EXHIBIT 2**

| Historical Period | Inflation Rate for Previous Year | Nominal Interest Rate | Inflation Rate for Loan Year | Real Interest Rate |
|---|---|---|---|---|
| 1946–1947 | 18.1% | 18.1% | 8.8% | 9.3 |
| 1978–1979 | 9.0 | 9.0% | 13.3 | −4.3 |
| 1993–1994 | 2.7 | 2.7% | 2.7 | 0 |
| 1920–1921 | 2.6 | 2.6% | −10.8 | 13.4 |

118

SECTION 9.6

# ECONOMIC FLUCTUATIONS

## KEY POINTS

- **Business cycles** refer to the short-term fluctuations in economic activity, not to the long-term trend in output, which in modern times has usually been upward.

- A business cycle has four phases: expansion, peak, contraction, and trough. The expansion phase usually is longer than the contraction, and in a growing economy, output (real GDP) will rise from one business cycle peak to the next.

- **Expansion** is when output is rising significantly, unemployment is falling, and both consumer and business confidence is high. Thus, investment is rising, as well as expenditures for expensive durable consumer goods, such as automobiles and household appliances. The **peak** is when the expansion comes to an end, when output is at the highest point in the cycle. The **contraction** is a period of falling real output, and is usually accompanied by rising unemployment and declining business and consumer confidence. Investment spending and expenditures on consumer durable goods fall sharply in a typical contraction. This contraction phase can also be called a **recession**. Usually a recession is said to occur if there are two quarters of declining real GDP. The **trough** is the point in time when output stops declining; it is the moment when business activity is at its lowest point in the cycle. Unemployment is relatively high at the trough, although the actual maximum amount of unemployment may not occur exactly at the trough. Often unemployment remains fairly high well into the expansion phase.

- Business cycles are not uniform in length. In both the 1980s and 1990s, the expansions were quite long by historical standards.

- The contraction phase is one of recession, a decline in business activity. Severe recessions are called **depressions.** Likewise, a prolonged expansion in economic activity is sometimes called a **boom.**

- Contractions seem to be getting shorter over time.

- Some fluctuation in economic activity also reflects seasonal patterns. Business activity tends to be high in the two months before the winter holidays, and somewhat lower in summertime when many families are on vacation. Within individual industries, of course, seasonal fluctuations in output often are extremely pronounced, agriculture being the best example. Often key economic statistics, like unemployment rates, are seasonally adjusted, meaning the numbers are modified to take account of normal seasonal fluctuations. Thus, seasonally adjusted unemployment rates in summer months are below actual unemployment rates because unemployment is normally high in summertime as a result of the inflow of school-age workers into the labor force.

- Studies have shown there is a strong correlation between the performance of the economy and the fate of an incumbent's bid for reelection. So it can be in the best interest of the incumbent to do everything in his power to stimulate the economy in the period leading up to the election. This might take the form of trying to pressure the Federal Reserve System to lower the interest rate or pressing Congress to cut taxes or increase government spending—anything that might generate more spending and thus greater employment. Of course, the negative side to all of this is that although the incumbent may get reelected, the economy may have been overstimulated, causing inflationary problems.

- Businesses, government agencies, and to a lesser extent, consumers, rely on economic forecasts to learn of forthcoming developments in the business cycles.

- Economists gather statistics on economic activity in the immediate past, and using past historical relationships between these factors and the overall level of economic activity (which form the basis of the economic theories used), they formulate **econometric models.** Statistics from the immediate past are plugged into the models and forecasts are made.

- We cannot correctly make assumptions about certain future developments, so economists' numbers are imperfect and their econometric forecasts are not always accurate. But while they are not perfect, they are helpful.

- One less sophisticated but very useful forecasting tool is watching trends in **leading economic indicators**, which tend to change before the economy as a whole changes. There are about a dozen such leading indicators, that are compiled into an index of leading indicators. If the index rises sharply for two or three months, it is likely (but not certain) that increases in the overall level of activity will follow.

- Since the development of the index of leading economic indicators, it has never failed to give some warning of an economic downturn. Unfortunately, the lead time has varied widely, which makes it less accurate and can cause timing and expectation problems with policy.

- While the economic indicators do provide a warning of a likely downturn, they do not provide accurate information on the depth or duration of the downturn.

## I    REVIEW

Short-term fluctuations in the level of economic activity are called business _____Cycles_____.

A business cycle usually has four phases. During the _____expansion_____ output is increasing and unemployment is falling. Output reaches its highest level at the _____peck_____. Unemployment rises and output falls during the _____Contraction_____. The _____trough_____ occurs when output reaches its lowest level. There is _____no_____ uniform length to a business cycle.

Recessions occur during the _____contraction_____ phase of the business cycle. When contractions are severe, they are called _____depression_____.

Business cycles are of interest to politicians. There is strong positive correlation between the performance of the _____economy_____ and the fate of an incumbent president's re-election.

Economists use historical relationships between things like consumer expenditures, the supply of money, and tax revenues and fluctuations in the overall level of economic activity to formulate _____econmetric_____ models.

Another useful economic forecasting tool is the index of _____ economic indicators.

## II    TRUE/FALSE

_F_ 1. Unemployment rises and falls with output over the business cycle.

_F_ 2. By promoting the conditions that result in long-term economic growth, countries will be able to avoid the ups and downs of the business cycle.

_T_ 3. Depressions are severe, long-term contractions in economic activity.

## III    MULTIPLE CHOICE

1. In Bill Clinton's first campaign for president, the mantra of his campaign was "It's the Economy Stupid." He believed his chances of defeating the incumbent, George Bush, were good because the economy had just experienced which phase of the business cycle?
   A) contraction
   B) peak
   C) trough
   D) expansion

2.  Which of the following correctly describes the identified phase of the business cycle?
    A)  Peak: output is falling and unemployment is rising.
    B)  Trough: output is at its highest point in the business cycle.
    C)  Expansion: output is rising and unemployment is falling.
    D)  Contraction: investment is rising and unemployment is falling.

## IV     APPLICATION AND DISCUSSION

1.  Exhibit 3 describes the real per capita gross domestic product for the country of Cyclia for the period 1981 to 1990.

### EXHIBIT 3

| Year | Real per Capita GDP |
|------|---------------------|
| 1981 | $3,000 |
| 1982 | 3,500 |
| 1983 | 4,300 |
| 1984 | 5,000 |
| 1985 | 4,950 |
| 1986 | 4,500 |
| 1987 | 3,500 |
| 1988 | 3,000 |
| 1989 | 2,400 |
| 1990 | 2,300 |

A)  The peak occurred in which year? The trough occurred in which year?

B)  How long was the expansion? How long was the contraction?

C)  If a new business cycle began in 1981, how long was this cycle?

Questions

1.  Who is counted as part of the labor force? Who isn't?

2.  Is Uncle Ed better off because he is no longer counted as "unemployed?"

121

# CHAPTER 10
# MEASURING ECONOMIC PERFORMANCE

# SECTION 10.1
# NATIONAL INCOME ACCOUNTING

## KEY POINTS

- There is a great desire to measure the performance of our economy so that private businesses and macroeconomic policy makers can set goals and develop policy recommendations.

- To fulfill the desire for a reliable, uniform method of measuring economic performance, **national income accounting** was born early in the twentieth century.

- Several measures of aggregate national income and output have been developed, the most important of which is **gross domestic product (GDP)**. GDP is defined as the value of all final goods and services produced in a country in a period of time, almost always one year. Only goods and services produced in the current period are included in this year's GDP.

- The value of a good or service is determined by the market prices at which goods and services sell. Underlying GDP calculations are the various equilibrium prices and quantities for the multitude of goods and services produced.

- A final good or service is one that is ready for its designated ultimate use, in contrast to intermediate goods or services that are used in the production of other goods.

- If we counted the value of intermediate goods as well as the full value of the final products in GDP, we would be **double counting** by adding the value of an intermediate good twice, first in its raw form and second in its final form.

# Chapter 10: Measuring Economic Performance

- There are two primary ways of calculating economic output: the expenditure approach and the income approach. Although these methods differ, their result (GDP) is the same, apart from minor "statistical discrepancies."

## I    REVIEW

National income accounting provides a ___Uniform___ means of accounting for a country's economic performance. The development of this methodology was so important that one of its earlier developers, Simon ___Kuznets___, won a Nobel Prize for his work.

The most widely used measure of aggregate national output is the Gross _____ Product. This is defined as the value of all _____ goods and services _____ within a country during a given period of _____.

The value of a good or service is determined by its market _____.

Final goods are goods that are purchased for their _____ use. Goods and services used to produce other goods and services are called _____ goods and services.

Only the value of _____ goods is counted in the Gross Domestic Product (GDP), because the value of intermediate goods and services is included in the value of the goods they are used to produce. Counting the value of intermediate goods in the GDP would be _____ counting.

Two methods can be used to calculate national economic output—the _____ and the _____ approaches. These two methods produce similar estimates of _____.

## II    TRUE/FALSE

___F___ 1. Estimates of GDP will differ significantly depending on whether the income or the expenditure approach is used.

___F___ 2. GDP is difficult to calculate because each person assigns a different value to the goods and services that they consume.

___F___ 3. The Bobby's Slaw Burger Drive-in buys $5,000 worth of hamburger, $1,000 of buns, and $500 worth of coleslaw each year. These purchases are included in the calculation of the GDP.

## III    MULTIPLE CHOICE

1. Goods and services that are used in the production of other goods and services are called
   A) ultimate goods.
   B) final goods.
   C) intermediate goods.
   D) gross domestic goods.

2. When economists from different countries discuss GDP, they are talking about the same measure because national income accounting provides a uniform method of measuring a country's economic performance. Which of the following is *not* part of the uniform approach?
   A) The value of a good or service is determined by the market price of the good or service.
   B) The value of all goods and services consumed are included.
   C) Only the value of final goods and services are included.
   D) Only goods and services produced within a country are included.

## IV   APPLICATION AND DISCUSSION

Which of the following expenditures would be counted in the calculation of the 2001 U.S. Gross Domestic Product?

| EXHIBIT 1 | | |
| --- | :---: | :---: |
| **Expenditure** | **Yes** | **No** |
| 1. I buy a new Ford F-150 pickup truck. | ☐ | ☐ |
| 2. Tina's construction company buys lumber to build 50 new homes. | ☐ | ☐ |
| 3. Ted and Janet buy dinner at the Weinershack. | ☐ | ☐ |
| 4. Emil buys Jenny's 1965 Corvette. | ☐ | ☐ |
| 5. Jarett buys a nesting doll from Russia. | ☐ | ☐ |

# SECTION 10.2
# THE EXPENDITURE APPROACH TO MEASURING GDP

## KEY POINTS

- With the **expenditure approach,** GDP is calculated by adding up the expenditures of market participants on final goods and services over a period of time.

- For convenience and analytical purposes, economists usually categorize expenditures into four categories: consumption, $C$; investment, $I$; government purchases, $G$; and net exports (which equals exports ($X$) minus imports ($M$), or $X - M$).

- Following the expenditure method, GDP $= C + I + G + (X - M)$

- **Consumption** refers to the purchase of consumer goods and services by households. It does not include purchases by business or government. A large percentage of GDP in a given year goes for consumer goods and services.

- Consumption spending is usually broken down into three subcategories: nondurable goods, durable consumer goods, and services.

- **Nondurable goods** include tangible consumer items that are typically consumed or used up in a relatively short period of time. **Durable goods** include longer-lived consumer goods, the most important single category of which is consumer vehicles. On occasion, it is difficult to decide whether a good is durable or nondurable, and the definitions are, therefore, somewhat arbitrary.

- The distinction between durables and nondurables is important because consumer buying behavior is somewhat different for each of these categories of goods. In boom periods, when GDP is rising rapidly, expenditures on durables often increase dramatically, while in years of stagnant or falling GDP, sales of durable goods often plummet. By contrast, sales of nondurables tend to be more stable over time because purchases of such goods are more difficult to shift from one time period to another.

- **Services** are intangible items of value, as opposed to physical goods. As incomes have risen, service expenditures have been growing faster than spending on goods; the share of total consumption going for services increased from 35 percent in 1950 to almost 60 percent by 1997.

- **Investment**, as used by economists, refers to the creation of capital goods whose purpose is to produce other goods. This definition of investment deviates from the popular use of that term. For instance, purchases of stock are not an investment as defined by economists (i.e., an increase in capital goods).

- There are two categories of investment purchases measured in the expenditure approach: fixed investment and inventory investment.

- **Fixed investments**, sometimes called **producer goods**, include all spending on capital goods, such as machinery, tools, and factory buildings, which increase our future production capabilities, as well as residential construction.

- **Inventory investment** includes all purchases by businesses that add to their inventories—stocks of goods kept on hand by businesses to meet customer demands.

- In recent years, investment expenditures have generally been around 15 percent of gross domestic product. Investment spending is the most volatile category of GDP, however, and tends to fluctuate considerably with changing business conditions. When the economy is booming, investment purchases tend to increase dramatically. In downturns, the reverse happens.

- Government expenditures on goods and services are included in GDP. However, transfer payments are not included in government purchases because that spending does not go to purchase newly produced goods or services. The government purchase proportion of GDP has grown rapidly over the last 30 years.

- Some of the goods and services that are produced in the United States are exported for use in other countries. The fact that these goods and services were made in the United States means that they should be included in a measure of U.S. production. Thus, we include the value of exports when calculating GDP. At the same time, however, some of our expenditures in other categories were for foreign-produced goods and services. These imports must be excluded from GDP in order to obtain an accurate measure of American production. Thus, GDP calculations measure net exports, which equals total exports ($X$) minus total imports ($M$). Net exports are a small proportion of GDP and are often negative for the United States.

## I       REVIEW

Using the expenditure approach, GDP is equal to the sum of all _____ on final goods and services by consumers, business, government, and foreigners over a period of time.

The purchase of goods like food, clothing, and home appliances by households is called _____.

Consumer goods like food and clothing that are used up in a relatively short period of time are referred to by economists as _____ goods, while goods that last longer, like appliances and automobiles, are referred to as _____ goods.

Intangible items like healthcare, legal help, and haircuts are called _____.

The creation of capital goods like machines and tools is called _____ by economists.

Also included as investment expenditure in the calculation of GDP is the value of all unsold business _____.

# Chapter 10: Measuring Economic Performance

In calculating GDP, the "government spending" category includes governments' purchases of goods and services and payments of salaries to its employees, but does not include _____ payments like welfare.

Net exports are calculated as exports minus _____.

## II     TRUE/FALSE

___F___ 1. When you buy a VCR to use at home, it is included in the investment component of GDP.

___F___ 2. As the incomes of Americans have grown over the past 50 years, they have spent larger portions of their incomes on goods like food, TVs, and home computers than they have on services like healthcare, education, and tourism.

___F___ 3. The expenditure category of GDP that fluctuates the most over time is consumption.

## III     MULTIPLE CHOICE

1. The largest single expenditure component of GDP is
   A) consumption.
   B) investment.
   C) government expenditure.
   D) net exports.

2. Residential construction is counted in the _____ category of GDP.
   A) consumption
   B) investment
   C) government expenditure
   D) net exports

3. Which of the following is *not* counted as part of GDP?
   A) the purchase of a loaf of bread by a consumer
   B) the unsold inventory of a furniture store
   C) the purchase of a snowplow by the City of Minneapolis
   D) the purchase of 100 shares of Microsoft stock by your grandmother

4. When your grandmother buys a bottle of French wine, it is included in which expenditure category of GDP?
   A) consumption
   B) investment
   C) government expenditure
   D) net exports

## IV    APPLICATION AND DISCUSSION

Using the expenditure approach, calculate GDP from the data in Exhibit 2.

| EXHIBIT 2 | |
| --- | --- |
| | **Amount (billions of dollars)** |
| Consumption | $4,500 |
| Consumption of Durable Goods | 500 |
| Consumption of Non-Durable Goods | 1,500 |
| Consumption of Services | 2,500 |
| Investment | 1,000 |
| Fixed Investment | 1,000 |
| Government Expenditures on Goods and Services | 1,300 |
| Government Transfer Payments | 300 |
| Exports | 750 |
| Imports | 850 |
| **GPD Equals** | |

# SECTION 10.3
# THE INCOME APPROACH TO MEASURING GDP

## KEY POINTS

- The **income approach** to measuring GDP involves summing the incomes received by producers of goods and services. When someone makes an expenditure for a good or service, that spending creates income for someone else. Someone receives the money spent, and that receipt of funds is called income. Therefore, by adding up all of the incomes received by producers of goods and services, we can calculate the gross domestic product because output creates income of equal value.

- The incomes received by persons providing goods and services are actually payments to the owners of productive resources. These payments are sometimes called **factor payments** and include wages for the use of labor services, rent for land, payments for the use of capital goods in the form of interest, and profits for entrepreneurs who put labor, land, and capital together.

- Before we can measure income, we must make three adjustments to GDP. The net income of foreigners must be subtracted from GDP to get **Gross National Product (GNP)**. Then **depreciation** of annual allowances set aside for the replacement of worn-out plant and equipment—must be subtracted to get **Net National Product (NNP).** Finally, **indirect business taxes,** sent by businesses to government, must be subtracted to get **National Income (NI).**

- National Income is a measure of the income earned by owners of resources—factor payments, including payments for labor services (wages, salaries, and fringe benefits), for use of land and buildings (rent), for money lent to finance economic activity (interest), and payments for use of capital resources (profits).

- **Personal Income (PI)** measures the amount of income received by individuals, rather than the income earned, because the income received reflects the amount available for spending after taxes and transfer payments. Personal Income measures the total amount of income received by households and noncorporate businesses.

- **Disposable Personal Income (DPI)** is the personal income available to individuals after taxes.

# Chapter 10: Measuring Economic Performance

## I     REVIEW

When someone buys a good or service, their spending creates _____ for someone else. The _____ approach to calculating Gross Domestic Product involves summing the incomes received by those producing the goods and services.

_____ payments are the incomes received by persons who own the resources used to produce goods and services. These include _____ for labor services, _____ for the services of natural resources, _____ for capital services, and _____ earned by business.

The difference between Gross Domestic Product and the net income of foreigners is called Gross _____ Product.

Sales taxes are an example of _____ business taxes.

National Income is a measure of the income earned by the owners of productive _____, while Disposable Personal Income is personal income available to individuals after _____.

## II     TRUE/FALSE

_T_ 1. In any given year, the total income earned by owners of factors of production is not equal to Gross Domestic Product.

_F_ 2. At the end of the year, when Millie does the books for Tu's Tree Services, she finds that Mr. Tu's profits were $2,215. These cannot be considered as a payment to a factor of production.

## III     MULTIPLE CHOICE

1. Gross Domestic Product measures the economy's total output. What is the measure of the income earned by owners of resources used in making final goods and services?
   A) Personal Income
   B) National Income
   C) Retained Earnings
   D) Gross Domestic Income

2. Balonia has no sales tax, foreign workers, or residents working over seas. In 2000, wages paid equaled $3,500, rent was $15, and interest paid was $3.25. If the 2000 GDP was $5,000, what can you say about the 2001 profits in the country of Balonia?
   A) They are less than $1481.75.
   B) They are equal to $1481.75.
   C) They are equal to $18.25.
   D) They are more than $18.25.

## IV     APPLICATION AND DISCUSSION

How does the simple model of the circular flow of income explain why we would expect Gross Domestic Product to equal both total expenditures and total income?

# SECTION 10.4
# PROBLEMS IN CALCULATING AN ACCURATE GDP

## KEY POINTS

- The primary problem in calculating accurate GDP statistics is that the "yardstick" used in adding together the values of different products, the U.S. dollar, also changes in value over time.

- In order to compare GDP values over time, a common or standardized unit of measure, which only money can provide, must be used in the calculations.

- We must adjust for the changing purchasing power of the dollar by constructing a **price index**, which attempts to provide a measure of the trend in prices paid for goods and services over time. The price index can be used to deflate the nominal or current dollar GDP values to a real GDP expressed in dollars of constant purchasing power.

- There are many different types of price indices. The most well-known index, the **consumer price index (CPI),** provides a measure of the trend in the prices of goods and services purchased for consumption purposes. The CPI is the price index that is most relevant to households trying to evaluate their changing financial position over time. The price index used to correct GDP statistics for changing prices is an even broader index called the **GDP deflator.** The GDP deflator measures the average level of prices of all final goods and services produced in the economy.

- Constructing a price index is complicated. To begin with, there are literally thousands of goods and services in our economy. Therefore, a "bundle" or "basket" of representative goods and services is selected by the index calculators.

- A price index that can be used to measure the inflation rate is equal to the cost of the chosen market basket in the current year divided by the cost of the same market basket in the base year, times 100.

- Unfortunately for our ability to calculate inflation, not all prices move by the same amount or in the same direction, so an average of the many price changes must be calculated. This is complicated by several factors, including quality changes in goods and services over time (so the observed price change may, in reality, reflect a qualitative change in the product rather than the purchasing power of the dollar), the creation of new products, and the disappearance of some old products. Calculating a price index is not a simple, direct process, and there are many factors that could potentially distort the CPI.

- The formula for converting any year's nominal GDP into real GDP (in base year dollars) is: Real GDP equals nominal GDP divided by the price level index times 100.

- In modern times, inflation has been prevalent. For most readers of this book, the price level (as measured by the consumer price index) has risen in every single year of their lifetime because the last year of a declining price level was 1955. Therefore, the adjustment of nominal (money) GDP to real GDP will tend to reduce the growth in GDP suggested by nominal GDP figures.

- The measure of economic welfare most often cited is **real per capita gross domestic product.** To calculate real per capita GDP, we divide the real GDP by the total population to get the value of real output of final goods and services per person. *Ceteris paribus*, people prefer more goods to fewer, so a higher GDP would seemingly make people better off.

- Because one purpose of using GDP as a crude welfare measure is to relate output to human desires, we need to adjust for population change. If we do not take population growth into account, we can be misled by changes in real GDP values.

## I    REVIEW

The primary problem in calculating U.S. GDP over time is the problem of a changing _____ level.

# Chapter 10: Measuring Economic Performance

Economists attempt to adjust for the changing purchasing power of the dollar by using price _____.

Our attempts to construct price indexes are complicated by several factors, including changes in the _____ of goods and services over time, the introduction of _____ products, and the disappearance of _____, outmoded products.

Price indexes are used to adjust nominal GDP in order to get _____ GDP.

The measure of economic welfare most often cited by economists is _____ per capita GDP.

## II    TRUE/FALSE

____ 1. If nominal GDP in 2000 is greater than nominal GDP in 1999, the economy's real output of goods and services must have risen.

____ 2. Economists believe that the Consumer Price Index tends to understate the actual rate of inflation.

____ 3. Nominal GDP is always greater than real GDP.

## III    MULTIPLE CHOICE

1. The Consumer Price Index (CPI) measures changes in the prices of
   A) all the goods and services included in the Gross Domestic Product.
   B) certain important commodities, including wheat, crude oil, and tin.
   C) certain goods and services purchased for consumption purposes.
   D) goods produced abroad but sold in the United States.

| EXHIBIT 3 | | | |
|---|---|---|---|
| Year | GDP Price Deflator | Nominal GDP (in billions of dollars) | Real GDP |
| 1991 | 97.3 | $5,917 | |
| 1992 | 100.0 | 6,244 | |
| 1993 | 102.6 | 6,553 | |
| 1994 | 105.0 | 6,936 | |
| 1995 | 107.6 | 7,254 | |

Use Exhibit 3, which shows U.S. nominal GDP from 1991–1995, to answer questions 2 and 3.

2. What was real GDP in 1995?
   A) $5,230 billion
   B) $6,742 billion
   C) $7,180 billion
   D) $8,123 billion

3. What was real GDP in 1992?
   A) $5,230 billion
   B) $6,244 billion

C) $7,254 billion

D) $8,613 billion

## IV    APPLICATION AND DISCUSSION

If GDP rises from $5,000 billion in Year 1 to $5,500 billion in Year 2, while the GDP deflator goes from 100 to 125, what happens to real GDP?

# SECTION 10.5

# PROBLEMS WITH GDP AS A MEASURE OF ECONOMIC WELFARE

## KEY POINTS

- Real GDP is often used as a measure of the economic welfare of a nation. The accuracy of this measure for that purpose is questionable because several important factors are excluded from its calculations, including nonmarket transactions, the underground economy, leisure, externalities, the types of goods purchased, the distribution of income, and expectations.

- Nonmarket transactions include the provision of goods and services outside of traditional markets for which no money is exchanged. We simply do not have reliable enough information on this output to include it in the GDP. The most important nonmarket transaction omitted from GDP are services provided directly in the home. (One example is that marrying one's housekeeper causes reported GDP to fall, although output does not change.) In less-developed countries, where a significant amount of food and clothing output is produced in the home, the failure to include nonmarket economic activity in GDP is a serious deficiency.

- It is impossible to know for sure the magnitude of the underground economy, which includes unreported income from both legal and illegal sources. The reason these activities are excluded results from the fact that most payments made for these services are not reported to governmental authorities nor go through normal credit channels. The estimates of the size of the underground economy vary from less than 4 percent to more than 20 percent of GDP, with a good portion of this unreported income from legal sources, such as self-employment.

- The value that individuals place on leisure is omitted in calculating GDP. This omission in GDP can be fairly significant in international comparisons, or when we look at one nation over time, because the amount of work and leisure varies considerably, usually falling with rising GDP.

- Positive and negative externalities can result from the production of some goods and services. As a result of these externalities, the equilibrium prices of these goods and services—the figure used in GDP calculations—does not reflect their true values to society (unless, of course, the externality has been internalized). GDP does not decrease to reflect pollution resulting from production, or increase to reflect external benefits to others in society. While GDP measures the goods and services that are produced, it does not adequately measure the "goods" and "bads" that result from production processes.

# Chapter 10: Measuring Economic Performance

- Conceptually, we would like a measure of economic activity that adds the value of positive externalities and subtracts the value of negative externalities to GDP. Two distinguished economists have developed such an indicator, called a **measure of economic welfare** or MEW. They (and others) have developed broader-based welfare measures that attempt to correct for the deficiencies in GDP, such as the failure to account for the spillover effects of pollution or the value of leisure. Work in the direction of developing a "quality of life" indicator may ultimately reduce reliance on GDP as a measure of performance. One difficulty is that construction of such indicators involves many subjective judgments (e.g., what is the value of leisure?).

- Real GDP has several defects as a welfare measure. Nonetheless, at the present time, there is no alternative measure that is generally accepted as better. The GDP indicator is useful in making comparisons of the market values over time and across countries, even if we cannot be completely sure of the welfare implications of the comparisons. We can be fairly confident about the welfare implications of changing GDP. An unexpectedly fast increase in GDP probably will lead to an increase in consumption relative to expectations, almost certainly increasing welfare. Likewise, a sharp fall in GDP leads to reduced consumption—a decline in the ratio of what people have compared to what they want—and therefore almost certainly a decline in human welfare.

## I     REVIEW

Although real GDP is often used as a measure of a nation's economic _____, it is a questionable measure. GDP does not include the value of _____ transactions, transactions in the _____ economy, _____, or _____. GDP also ignores the _____ of income.

Nonmarket activities provide goods and services _____ the market. _____ is not exchanged for these goods and services. _____ is an important nonmarket activity in the United States.

The underground economy includes all legal and illegal _____ income. Underground activity is omitted, not because it is illegal, but because there is no _____ of the payments.

Leisure has a positive value that is _____ in calculating the GDP. When the amount of leisure consumed varies, either over time or between countries, GDP is an _____ tool for making welfare comparisons.

When positive or negative _____ are present, market prices will not reflect the true value of goods and services to society. Since market prices are used to value output in national income accounts, externalities mean that _____ will misrepresent the true value of output to society.

In order to correct for the failure of GDP to account for things like negative externalities and the value of leisure, economists have developed an indicator called the Measure of Economic _____.

Although GDP is not a perfect measure of welfare for society, no widely _____ alternative has won acceptance. GDP can be used to make comparisons of market values over _____ and across _____. In general, increases in GDP are associated with increased consumption and _____ welfare, while _____ in GDP are associated with lower consumption and _____ economic welfare.

## II     TRUE/FALSE

____ 1. The GDP in MBAland is $40 million and the average MBA works 84 hours a week. In Surferland, the GDP is only $25 million and the average Surfer works 20 hours per week. People in MBAland are not necessarily better off because they have a higher GDP.

F ___2. Nonmarket transactions and transactions in the underground economy are not part of the GDP for ethical and methodological reasons.

F ___3. Economists subtract the dollar amounts of damage that result from pollution from the dollar value of output when they calculate GDP.

## III    MULTIPLE CHOICE

1.  In some rural U.S. regions, residents harvest much of their food supplies directly from nature by hunting, fishing, and gathering. The importance of these subsistence activities means that GDP will
    A) overestimate the true value of the nation's production of final goods and services.
    B) underestimate the true value of the nation's production of final goods and services.
    C) correctly estimate the true value of the nation's production of final goods and services.
    D) overestimate the true value of the nation's production of final goods and services only when the income approach is used.

2.  Prohibition began in 1920 when the Volstead Act was passed to implement the Eighteenth Amendment to the Constitution prohibiting the production and sale of liquor and beer. In 1920 much of this economic activity went underground, and Al Capone became a leading illegal entrepreneur. Assuming the amount of liquor and beer produced stayed the same, what was the effect of the Volstead Law on the GDP in 1920?
    A) GDP would decline since activities in the underground economy were not included.
    B) GDP would have remained the same because only the organization producing the goods changed.
    C) GDP would increase because it would increase production in the underground economy.
    D) GDP would not be affected because these goods were now intermediate goods.

## IV    APPLICATION AND DISCUSSION

Briefly explain how each of the following hypothetical changes would affect the country's GDP, production, and welfare.

A)  Biotech entrepreneur, Dr. Pool, marries her chef, who continues to do the cooking at home.

B)  For health reasons, the government makes the production and sale of pizza illegal, but the same number of pizzas can still be found in the blackmarket.

C)  Blanche Flowers, whose company produces car batteries, changes the production process so that production now produces emissions that kill trees and shrubs in the area around her plant.

D)  Karen Grace retires from her job as an accountant but continues to work as much as a volunteer accountant for her church and a local non-profit organization.

E)  Bob decides he is working too much and quits his second job at the Wheel-O-Dog restaurant.

Questions

1. How does this comic strip represent the circular flow model?

2. Which transactions shown are made in product markets? Which in factor markets?

# CHAPTER 11
# ECONOMIC GROWTH IN THE GLOBAL ECONOMY

# SECTION 11.1
# ECONOMIC GROWTH

## KEY POINTS

- John Maynard Keynes, primarily concerned with explaining and reducing short-term fluctuations in the level of business activity, once said that "in the long run we are all dead." He wanted to smooth out the business cycle, largely because of the implications that cyclical fluctuations had for buyers and sellers in terms of unemployment and price instability.

- Keynes' concerns were important and legitimate. At the same time, his flippant remark about the long run ignores the fact that human welfare is greatly influenced by long-term changes in a nation's capacity to produce goods and services. Emphasis on the short run of the business cycle ignores the longer term dynamic changes that affect output, leisure, real incomes, and lifestyles. Many would argue that in the long run, economic growth is a crucial determinant of people's well-being.

- **Economic growth** is usually measured by the annual percent change in real output of goods and services per capita (real GDP per capita).

- Along the production possibilities curve, the economy is producing at its potential output. How much the economy will produce at its potential output, sometimes called its **natural level of output**, depends on the quantity and quality of an economy's resources, including labor, capital, and natural resources. In addition, technology can increase the economy's production capabilities. Improvements in and greater stocks of land, labor, and capital can shift out the production possibilities curve. Another way of saying that economic growth has shifted the production possibilities curve out is to say that growth has increased potential output.

# Chapter 11: Economic Growth in the Global Economy

- A nation with greater economic growth will end up with a much higher standard of living, *ceteris paribus*.

- A simple formula called the Rule of 70 can tell how long it will take a nation to double its output. The number of years necessary is approximately equal to the nation's growth rate divided into 70.

- The "richest" or "most developed" countries today have many times the per capita output of the "poorest" or "least-developed" countries. The international differences in income, output and wealth are striking and have caused a great deal of friction between developed and less-developed countries.

- Growth in a country's standard of living depends on productivity growth. **Productivity** is the amount of goods and services a worker can produce per hour.

## I        REVIEW

Economic _____ is measured by the annual percentage change in the per capita real output of a country's goods and services. In the long run, economic growth is a crucial determinant of the _____- being of a nation's population.

A country's production _____ curve defines the economy's potential output. Growth results in a(n) _____ shift in a country's production possibilities curve.

Increases in the quantity and _____ of an economy's resources, improved _____, and _____ entrepreneurial activity will result in an increase in its potential output.

Small differences in countries' rates of economic growth will result in _____ disparities in those countries' standards of living in the long run.

There are significant _____ in income, output, and wealth among countries of the world.

_____ is the amount of goods and services a worker can produce per hour.

## I        TRUE/FALSE

**F** 1. In any country the population will generally be better off as long as real output increases over time.

**T** 2. The long-run consequence of college students sacrificing income and earning their college degrees is that the country's production possibilities curve shifts out and its potential output increases.

## III        MULTIPLE CHOICE

1. Which of the following did *not* result in economic growth?
   A) Using a system of dikes, the Dutch increased the amount of arable land in the country.
   B) James Watt introduced the steam engine to the country's manufacturers.
   C) Botswana doubled the number of school age children who graduate from high school.
   D) During the Civil War, the Union Army destroyed the railroads and most of the manufacturing facilities in the South.

2. Which of the following is a true statement about the variation in GDP among countries of the world?
   A) Differences in GDP and standard of living among countries are not that great.
   B) Differences in GDP and standard of living between the developed and least-developed countries have existed for a long time.
   C) Measured by GDP, the U.S. economy is only 50 times as large as the Egyptian economy.
   D) In 1997, the Russian economy, measured by GDP, was twice as large as the Indian economy.

## IV    APPLICATION AND DISCUSSION

The ants and the grasshoppers have a difference of opinion. The ants believe they should save today and invest in capital in order to produce more in the long run. The grasshoppers want to consume it all today because "In the long run, we're all dead."

Imagine a discussion between an ant and a grasshopper economist. What do you think would be the most important point each would make in supporting their view? How would their feelings about future population affect their views? How would the level of output in their economies affect their views?

# SECTION 11.2
# DETERMINANTS OF ECONOMIC GROWTH

## KEY POINTS

- Economists have had different theories of economic growth.

- Many separate explanations of economic growth have been proposed, but none of them, by themselves, can completely explain economic growth. However, each of the explanations may be part of a more complicated reality. Economic growth is a complex process involving many important factors, no one of which completely dominates.

- There are several factors that nearly everyone agrees have contributed to economic growth in some or all countries: 1) growth in the quantity and quality of labor resources used (human capital); 2) increase in the use of inputs provided by the land (natural resources); 3) growth in physical capital inputs (machines, tools, buildings, inventories); 4) technological knowledge (new ways of combining given quantities of labor, natural resources, and capital inputs) allowing greater output than previously possible.

- Labor is needed in all forms of productive activity. But other things being equal, an increase in labor input does not necessarily increase output per capita. If the increase in labor input results from an increase in population, per capita growth might not occur because the increase in output could be offset by the increase in population. However, if a greater proportion of the population works (that is, the labor force participation rate rises) or if workers put in longer hours, output per capita will increase—assuming that the additional work activity adds something to output. Qualitative improvements in workers (learning new skills, for example) can also enhance output. Indeed, it has become popular to view labor as "**human capital**" that can be augmented or improved by education and on-the-job training.

- Abundant natural resources also can enhance output whereas a limited resource base is an important obstacle to economic growth. Resources are, however, not the whole story. The natural resource base can affect the initial development process, but sustained growth is influenced by other factors.

- There is nearly universal agreement that capital formation has played a significant role in the economic development of nations.

- Technological advances stem from human ingenuity and creativity in developing new ways of combining the factors of production to enhance the amount of output from a given quantity of resources. It involves invention and innovation. **Innovation** is the adoption of a new product or process. New technology, however, must be introduced into productive use by managers or entrepreneurs who must weigh their estimates of benefits of the new technology against their estimates of costs. Thus, the entrepreneur is an important economic factor in the growth process.

- Technological advances permit us to economize on one or more inputs used in the production process. It can permit savings of labor, as occurs when a new machine is invented that does the work of many workers. It can also be land (natural resource) saving or even capital saving. For example, nuclear fission has permitted us to build power plants that economize on the use of coal, a natural resource. The reduction in transportation time that accompanied the invention of the railroad allowed businesses to reduce the capital they needed in the form of inventories. Because goods could be obtained quickly, businesses could reduce the stock kept on their shelves.

## II       REVIEW

There are _____ theories on the causes of economic growth.

Economic growth is a _____ process created by many different factors. Nearly everyone would agree that four important factors resulting in economic growth have been:

1. Growth in the quantity and _____ of labor resources.

2. Increased use of _____ resources.

3. _____ physical capital.

4. _____ knowledge.

Increasing population will not necessarily increase per _____ output. However, per capita output will increase if _____ of the population works or works _____ hours or if the population's "_____ capital" is improved.

The abundance of _____ resources has been cited as a major contributor to U.S. economic growth. If each worker has more natural resources to work with, *ceteris paribus,* they will produce _____ goods and services.

There is almost universal agreement that _____ formation plays a significant role in economic growth.

Technological change reflects people's creativity in finding new ways to _____ factors of production. Technological advance permits us to economize on _____ used in production. _____ is the adoption of technological advances to produce goods and services. Innovation is an important role of the _____.

## II       TRUE/FALSE

_____ 1. Most modern economists agree that there is a single factor that can be used to explain economic growth.

_____ 2. The talent for creating scientific advances and inventions is not the only talent necessary for technological change to create economic growth.

_____ 3. Improving the health and education of a nation's population increases its "human capital." Increasing a country's human capital is more likely to increase per capita output than increases in a nation's population.

## III    MULTIPLE CHOICE

1.  Which of the following is *not* one of the factors that contributes to economic growth?
    A)  an increase in the stock of physical capital
    B)  an improvement in the skills and education of workers
    C)  a decrease in the proportion of the population that works
    D)  an increase in innovation and the rate of technological change

2.  If Country A and Country B are identical in every way except that labor force growth is faster in Country A,
    A)  Country B will experience higher overall economic growth than Country A.
    B)  Country A will experience higher overall growth, as well as higher per capita growth.
    C)  Country A will experience higher overall growth, but may actually have less growth in per capita output.
    D)  There will be no difference in the overall growth or per capita growth between the two countries.

## IV    APPLICATION AND DISCUSSION

1.  Economic problems in Russia are of concern to people throughout the world. How do you think each of the hypothetical actions described in Exhibit 1 contributes to Russian economic growth? Check the box indicating whether the action contributes to economic growth (+), results in a decrease in per capita output (–), or has no growth effect (0).

| EXHIBIT 1 | | | |
|---|---|---|---|
| **Action** | **+** | **–** | **0** |
| 1. The government expands the capacity of the nation's universities and increases the number of college graduates. | ☐ | ☐ | ☐ |
| 2. Falling incomes reduce the amount that the average Russian is willing to save. | ☐ | ☐ | ☐ |
| 3. The Russian economy shifts from producing military equipment to producing consumer goods. | ☐ | ☐ | ☐ |
| 4. High taxes discourage businesses from making new capital investments. | ☐ | ☐ | ☐ |

# SECTION 11.3
# RAISING THE LEVEL OF ECONOMIC GROWTH

## KEY POINTS

- Economic growth means more than an increase in the real income (output) of the population. Changes in output are accompanied by a number of other important changes. A nation can pursue a number of policies to increase economic growth.

- One of the most important determinants of economic growth is the saving rate. In order to consume more in the future, we must save more now. Generally speaking, higher levels of saving will lead to higher levels of investment and capital formation and, therefore, to greater economic growth.

- Sustained rapid economic growth is associated with high rates of saving and investment around the world. However, investment alone does not guarantee economic growth, which hinges importantly on the quality and the type of investment as well as on investment in human capital and improvements in technology.

- Some scholars believe that the importance of **research and development** (R&D)—which can include new products, management improvements, production innovations, or simply learning by doing—is understated. It is clear that investments in R&D and rewarding innovators with patents has paid big dividends in the past 50 to 60 years. In addition, there is an important link between research and development and capital investment. When capital depreciates over time, it is replaced with new equipment that embodies the latest technology. Consequently, R&D may work hand-in-hand with investment to improve growth and productivity.

- Economic growth rates tend to be higher in countries where the government enforces property rights. In most developed countries, property rights are effectively protected by the government, but in developing countries, this is not normally the case. And if the government is not enforcing property rights, the private sector must respond in costly ways that stifle economic growth.

- Free trade can lead to greater output because of the principle of comparative advantage. Essentially, it suggests that if two nations or individuals with different resource endowments and production capabilities specialize in producing a smaller number of goods and services, then they are relatively better at and engage in trade. Both parties will benefit as total output rises.

- Education, investment in human capital, is just as important as improvements in physical capital. Accepting a reduction in current income to acquire education and training can increase future earning ability, which can raise the standard of living.

- With economic growth, illiteracy rates fall and formal education grows. The correlation between per capita output and the proportion of the population that is unable to read or write is striking. Improvements in literacy stimulate economic growth by reducing barriers to the flow of information and raise labor productivity.

- One problem of providing enough education in poorer countries is that since children in developing countries are an important part of the labor force at a young age, there is a higher opportunity cost of education in terms of forgone contribution to family income.

- Education is a consequence of economic growth, becoming a consumption good as well as a cause of economic growth, and creating human capital.

## I     REVIEW

Individuals can either consume or _____ their income.  Generally speaking, higher levels of saving lead to higher levels of _____ formation and economic _____.  Some scholars believe that _____ and development activities work hand-in-hand with investment to spur economic _____.

Economic growth rates tend to be higher in countries that enforce _____ rights. Free _____ can also lead to greater output because of the principle of _____ advantage.

Education, sometimes known as investment in _____ capital may be just as important as improvements in physical capital.

## II     TRUE/FALSE

____F____1. If a country's rate of saving increases, its levels of investment and capital formation will necessarily fall.

____T____2. There is a positive relationship between literacy rates and output per capita.

## III    MULTIPLE CHOICE

1.  During the Klondike gold rush, the first prospectors in the region arrived before any government authority. They followed a long goldfield tradition and created "miners' laws" that described how gold claims could be staked and how these claims would be enforced. The creating of miners' laws showed that these prospectors recognized the importance of which of the following factors that affect economic growth?
    A)  increasing physical capital
    B)  free trade
    C)  well-defined and enforced property rights
    D)  technological advance

2.  Which of the following is not an argument for government to subsidize education?
    A)  Education can increase the skill level of the population and raise the general standard of living.
    B)  Education may lead to lower crime rates.
    C)  Education may produce better-informed voters.
    D)  Individuals who become better educated will benefit financially.

## IV    APPLICATION AND DISCUSSION

When the Pilgrims first came to America in 1620, the property rights of individuals were not well defined. For the first several years of the Plymouth Colony, everything that was produced, including corn, fish and housing, was held in common and divided equally. After nearly starving, the Pilgrims adopted private property in 1623 and allowed each family to own their own land and agricultural produce. Following the institution of property rights the colony flourished. (Tom Bethell, "How Private Property Saved the Pilgrims," *Hoover Digest 1999*, No. 1. http://www.hoover.org).

What kinds of problems do you think the Pilgrims encountered under the system of communal property? Why did the establishment of private property improve their situation?

# SECTION 11.4
# POPULATION AND ECONOMIC GROWTH

## KEY POINTS

*   The impact of population growth on per capita economic growth is far from obvious. If population were to expand faster than output, per capita output would fall; population growth would be growth inhibiting. With a greater population, however, comes a greater labor force. Also, economies of large scale production may exist in some forms of production, so larger markets associated with greater populations lead to more efficient-sized production units.

*   Certainly very rapid population growth did not seem to impede American economic growth in the mid-nineteenth century. America's economic growth until at least World War I was accompanied by population growth that was among the highest in the world for the time.

*   In many of the less-developed countries today, rapid population growth threatens sustained economic growth. These are countries that are predominantly agricultural with very modest natural resources, especially land. The land–labor ratio is very low, fitting the model developed by the English economist, the Rev. Thomas Malthus.

- Malthus's model predicted that per capita economic growth would eventually become negative, and that wages would ultimately reach an equilibrium at a subsistence level, or just large enough to provide enough income to stay alive. Malthus assumed an agricultural society where goods were produced by two inputs, land and labor. He assumed that the supply of land was fixed in quantity. Further, he assumed that the sexual desires of humans would work to increase population.

- As population increased, the number of workers would increase and, thus, with greater labor inputs available, output would also go up. At some point, however, output would increase by diminishing amounts because of the law of diminishing returns, which states that if you add variable amounts of one input (in this case labor) to fixed quantities of another input (in this case land), output would rise but by diminishing amounts. As the land–labor ratio falls, there is less land per worker.

- Fortunately, Malthus' theory proved spectacularly wrong for much of the world. While the law of diminishing returns is a valid concept, Malthus' other assumptions were unrealistic. Agricultural land is not completely fixed in quantity or quality. Irrigation, fertilizer, and conservation techniques have increased arable land. More important, Malthus implicitly assumed there would be no technological advance, and ignored the real possibility that improved technology, often embodied in capital, could overcome the impact of the law of diminishing returns. Moreover, the Malthusian assumption that sexual desire would necessarily lead to population increase did not take birth control techniques into account.

- Unfortunately, the Malthusian assumptions are not too widely at variance with several less-developed countries today. Some nations are having substantial population increases, with a virtually fixed supply of land and little technological advance. Population growth has a negative impact on per capita output in this case, since the added output derived from having more workers on the land is very small. In short, for some places in the modern world, the Malthusian model may be relevant.

- In this situation, it is scarcely surprising that population control is considered to be critical in many less-developed countries. The implementation of birth control has been far from routine, however. While greater population may lower per capita output, other things equal, from the perspective of an individual family, the production of children means greater security in old age, more labor for the farm now, etc. In most countries, population control efforts have been only modestly successful. It remains a key factor in the growth patterns in countries with high populations in relation to natural resources and capital equipment.

## I      REVIEW

If population growth increases faster than output, per capita output will _____.

A greater population generally results in a _____ labor force.

A larger population can result in economic benefits because larger markets associated with large populations can lead to _____ of large-scale production.

Rapid population growth, however, can threaten sustained economic growth if it leads to _____ returns in production.

## II      TRUE/FALSE

_F_ 1. Rapid population growth was a major impediment to U.S. economic growth in the mid-nineteenth and early twentieth centuries.

_T_ 2. If Latvia's output increases by 3 percent while its population rises by 1 percent, Latvia's per capita output will rise.

## III    MULTIPLE CHOICE

1. The population of the world is approximately _____ people.
   A) 600 million
   B) 1 billion
   C) 6 billion
   D) 12 billion

2. In the 1700s, Reverend Thomas Malthus predicted that
   A) per capita economic growth would eventually become negative because population growth would tend to outstrip production.
   B) per capita economic growth would tend to rise in the future because technological advances in production would assume that output outstripped population growth.
   C) per capita economic growth would tend to rise as modern birth control techniques caused the rate of population growth to decline.
   D) per capita economic growth would not change very much because humans were already content with their standards of living.

3. In making the "Malthusian Prediction," Reverend Malthus assumed that
   A) technological advance would be rapid; the supply of capital was unlimited; and birth control techniques would limit population growth.
   B) there would be little, if any technological advance; the supply of capital was fixed; and birth control techniques would limit population growth.
   C) the supply of land was fixed in quantity; there would be little, if any technological advance; and the sexual desires of humans would work to increase population.
   D) the supply of land was fixed in quantity; technological advances would be rapid; the sexual desire of humans would lead to rapid population growth.

## IV    APPLICATION AND DISCUSSION

Economist Julian Simon once said that "The most important economic effect of population size and growth is the contribution of additional people to our stock of useful knowledge. And this contribution is great enough in the long run to overcome all the costs of population growth." (*The Ultimate Resource 2,* Princeton University Press, 1996, pp. 3–4.)

What do you think? Was Simon correct? What are the *costs* to society of an additional person? What are the benefits? Would Malthus have agreed with Simon?

Questions

1.  Who do you agree with, the Malthusian or Guy DePuy?

2.  What are the pros and cons of economic growth?

# CHAPTER 12
# INVESTMENT AND SAVING

SECTION 12.1 FINANCIAL MARKETS

SECTION 12.2 INVESTMENT DEMAND AND SAVING SUPPLY

## SECTION 12.1
# FINANCIAL MARKETS

### KEY POINTS

- Financial markets facilitate the interaction between households, firms, governments, banks, and other financial institutions that borrow and lend funds.

- Financial markets are global

- The owners of corporations own shares of **stock** in the company and are called **stockholders**. Each stockholder's ownership of the corporation and voting rights in the selection of corporate management is proportionate to the number of shares owned.

- Shares of stock are bought and sold by individuals and institutions in the **stock market**, usually on one of the organized stock exchanges. The price that shares sell for will fluctuate with changes in demand and/or supply. Corporations sometimes use proceeds from new sales of stock to finance expansion of their activities.

- There are actually two primary types of stock: preferred stock and common stock.

- Owners of **preferred stock** receive a fixed regular dividend payment; the payment remains the same regardless of the profits of the corporation. No dividends can generally be paid to holders of common stock until the preferred stockholders receive a specified fixed amount per share of stock, assuming that funds are available after the debts of the corporation are paid.

- Owners of **common stock** are the residual claimants on the resources of the corporation. They share in all profits remaining after expenses are paid, including interest payments to owners of debt obligations of the corporation and dividend payments to owners of preferred stock.

- Dividends in common stock frequently vary with profits, often going up in years of prosperity and down in less prosperous years. If the corporation is sold or liquidated, the common stockholders receive all the corporate assets after all debts are paid and preferred stockholders are paid a fixed amount per share. Owners of common stock assume greater risks than preferred stockholders, doing so because the potential rewards are then greater if the company is in fact successful.

- Individuals as well as institutions such as insurance companies, pension funds, mutual funds, trust departments of banks, and university and foundation endowment funds, all hold corporate stocks. General Motors, IBM, and Microsoft have millions of individual stockholders. Indirectly, millions more are involved in stocks through mutual funds, ownership of life insurance, vested rights in private pension funds, and so on.

- Another important way that corporations finance their growth is by borrowing money. While corporate borrowing takes different forms, corporations primarily borrow by issuing **bonds.** The holder of a bond is not a part owner of a corporation; rather, he is a creditor to whom the corporation has a debt obligation.

- The obligation to bondholders is of higher legal priority than that of stockholders. Before any dividends can be paid, even to owners of preferred stock, the interest obligations to bondholders must be met. If a company is liquidated, bondholders must be paid in full the face value of their bond holding before any disbursements can be made to stockholders. Bondholders have greater financial security than stockholders, but receive a fixed annual interest payment, with no possibility to receive increased payments as the company prospers. The possibility a bond value increasing greatly—a capital gain—is limited compared to that of stocks.

- The values of **securities** (stocks and bonds) sold in financial markets change with expectations of benefits and costs.

- Most economists believe that it is very difficult, without illegal inside information or a lot of luck, to consistently pick winners in the stock market.

## I      REVIEW

_____ are the owners of corporations. They own shares of stock in the company and their voting rights and dividend income are _____ to the proportion of total stocks that they own.

Holders of _____ stock receive a regular, fixed dividend, which is the same regardless of the company's profits. Dividends are paid to preferred stockholders _____ the holders of common stock. Common stock owners are the _____ claimants on the resources of the corporation.

Companies issue _____ when they borrow. The bondholder is a _____, not an owner of the company.

The _____ walk theory of the stock market holds that it is very difficult to consistently pick winning stocks without illegal inside information.

The _____-_____ ratio is the current price of the stock divided by last year's earnings per share.

## II      TRUE/FALSE

F 1. Since Jerry has purchased one share of the Organic Farm Corporation stock, he will have equal voting rights with Chandra who owns 1,000 shares.

T 2. If a corporation is successful, the potential rewards for holders of common stock are greater than for holders of preferred stock.

___ 3. If investors believe a change in government policy will reduce a corporation's profits, they will reduce the price they are willing to pay for that firm's stock.

## III    MULTIPLE CHOICE

1. Which of the following describes the legal priority for payoff in the event that a corporation goes out of business?
   A)  preferred stockholders, common stockholders, and bondholders
   B)  bondholders, preferred stockholders, and common stockholders
   C)  common stockholders, preferred stockholders, and bondholders
   D)  preferred stockholders, bondholders, and common stockholders

2. When a corporation issues a bond, it is
   A)  selling an ownership share in the company.
   B)  investing in another company.
   C)  creating a new set of preferred stock.
   D)  borrowing money and promising to pay the lender back.

3. The Swedish monkey that recently picked a better stock portfolio than the country's top stock market analysts simply be throwing darts proved that
   A)  he was one smart monkey.
   B)  a diversified portfolio is best.
   C)  a randomly picked portfolio is not a very good one.
   D)  in efficient markets consistent, extraordinary profit opportunities do not exist.

4. Investors believe that a company's earnings will be higher in the current year than they were last year. How will this show up in the stock tables?
   A)  relatively high price-earnings ratio
   B)  relatively low price-earnings ratio
   C)  relatively high dividend
   D)  relatively low dividend

## IV    APPLICATION AND DISCUSSION

One day on Gilligan's Island, Mr. Howell was out beachcombing when he came upon a torn piece from the *Wall Street Journal* (the paper and printing are unmistakable). You can help Mr. Howell check at least part of his investment portfolio. The following information is on the piece from the *Journal;* unfortunately none of the headings were attached.

| -4.4 | 49.66 | 40 | General Mills GIS | 1.10 | 2.5 | 18 | 26101 | 44.87 | -0.10 |
| 8.5 | 35.88 | 26.67 | Heinz HNZ | 1.08 | 3.0 | 19 | 6865 | 35.67 | 0.02 |
| 12.1 | 75.28 | 60.69 | Hershey HSY | 1.58 | 2.1 | 24 | 2564 | 75.57 | 0.30 |
| 23.2 | 23.90 | 11.67 | Hewlett Packard HPQ | .32 | 1.5 | 44 | 68090 | 21.39 | 0.15 |

A)  Which stock's price has changed most in the current calendar year?

B)  Which company paid the highest dividend per share last year?  Which paid the lowest?

C)  Which stock has the highest price to earnings ratio?  Which has the lowest?

# INVESTMENT DEMAND AND SAVING SUPPLY

## KEY POINTS

- If we put the investment demand for the whole economy and national savings together, we can establish the real interest rate in the saving and investment market.

- The investment demand curve (*ID*) is downward sloping, reflecting the fact that investment spending varies inversely with the real interest rate—the amount borrowers pay for their loans.

- At high real interest rates, firms will only pursue those few investment activities with even higher expected rates of return. As the real interest rate falls, additional projects with lower expected rates of return become profitable for firms, and the quantity of investment demanded rises. The investment demand curve shows the dollar amount of investment forthcoming at different real interest rate.

- Because lower interest rates stimulate the quantity of investment demanded, governments often try to combat recessions by lowering interest rates.

- Several determinants other than interest rates will shift the investment demand curve. If firms expect higher rates of return on their investments, for a given interest rate, the *ID* curve will shift to the right. If firms expect lower rates of return on their investments, for a given interest rate, the *ID* curve will shift to the left. Possible investment demand curve shifters include changes in technology, inventory, expectations, business taxes, or the supply of national savings.

- Product and process innovation can cause the *ID* curve to shift out. The development of new machines that can improve the quality and the quantity of products or lower the costs of production will increase the rate of return on investment, independent of the interest rate. The same is true for new products.

- When inventories are high and goods are stockpiled in warehouses all over the country, there is a lower expected rate of return on new investment and *ID* shifts to the left. Firms with excess inventories of finished goods have very little incentive to invest in new capital. Alternatively, if inventories are depleted below the levels desired by firms, the expected rate of return on new investment increases, as firms look to replenish their shelves to meet the growing demand and *ID* shifts to the right.

- If higher expected sales and a higher profit rate are forecast, firms will invest in plant and equipment and the *ID* curve shifts to the right and more investment will be desired at a given interest rate. If lower expected sales and a lower profit rate are forecasted, the *ID* curve shifts to the left and fewer investments will be desired at a given interest rate.

- If business taxes are lowered—such as with an investment tax credit—potential after-tax profits on investment projects will increase and shift the *ID* curve to the right. Higher business taxes will lead to lower potential after-tax profits on investment projects and shift the *ID* curve to the left.

- The supply of national saving is composed of both private saving and public saving. Households, firms, and the government can supply savings. The supply curve of savings is upward sloping. At a higher real interest rate, there is a greater quantity of savings supplied. Think of the interest rate as the reward for saving and supplying funds to financial markets. At a lower real interest rate, a lower quantity of savings is supplied.

- As with the investment demand curve, there are noninterest determinants of the saving supply curve.

- If disposable (after-tax) income were to rise, the supply of savings would shift to the right—and more savings would occur at any given interest rate. If disposable income fell, there would be less saving at any given interest rate.

- If you expected lower future earnings, you would tend to save more now at any given interest rate—shifting the saving supply curve to the right. If you expected higher future earnings, you would tend to consume more and save less now, knowing that more income is right around the corner—shifting the saving supply curve to the left.

- In equilibrium, desired investment equals desired national saving at the intersection of the investment demand curve and the saving supply curve. The real equilibrium interest rate is determined by the intersection of these two curves. If the real interest rate is above the equilibrium real interest rate, forces within the economy would tend to restore the equilibrium.

- At a higher than real equilibrium interest rate, the quantity of savings supplied would be greater that quantity of investment demanded—and there would be a surplus of savings at this real interest rate. As savers (lenders) compete against each other to attract investment demanders (borrowers), the real interest rate falls. Alternatively if the real interest rate is below the equilibrium real interest rate, the quantity of investment demanded is greater than the quantity of saving supplied at that interest rate—and a shortage of saving occurs. As investment demanders (borrowers) compete against each other for the available saving, the real interest rate is bid up.

- A firm making an investment decision must consider the price of the new capital that they must pay now with the additional revenue the firm anticipates to make over time. That is, the firm must compare current cost with future benefits. To figure out how much those future benefits are worth today, economists use a concept called present value.

- The **present value** of future income is the value of having that future income now. People prefer to have money now rather than later; that is why they are willing to pay interest to borrow it.

$PV = \$X/(1 + r)^t$

- Because the discount rate varies from person to person, a good proxy is the market rate of interest.

- An investor will buy capital if the expected discounted present value of the capital exceeds the current price. Therefore, falling interest rates lead to greater investment.

- **Private saving** is the amount of income households have left over after consumption and net taxes.

- **Public saving** is the amount of income the government has left over after paying for is spending.

- **National saving** is the sum of private and public saving.

- A budget surplus increases national saving and results in a lower real interest rate.

- A budget deficit reduces national saving and results in a higher real interest rate.

- In an **open economy** capital inflows from abroad encourage capital formation and economic growth, while capital outflows hinder capital formation and reduce the rate of economic growth.

## I     REVIEW

The investment demand curve is _____ sloping, reflecting the fact that investment spending varies _____ with the real interest rate.

If firms expect higher rates of return on their investments, for a given interest rate, the _____ demand curve will shift to the _____. If firms expect lower rates of return, the investment _____ curve will shift to the _____.

The supply of national saving is composed of both private and _____ saving.

In equilibrium, desired _____ equals desired national _____ at the intersection of the investment _____ and saving _____ curves. The intersection of these curves determines the real equilibrium _____ rate.

# Chapter 12: Investment and Saving

People would rather have money now than in the future. They are willing to pay _____ to have money today. The present value of $1,000 in the future depends on the _____ you have to wait and the market _____ rate.

If the present value of the benefits of an investment _____ the cost, it is a profitable investment. If the cost exceeds the present value of the benefits of an investment, it is a _____ investment.

From our knowledge of the circular flow in a closed economy, we know that the total income of households must equal the total _____ of the economy.

Private saving is the amount of income that households have left over after _____ and net taxes, while public saving is the amount of income that government has left over after paying its _____.

If the government collects more in taxes than it spends it will run a budget _____. If it spends more than it collects in tax revenue it will run a budget _____.

Budget surpluses on the part of government cause interest rates to _____, while budget deficits cause interest rates to _____.

## II    TRUE/FALSE

___T___ 1. Investment spending and interest rates are inversely related.

___F___ 2. Because higher interest rates stimulate investment spending, the government often tries to raise interest rates to combat a recession.

___F___ 3. Stegman is willing to sell you a commercial oven for $10,000. You know that you could earn $1,200 for each of the next ten years before the oven needs to be replaced. This would always be a good investment.

___T___ 4. Roy offers to pay you $1,000 in one year if you loan him $950 today. Sigfrid says he will pay you $1,000 in two years if you loan him $950 today. These deals are not equivalent even though you are paid back the same amount.

___F___ 5. If the federal government runs a budget surplus, national saving will decline and interest rates will rise.

## III    MULTIPLE CHOICE

1. Which of the following will *not* cause the investment demand curve to shift to the right?
   A) Businesses forecast lower expected sales.
   B) New cost-saving technologies are introduced.
   C) Congress cuts business taxes.
   D) The interest rate falls.

2. Which of the following is likely to cause a rightward shift in the saving supply curve?
   A) a decrease in disposable income
   B) an increase in disposable income
   C) an increase in federal income tax rates
   D) lower business profits

3.  Guy and his sister, Dolly, decide not to open "Guy's and Dolly's Espresso Emporium" because only the local loan shark, Nathan Toledo, will loan them the $10,000 needed to buy the coffee machine. Nathan would charge 50 percent interest. What can we say about Guy and Dolly's expectation about the coffee business?
    A)  They expect the machine's yearly marginal revenue product will be more than $5,000.
    B)  They expect the machine's yearly marginal revenue product will be less than $5,000.
    C)  They expect the machine's yearly marginal resource cost will be $10,000.
    D)  They expect to get burnt working with Nathan Toledo.

4.  Which of the following will result from chronic budget deficits on the part of the federal government?
    A) Increased national saving and higher interest rates.
    B) Increased national saving and lower interest rates.
    C) Decreased national saving and higher interest rates.
    D) Decreased national saving and lower interest rates.

## IV     APPLICATION AND DISCUSSION

1.  In 2001 the Japanese economy deteriorated. Consumer spending was weak, business profits fell, and falling demand for exports resulted in a buildup of unsold inventories. In this atmosphere, what do you think happened to investment spending in Japan? Explain. If you drew a graph of Japan's investment demand curve, which way would it shift?

2.  Heather has given you a contract in which she promises to pay you $1,000 if you would loan her $900. The ink on the contract has run so the date is hard to read. She will either pay you back in two years or ten. Is this a wise investment for you with either payback period? Calculate the present value of a payment of $1,000 in two years and ten years when the interest rate is 5 percent. How do the results change when the interest rate is 1 percent?

# CHAPTER 13
# AGGREGATE DEMAND AND AGGREGATE SUPPLY

## SECTION 13.1
# THE DETERMINANTS OF AGGREGATE DEMAND

### KEY POINTS

- **Aggregate Demand (*AD*)** is the sum of the demand for all goods and services in the economy. It can also be seen as the quantity of real GDP demanded at different price levels.

- Aggregate Demand ($AD$) = Consumption ($C$) + Investment ($I$) + Government purchases ($G$) + Net Exports ($X - M$).

- Consumption is by far the largest component of *AD*, typically almost 70 percent of total economic activity, measured by GDP. Understanding the determinants of consumption is critical to an understanding of the forces leading to changes in aggregate demand which, in turn, change total output and income.

- The higher a nation's income, the more it spends on consumption. At the level of individuals, consumption increases with after-tax income, also called **disposable income**. In addition to income, other factors, such as the "lumpiness" of some goods' purchases, such as cars and interest rates—at higher real interest rates, consumers save more and consume less—also influence consumption.

- Households typically spend a large portion of their total disposable income and save the rest. The fraction of their total disposable income that households spend on consumption is called the **average propensity to consume (APC)**. The additional consumption that results from an additional dollar of disposable income is the **marginal propensity to consume (MPC)**.

## I    REVIEW

Aggregate demand is the sum of the demand for _____ goods and services in the economy. It describes the quantity of real GDP demanded at different _____ levels.

The four major components of aggregate demand are _____, investment, _____ purchases, and net _____.

_____ is the largest component of aggregate demand. It accounts for almost _____ percent of GDP.

At the individual and national level, the greater our income the _____ will be consumption spending. The level of our _____ or after-tax income will affect consumption.

The national level of consumption will also be affected by _____ rates. Higher interest rates make saving _____ attractive and borrowing less attractive, so people consume _____.

If people expect higher incomes in the future, they may consume _____ than their current incomes allow. When they consume more than their income, they _____. College age and older people consume more than their _____ incomes allow; their spending decisions reflect their lifetime earnings expectations.

The fraction of their total income that households spend on consumption is called the average _____ to consume.

Marginal propensity to consume is a measure of the _____ consumption that results from a one dollar increase in income. A household's marginal propensity to consume and its average propensity to consume are not necessarily _____.

_____ expenditures are the most unstable category of GDP. _____ purchases is spending by federal, state, and local governments on new _____ and services.

Goods and services that we sell to foreigners are called _____, while goods and services we buy from foreigners are called _____.

Exports minus imports $(X - M)$ is called _____ exports.

## II    TRUE/FALSE

F 1. College graduates, because they are just starting their careers, have a lower average propensity to consume than older, more experienced workers.

T

2.  Rose and Kareem expect that their state, local, and federal taxes will increase by $300 in 2002 and they expect pay increases of about $250. Even though their total income increases, Rose and Kareem will not increase their consumption spending in 2002.

## III    MULTIPLE CHOICE

1.  The largest component of aggregate demand is
    A)  consumption.
    B)  investment.
    C)  net exports.
    D)  government spending.

2.  Marcus Homer earned $250,000 in 2000 as a baseball rookie; he spent 75 percent of his earnings. In 2001 with a new contract he earned $2,000,000 per year. His consumption increased by $1,000,000. Which of the following statements is *not* true?
    A)  His 2000 average propensity to consume is .75.
    B)  His average propensity to consume falls between 2000 and 2001.
    C)  His marginal propensity to consume is .57.
    D)  His marginal propensity to consume equals .75.

3.  Why would we, *ceteris paribus,* expect aggregate demand to increase when national income increases?
    A)  An increase in income will result in a decrease in consumption but an increase in other components of aggregate demand.
    B)  An increase in income will result in an increase in consumption, which is the major component of aggregate demand.
    C)  An increase in income will result in an increase in U.S. exports to other countries.
    D)  An increase in income will result in a decrease in interest rates.

## IV    APPLICATION AND DISCUSSION

Indicate how each of the following would affect the overall level of aggregate demand by putting either a plus (+) or a minus (-) in the AD column.  Using C, I, G, or (X-M) for consumption, investment, government spending and net exports respectively, indicate which component(s) of aggregate demand would change.

|  | AD | Component(s) |
|---|---|---|

1.  Congress passes a reduction in personal income tax rates.

2.  Interest rates rise.

3.  U.S. runs a trade deficit.

4.  Government education spending rises.

SECTION 13.2
# THE AGGREGATE DEMAND CURVE

## KEY POINTS

- The aggregate demand curve reflects the total amounts of real goods and services that all groups together want to purchase in a given time period. It indicates the quantities of real GDP (RGDP) demanded at different price levels.

- *AD* is different than the demand curve presented in Chapter 4, which looked at the relationship between the relative price of a good and the quantity demanded.

- The *AD* curve slopes downward, which means that there is an inverse (or opposite) relationship between the price level and real gross domestic product (RGDP) demanded. An increase in the price level causes RGDP demanded to fall. Conversely, if there is a reduction in the price level, the quantity of RGDP demanded rises.

- Three complementary explanations exist for the negative slope of the aggregate demand curve: the real wealth effect, the interest rate effect, and the open economy effect.

- The **real wealth effect** reflects the fact that the real (adjusted for inflation) value of any asset of fixed dollar value, like cash, falls as the price level increases. That reduces people's real wealth, and therefore their planned purchases of goods and services, lowering the quantity of RGDP demanded. If the price level falls, people's real wealth in such forms will increase, increasing the quantity of RGDP demanded.

- The real wealth effect can be summarized as:

  A higher price level: reduced real wealth; reduced purchasing power; reduced RGDP demanded;

  A lower price level: increased real wealth; increased purchasing power; increased RGDP demanded.

- The effect of the price level on interest rates can also cause the *AD* curve to have a negative slope. At a higher price level, consumers will wish to hold more dollars in order to purchase those items that they want to buy. That will increase the demand for money. If the demand for money increases, and the Federal Reserve System does not alter the money supply, then interest rates will rise. In other words, the demanders of dollars will bid up the price of those dollars—the interest rate. At higher interest rates, the opportunity cost of borrowing rises, and fewer interest-sensitive investments will be profitable, reducing the quantity of investment goods demanded by firms, as well as the quantity of consumer durable goods demanded by households. This **interest rate effect** will cause fewer investment goods to be demanded and, consequently, a lower RGDP demanded. On the other hand, if the price level fell, and people demanded less money as a result, then the interest rates would fall. Lower interest rates would trigger greater investment and consumer durable spending and a larger real GDP would result.

- The interest rate effect process can be summarized as:

  A higher price level: increases money demand (money supply unchanged); increases the interest rate; reduces investments; reduces RGDP demanded;

  A lower price level: decreases money demand (money supply unchanged); decreases the interest rate; increases investments; increases RGDP demanded.

- Many goods and services are bought and sold in global markets. If the prices of goods and services in the domestic market rise relative to those in global markets due to a higher domestic price level, consumers and businesses will buy more from foreign producers and less from domestic producers. Because real GDP is a measure of domestic output, the reduction in the willingness of consumers to buy from domestic producers leads to a lower level of real GDP demanded at the higher domestic price level. And if domestic prices of goods and services fall relative to foreign prices, more domestic products will be bought, increasing RGDP demanded.

- The **open economy effect** can be summarized as:

  An increased price level: decreases the demand for domestic goods; decreases RGDP demanded;

  A decreased price level: increases the demand for domestic goods; increases RGDP demanded.

# Chapter 13: Aggregate Demand and Aggregate Supply

## I    REVIEW

The _____ demand curve shows the quantities of real gross domestic product that people wish to purchase at different price levels. It shows the relationship between the total quantity of goods and services demanded in a given time period and the _____ level.

There is a(n) _____ relationship between the price level and the quantity of goods and services people demand.

The aggregate demand curve is _____ from the demand curve for a particular good. The quantity of a particular good demanded is inversely related to the good's _____ price, while aggregate demand describes the relation between the total output demanded and the average level of _____ prices.

The real _____ effect is one explanation of the negative slope of the aggregate demand curve. Changes in the price level will reduce the _____ value of consumers' money assets, which decreases their real _____. A reduction in real wealth causes consumers to buy _____ goods and services which leads to a reduction in real GDP demanded.

The _____ rate effect is another way to explain the relation between the average price level and the total output demanded. If the price level increases, consumers will need _____ money to buy the same amount of the more expensive goods and services. An increase in the _____ for money without an _____ in supply will cause money's price, the _____ rate, to increase. Higher interest rates will _____ investment and cause a reduction in the quantity of goods and demanded.

If U.S. price levels increase, domestic goods will be relatively _____ expensive than foreign goods. Consumers will _____ more and _____ the quantity of domestic goods and services they buy. This _____ economy effect provides another explanation for the _____ relation between the average price level and the quantity of output demanded described by the aggregate demand curve.

## II    TRUE/FALSE

__T__ 1. When the average price level in a country decreases, we would, *ceteris paribus,* expect to see an increase in investment spending, which would increase aggregate demand.

__F__ 2. Changes in the relative price of pistachios will change both the quantity demanded of pistachios and the total quantity of goods and services demanded.

## III    MULTIPLE CHOICE

1. During the 1970s, U.S. prices generally rose faster than prices in other parts of the world. Which of the following changes would the open economy effect predict took place in response to these price level changes?
   A) Americans reduced the proportion of foreign goods bought since domestic prices were relatively lower.
   B) Americans reduced the amount of investment they undertook because interest rates increased.
   C) Americans reduced the amount of goods and services they wanted to consume because they felt less wealthy.
   D) Americans reduced the proportion of domestic goods and services bought because domestic prices were relatively higher.

2.  Ron prefers to keep his $10,000 retirement savings buried in the backyard. After an increase in the price level, Ron reduces the amount of goods and services he wants to purchase. Ron's rationalization, that now his retirement savings won't buy as much, is consistent with which explanation of the aggregate demand curve's negative slope?
    A) open economy effect
    B) real wealth effect
    C) interest rate effect
    D) the inflation effect

3.  The interest rate effect suggests that the negative slope of the aggregate demand curve results because changes in the price level affect
    A) the purchases of foreign goods.
    B) the demand for money.
    C) the real purchasing power of assets.
    D) the level of income.

## IV    APPLICATION AND DISCUSSION

Complete each of the following statements using □ for an increase and a □ for a decrease.

A(n) _____ in the price level will result in an decrease in the demand for money, a(n) _____ in the interest rate, a(n) _____ investment, and a(n) _____ in real GDP demanded.

An increase in the price level will result in a(n) _____ in imports and a(n) _____ in real GDP demanded.

A(n) _____ in the price level will result in a decrease in the real value of money assets, a(n) _____ in purchasing power, and a(n) _____ in real GDP demanded.

An increase in the price level will result in a(n) _____ in the demand for money, a(n) _____ in the interest rate, and a(n) _____ in real GDP demanded.

A(n) _____ in the price level will result in a decrease in imports and a(n) _____ in real GDP demanded.

A decrease in the price level will result in a(n) _____ in the real value of money assets, a(n) _____ in purchasing power, and a(n) _____ in real GDP demanded.

# SECTION 13.3
# SHIFTS IN THE AGGREGATE DEMAND CURVE

## KEY POINTS

-   As for the supply and demand curves in Chapter 4, there can be both shifts in and movements along the *AD* curve. The previous section discussed three factors—the real wealth effect, the interest rate effect, and the open (or foreign) economy effect—that result in the downward slope of the *AD* curve (not a shift in *AD*). Each of these factors generates a movement along the *AD* curve because the general price level changed.

-   The whole *AD* curve can shift to the right or left. If some nonprice level determinant causes total spending to increase, then the *AD* curve will shift to the right. If a nonprice level determinant causes the level of total spending to decline, then the *AD* curve will shift to the left.

# Chapter 13: Aggregate Demand and Aggregate Supply

- Anything that changes the amount of total spending in the economy (holding price levels constant) will impact the *AD* curve. An increase in any component of GDP (*C, I, G,* and *X – M*) can cause the *AD* curve to shift rightward. Conversely, decreases in *C, I, G,* or *X – M* will shift *AD* leftward.

- A whole host of changes could impact consumption patterns.

- An increase in consumer confidence, an increase in wealth, or a tax cut each can increase consumption and shift *AD* to the right. An increase in population would also increase *AD,* as there are now more consumers spending more money on goods and services.

- The *AD* could also shift to the left due to decreases in consumption demand. If consumers sensed the economy was headed for a recession or the government imposed a tax increase, this would result in a leftward shift of the *AD* curve. Since consuming less is saving more, an increase in savings, *ceteris paribus*, would shift *AD* to the left. Consumer debt may also be a reason why some consumers might put off additional spending.

- Investment is also an important determinant of aggregate demand. Increases in demand for investment goods occur for a variety of reasons. If business confidence increases or real interest rates fall, business investment will increase and *AD* will shift to the right. A reduction in business taxes would also shift *AD* to the right because businesses would now retain more of their profits to invest. However, if real interest rates or business taxes rise, then we would expect to see a leftward shift in *AD*.

- Government purchases is also part of total spending and therefore must impact *AD*. An increase in government purchases, other things equal, shifts *AD* to the right, while a reduction shifts *AD* to the left.

- Global markets are also important in a domestic economy. If major trading partners are experiencing economic slowdowns, then they will demand fewer U.S. imports. This causes net exports (*X – M*) to fall, shifting *AD* to the left. Alternatively, an economic boom in the economies of major trading partners may lead to an increase in our exports to them, causing net exports (*X – M*) to rise and *AD* to increase.

## I    REVIEW

If a non-price level determinant causes total spending to increase, the aggregate demand (*AD*) curve will shift to the _____. If, on the other hand, a non-price determinant causes total spending to fall, the *AD* curve will shift to the _____.

An increase in consumer confidence, an increase in wealth, or a tax cut can _____ consumption and shift the *AD* curve to the _____.

If consumers fear that the economy is headed for a recession, if the government raises taxes, or if wealth decreases, consumption will _____ and the *AD* curve will shift _____.

If business confidence increases, or if real interest rates fall, business investment will _____ and the *AD* curve will shift to the _____. If government raises taxes on business, or if interest rates rise, business investment will _____ and the *AD* curve will shift to the _____.

If government spending goes up, the *AD* curve will shift to the _____. If government spending declines, the *AD* curve will shift to the _____.

If net exports fall, the *AD* curve will shift to the _____. If net exports increase, the *AD* curve will shift to the _____.

# Chapter 13: Aggregate Demand and Aggregate Supply

## II     TRUE/FALSE

F  1. A reduction in the price level will cause the *AD* curve to shift to the left.

T  2. Holding price levels constant, anything that changes the amount of total spending in the economy will cause the *AD* curve to shift.

## III     MULTIPLE CHOICE

1.  An economic boom in China is likely to lead to a
    A)  decrease in U.S. exports.
    B)  increase in U.S. exports.
    C)  decrease in U.S. imports.
    D)  decrease in U.S. consumption spending.

2.  An increase in the money supply that leads to a decrease in interest rates is likely to result in a(n)
    A)  decrease in consumption spending.
    B)  decrease in investment spending.
    C)  increase in investment spending.
    D)  decrease in government expenditure.

## IV     APPLICATION AND DISCUSSION

In each of the following, identify the component of aggregate demand (AD) that would be affected and use the accompanying graphs to show the effect of each on the AD curve.

A)  Federal government cuts income tax rates.          B)  Consumer confidence soars.

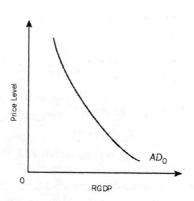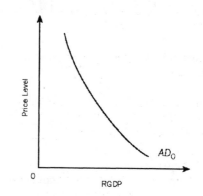

159

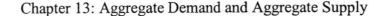

C)  Real interest rates plummet.

D)  Government cuts spending.

E)  Business leaders become pessimistic over the future of the U.S. economy.

F)  U.S. exports to Asia rise dramatically.

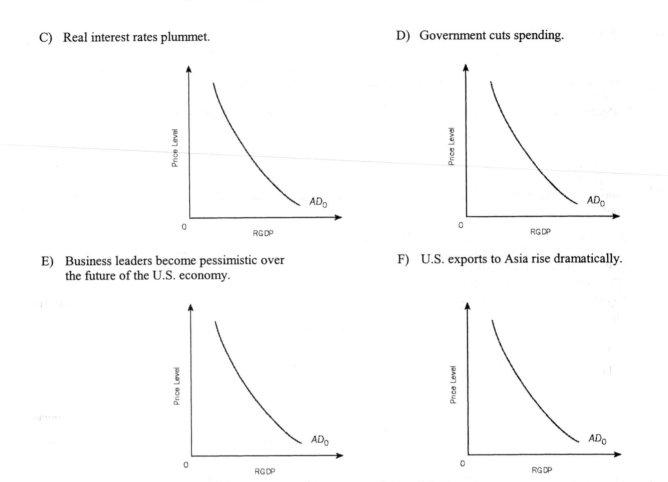

# SECTION 13.4
# THE AGGREGATE SUPPLY CURVE

## KEY POINTS

- The **aggregate supply (AS)** curve is the relationship between the total quantity of final goods and services that suppliers are willing and able to produce and the overall price level. The aggregate supply curve represents how much RGDP suppliers will be willing to produce at different price levels.

- In fact, there are two aggregate supply curves—a **short-run aggregate supply (SRAS)** curve and a **long-run aggregate supply (LRAS)** curve. The short-run relationship refers to a period when output can change in response to supply and demand, but input prices have not yet been able to adjust (for example, nominal wages are assumed to adjust slowly in the short run). The long-run relationship refers to a period long enough for the prices of outputs and all inputs to fully adjust to changes in the economy.

- In the short run, the aggregate supply curve is upward sloping. This means that at a higher price level, producers are willing to supply more real output, and at lower price levels, they are willing to supply less real output.

- Why would producers be willing to supply more output just because the price level increases? There are two possible explanations: the **profit effect** and the **misperception effect**.

160

# Chapter 13: Aggregate Demand and Aggregate Supply

- To many firms, input costs—like wages and rents—are relatively constant in the short run. The slow adjustments of input prices are due to the longer-term input contracts that do not adjust quickly to price changes. So when the price level rises, output prices rise relative to input prices (costs), raising producers' short-run profit margins. These increased profit margins make it in the producers' self-interest to expand their production and sales at higher price levels. If the price level falls, output prices fall and producers' profits tend to fall. When output prices fall, producers will find it more difficult to cover their input costs and, consequently, will reduce their level of output.

- The second explanation of the upward-sloping short-run aggregate supply curve is that producers can be fooled by price changes in the short run. Say a producer sees the price of his output rising. If he thinks that the relative price of his output is rising (i.e., that his product is becoming more valuable in real terms), he will supply more. In actuality, however, it might be that it was not just his goods' prices that were rising; the prices of many other goods and services could also be rising at the same time as a result of an increase in the price level. The relative price of his output, then, was not actually rising, although it appeared so in the short run. In this case, the producer was fooled into supplying more based on his short-run misperception of relative prices.

- Along the short-run aggregate supply curve, we assume that wages and other input prices are constant. This is not the case in the long run, which is a period long enough for the price of all inputs to fully adjust to changes in the economy.

- Along the long-run aggregate supply curve, we are looking at the relationship between RGDP produced and the price level, once input prices have been able to respond to changes in output prices. That is, along the *LRAS* curve, two sets of prices are changing—the prices of outputs and the price of inputs. That is, along the *LRAS* curve, a 10 percent increase in the price of goods and services is matched by a 10 percent increase in the price of inputs.

- The long-run aggregate supply curve is insensitive to the price level, reflecting the fact that the level of RGDP producers are willing to supply is not affected by changes in the price level. The vertical *LRAS* curve will always be positioned at the natural rate of output, where all resources are fully employed. That is, in the long run, firms will always produce at the maximum sustainable level allowed by their capital, labor, and technological inputs, regardless of the price level.

- The long-run equilibrium level is where the economy will settle when undisturbed, and all resources are fully employed. Remember that the economy will always be at the intersection of *AS* and *AD* but that will not always be at the natural rate of output. Long-run equilibrium will only occur where *AS* and *AD* intersect along the long-run aggregate supply curve at the natural, or potential, rate of output.

## I        REVIEW

The aggregate _____ curve represents how much RGDP suppliers are willing to produce at different price levels.

In the short run, the aggregate supply curve is _____ sloping, which means that at a higher price level, producers are willing to supply _____ real output and at lower prices they are willing to supply _____ real output.

There are two possible explanations for an upward-sloping short-run aggregate supply curve: the _____ effect and the _____ effect.

In the long run, the aggregate supply curve is drawn as a perfectly _____ line, indicating that output is insensitive to the _____ level.

The long-run aggregate supply curve is positioned at the _____ rate of output, where all resources are fully employed.

Chapter 13: Aggregate Demand and Aggregate Supply

## II    TRUE/FALSE

**F** 1. According to the profit effect explanation of short-run aggregate supply, firms will *not* increase output as the price level rises because they have no incentive to do so.

**T** 2. According to the misperception effect explanation of short-run aggregate supply, firms increase output as the price level rises because they mistake the increase in overall prices for an increase in the relative price of their own output.

## III    MULTIPLE CHOICE

1.  The short-run is
    A)  any time period of less than a year.
    B)  a time period in which the prices of output cannot change, but in which the prices of inputs have time to adjust.
    C)  a time period in which output prices can change in response to supply and demand, but in which all input prices have not yet been able to adjust.
    D)  a time period in which neither the prices of outputs nor the prices of inputs are able to change.

2.  The long-run is
    A)  any time period of more than a year.
    B)  a time period in which output prices can change but input prices have not had time to adjust.
    C)  a time period in which input prices can change, but output prices have not had time to adjust.
    D)  a time period long enough for the prices of both outputs and inputs to adjust to changes in the economy.

## IV    APPLICATION AND DISCUSSION

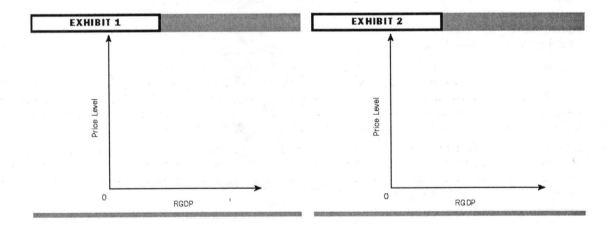

1.  If the aggregate supply curve is upward-sloping, what affect will an increase in consumption or government spending have on the levels of output, employment, and prices? Use the blank graph in Exhibit 1 to illustrate your answer.

2.  If the aggregate supply curve is perfectly vertical, what affect will an increase in consumption or government spending have on the levels of output, employment, and prices? Use the blank graph in Exhibit 2 to illustrate your answer.

SECTION 13.5

# SHIFTS IN THE AGGREGATE SUPPLY CURVE

## KEY POINTS

- The underlying determinant of shifts in short-run aggregate supply is production costs. *Ceteris paribus*, lower production costs will motivate producers to produce more at any given price level, shifting *AS* rightward. Likewise, higher production costs will motivate producers to produce less at any given price level, shifting *AS* leftward.

- Any change in the quantity of any factor of production available—capital, entrepreneurship, land, or labor—can cause a shift in both the long-run and short-run aggregate supply curves. An increase in any of these factors can shift both the *LRAS* and *SRAS* curves to the right. A decrease in any of these factors can shift both the *LRAS* and *SRAS* curves to the left.

- Changes in the stock of capital will alter the amount of goods and services the economy can produce. Investing in capital improves the quantity and quality of the capital stock. And more and better quality capital will lower the costs of production in the short run, shifting the short-run aggregate supply curve rightward, and allow output to be permanently greater than before, shifting the *LRAS* rightward, *ceteris paribus*.

- Changes in human capital can also alter the aggregate supply curve. Investments in human capital may include educational or vocational programs or on-the-job training. All of these investments in human capital would cause productivity to rise. As a result, the short-run aggregate supply curve would shift to the right because a more skilled workforce will lower the costs of production, and the *LRAS* curve would shift to the right because greater output is achievable on a permanent, or sustainable, basis, *ceteris paribus*.

- Entrepreneurs, through their inventive activity, lower costs and expand real output possibilities. If entrepreneurial activities lower the costs of production and expand what can be produced with the resources available to the economy, then the short-run and long-run aggregate supply curves both shift to the right.

- Land is an all-encompassing definition that includes all natural resources. An increase in usable natural resources, such as successful oil exploration, would lower the costs of production and expand the economy's sustainable rate of output, shifting both *SRAS* and *LRAS* to the right. Likewise, a decrease in the amount of natural resources available would result in a leftward shift of both *SRAS* and *LRAS*.

- The addition of workers to the labor force, *ceteris paribus,* can increase aggregate supply, as with women and baby boomers during the 1960s. It tends to depress wages and increase short-run aggregate supply, *ceteris paribus*. An expanded labor force also increases the economy's potential output, increasing *LRAS*. Increases or decreases in labor productivity will also affect the aggregate supply curve. Lower output per worker causes production costs to rise and potential real output to fall, resulting in a leftward shift in both *SRAS* and *LRAS*.

- Increases in government regulations can make it more costly for producers; this increase in production costs results in a leftward shift of *SRAS*, and the reduction in society's potential output would shift *LRAS* left as well. Likewise, a reduction in government regulations on businesses would lower the costs of production and expand potential real output, causing both *SRAS* and *LRAS* to shift to the right.

- Some factors shift *SRAS* but do not impact *LRAS*. The most important of these factors are changes in input prices and natural disasters.

- The price of factors, or inputs, that go into producing outputs will affect only *SRAS* if they don't reflect permanent changes in the suppliers of some factors of production.

- If wages increase without a corresponding increase in labor productivity, then it will become more costly for suppliers to produce goods and services at every price level, causing *SRAS* to shift to the left. *LRAS* will not shift, however, because with the same supply of labor as before, potential output does not change.

- If the price of steel rises, automobile producers will find it more expensive to do business because their production costs will rise, again resulting in a leftward shift in *SRAS*. The *LRAS* will not shift, however, as long as the capacity to make steel has not been reduced.

- It is supply and demand in factor markets (like capital, land, and labor) that cause input prices to change. The reason that changes in input prices only affect *SRAS* and not *LRAS*, unless they reflect permanent changes in the supplies of those inputs, lies in our definition of long-run aggregate supply. The *LRAS* is vertical at the natural level of real output, determined by the supplies of the various factors of production. A fall in input prices, which shifts *SRAS* right, only shifts *LRAS* right if potential output has risen, and this only occurs if the supply of those inputs is increased.

- Adverse supply shocks, such as natural disasters, can increase the costs of production. They could cause *SRAS* to shift to the left, *ceteris paribus*. However, once the temporary effects of these disasters have been felt, no appreciable change in the economy's productive capacity has occurred, so *LRAS* doesn't shift as a result.

## I      REVIEW

Change in the quantity of any factor of _____ can cause a shift in both the long- and short-run aggregate supply curves.

The underlying determinant of shifts in short-run aggregate supply is production _____. Lower production costs will, *ceteris paribus*, result in _____ production at every price level.

More and better quality capital will _____ the costs of production in the short run and shift the short-run aggregate supply curve to the _____. Investing in capital will also shift the long-run aggregate supply curve to the _____ and provide a _____ increase in potential output. Investment in _____ capital will have the same affect because it increases the _____ of labor.

Because they introduce new technology, _____ can increase both the short-run and long-run aggregate supply curves by _____ the cost of production and expanding real output _____. New technology allows _____ to be produced with the resources available to the economy.

An increase in natural resources will expand an economy's _____ rate of output and lower its costs of production, shifting both short- and long-run aggregate supply curves to the _____.

Additional workers will _____ wages, *ceteris paribus*, and increase short-run aggregate supply. The economy's potential output and _____-run aggregate supply will also increase with an increase in its labor force.

Increased government _____ can make it more costly to produce goods and services and _____ short-run aggregate supply. Regulations will also reduce society's potential output, which will shift the long-run aggregate supply curve to the _____.

Changes in _____ prices and natural _____ affect the short-run aggregate supply curve but do not impact the long-run aggregate supply curve.

Changes in _____ prices will affect the short-run aggregate supply curve. _____ input prices will reduce short-run aggregate supply while a _____ in input prices will have the opposite effect. The economy's potential output and its _____-run aggregate supply curve will not change unless the price changes reflect _____ changes in factor supplies.

Natural disasters, such as flooding, earthquakes, and droughts, cause _____ changes in an economy's productive capacity. Disasters will cause the short-run aggregate supply curve to shift to the _____ but cause no change in the long-run aggregate supply curve.

# Chapter 13: Aggregate Demand and Aggregate Supply

## II    TRUE/FALSE

_T_ 1. In the aggregate, producers will respond to a reduction in nominal wage rates by increasing their total output.

_F_ 2. The 1993 Midwest floods significantly reduced that year's harvest of wheat, corn, and soybeans. The floods produced a leftward shift in the U.S. long-run aggregate supply curve.

_F_ 3. Immigration to the United States at the turn of the century was sizable. Immigration caused the U.S. potential output to increase, which shifted the long-run aggregate supply curve to the right, but it had no effect on the short-run aggregate supply curve.

## III    MULTIPLE CHOICE

1. In a moment of euphoria after an exciting Super Bowl, employers agree to raise everyone's wages by 25 percent. Which of the following changes will result from the employers' gesture?
   A) The long-run aggregate supply curve will shift to the left.
   B) The short-run aggregate supply curve will shift to the right.
   C) The short-run aggregate supply curve will shift to the left.
   D) Both A and C.

2. Which of the following would *not* cause the long-run aggregate supply curve to shift to the right?
   A) Oil companies find major new oil and gas deposits in the Ozark Mountains.
   B) New technology allows oil companies to produce oil in greater ocean depths in the Gulf of Mexico.
   C) The U.S. Minerals Management Service increases the number of inspections required on drilling rigs off the coast of the United States.
   D) The federal government opens up a portion of the National Petroleum Reserve in Alaska to exploration and development.

3. Many observers have predicted the twenty-first century will be the new age of the entrepreneur with social, legal, and economic conditions changing to promote entrepreneurs. If these predictions are correct, what effect will these changing conditions have, *ceteris paribus,* on the long-run aggregate supply curve?
   A) *LRAS* will decline because entrepreneurs make lots of mistakes.
   B) *LRAS* will increase because entrepreneurs increase the productivity of existing resources.
   C) The *SRAS* will decrease because the wages of entrepreneurs will rise.
   D) The *LRAS* and *SRAS* will move in opposite directions because entrepreneurs will only be effective in the long run.

## IV    APPLICATION AND DISCUSSION

In 1998, Hurricane Mitch devastated much of the Central American country of Honduras. While natural disasters usually have only temporary effects on a country's economy, under certain catastrophic circumstances, they may also have serious long-term effects. How would each of the following potential consequences of a major hurricane affect a country's economy? Decide whether the consequence will increase (+), decrease (–), or have no affect on the LRAS and SRAS.

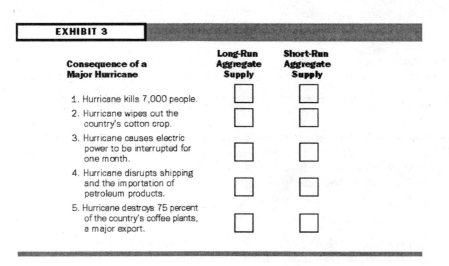

**EXHIBIT 3**

| Consequence of a Major Hurricane | Long-Run Aggregate Supply | Short-Run Aggregate Supply |
|---|---|---|
| 1. Hurricane kills 7,000 people. | ☐ | ☐ |
| 2. Hurricane wipes out the country's cotton crop. | ☐ | ☐ |
| 3. Hurricane causes electric power to be interrupted for one month. | ☐ | ☐ |
| 4. Hurricane disrupts shipping and the importation of petroleum products. | ☐ | ☐ |
| 5. Hurricane destroys 75 percent of the country's coffee plants, a major export. | ☐ | ☐ |

SECTION 13.6

# MACROECONOMIC EQUILIBRIUM

## KEY POINTS

- The short-run equilibrium level of real output and the price level are determined by the intersection of the aggregate demand curve and the short-run aggregate supply curve. When this equilibrium occurs at the potential output level, on the long-run aggregate supply curve, the economy is operating at full employment.

- Only a short-run equilibrium that is at potential output is also a long-run equilibrium. Short-run equilibrium can change when the aggregate demand curve or the short-run aggregate supply curve shifts rightward or leftward, but the long-run equilibrium level of RGDP only changes when the *LRAS* shifts. Sometimes, these supply or demand changes are anticipated; at other times, however, the shifts occur unexpectedly. Economists call these unexpected shifts **shocks**.

- Short-run equilibrium can occur at less than the potential output of the economy, resulting in a **recessionary gap**. Or it can temporarily occur beyond potential output, resulting in an **expansionary gap**.

# Chapter 13: Aggregate Demand and Aggregate Supply

- Demand-pull inflation occurs when the price level rises as a result of an increase in aggregate demand. The increase in *AD* causes an increase in the price level and an increase in real output, illustrated by a movement up along the *SRAS* curve. This causes an expansionary gap. The increase in output as a result of the increase in the price level is a result of its effect on producers' profits; firms have an incentive to increase real output when the prices of the goods they are selling are rising faster than the costs of the inputs they use in production.

- The short-run result of an increase in *AD* is a level of RGDP beyond full employment. The potential output is an expansionary gap. It seems peculiar that the economy can operate beyond its potential, but this is possible, temporarily, as firms encourage workers to work overtime, extend the hours of part-time workers, hire recently retired employees, reduce frictional unemployment through more extensive searches for employees, and so on. However, short-run real output beyond potential output (and employment beyond full employment) cannot be sustained in the long run.

- In the expansionary gap situation, because the price level is now higher, workers (and other input suppliers) become disgruntled with real wages that have not yet adjusted to the new price level. Recall that along the *SRAS* curve, wages and other input prices are assumed to be constant. Therefore, workers' and input suppliers' purchasing power falls as output prices rise. (If prices have risen, but wages have not risen as much, real wages have fallen.) Because real (adjusted for inflation) wages have fallen, workers and other suppliers demand higher prices in order to supply their inputs. As input prices respond to the higher level of output prices, the *SRAS* curve shifts to the left. Suppliers will continually seek higher prices for their inputs until they reach the new long-run equilibrium. At that point, input suppliers' purchasing power is restored at full-employment equilibrium. The only long-run difference from the initial equilibrium is the new, higher price level.

- The 1970s and early 1980s witnessed a phenomenon known as **stagflation,** where lower growth and higher prices occurred together. Some economists believe that this was caused by a leftward shift in the aggregate supply curve. If aggregate demand did not change significantly and the price level increased, then the inflation was caused by supply-side forces, not demand. This is called **cost-push inflation.**

- The primary culprits responsible for the leftward shift in *SRAS* in the 1970s were oil price increases. An increase in input prices can cause the *SRAS* curve to shift to the left, and this spelled big trouble for the U.S. economy—higher price levels, lower output, and higher rates of unemployment.

- Starting with the economy initially at full-employment equilibrium, suppose there is a sudden increase in input prices, such as an increase in the price of oil. This increase would shift the *SRAS* curve to the left. As a result, the price level rises and real output falls below potential output. Now firms may demand fewer workers as a result of the higher input costs that cannot be passed on to the consumers. The result is higher prices, lower real output, more unemployment, and a recessionary gap.

- As far as energy prices are concerned, the 1980s witnessed falling oil prices as OPEC lost some of its clout, and many non-OPEC oil producers increased production. The net result was a rightward shift in the *SRAS* curve. Holding *AD* constant, this rightward shift in *SRAS* would lead to lower prices, greater output, and lower rates of unemployment.

- Just as cost-push inflation can cause a recession, so can a decrease in *AD*. A fall in *AD* would reduce real output and the price level, and increase unemployment in the short run—a recessionary gap.

- Many recoveries from recessions occur because of increases in aggregate demand that take the economy back to potential output.

- However, it is possible that the economy would self-correct through declining wages and prices. In a recession, unemployed workers and other input suppliers will bid down wages and prices, and the resulting reduction in production costs shifts the short-run aggregate supply curve to the right. Eventually, the economy returns to a long-run equilibrium at potential output and a lower price level.

- Many economists believe that wages and prices may be very slow to adjust, especially downward. This downward wage stickiness may lead to prolonged periods of recession, by making the economy's adjustment mechanism slower.

- Wages and prices may be sticky downward because of long-term labor contracts, a legal minimum wage, employers paying efficiency wages, and menu costs.

# Chapter 13: Aggregate Demand and Aggregate Supply

- If the economy is currently in an expansionary gap, with output greater than potential output, the price level is higher than workers anticipated, and workers' and input suppliers' purchasing power has fallen. Consequently, workers and other suppliers demand higher prices to be willing to supply their inputs, shifting the short-run aggregate supply to the left, until they reach the long-run equilibrium at potential output. Input suppliers' purchasing power is restored at a higher price level.

- In this chapter, we have been shifting the *AS* and *AD* curves around as if we knew exactly what we were doing. But it is very important to mention that the AD/AS model is a crude tool.

- In the supply and demand curves covered in Chapter 6, we saw how this simple tool is very rich in explanatory power. While supply and demand analysis does not always provide precise estimates of the shifts or of the exact price and output changes that accompany those shifts, it does provide a framework to predict the direction that certain important variables will change under different circumstances.

- The same is true in the AD/AS model, but it is less precise because of the complexities and interrelationships that exist in the macroeconomy. The slopes of the *AD* and *AS* curves, the magnitudes of the shifts, and the interrelationship of the variables are to some extent a mystery. For example, if a reduction in aggregate demand leads to lower real GDP and, as a result, there are fewer workers that are willing to look for work, it impacts the *AS* curve. There are other examples of the interdependence of the *AD* and *AS* curves that make this analysis not completely satisfactory. Nevertheless, the framework still provides some important insights into the workings of the macroeconomy.

## I     REVIEW

The short-run equilibrium level of real output and the price level are determined by the intersection of the aggregate demand curve and the short-run aggregate _____ curve.

Short-run equilibrium can change when either the aggregate demand curve or the short-run aggregate supply curve shifts, but the long-run level of RGDP changes only when the long-run aggregate _____ curve shifts.

When equilibrium occurs at less than full-employment output, we call the gap between actual equilibrium and full-employment output a(n) _____ gap. When equilibrium occurs beyond full-employment output we call the gap between full-employment output and actual equilibrium a(n) _____ gap.

When the price level rises as a result of an increase in aggregate demand, it is called _____-pull inflation.

When the price level rises as a result of a decrease in aggregate supply, it is called _____-push inflation.

In the 1970s and early 1980s, the United States experienced a phenomenon known as _____, where lower growth of RGDP and higher prices occurred together.

When the economy is in a recession, it may _____-correct through declining wages and _____.

When the economy is experiencing an inflationary gap the economy will self-correct through _____ wages and prices.

## II     TRUE/FALSE

_____ F 1. A frequent cause of demand-pull inflation during the 1970s and early 1980s was higher oil prices.

_____ T 2. Cost-push inflation is shown as a leftward shift in the short-run aggregate supply curve.

F

3. An expansionary gap exists when actual macroeconomic equilibrium occurs at a level of RGDP that is below potential RGDP.

## III    MULTIPLE CHOICE

1.  Stagflation occurs when output
    A) rises and the price level falls.
    B) rises and the price level rises.
    C) falls and the price level falls.
    D) falls and the price level rises.

2.  A recession could result from a(n)
    A) increase in aggregate demand.
    B) decrease in aggregate demand.
    C) increase in short-run aggregate supply.
    D) increase in long-run aggregate supply.

3.  When the economy is in a recession, it is possible for the economy to self-correct through a(n)
    A) increase in wages with a corresponding decrease in the price level.
    B) increase in wages and a corresponding increase in the price level.
    C) decrease in wages with a corresponding increase in the price level.
    D) decrease in wages and a corresponding decrease in the price level.

## IV    APPLICATION AND DISCUSSION

1.  Use the graph in Exhibit 4 to show the *short-run* effect of an increase in aggregate demand.

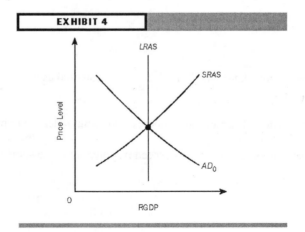

169

2.     Now use the graph in Exhibit 5 to show the *long-run* effect of an increase in aggregate demand.

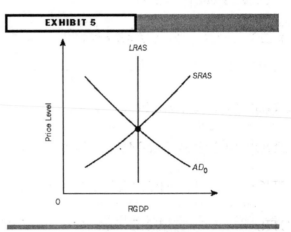

Questions

1.  What factors determined Julie's long-run potential as a runner? What caused Julie to temporarily exceed her long-run potential?

2.  What factors determine an economy's long-run potential to produce?

3.  What causes an economy to exceed its potential in the short run?

# CHAPTER 14
# FISCAL POLICY

# SECTION 14.1
# FISCAL POLICY

## KEY POINTS

- **Fiscal policy** is the use of government purchases, taxes, and transfer payments to alter real GDP and price levels.

- When government spending (for purchases of goods and services and transfer payments) exceeds tax revenues, there is a **budget deficit**. When tax revenues are greater than government spending, a **budget surplus** exists. A balanced budget, where government expenditures equal tax revenues, may seldom occur unless efforts are made to deliberately balance the budget as a matter of public policy.

# Chapter 14: Fiscal Policy

- When the government wishes to stimulate the economy by increasing aggregate demand, it will increase government purchases of goods and services, increase transfer payments, lower taxes, or use some combination of these approaches. Any of those options will increase the budget deficit (or reduce the budget surplus). Thus, **expansionary fiscal policy** is associated with increased government budget deficits. Likewise, if the government wishes to dampen a boom in the economy by reducing aggregate demand, it will reduce its purchases of goods and services, increase taxes, reduce transfer payments, or even some combination of these approaches. Thus, **contractionary fiscal policy** will tend to create or expand a budget surplus, or reduce a budget deficit, if one exists.

## I    REVIEW

_Fiscal_ policy is the use of the government's purchases, taxes, and transfer payments to alter the equilibrium level of real GDP and the price level.

In 2001 a large tax _cut_ was implemented to combat an economic _slow down_ and to promote long-term economic growth.

When government spending exceeds government revenues there is a government budget _deficit_. When government revenues exceed government spending there is a budget _surplus_. A balanced budget occurs when government revenue _equals_ government spending.

When the government wants to stimulate the economy it can _increase_ the budget deficit by increasing government purchases, increasing transfer payments, or lowering taxes. _Expansionary_ fiscal policy is associated with government budget deficits.

If the government wishes to dampen a booming economy it can _reduce_ spending, _reduce_ transfer payments, or _increase_ taxes. _Contractionary_ fiscal policy will tend to create budget surplus or reduce a budget deficit.

## II    TRUE/FALSE

_T_ 1. Expansionary fiscal policy will increase the budget deficit (or reduce a budget surplus) through greater government spending, lower taxes, or both.

_F_ 2. Contractionary fiscal policy would be the government's policy of choice when the economy is in a recession.

## III    MULTIPLE CHOICE

1. When the government uses fiscal policy, it uses government purchases, taxes, and transfers to
   A) affect the aggregate supply curve and change equilibrium real GDP and price levels.
   B) change the country's potential output and change equilibrium real GDP and price levels.
   C) shift the aggregate demand curve and change equilibrium real GDP and price levels.
   D) alter the country's production possibilities curve.

2. In the early 1980s, U.S. unemployment rates reached their highest levels since the Great Depression. If the government wished to move the economy out of recession, which of the following would have been an appropriate policy action?
   A) increase government spending
   B) increase taxes
   C) decrease government spending
   D) decrease labor supplies

## IV    APPLICATION AND DISCUSSION

How would you use each of the three tools of fiscal policy in each of the situations in Exhibit 1? Use (+) for an increase and (−) for a decrease in the level.

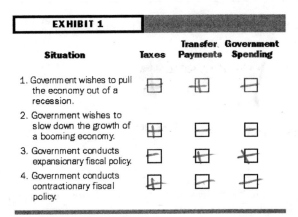

| Situation | Taxes | Transfer Payments | Government Spending |
|---|---|---|---|
| 1. Government wishes to pull the economy out of a recession. | | | |
| 2. Government wishes to slow down the growth of a booming economy. | | | |
| 3. Government conducts expansionary fiscal policy. | | | |
| 4. Government conducts contractionary fiscal policy. | | | |

# SECTION 14.2
# GOVERNMENT: SPENDING AND TAXATION

## KEY POINTS

- The public sector (federal, state, and local governments) plays a pivotal role in the allocation of resources and the distribution of income.

- It is impossible to precisely measure the degree of governmental involvement in the economy with any single number. But measured in terms of total government spending as a percentage of output, the growth of the government sector has been substantial, from about 11 percent in 1929 to over 30 percent today, with a large part of the growth between 1930 and 1975.

- State and local spending is very different than federal spending. Education and public welfare account for over 50 percent of their expenditures. Other important areas of spending include highways, utilities, police, and fire protection.

- How do governments obtain revenue? Two major avenues are open: taxation and borrowing. A large majority of government activity is financed by taxation. At the federal level, most taxes are on personal income and corporate income. Most remaining revenue comes from payroll taxes, which are used to pay for Social Security and Medicare.

- Some consider **excise taxes** to be the least fair type of taxes. A **consumption tax** (a tax on consumer goods rather than income) on these specific items will impose a far greater burden, as a percentage of income, on the poor and middle class than on the wealthy because low-income families spend a greater proportion of their income on such goods than do high income families. In addition, excise taxes may lead to economic inefficiencies.

- **Progressive taxes,** such as the federal income tax, require those with higher incomes to pay a greater proportion of their income in taxes. **Regressive taxes,** such as payroll taxes, take a greater proportion of the income of lower-income groups than higher-income groups. Adding together all taxes, the federal tax system is probably only slightly progressive.

- State and local revenue sources include property taxes, sales and state income taxes, federal government grants, and license fees and user charges (e.g., utilities and tuition).

## I    REVIEW

One way to gauge the degree of government involvement in the economy is to examine the ratio of government _Spending_ to total output.

Over the past 80 years government spending as a share of total output has _increased_.

In most years, the way the United States pays for government activity is through _taxation_.

Most tax revenues come to the U.S. government through personal and corporate _income_ taxes.

The taxes that are used to fund Social Security and Medicare are called _payroll_ taxes.

Some people consider _excise_ taxes to be the least fair type of taxes since low-income families pay a greater proportion of their income on these taxes than do high-_income_ families.

Taxes that require those with higher incomes to pay a greater proportion of their income in taxes are called _progressive_ taxes.

Taxes that take a greater proportion of the income of lower-income groups than higher-income groups are called _regressive_ taxes.

## II    TRUE/FALSE

_F_ 1. Since the 1970s, the biggest single area of growth in government spending has been in defense spending.

_F_ 2. State and local governments spend their money on the same sorts of things that the federal government does.

_F_ 3. The federal government gets most of its money from tariffs on imported goods.

_T_ 4. Excise taxes are regressive.

## III    MULTIPLE CHOICE

1.  When did the largest growth in government as a share of total U.S. output occur?
    A)  1935-1940
    B)  1940-1945
    C)  1945-1960
    D)  1990–2000

2.  Currently, the largest single component of federal expenditure is
    A)  interest on the national debt.
    B)  Social Security.
    C)  defense spending.
    D)  foreign aid.

3.  The largest single component of state and local spending is
    A)  police and fire protection.
    B)  public welfare.
    C)  education.
    D)  highways.

## IV    APPLICATION AND DISCUSSION

Below are income and income tax information for four hypothetical families.

| Family | Total Income | Total Income Tax | Average Tax Rate |
|--------|--------------|------------------|------------------|
| 1 | $10,000 | $ 1,000 | 10 |
| 2 | $50,000 | $10,000 | 20 |
| 3 | $90,000 | $27,000 | 30 |
| 4 | $130,000 | $52,000 | 40 |

A)  Calculate the average tax rate for each family and fill in the "Average Tax Rate" column.

B)  Is the income tax progressive or regressive?

**QUESTION**

1.How do helmet laws affect the costs of motorcycle riding?

S E C T I O N   1 4 . 3

# THE MULTIPLIER EFFECT

## KEY POINTS

- Real GDP will change any time the amount of any one of the four forms of purchases—consumption, investment, government purchases, and net exports—changes. If, for any reason, people generally decide to purchase more in any of these categories out of given income, aggregate demand will shift rightward.

- Any one of the components of purchases of goods and services ($C$, $I$, $G$, or $X - M$) can initiate changes in aggregate demand, and thus a new short-run equilibrium. Changes in total output are very often brought about by alterations in investment plans because investment purchases are a relatively volatile category of expenditures. However, if policy makers are unhappy about the present short-run equilibrium GDP, perhaps because they view unemployment as being too high, they can deliberately manipulate the level of government purchases in order to obtain a new short-run equilibrium value. Similarly, by changing taxes or transfer payments, they can alter the amount of disposable income of households and thus bring about changes in consumption purchases.

- Usually, when an initial increase in purchases of goods or services occurs, the ultimate increase in total purchases will tend to be greater than the initial increase. This is called the **multiplier effect.**

- The multiplier effect is illustrated by the government increasing its defense budget by $10 billion to buy aircraft carriers. When the government purchases the aircraft carriers, not only does it add to the total demand for goods and services directly, it also provides $10 billion in added income to the companies that actually construct the aircraft carriers. Those companies will then hire more workers and buy more capital equipment and other inputs in order to produce the new output. The owners of these inputs, therefore, receive more income because of the increase in government purchases. And what will they do with this additional income? While behavior will vary somewhat among individuals, collectively they will probably spend a substantial part of the additional income on additional consumption purchases, pay some additional taxes incurred because of the income, and save a bit of it as well. The additional consumption purchases made as a portion of the additional income is measured by the **marginal propensity to consume (MPC).**

- The multiplier effect is worked out for an assumed MPC of two-thirds. The initial $10 billion increase in government purchases causes both a $10 billion increase in aggregate demand and an income increase of $10 billion to suppliers of the inputs used to produce aircraft carriers; the owners of those inputs, in turn, will spend an additional $6 2/3 billion (two-thirds of $10 billion) on additional consumption purchases. A chain reaction has been started. The added $6.67 billion in consumption purchases by those deriving income from the initial investment brings a $6.67 billion increase in aggregate demand and in new income to suppliers of the inputs that produced the goods and services. These persons, in turn, will spend some two-thirds of their additional $6.67 billion in income, or $4.44 billion on consumption purchases. This means a $4.44 billion more in aggregate demand and income to still another group of persons, who will then proceed to spend two-thirds of that amount, or $2.96 billion on consumption purchases. The chain reaction continues, with each new round of purchases providing income to a new group of persons who, in turn, increase their purchases. At each round, the added income generated and the resulting consumer purchases gets smaller because some of each round's increase in income goes to savings and tax payments.

- The multiplier is equal to 1 divided by 1 minus the marginal propensity to consume (1/1–- MPC).

- Note that the larger the marginal propensity to consume, the larger the multiplier effect because relatively more additional consumption purchases out of any given income increase generates relatively larger secondary and tertiary income effects in successive rounds of the process.

- Because an initial increase in one of the AD components results in greater income, including higher profits for suppliers, it will lead to increased consumer purchases. So the effect of the initial increase will tend to have a multiplied effect on the economy. The initial impact of a $10 billion additional purchase by the government directly shifts AD right by $10 billion. The multiplier effect then causes AD to shift $20 billion further to the right. The total effect on AD of a $10 billion increase in government purchases is therefore $30 billion, if the marginal propensity to consume equals 2/3.

- The multiplier process is not instantaneous. Time lags mean that the ultimate increase in purchases may not be achieved for a year or more. The extent of the multiplier effect visible within a short time period will be less than the total effect indicated by the multiplier formula. In addition, savings, taxes, and money spent on import goods (which are not part of aggregate demand for domestically produced goods and services) will reduce the size of the multiplier because each of them reduces the fraction of a given increase in income that will go to additional purchases of domestically produced consumption goods.

---

I      REVIEW
_____

A change in any one of the components of purchases of goods and services (C, I, G, or X – M) can initiate changes in _aggregate_ demand.

The _multiplier_ effect is a chain reaction of additional income and purchases that results in an ultimate increase in total purchases that is _greater_ than the initial increase in purchases.

The additional consumption made as a portion of additional income is measured by the marginal _propensity_ to consume.

The larger the marginal propensity to consume, the larger the _multiplier_ effect.

## II    TRUE/FALSE

_F_ 1. The multiplier effect is generated only by changes in investment or government spending.

_F_ 2. The multiplier effect is virtually instantaneous.

## III    MULTIPLE CHOICE

1.  If the marginal propensity to consume is 4/5, the multiplier is
    A)  1/5.
    B)  1.
    C)  5.
    D)  20.

2.  If the marginal propensity to consume is 9/10, the multiplier is
    A)  9/10.
    B)  9.
    C)  10.
    D)  90.

## IV    APPLICATION AND DISCUSSION

If the marginal propensity to consume is 2/3, show the multiplier effect of a $10 billion increase in defense spending on the AD curve in Exhibit 2.

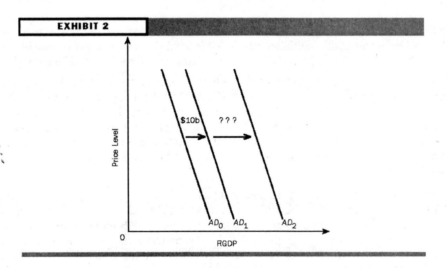

# SECTION 14.4
# FISCAL POLICY AND THE AD/AS MODEL

## KEY POINTS

- The primary tools of fiscal policy, government purchases, taxes, and transfer payments, can be presented in the context of the aggregate supply and demand model.

- When the government purchases more, taxes less, and increases transfer payments, the size of the government's budget deficit will grow. While budget deficits are often thought to be bad, a case can be made for using budget deficits to stimulate the economy when it is operating at less than full capacity. Such expansionary fiscal policy has the potential to move an economy out of a recession and closer to full employment.

- If the government decides to purchase more, cut taxes, and/or increase transfer payments, other things constant, total purchases will rise, shifting the aggregate demand curve to the right. The effect of this increase in aggregate demand depends on the position of the macroeconomic equilibrium prior to the government stimulus.

- Starting from an initial recession equilibrium, with real output below potential RGDP, an increase in government purchases, a tax cut, and/or increase in transfer payments would increase the size of the budget deficit and lead to an increase in aggregate demand, ideally to a new short-run equilibrium at potential RGDP. This result of such a change would be an increase in the price level and an increase in RGDP. Remember, of course, that much of this increase in aggregate demand is caused by the multiplier process, so that the magnitude of the change in aggregate demand will be much larger than the magnitude of the stimulus package of tax cuts, increases in transfer payments, and/or government purchases. If the policy change is of the right magnitude and timed appropriately, the expansionary fiscal policy could stimulate the economy, pulling it out of recession, and resulting in full employment.

- When the economy is operating at full employment, an increase in government spending, an increase in transfer payments, and/or a tax cut causes an increase in aggregate demand. Moving up along the short-run aggregate supply curve, the price level rises and real output rises as we reach a new short-run equilibrium. The high level of aggregate demand at beyond full capacity will put pressure on input markets, sending wages and other input prices higher. The higher costs will shift the short-run aggregate supply curve leftward, until a sustainable long-run equilibrium is reached. Real output returns to the full-employment level, and the long-term effect is an increase in the price level.

- When the government purchases less, taxes more, or decreases transfer payments, the size of the government's budget deficit will fall or the size of the budget surplus will rise, other things equal. Sometimes such a change in fiscal policy may help "cool off" the economy when it has overheated and inflation has become a serious problem.

- When initial short-run equilibrium is at a point beyond full-employment output, the government decides to reduce its purchases, increase taxes, or reduce transfer payments, which will directly affect aggregate demand. A tax increase on consumers or a decrease in transfer payments will reduce households' disposable incomes, reducing purchases of consumption goods and services, and higher business taxes will reduce investment purchases. The reductions in consumption, investment, and/or government purchases will shift the aggregate demand curve leftward, ideally to a long-run full-employment level of RGDP. The result is a lower price level and full-employment output and a new short- and long-run equilibrium.

- Now consider the case of an initial short- and long-run equilibrium at full employment, where *AD* intersects both the *SRAS* curve and the *LRAS* curve. A decrease in aggregate demand from that results from a reduction in government purchases, higher taxes, or lower transfer payments and leads to a short-run equilibrium with lower prices and real output reduced below its full-employment level. As prices fall, input suppliers then revise their price level expectations downward. That is, laborers and other input suppliers are now willing to take less for the use of their resources, and the resulting reduction in production costs shifts the short-run supply curve right. The resulting eventual long-run equilibrium is a reduction in the price level, with real output returning to its full-employment level.

# Chapter 14: Fiscal Policy

## I    REVIEW

Budget deficits can be used to ___*stimulate*___ the economy when it is operating at less than full capacity.

Increasing government spending, reducing taxes, and expanding transfer payments increases consumption, investment and government spending and causes the aggregate demand curve to shift to the ___*right*___.

The effect of this increased aggregate demand depends on the position of the initial macroeconomic ___*equilibrium*___. If policy change is of the right ___*magnitude*___ and timing, expansionary fiscal policy can move an economy out of ___*recession*___ to full employment.

When the economy is at full employment, expansionary fiscal policy will only result in a(n) ___*increase*___ in the price level in the long run. Increases in aggregate demand cause output to rise above the ___*full*___ employment level in the short run. Pressure on input markets causes wages and other input prices to ___*increase*___, which shifts the SRAS curve to the ___*left*___ until a new short-run equilibrium is reached at the ___*full*___ capacity level of output.

Contractionary fiscal policy has the potential to ___*dampen*___ the inflationary pressure of an overheated economy. Decreased government spending, increased taxes, or reductions in transfer payments will shift the aggregate demand curve to the ___*left*___. If the initial short-run equilibrium is at a level of output ___*greater*___ than the economy's full productive capacity, such policies will move the economy back toward full employment real GDP and dampen the inflationary pressure.

If the initial equilibrium is at the full employment real GDP, contractionary fiscal policy will result in a short-run equilibrium at a ___*lower*___ level of output. The prices of labor and other inputs ___*fall*___, which causes the SRAS curve to shift to the ___*right*___. Input prices will continue to fall until new short-run equilibrium is reached at the ___*full*___ employment level of output. The only change in the long run will be a decrease in the ___*price*___ level.

## II    TRUE/FALSE

___F___ 1. If the government cuts taxes, total spending will fall and the aggregate demand curve will shift to the left.

___T___ 2. When the economy is at the full-employment level of real GDP, increased government spending will not increase the economy's total output in the long run.

## III    MULTIPLE CHOICE

Answer questions 1 through 2 by referring to Exhibit 3.

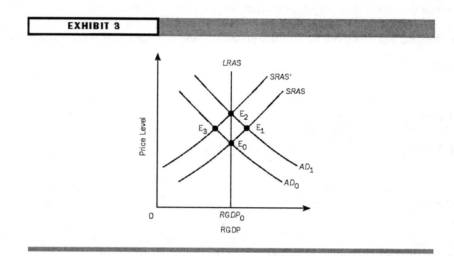

EXHIBIT 3

1.  If the economy is at full-employment real GDP, expansionary fiscal policy, which increases aggregate demand from $AD_0$ to $AD_1$, will result in the new short-run equilibrium
    A)  $E_0$.
    B)  $E_1$.
    C)  $E_2$.
    D)  $E_3$.

2.  The expansionary fiscal policy shown in Exhibit 3 will result in the new long-run equilibrium
    A)  $E_0$.
    B)  $E_1$.
    C)  $E_2$.
    D)  $E_3$.

3.  If government policy makers are worried about the inflationary potential of the economy, they believe the economy is at which of the following?
    A)  a short-run equilibrium with output less than full-employment real GDP
    B)  a short-run equilibrium with output greater than full-employment real GDP
    C)  a short-run equilibrium with output equal to full-employment real GDP
    D)  a short-run equilibrium which is the same as long-run equilibrium

4.  If government policy makers were worried about the inflationary potential of the economy, which of the following would *not* be a correct fiscal policy change?
    A)  increase consumption taxes
    B)  increase government spending
    C)  reduce transfer payments
    D)  reduce the budget deficit

## IV    APPLICATION AND DISCUSSION

When governments go to war they dramatically expand government spending. Unless tax revenues increase at the same rate, the deficit will rise. When the United States entered World War II, following the Great Depression, the economy was producing at less than the full-employment level of output. The U.S. military buildup during the Vietnam War, on the other hand, took place when the economy was producing near full employment. Use your understanding of the AD/AS model to explain why we would expect more inflationary pressure in the economy during the Vietnam War.

# SECTION 14.5
# AUTOMATIC STABILIZERS

## KEY POINTS

- Some changes in government transfer payments and taxes take place automatically as business cycle conditions change, without deliberations in Congress or the executive branch of the government. Changes in government transfer payments or tax collections that automatically tend to counter business cycle fluctuations are called **automatic stabilizers.**

- The most important automatic stabilizer is the tax system. For example, with the personal income tax, as incomes rise, tax liabilities also increase automatically. Personal income taxes vary directly with income, and in fact rise or fall by greater percentage terms than income itself rises or falls. Big increases and big decreases in GDP are both lessened by automatic changes in income tax receipts. For example, if GDP declines, tax liabilities decline, increasing disposable incomes and stimulating consumption spending, partly offsetting the initial decline in aggregate demand.

- Other income-related payroll taxes, notably Social Security taxes, the corporate profit tax, and the unemployment compensation program also act as automatic stabilizers. Because incomes, earnings, and profits all fall during a recession, the government collects less in taxes. This reduced tax burden partially offsets any recessionary fall in aggregate demand. Similarly, during recessions, unemployment rises and more people become eligible for public assistance (welfare). Unemployment compensation and public assistance payments increase. During boom periods, such payments will fall as the number of the unemployed declines. Both these tax and spending programs act as automatic stabilizers, stimulating aggregate demand during recessions and reducing aggregate demand during booms.

## I    REVIEW

Automatic _stabilizers_ are changes in government transfer payments and tax collections that automatically counter business cycle fluctuations. They work _without_ legislative or executive branch action.

The personal income _tax_ is an automatic stabilizer. Income taxes vary _directly_ with income. Taxes change by a _greater_ percent than income when income increases or decreases, so changes in _disposable_ income are not as great as changes in income.

Other income and profit-based taxes also _fall_ during a recession partially offsetting the effects of declining income and profits on the economy.

# Chapter 14: Fiscal Policy

The unemployment _compensation_ program is another automatic stabilizer. During recessions as unemployment _rises_, unemployment compensation provides _income_ to the unemployed. During boom times as unemployment _falls_, these government payments also decline.

The system of _public_ assistance provides another example of an automatic stabilizer.

## II    TRUE/FALSE

_T_  1. During the last recession Ophelia lost her job and her yearly income fell by 20 percent. Her disposable income fell by less than 20 percent.

_F_  2. The significant time it takes for Congress to respond to the fluctuations of the business cycle and enact appropriate automatic stabilizers makes them ineffective tools.

## III    MULTIPLE CHOICE

1.  During a recession, public assistance payments and unemployment compensation payments automatically increase while income taxes automatically decrease. Which of the following best describes the effect of these changes on aggregate demand?
    A)  Aggregate demand will be greater than it was before the recession.
    B)  Aggregate demand will be less than it was before the recession.
    C)  Aggregate demand will be the same as it was before the recession.
    D)  Aggregate demand will be less than it would be without these automatic stabilizers.

2.  Martha and George spend all of their disposable income on consumption. During the last recession their total income fell from $50,000 to $25,000. The decline in income caused their tax rate to fall from 20 percent to 10 percent. Martha and George reduced consumption spending by
    A)  $25,000.
    B)  $22,500.
    C)  $20,000.
    D)  $17,500.

## IV    APPLICATION AND DISCUSSION

Senator Zedler thinks America should always have a balanced budget. To this end she proposes the "Balance Budget Tax." The tax would be automatically calculated each year so that each person pays his or her share of the tax that would eliminate the current year deficit. Each person would get a similar rebate when there is a budget surplus. Would this "Balanced Budget Tax" proposal add another automatic stabilizer? Explain why or why not?

SECTION 14.6

# POSSIBLE OBSTACLES TO EFFECTIVE FISCAL POLICY

## KEY POINTS

- The multiplier effect of an increase in government purchases implies that the increase in aggregate demand will tend to be greater than the initial fiscal stimulus, other things equal. However, this may not be true because all other things will not tend to stay equal in this case.

- When the government borrows money to finance a deficit, it increases the overall demand for money in the money market, driving interest rates up. As a result of the higher interest rate, consumers may decide against buying some interest-sensitive goods, and businesses may cancel or scale back plans to expand or buy new capital equipment. In short, the higher interest rate will choke off private spending on goods and services, and as a result, the impact of the increase in government purchases may be smaller than we first assumed. Economists call this the **crowding-out effect**.

- An additional $10 billion of government spending on aircraft carriers, other things equal, would shift the aggregate demand curve right by $10 billion times the multiplier. However, as this process takes place, interest rates are bid up, crowding out some investments and other interest-rate-sensitive purchases at the same time. By itself, this would reduce aggregate demand by the purchases crowded out times the multiplier. Since both these processes are taking place at the same time, the net effect is the difference between the expansion of government purchases and the private sector purchases crowded out, times the multiplier. The crowding-out effect also occurs with a tax change.

- Critics of the crowding-out effect analysis argue that the increase in government purchases (or tax cut), particularly if the economy is in a severe recession, could actually improve consumer and business expectations and actually encourage private investment spending. It is also possible that the monetary authorities could increase the money supply to offset the higher interest rates from the crowding-out effect.

- Another form of crowding out can take place in international markets. Expansionary fiscal policy increases the federal budget deficit. To finance the deficit, the U.S. government borrows more money, driving up the interest rate (the basic crowding-out effect). However, the higher interest rates will attract funds from abroad, and funds foreigners will first have to convert from their currencies into dollars. The increase in the demand for dollars relative to other currencies will cause the dollar to appreciate in value. This will cause net exports to fall, by making foreign imports relatively cheaper in the United States, increasing imports, and by making U.S.-made goods more expensive to foreigners, decreasing exports. This reduction in net exports causes a fall in *AD,* partly crowding out the effects of expansionary fiscal policy.

- The larger the crowding-out effect, the smaller the actual effect of a given change in fiscal policy.

- It is important to recognize that fiscal policy is implemented through the political process, requiring both congressional and presidential action and that process takes time. Often, the lag between the time that a fiscal response is desired and the time an appropriate policy is implemented and its effects felt is considerable. Sometimes a fiscal policy designed to deal with a contracting economy may actually take effect during a period of economic expansion, or vice versa, resulting in a stabilization policy that actually destabilizes the economy.

- The timing of fiscal policy is crucial. Because of the significant lags before the fiscal policy has its effect, the increase in aggregate demand may occur at the wrong time. In response to current low levels of output and high rates of unemployment, policy makers may decide to increase government purchases and implement a tax cut. But during the period from when policy makers recognized the problem to when the policies had a chance to work themselves through the economy, say there was a large increase in business and consumer confidence, shifting the aggregate demand curve rightward, increasing real GDP and employment. Now when the fiscal policy takes effect, the policies will have the undesired effect of causing inflation, with little permanent effect on output and employment. The same timing problems exist for fiscal policy designed to combat high inflation rates. Timed correctly, contractionary fiscal policy could correct an inflationary boom; timed incorrectly, it could cause a recession.

## I   REVIEW

If government borrows to pay for deficit spending it increases the overall demand for loanable funds and drives interest rates ___*up*___.

*Ceteris paribus*, higher interest rates will result in less ___*private*___ spending on goods and services.

When increased government spending drives up interest rates and chokes off private spending it is called ___*crowding*___ out.

In the open economy, budget deficits ___*increase*___ the demand for loanable funds, raise interest rates, and lead to an ___*appreciation*___ in the value of the dollar relative to other currencies.

The ___*lag*___ between the time that a fiscal response is desired and the time an appropriate policy is implemented and its effects felt is considerable.

## II      TRUE/FALSE

___F___ 1. Higher interest rates lead to higher levels of private spending.

___T___ 2. In an open economy higher interest rates in the U.S. cause the dollar to appreciate in value.

## III     MULTIPLE CHOICE

1.  If the federal government borrows to finance deficit spending, the
    A) supply of loanable funds will increase, driving interest rates up.
    B) supply of loanable funds will decrease, driving interest rates down.
    C) demand for loanable funds will increase, driving interest rates up.
    D) demand for loanable funds will decrease, driving interest rates down.

2.  Which of the following is true about time lags and fiscal policy?
    A) Once an appropriate fiscal policy has been determined it can be implemented quickly.
    B) The lag time between when a fiscal policy is needed and when it is actually implemented is considerable.
    C) Changes in federal taxes can by implemented easily by the president, without the approval of Congress.
    D) Changes in fiscal policy that involve changes in government spending on public works projects do not involve significant time lags.

3.  If U.S. budget deficits raise interest rates and attract investment funds from abroad, the foreign exchange value of the dollar will
    A) appreciate and U.S. net exports $(X - M)$ will increase.
    B) appreciate in value and U.S. net exports $(X - M)$ will decrease.
    C) depreciate and U.S. net exports $(X - M)$ will decrease.
    D) depreciate and U.S. net exports $(X - M)$ will increase.

## IV     APPLICATION AND DISCUSSION

Critics of the $1.35 trillion tax cut passed by Congress in 2001 say it will lead to higher interest rates. Is such a claim reasonable? How can a tax cut lead to higher interest rates?

SECTION 14.7
# SUPPLY-SIDE FISCAL POLICY

## KEY POINTS

- When policy makers discuss methods to stabilize the economy, the traditional focus has been on managing the economy through demand-side policies. But there are economists who believe that we should be focusing on the supply side of the economy as well, especially in the long run, rather than just on the demand side. In particular, they believe that individuals will save less, work less, and provide less capital when taxes, government transfer payments (like welfare), and regulations are too burdensome on productive activities. In other words, they believe that fiscal policy can work on the supply side of the economy as well as the demand side.

- Supply-siders would encourage government to reduce individual and business taxes, deregulate, and increase spending on research and development. Supply-siders believe that these types of government policies could cause greater long-term economic growth by stimulating personal income, savings, and capital formation.

- High tax rates could conceivably reduce work incentives to the point that government revenues are lower at high marginal tax rates than they would be at somewhat lower rates. Economist Arthur Laffer has argued that point graphically in what has been called the **Laffer curve**.

- When tax rates are low, increasing the federal tax rate will increase federal revenues. However, at very high federal tax rates, disincentive effects and increased tax evasion may actually reduce federal tax revenue. Over this range of tax rates, lowering them may actually increase federal tax revenue.

- A very high marginal tax rate on the rich actually might reduce the incentive to work, save, invest, produce, and perhaps as important, lead to illegal shifts in transactions to what has been termed the underground economy. If tax evasion becomes common, the equity and revenue-raising efficiency of the tax system suffers, as does general respect for the law.

- While all economists believe that incentives matter, there is considerable disagreement on the shape of the Laffer curve and where the economy actually is on the Laffer curve.

- Some economists believe that investment in research and development will have long-run benefits for the economy. In particular, greater research and development will lead to new technology and knowledge, which will permanently shift the short- and long-run aggregate supply curves to the right. The government encourages investments in research and development by giving tax breaks or subsidies to firms.

- Rather than being primarily concerned with short-run economic stabilization, supply-side policies are aimed at increasing both the short-run and long-run aggregate supply curves. If these policies are successful and maintained, both short- and long-run aggregate supply will increase over time, as the effects of deregulation and major structural changes in plant and equipment work their way through the economy, which takes some time.

- Critics of supply-side economics are skeptical of the magnitude of the impact of lower taxes on work effort and the impact of deregulation on productivity. They claim that the tax cuts of the 1980s led to moderate real output growth but only through a reduction in real tax revenues, inflation, and large budget deficits. They question whether people will save and invest much more if capital gains taxes are reduced, whether they will work much more if marginal tax rates are lowered, and whether the new production that occurs from deregulation be enough to offset the benefits of regulation.

- Supply-side initiatives affect aggregate demand as well as aggregate supply. If tax rates are reduced, it is quite possible that the demand-side stimulus from the increased disposable income (income after taxes) that results may be equal to, or even greater than the supply-side effects, causing higher price levels, and even greater short-run real output levels, although the long-run real output level increases with the long-run aggregate supply curve.

- Defenders of the supply-side approach argue that the real tax revenues of those in the highest marginal tax brackets actually increased as their tax rates fell in the 1980s (as they also had for earlier reductions in tax rates on the most heavily taxed high income groups) and that, compared to other developed countries in the world, the United States had very prosperous growth from 1982 to 1989. In addition, many supply-siders argue that most of their policy prescriptions were never really even tried for at least three reasons. First, many supply-siders' proposals for improving productive incentives were ignored and, in some cases, productive incentives were made worse rather than better. Second, the real output effects of the initial tax cuts were minimized by the restrictive, inflation-fighting policies of the Federal Reserve in the early 1980s. Third, Congress did not reduce federal expenditures, which was at least partially responsible for the growing deficit.

## I    REVIEW

Supply-side economists encourage government to __reduce__ taxes, deregulate, and increase spending on research and development because they think that these types of policies lead to __greater__ economic growth.

Supply-siders believe that savings and investment could be improved through __lower__ taxes.

Supply-siders believe that lower marginal tax rates will __raise__ after-tax earnings and lead people to work __more__ than they would otherwise.

According to supply-side economists, higher tax rates __discourage__ investment and encourage investors to spend more time and effort seeking tax __shelters__.

According to the Laffer curve, an increase in tax rates when taxes are low will __increase__ tax revenues. When tax rates are high, however, an increase in taxes will __reduce__ tax revenue.

A tax cut can lead to increases in short-run aggregate __supply__, long-run aggregate __supply__, and to an increase in __aggregate__ demand.

## II    TRUE/FALSE

__F__ 1. Supply-side economists believe that fiscal policy works only on the supply side of the economy, leaving aggregate demand unaffected.

__F__ 2. In order to combat high unemployment in the early 1960s, President John F. Kennedy proposed an increase in income tax rates combined with a decrease in government spending.

## III    MULTIPLE CHOICE

1. According to proponents of supply-side economics, a decrease in marginal tax rates will
   A) shift the aggregate demand curve to the left.
   B) encourage investors to spend valuable time and energy looking for tax shelters.
   C) discourage work effort and dampen productive investment.
   D) encourage work effort and spur productive investment.

2.  According to supply-side economists, their policies will shift
    A)  the aggregate demand curve to the right while leaving short-run aggregate supply and long-run aggregate supply unaffected.
    B)  the long-run aggregate supply curve and the short-run aggregate supply curves to the left while leaving aggregate demand unaffected.
    C)  the aggregate demand curve to the left, leaving short-run aggregate supply and long-run aggregate supply unaffected.
    D)  all three of the curves, aggregate demand, short-run aggregate supply, and long-run aggregate supply, to the right.

3.  Presidents John F. Kennedy and Ronald Reagan were alike in that they both advocated
    A)  higher marginal tax rates and cuts in government spending in order to reduce interest rates.
    B)  lower marginal tax rates and reductions in government spending in order to reduce interest rates.
    C)  lower marginal tax rates in order to stimulate the economy.
    D)  higher marginal tax rates in order to stimulate the economy.

## IV      APPLICATION AND DISCUSSION

Which policy would a supply-sider prefer, an across-the-board tax reduction in income tax rates or a package of tax-relief measures that would give every household a $300 tax rebate and allow them to deduct the interest they pay on credit card purchases?

# SECTION 14.8
# THE NATIONAL DEBT

## KEY POINTS

- Historically the largest budget deficits and a growing government debt occur during war years, when defense spending escalates, and during recessions as taxes are cut and government spending is increased. However, in the 1980s, deficits and debt soared in a relatively peaceful and prosperous time.

- Recall that when the government borrows to finance a budget deficit, it causes the interest rate to rise, which crowds out private investment, reducing capital formation. But a budget surplus adds to national savings and lowers the interest rate, stimulating private investment and capital formation.

- During the late 1990's, after nearly a decade of uninterrupted growth in the economy, chronic deficits in the federal budget turned to surpluses.

- Recently, due to tax cuts, the war on terrorism, and the 2001 recession, federal budget surpluses have been replaced by deficits.

- Policy makers now have to decide what to do with budget surpluses. Some favor continuing to pay down the national debt to drive interest rates down further and stimulate investment. Others favor cutting taxes, to reduce their misallocation of resources and the temptation toward special interest spending. These raise an important question: are we getting government goods and services with benefits that are greater than the costs?

- For many years, the government ran continuous budget deficits and built up a large federal debt. How did it pay for those budget deficits? After all, it has to have some means of paying out the funds necessary to support government expenditures that are in excess of the funds derived from tax payments. One thing the government could do is simply print money. However, printing money to finance activities is highly inflationary and also undermines confidence in the government. Typically, the budget deficit is financed by issuing debt. The federal government in effect borrows an amount necessary to cover the deficit by issuing bonds, or IOUs, payable typically at some maturity date. The sum total of the values of all bonds outstanding constitutes the federal debt. The tendency of the federal government to engage in budget deficits has led to increasing federal debt over time.

- From 1960 through 1997, the federal budget was in deficit every year except one. Deficits can be important because they provide the federal government with the flexibility to respond appropriately to changing circumstances, such as special emergencies or to avert an economic downturn.

- The "burden" of the national debt is a topic that has long interested economists, particularly whether it falls on present or future generations. Arguments can be made that the generation of taxpayers living at the time that the debt is issued shoulder the true cost of the debt because the debt permits the government to take command of resources that might be available for other, private uses. In a sense, the resources its takes to purchase government bonds might take away from private activities, such as private investment financed by private debt. The issuance of debt does involve some intergenerational transfer of incomes, however, because long after federal debt is issued, a new generation of taxpayers is making interest payments to persons of the generation that bought the bonds issued to finance that debt. If public debt is created intelligently, however, the "burden" of the debt should be less than the benefits derived from the resources acquired as a result; this is particularly true when the debt permits an expansion in real economic activity or for the development of vital infrastructure for the future. The opportunity cost of expanded public activity may also be small in terms of private activity that must be forgone to finance the public activity, if unemployed resources are put to work.

## I     REVIEW

Typically, the federal government funds deficit spending by issuing __bonds__, or IOUs. The sum total of the values of all outstanding bonds constitutes the federal __debt__.

From 1960 through 1997, the federal budget was in __deficit__ every year except 1969, when the government ran a small __surplus__.

Historically, the largest budget deficits occur during __war__ years. In the 1980s, however, deficits soared because tax __cuts__ were not matched by reductions in government __spending__.

During the late 1990's the federal government ran __surpluses__ in its budget. Recently, however, due to tax cuts, the war on terrorism, and the 2001 recession, the federal government has run budget __deficits__.

Although arguments can be made that the generation of __taxpayers__ living at the time that the debt is issued shoulders the true cost of the debt, there is no denying that issuance of debt involves some __intergenerational__ transfer of incomes. Long after the debt is issued a new generation of taxpayers must make __interest__ payments on the debt.

Future generations, however, may also receive __benefits__ from debt incurred by prior generations, especially if the debt is used to promote __expansion__ of economic activity or provide vital __infrastructure__ for the future.

## II     TRUE/FALSE

__F__ 1. The current size of the national debt presents a serious threat to the economic well-being of the United States.

__T__ 2. Increased public debt places a burden on future generations.

## III    MULTIPLE CHOICE

1.  Currently, the national debt amounts to about _____ percent of GDP.
    A)  5
    B)  25
    C)  60
    D)  250

2.  When the federal government runs a budget surplus, national savings goes _____, interest rates go _____, and private investment _____.
    A)  down; up; decreases
    B)  down; down; decreases
    C)  up; up; decreases
    D)  up; down; increases

3.  Chronic budget deficits and a large national debt will cause future generations to inherit
    A)  lower tax burdens.
    B)  higher tax burdens.
    C)  lower interest payment liabilities.
    D)  a smaller money supply.

## IV    APPLICATION AND DISCUSSION

"One problem with a large national debt is that is promotes deficits in our balance of trade." From what you know about debt, government borrowing, interest rates, and foreign exchange rates, how do you evaluate this statement?

Questions

1.  What effect does the tax cut have on Julie? Does it affect the aggregate demand curve?

2.  How could a tax cut affect the aggregate supply curve?

# CHAPTER 15
# MONEY AND THE BANKING SYSTEM

# SECTION 15.1
# MONEY

## KEY POINTS

- **Money** is anything that is generally accepted in exchange for goods or services.

- Many things, including tobacco, wampum (Indian trinkets), cigarettes, and whiskey have been used as money. But commodities have several disadvantages when used as money, the most important of which is that they deteriorate easily after a few trades. Precious metal coins have for millennia been used for money, partly because of their durability.

- **Currency** consists of coins and/or paper that some institution or government has created to be used in the trading of goods and services and the payment of debts. Currency in the form of metal coins is still used as money throughout the world today. But metal currency has a disadvantage: It is bulky. Also, certain types of metals traditionally used in coins, like gold and silver, are not available in sufficient quantities to meet our demands for a monetary instrument. For these reasons, metal coins have for centuries been supplemented by paper currency, often in the form of bank notes.

# Chapter 15: Money and Banking

- In the United States, the Federal Reserve System issues Federal Reserve Notes in various denominations, and this paper currency, along with coins, provides the basis for most transactions of relatively modest size in the United States today.

- In the United States and in most other nations of the world, metallic coins and paper currency are the only forms of **legal tender.** In other words, coins and paper money have been officially declared to be money—to be acceptable for the settlement of debts incurred in financial transactions. In effect, the government says, "We declare these instruments to be money, and citizens are expected to accept them as a medium of exchange." Legal tender is **fiat money**—a means of exchange that has been established not by custom and tradition, or because of the value of the metal in a coin, but by government fiat or declaration.

- Most of the money that we use for day-to-day transactions is not official legal tender. Rather, it is a monetary instrument that has become "generally accepted" in exchange over the years and has now, by custom and tradition, become money.

- **Demand deposits** are deposits in banks that can be withdrawn on demand, by simply writing a check. Some other forms of accounts in financial institutions also have virtually all of the attributes of demand deposits. For example, there are also other checkable deposits that earn interest but have some restrictions, such as higher monthly fees or minimum balance requirements. These interest-earning checking accounts effectively permit the depositors to write "orders" similar to checks and assign the rights to deposit to other persons, just as we write checks to other parties. Practically speaking, funds in these accounts are the equivalent of demand deposits and have become an important component in the supply of money. Both of these types of accounts are forms of **transaction deposits** because they can be easily converted into currency or used to buy goods and services directly. **Travelers' checks**, like currency and demand deposits, are also easily converted into currency or used directly as a means of payment.

- Demand deposits and other checkable deposits have replaced paper and metallic currency as the major source of money used for transactions in the United States and in most other relatively well-developed nations. There are several reasons, including ease and safety of transactions, lower transaction costs, and transaction records.

- Paying for goods and services with a check is easier (meaning cheaper) and less risky than paying with paper money. Paper money is readily transferable: If someone takes a $20 bill from you, it is gone, and the thief can use it to buy goods with no difficulty. If, however, someone steals a check that you have written, that person probably will have great difficulty using it to buy goods and services. If your checkbook is stolen, a person can use your check as money only if he or she can successfully forge your signature and provide some identification. Hence, transacting business by check is much less risky than using legal tender; there is, then, an element of insurance or safety in the use of transaction deposits instead of currency.

- Transactions deposits are a popular monetary instrument precisely because they lower transaction costs compared with the use of metal or paper currency. In very small transactions, the gains in safety and convenience of checks are outweighed by the time and cost required to write and process them; in these cases, transaction costs are lower with paper and metallic currency. It is unlikely that the use of paper or metallic currency will entirely disappear for that reason.

- Another useful feature of transactions deposits is that they provide a record of financial transactions. In an age where detailed records are often necessary for tax purposes, this is a useful feature. Of course, paper currency transactions are also popular, in part, probably because a substantial amount of business activity is going on with cash payments so that no record will be available for the tax collectors to review.

- Credit cards are "generally acceptable in exchange for goods and services." However, credit card payments are actually guaranteed loans available on demand to users, which merely defers customer payment for transactions using a demand deposit. Ultimately, things purchased with a credit card must be paid for with a check. Credit cards are not money, but rather a convenient means to carry out transactions that minimizes the physical transfer of checks and currency. In that sense, they are substitutes for the use of money in exchange.

- Economists are not completely in agreement on what constitutes money for all purposes. Coins and paper currency, demand and other checkable deposits, and travelers' checks are certainly forms of money because all are accepted as direct means of payment for goods and services. Some economists, however, argue that for some purposes "money" should be more broadly defined to include nontransaction deposits.

- **Nontransaction deposits** are fund accounts against which the depositor cannot directly write checks. People use these accounts primarily because they generally pay higher interest rates than transactions deposits.

- Two primary types of nontransaction deposits exist—savings accounts and time deposits (certificates of deposit or CDs). Nontransaction deposits are **near money** assets but not money itself. Savings accounts and time deposits cannot directly be used to purchase a good or service. They are not a direct medium of exchange. You must convert funds from your savings account into currency or demand deposits before you can buy goods and services. Savings accounts are assets that can be quickly converted into money at the face value of the account, so savings accounts are highly liquid assets. However, early withdrawal from some time deposits, especially certificates of deposit, may require the depositor to forgo some interest income as a penalty.

- **Money market mutual funds** are interest-earning accounts provided by brokers who pool funds into investments like Treasury bills. These funds are invested in short-term securities, and the depositor is allowed to write checks against his or her account subject to certain limits. Money market mutual funds are highly liquid assets that have experienced tremendous growth over the last 20 years. They are considered near money because they are relatively easy to convert into money for the purchase of goods and services.

- Stocks and bonds are among the many forms of financial assets that virtually everyone agrees are not "money." First, they cannot be turned into cash as quickly as a savings deposit. Second, and more important, the value of the stock fluctuates over time with no guarantee that the owner of the asset can obtain his original nominal value at any moment in time. Thus, stocks and bonds are not sufficiently liquid assets to be considered "money."

- Money is an asset that we generally use to buy goods or services. It is so easy to convert money into goods and services that we say it is the most liquid of assets. **Liquidity** refers to the ease with which one asset can be converted into another asset or goods and services.

- Because a good case can be made both for including and for excluding savings accounts, CDs, and money market mutual funds from our operational definition of the money supply for different purposes, we do both. Economists call the narrow definition of money—currency, checkable deposits, and travelers' checks—**M1.** The broader definition of money, encompassing M1, plus saving accounts, time deposits (except for some large-denomination certificates of deposits), and money market mutual funds is called **M2.** M2 is more than three times the magnitude of M1, meaning that people prefer to keep the bulk of their liquid assets in the form of savings accounts of various kinds, rather than as currency or in transactions accounts.

## I     REVIEW

Money is anything that is generally accepted in _____ for goods and services.

In colonial America, _____ such as tobacco and wampum were sometimes used as money. The main disadvantage of using commodities as money is that they tend to _____ after a few trades.

Coins made of precious metal such as gold and silver have been used as _____ for thousands of years due to their durability.

Currency consists of coins and _____ that institutions or governments have created to be used as money. In the United States, the Federal Reserve System issues paper currency in various denominations called Federal Reserve _____.

Currency that has been officially declared to be money is a form of _____ tender.

Most of the money that Americans use for day-to-day transactions are assets in checking accounts called _____ deposits.

In the United States, checking accounts have replaced paper and metallic currency as the major form of money used in large transactions for several reasons, including ease and _____ of transactions, lower _____ costs, and transaction _____.

# Chapter 15: Money and Banking

Nontransaction deposits are fund accounts against which the depositor cannot directly write
_____ .

Money market mutual funds are interest-earning accounts provided by brokers who pool funds into
_____ -term investments like _____ bills.

Stocks and bonds are considered nonmonetary _____ .

The ease with which one asset can be converted into another asset or into goods and services is referred to as
_____ . Money is a more _____ asset than stocks and
bonds.

The narrow definition of money, called _____ , consists of currency, checkable deposits,
and travelers' checks, while a broader measure, called _____ consists of M1 plus savings
account, _____ deposits, and money market mutual funds.

## II    TRUE/FALSE

___T___ 1. Another name for "time deposit" is "certificate of deposit" or "CD."

___F___ 2. Economists consider stocks and bonds to be a form of money.

___F___ 3. The U.S. money supply is "backed" by the gold at Fort Knox.

## III    MULTIPLE CHOICE

1. Checkable deposits like demand deposits and interest-earning checking accounts are
   A) transactions accounts.
   B) savings accounts.
   C) travelers' checks.
   D) legal tender.

2. Which of the following is *not* money?
   A) demand deposits
   B) currency
   C) travelers' checks
   D) credit cards

3. The sum of currency, checkable deposits, and travelers' checks is called
   A) near money.
   B) fiat money.
   C) savings accounts.
   D) M1.

4. Which of the following is a difference between M1 and M2?
   A) M1 is near money while M2 is fiat money.
   B) M1 is mostly in savings accounts while M2 is in checking accounts.
   C) M2 includes time deposits while M1 does not.
   D) M2 is money held outside the United States while M1 measures the money supply within the United States.

## IV    APPLICATION AND DISCUSSION

```
┌─────────────────────┐
│   EXHIBIT 1         │░░░░░░░░░░░░░░░
└─────────────────────┘
   Rank              Asset
   ____      Currency
             An Automobile
   ____      Checkable Deposit
   ____      A House
   ____      A Six-Month Certificate of Deposit
   ____
```

Rank the assets in Exhibit 1 in terms of their "liquidity," ranking the most liquid asset number 1 and the least liquid number 5. Justify your ranking.

# SECTION 15.2
# THE FUNCTIONS OF MONEY

## KEY POINTS

- The primary function of money is to serve as a **medium of exchange**, to facilitate transactions, and to lower transactions costs. However, money is not the only medium of exchange; rather, it is the only medium that is generally accepted for most transactions.

- **Barter** is expensive and inefficient and generally prevails only where limited trade is carried out over short distances, which generally means in relatively primitive economies. The more complex the economy (e.g., the higher the real per capita GDP), the greater the economic interactions between people, and consequently, the greater the need for one or more universally accepted assets serving as money.

- Besides serving as a medium of exchange, money is also a standard of value. With money, a common "yardstick" exists so that the values of diverse goods and services can be very precisely compared. By providing a universally understood measure of value, money serves to lower the information costs involved in making transactions. Without money, a person might not know what a good price for a particular good is because so many different commodities can be bartered for it. With money, there is but one price of a particular good, and that price is readily available as information to the potential consumer.

- Money serves as a store of value. It can provide a means of saving or "storing" things of value in an efficient manner. It is both cheaper and safer to store paper rather than wheat.

- Money is also a **means of deferred payment**. Money makes it much easier to borrow and to repay loans. With barter, lending is cumbersome and riskier. Fluctuations in the value of money can occur, and indeed, inflation has been a major problem. But the value of money fluctuates far less than the value of many individual commodities, so lending in money imposes fewer risks on buyers and sellers than lending in commodities.

## I    REVIEW

The primary function of money is to serve as a medium of _____. Money facilitates _____, and lowers _____ costs.

# Chapter 15: Money and Banking

In the absence of money, when individuals pay for goods and services by offering other goods and services in exchange, it is called _____.

Barter is _____ because several trades may be necessary before individuals are able to get the goods or services they desire.

Besides serving as a medium of exchange, money is also both a _____ of value and a _____ of value.

Because money makes it easier to borrow and repay loans, it also serves as a means of _____ payment.


## II      TRUE/FALSE

_F_ 1. When a miser buries his money in his backyard, he is using money as a medium of exchange.

_T_ 2. When Joy buys her morning coffee with a dollar bill, she is using money as a medium of exchange.


## III      MULTIPLE CHOICE

1. Which of the following is *not* a correct statement about money?
   A)  Money serves as a medium of exchange.
   B)  Money serves as a store of value.
   C)  Money is a means of deferred payment.
   D)  The value of money generally fluctuates much more than the prices of individual commodities like oil or wheat.

2. A barter system is one in which individuals
   A)  use money as a medium of exchange, but not as a unit of account.
   B)  use nothing but fiat money in transactions.
   C)  pay for goods and services by offering other goods and services in exchange.
   D)  buy and sell, but not in markets.


## IV      APPLICATION AND DISCUSSION

In a barter economy, how would you pay your university tuition?

SECTION 15.3

# HOW BANKS CREATE MONEY

## KEY POINTS

- The biggest players in the banking industry are **commercial banks.** Commercial banks account for more than two-thirds of all the deposits in the banking industry; they maintain almost all of the demand deposits and close to half of the savings accounts.

- The United States has nearly 1,000 commercial banks, in marked contrast to most other nations where the leading banks operate throughout the country and where a large proportion of total bank assets are held in a handful of banks. Until recently, banks were restricted by federal law from operating in more than one state. This has now changed, and the structure of banking as we now know it will inevitably change with the emergence of interstate banking, mergers, and "hostile" takeovers.

- Aside from commercial banks, the banking system includes two other important financial institutions: **Savings and loan associations** and **credit unions**. Savings and loan associations provide many of the same services as commercial banks, including checkable deposits, a variety of time deposits, and money market deposit accounts. The almost 2,000 members of savings and loan associations have typically invested most of their savings deposits into home mortgages. Credit unions are cooperatives, made up of depositors with some common affiliation, like the same employer or union.

- Financial institutions offer a large number of financial functions. Most important, they are depositories for savings and liquid assets that are used by individuals and firms for transaction purposes. They can create money by making loans. In making loans, financial institutions act as intermediaries between savers, who supply funds, and borrowers seeking funds to invest.

- Most money, narrowly defined, is in the form of transaction deposits, assets that can be directly used to buy goods and services. When a bank lends to a person, it typically gives the borrower the funds by a check or by adding funds to an existing checking account of the borrower. If you go into a bank and borrow $1,000, the bank probably will simply add $1,000 to your checking account at the bank. In doing so, a new checkable deposit—money—is created.

- Banks make loans and create checkable deposits in order to make a profit. They make their profit by collecting higher interest payments on loans than they pay their depositors for those funds. If you borrow $1,000 from Loans R Us National Bank, the interest payments you make, less the expenses the bank incurs in making the loan, including their costs of acquiring the funds, represents profit to the bank.

- Because the way to make more profit is to make more loans, banks want to make a large volume of loans. Government regulatory authorities limit the loan issuance of banks by imposing **reserve requirements**. Reserve requirements require banks to keep on hand a quantity of cash or reserve accounts with the Federal Reserve equal to a prescribed proportion of their checkable deposits.

- Even in the absence of regulations restricting the creation of checkable deposits, a prudent bank would put some limit on their loan (and therefore deposit) volume. For people to accept checkable deposits as money, the checks written must be generally accepted in exchange for goods and services. People will accept checks only if they know that they are quickly convertible at face value into legal tender. For this reason, banks must have adequate cash reserves on hand (including reserves at the Fed that can be almost immediately converted to currency, if necessary) to meet the needs of customers who wish to convert their checkable deposits into currency or spend them on goods or services.

- Our banking system is sometimes called a **fractional reserve system** because banks, by law as well as by choice, find it necessary to keep cash on hand and reserves at the Federal Reserve equal to some fraction of their checkable deposits. Even in the absence of reserve regulations, few banks would risk maintaining fewer reserves on hand than they thought prudent for their amount of deposits (particularly demand deposits).

- Reserve requirements exist primarily to control the amount of demand and time deposits, and thus the size of the money supply; they do not exist simply to prevent bank failures.

- While banks must meet their reserve requirements, they do not want to keep any more of their funds as additional reserves than necessary for safety because cash assets do not earn any interest. In order to protect themselves but also earn some interest income, banks usually keep some of their assets in highly liquid investments such as United States government bonds. These types of highly liquid, interest-paying assets are often called **secondary reserves**.

- Money is created when banks make loans. To get a good picture of the size of the bank, what it owns, and what it owes, we look at its **balance sheet**.

- The assets of a bank are those things of value that the bank owns (e.g., cash, reserves at the Federal Reserve, bonds, or its buildings), including contractual obligations of individuals and firms to pay funds to the bank (loans). The largest asset item for most banks is loans. Banks maintain most of their assets in the form of loans because interest payments on loans are the primary means by which they earn revenue.

- Some assets are kept in the form of noninterest-bearing cash and reserve accounts at the Federal Reserve, in order to meet legal reserve requirements (and to meet the cash demands of customers). Typically, relatively little of a bank's reserves, or cash assets, is physically kept in the form of paper currency in the bank's vault or at tellers' windows. Most banks keep a majority of their reserves as reserve accounts at the Federal Reserve. Banks usually also keep some assets in the form of bonds that are quickly convertible into cash if necessary (secondary reserves).

- All banks have substantial liabilities, which are financial obligations that the bank has to other people. The predominant liability of virtually all banks is deposits. If you have money in a demand deposit account, you have the right to demand cash for that deposit at any time. Basically, the bank owes you the amount in your checking account. Time deposits similarly constitute a liability of banks.

- For a bank to be healthy and solvent, its assets must exceed its liabilities. This difference between a bank's assets and its liabilities constitutes the bank's capital, or net worth. Capital is included on the right side of the balance sheet so that both sides of the balance sheet (assets and liabilities plus capital) are equal. Any time the aggregate amount of bank assets changes, the aggregate amount of liabilities and capital also must change by the same amount, by definition.

- Suppose a bank faces a **required reserve ratio** of 10 percent. This means that the bank must keep cash on hand or at the Federal Reserve Bank equal to 10 percent of its deposits. Required reserves equal deposits times required reserve ratio.

- **Excess reserves** = actual reserves – required reserves. Reserves in the form of cash and reserves at the Federal Reserve earn no revenue for the bank; there is no profit to be made from holding cash. Whenever excess reserves appear, banks will convert the noninterest earning reserves into other interest-earning assets, sometimes bonds but usually loans.

- What happens to a new deposit of $100,000? The bank is required to hold $10,000 in required reserves. The remaining 90 percent, or $90,000, becomes excess reserves, and most of this will likely become available for loans. Say the bank lends out all of its excess reserves of $90,000. At the time the loan is made, the money supply will increase by $90,000, as that amount is added to the borrower's checking account. Since demand deposits are money, the issuers of the loan have created money.

- Further, borrowers are not likely to keep the money in their checking accounts for long since you usually take out a loan to buy something. When the borrower pays for the desired goods, the recipient will likely deposit the money in his account at another bank to add even more funds to additional money expansion.

- When banks create more money, they make the economy more liquid, but they do not directly create wealth. Borrowers have more money, but they also have a new liability—loans.

- In short, banks create money when they increase demand deposits through the process of creating loans. In the next section, we will see how the process of loans and deposits has a multiplying effect throughout the banking industry.

I      **REVIEW**

The biggest players in the banking industry are _____ banks. They are distinct from most other financial institutions in that they can create _____ deposits.

# Chapter 15: Money and Banking

Aside from commercial banks, the banking system includes two other types of financial institutions: savings and _____ associations, and _____ unions.

Financial institutions serve as depositories for savings and liquid assets that are used by individuals and firms for _____ purposes. In making loans, financial institutions act as _____ between savers, who supply funds, and borrowers seeking to invest.

If someone borrows $1,000 from a bank, the bank usually will simply add $1,000 to their checking account, and in doing so will create new _____.

Banks make profits by collecting higher interest payments on the _____ they make than the interest they pay their depositors for those funds. The more loans a bank makes, the more _____ it makes.

Reserve _____ require banks to keep on hand a quantity of cash or reserve accounts with the Federal Reserve equal to a prescribed proportion of their _____ deposits.

Our banking system is sometimes called a _____ reserve system because banks are required to maintain cash and other reserves equal to some specified fraction of their checkable deposits.

The _____ of a bank are those things of value that the bank owns, including cash, bonds, buildings and outstanding loans. Financial obligations that banks have to others are called _____.

Banks create new _____ when they increase demand deposits through the process of creating loans.

## II    TRUE/FALSE

_F___ 1. Reserve requirements exist primarily to prevent bank failures.

_T___ 2. The largest asset item for most banks is loans.

## III    MULTIPLE CHOICE

1.  A bank's "capital" is the
    A) value of all its assets, including loans.
    B) value of all its assets, excluding loans.
    C) value of its physical plant, including buildings, computers, and automatic teller machines.
    D) difference between its assets and liabilities.

2.  The required reserves of banks are a specified percentage of their
    A) deposits.
    B) loans.
    C) cash on hand.
    D) total assets.

3. Which of the following will lead to an increase in the money supply?
    A) You pay back a $10,000 loan that you owe to your bank.
    B) Your bank gives you a $10,000 loan by adding $10,000 to your checking account.
    C) You pay $10,000 in cash for a new motorcycle.
    D) You bury $10,000 in cash in your backyard.

## IV    APPLICATION AND DISCUSSION

If you deposit $1,000 in a bank, calculate how much the bank must keep as required reserves and how much it can loan out under each of the required reserve ratios in Exhibit 2.

| EXHIBIT 2 | | |
|---|---|---|
| Required Reserve Ratio | Amount of Required Reserves | Amount of Loanable Funds |
| 1. 5% | | |
| 2. 10% | _____ | _____ |
| 3. 15% | _____ | _____ |
| 4. 20% | _____ | _____ |
| 5. 25% | _____ | _____ |

# SECTION 15.4
# THE MONEY MULTIPLIER

## KEY POINTS

- Banks can create money (demand deposits) by making loans, and the monetary expansion of an individual bank is limited to its excess reserves. While this is true, it ignores the further effects of a new loan and the accompanying expansion in the stock of money. New loans create new money directly, but they also create excess reserves in other banks, which leads to still further increases in both loans and the stock of money, increasing purchases of goods and services in the process. This is the multiple expansion effect, where a given volume of bank reserves creates a multiplied amount of money.

- The following formula can be used to measure the total maximum potential impact on the supply of money: potential money creation = initial deposit money multiplier. The **money multiplier** is simply 1 divided by the reserve ratio; it is the amount of money that the banking system generates with each dollar of reserves.

- The higher the required reserve ratio, the smaller the banking multiplier. Thus, a required reserve ratio of 25 percent, or one-fourth, means a banking multiplier of 4. Likewise, a required reserve ratio of 10 percent, or one-tenth, means a banking multiplier of 10. Using the money multiplier, we can calculate the total impact of any initial deposit on the amount of new money that can be created as a result.

- "Potential money creation" described the impact of creating loans and deposits out of excess reserves. Some banks may choose not to lend all of their excess reserves. Some banks may simply be extremely conservative and keep some extra newly acquired cash assets in that form. When that happens, the chain reaction effect is reduced by the amount of excess reserves not loaned out. Moreover, some borrowers may not spend all their newly acquired bank deposits, or they may wait a considerable period of time before doing so. Others may put their borrowed funds into time deposits rather than checkable deposits, which would reduce the M1 expansion process but not the M2 money expansion process. Still others may choose to keep some of their loans as currency in their pockets.

- The leakages and time lags in the bank money expansion process usually mean that the actual monetary impact of an initial deposit created out of excess reserves within a short time period is less than indicated by the money multiplier. Still, the multiplier principle does work, and a multiple expansion of deposits will generally occur if the banking system is characterized by fractional reserves.

- The process of money creation can be reversed, and in the process, money is destroyed. When a person pays a loan back to a bank, she usually does so by writing a check to the bank for the amount due. As a result, demand deposits decline, directly reducing the money supply, and setting in motion a multiple contraction through the banking system.

## I     REVIEW

New loans create money directly, but they also create _____ reserves in other banks, which leads to still further increases in both loans and the stock of _____.

When borrowers get their loans, the borrowed money will likely be _____ on something, such as new machinery, a new house, or greater store inventories.

The money _____ is 1 divided by the reserve requirement. The larger the reserve requirement, the _____ the money multiplier.

In all, the potential impact of a new checkable deposit on the money supply is equal to the amount of the initial deposit times the _____ multiplier.

If borrowers do not spend all of their newly acquired checkable deposits, or if they wait a considerable period of time before doing so, the actual impact of an initial deposit is _____ than that indicated by the money multiplier.

When a person pays a loan back to a bank by writing a check for the amount due, demand deposits _____ and the money stock is _____.

## II     TRUE/FALSE

_F_ 1. If banks are required to keep 100 percent of their deposits on reserve, a $1,000 deposit in a checking account would lead to a $100,000 increase in the money supply.

_T_ 2. An increase in the reserve requirement reduces the value of the money multiplier.

## III     MULTIPLE CHOICE

1.  A reserve requirement of 20 percent means a money multiplier of
    A) 1.
    B) 2.
    C) 5.
    D) 20.

2. A reserve requirement of 25 percent means a money multiplier of
   A) 1.
   B) 4.
   C) 25.
   D) 1/25.

---

## IV    APPLICATION AND DISCUSSION

What if currency were the only money and there were no banks. What is the potential impact on the money supply of the creating of $10,000 in new currency?

What would the potential impact be if there *were* banks and the reserve requirement was 10 percent?

SECTION 15.5

# THE COLLAPSE OF AMERICA'S BANKING SYSTEM, 1920–1933

## KEY POINTS

- The day President Franklin D. Roosevelt assumed office in 1933, he declared, "The only thing we have to fear is fear itself." Those ten words succinctly summarize the problems that led the world's leading economic power to a total collapse in its system of commercial banking and, with that, to an abrupt and unprecedented decline in the supply of money. The decline in the money supply, in turn, contributed to an economic downturn that had dire consequences for many, especially for the one-fourth of the labor force unemployed at the time of Roosevelt's first inaugural address.

- In 1920, there were 30,000 banks in the United States; by 1933, the number had declined to about 15,000. During the prosperous 1920s, nearly 6,000 banks closed their doors. In some cases, bank failure reflected imprudent management or even criminal activity on the part of bank officers (stealing from the bank). A few banks had a sufficient amount of resources stolen by others to make them insolvent (the Bonnie and Clyde effect). More often, though, banks in rural areas closed as a consequence of having large sums of assets tied up in loans to farmers who, because of low farm prices, were not in a position to pay off the loans when they came due. Rumors spread that a bank was in trouble, and these rumors, even if false, became self-fulfilling prophecies. Bank "runs" developed and even conservatively run banks with cash equal to 15 or 20 percent of their deposit liabilities found themselves with insufficient cash reserves to meet the withdrawal requests of panicky depositors.

- The bank failures of the 1920s, while numerous, were generally scattered around small towns in the country. Confidence in banks actually generally increased in that decade, and by the fall of 1929, there were $11 in bank deposits for every $1 in currency in circulation.

- The first year following the stock market crash of 1929 saw little dramatic change to the banking system, but in late 1930, a bank with the unfortunately awesome sounding name of the Bank of the United States failed, the largest bank failure in the country to that time. This failure had a ripple effect. More bank "runs" occurred as depositors began to get jittery. Banks, fearing runs, began to not lend their excess reserves, thereby aggravating a fall in the money stock and reducing business investment.

- As depositors converted their deposits to currency, bank reserves fell, and with that the ability of banks to support deposits. The situation improved a bit in 1932, when a newly created government agency, the Reconstruction Finance Corporation (RFC), helped banks in distress with loans. By early 1933, however, the depositor confidence decline had reached such a point that the entire banking system was in jeopardy.

- On March 4, newly inaugurated President Roosevelt declared a national bank holiday, closing every bank in the country for nearly two weeks. Then, only the "good" banks were allowed to reopen, an action that increased confidence. By this time the deposit-currency ratio had fallen from 11 to 1 (in 1929) to 4 to 1 (in 1933). Passage of federal deposit insurance in mid-1933 greatly strengthened depositor confidence and led to money reentering the banks. The recovery process began.

- The collapse occurred for several reasons.

  First, the nation had thousands of relatively small banks. Customers believed that depositor withdrawals could force a bank to close, and the mere fear of bank runs made them a reality. Canada, with relatively few banks that were mostly very large with many branches, had no bank runs.

  Second, governmental attempts to stem the growing distress were weak and too late. Financial aid to banks was nonexistent from the Federal Reserve System and other governmental efforts began only in 1932—well into the decline.

  Third, deposit insurance did not exist. The financial consequences of bank failures were correctly perceived by the public to be great.

  Fourth, growing depositor fear was enhanced by the fact that the economy was in a continuous downward spiral—there was no basis for any optimism that bank loans would be safely repaid.

- The combination of the Federal Deposit Insurance Corporation (FDIC) and the government's greater willingness to assist distressed banks has largely eliminated bank runs and failures in recent times. Now when a bank runs into financial difficulty, the FDIC may assist another bank in taking over the assets and liabilities of the troubled bank so that no depositor loses a cent. Thus, changes in the money supply resulting from a loss of deposits from failed banks are no longer a big problem. Better bank stability means a greater stability in the money supply, which means a greater level of economic stability.

- However, in the 1980s we did have a savings and loan crisis. Savings and loans had made many real estate loans in the early 1970s, when the inflation rate was relatively low. Then inflation rates rose rapidly and nominal interest rates soared. The savings and loans were in a squeeze—they had to pay high interest rates to attract depositors, but were earning low interest rates on their real estate loans from the early 1970s—a disastrous combination for them. Many went belly up.

- Then the government eased regulations to make it easier for savings and loans to compete for deposits.

- Deregulation, coupled with deposit insurance, put savings and loans in a gambling mood, and many poured money into high-risk real estate loans and other risky ventures. Depositors did not have an incentive to monitor their banks because they knew they would be protected up to $100,000 on their accounts by the government. Eventually, more than 1,000 thrift institutions went bankrupt. While depositors were saved, taxpayers were not. They ended up paying much of the bill for the debacle, estimated at more than $150 billion. The Thrift Bailout Bill of 1989 provided funds for the bailout and new stricter provisions for banks.

## I    REVIEW

From the stock market crash of 1929 until 1933, the U.S. economy contracted and the entire banking system nearly collapsed, leading to an unprecedented _____ in the money stock.

As depositors lost confidence in banks and converted their deposits to currency, bank reserves

_____ .

# Chapter 15: Money and Banking

In early 1933, newly elected President Franklin Roosevelt declared a national bank _____, closing every bank in the country for nearly two weeks. In mid-1933, passage of federal _____ insurance greatly strengthened depositor confidence in banks.

The combination of the Federal Deposit _____ Corporation (FDIC) and the government's greater willingness to assist distressed banks has largely eliminated bank _____.

## II    TRUE/FALSE

_F_____1. When the U.S. banking system collapsed during 1929–1933, the money supply skyrocketed.

_F_____2. Despite federal deposit insurance and greater governmental willingness to assist distressed banks, bank runs are still a common occurrence.

## III    MULTIPLE CHOICE

1. Which of the following did *not* contribute to the U.S. banking collapse of 1929–1933?
   A) The Federal Reserve System and other government agencies did not act quickly or decisively enough.
   B) Deposit insurance did not exist at that time.
   C) The banking industry consisted of only a few very large banks.
   D) The fact that the economy was in a continuous downward spiral during this period undermined depositors' confidence in the solvency of banks.

2. At the time of Franklin Roosevelt's inauguration as president in 1933, the U.S. unemployment rate was
   A) 5 percent.
   B) 10 percent.
   C) 25 percent.
   D) 50 percent.

3. In the aftermath of the savings and loan crisis of the 1980s
   A) more than a thousand savings and loan institutions went bankrupt.
   B) people who had deposits in failed thrift institutions lost their money.
   C) taxpayers were exempt from paying for the costs of the crisis.
   D) All of the above are true.

## IV    APPLICATION AND DISCUSSION

During the bank runs that occurred during the Great Depression many depositors who tried to withdraw funds were surprised to learn that their money wasn't in the bank's safe. Bankers told their outraged depositors that their money wasn't in the bank, but rather "out there working in the community, building businesses and providing jobs."

Why wasn't depositors' money in the bank's safe? How can money be "out there working in the community?"

## Questions

1. What characteristics make fei useful as money?

2. What are the drawbacks of stone money?

# CHAPTER 16

# FEDERAL RESERVE SYSTEM AND MONETARY POLICY

# SECTION 16.1

# THE FEDERAL RESERVE SYSTEM

## KEY POINTS

- In most countries of the world, the job of manipulating the supply of money belongs to the central bank.

- A central bank has many functions.

  First, a central bank is a "banker's bank." It serves as a bank where commercial banks maintain their own reserves.

  Second, a central bank performs service functions for commercial banks, such as transferring funds and checks between various commercial banks in the banking system.

  Third, the central bank typically serves as the major bank for the central government.

  Fourth, the central bank buys and sells foreign currencies and generally assists in the completion of financial transactions with other countries.

  Fifth, it serves as a "lender of last resort" that helps banking institutions in financial distress.

Sixth, the central bank is concerned with the stability of the banking system and the supply of money. The central bank can and does impose regulations on private commercial banks; it thereby regulates the size of the money supply and influences the level of economic activity. The central bank also implements monetary policy, which along with fiscal policy, forms the basis of efforts to direct the economy to perform in accordance with macroeconomic goals.

- In most countries, the central bank is a single bank. In the United States, however, the central bank is 12 institutions, spread all over the country, closely tied together and collectively called the Federal Reserve System. Each of the 12 banks has branches in key cities in its district. Each Federal Reserve bank has its own board of directors and, to some limited extent, can set its own policies. Effectively, however, the 12 banks act largely in unison on major policy issues, with effective control of major policy decisions resting with the Board of Governors and the Federal Open Market Committee of the Federal Reserve System, headquartered in Washington, D.C. The Chairman of the Federal Reserve Board of Governors is generally regarded as one of the most important and powerful economic policy makers in the country.

- The Federal Reserve was created in 1913 because the U.S. banking system had little stability and no central direction. Technically, the Fed is privately owned by the banks that "belong" to it. All banks are not required to belong to the Fed; but since new legislation was passed in 1980, there is virtually no difference in the requirements of member and nonmember banks. The private ownership of the Fed is essentially meaningless because the Board of Governors of the Federal Reserve, which controls major policy decisions, is appointed by the president of the United States, not by the stockholders.

- Historically, the Fed has had a considerable amount of independence from both the executive and legislative branches of government. The president appoints the seven members of the Board of Governors, subject to Senate approval, but the term of appointment is 14 years. This means that no member of the Federal Reserve Board will face reappointment from the president who initially made the appointment because presidential tenure is limited to two four-year terms. Moreover, the terms of board members are staggered, so a new appointment is made only every two years. It is practically impossible for a single president to appoint a majority of the members of the board, and even if it were possible, members have little fear of losing their jobs as a result of presidential wrath. The Chair of the Federal Reserve Board is a member of the Board of Governors who serves a four-year term. The Chair is truly the chief executive officer of the system, and he effectively runs it with considerable help from the presidents of the 12 regional banks.

- Many of the key policy decisions of the Federal Reserve are actually made by its Federal Open Market Committee (FOMC), which consists of the seven members of the Board of Governors; the president of the New York Federal Reserve Bank, and four other presidents of Federal Reserve Banks, who serve on the committee on a rotating basis. The FOMC makes most of the key decisions influencing the direction and size of changes in the money stock, and their regular, secret meetings are accordingly considered very important by the business community and government.

## I      REVIEW

In most countries, the job of manipulating the supply of money belongs to the _____ bank. In the United States, this function is performed by the Federal _____ System or "Fed."

The Fed is governed by a seven-member Board of _____. Each member is appointed by the _____ of the United States.

An important aspect of the Fed's operation is that it has a considerable amount of _____ from both the executive and legislative branches of government.

Many key policy decisions of the Federal Reserve are actually made by its Federal Open _____ Committee.

# Chapter 16: The Federal Reserve System and Monetary Policy

## II  TRUE/FALSE

F  ____ 1. The central bank of the United States is the U.S. Treasury Department.

T  ____ 2. The Federal Reserve System consists of 12 Federal Reserve Banks, spread all over the country.

## III  MULTIPLE CHOICE

1. Which of the following is *not* a function of a central bank?
   A) controlling the nation's money supply
   B) serving as a "lender of last resort" to help banking institutions in distress
   C) collecting taxes for the federal government
   D) buying and selling foreign currency

2. The Federal Reserve System was created in
   A) 1776.
   B) 1789.
   C) 1913.
   D) 1933.

## IV  APPLICATION AND DISCUSSION

Below are profiles of three prominent people. Who do you think is the current Chairman of the Federal Reserve Board of Governors? (Can you identify the other two people?)

**Person A** _____

Born in 1952, he served in the U.S. Navy as a member of an Underwater Demolition Team for six years, attended North Hennepin Minnesota Community College, and was a professional wrestler for 11 years. Acted in several motion pictures including *Predator* and *Running Man* and was mayor of Brooklyn, Minnesota, from 1991–1995. He is married with two children.

**Person B** _____

Born in 1946, she earned a bachelor's degree in government from Wheaton College in Norton, Massachusetts, and was a director of the Somerset County Board of Freeholders and President of the New Jersey Board of Public Utilities. She was the first woman to become Governor of New Jersey and is currently head of the Environmental Protection Agency. She is married with two children.

**Person C** _____

Born in 1926, he received Bachelor's, Master's, and Ph.D. degrees in economics, all from New York University, and was chairman and president of an economic consulting firm for 30 years, and Chairman of the Council of Economic Advisors under President Gerald Ford from 1974 to 1977. He served as Chairman of the National Commission on Social Security Reform, was a member of President Ronald Reagan's Economics Policy Advisory Board, and was a consultant to the Congressional Budget Office. He is married to Andrea Mitchell, NBC Chief Foreign Affairs Correspondent.

SECTION 16.2

# THE EQUATION OF EXCHANGE

## KEY POINTS

- Perhaps the most important function of the Federal Reserve is its ability to regulate the money supply. In order to fully understand the significant role that the Federal Reserve plays in the economy, we will first examine the role of money in the national economy.

- In the early part of this century, economists noted a useful relationship that helps our understanding of the role of money in the national economy. That relationship is called **the equation of exchange**, which can be presented as: $MV = P\ Q$, where $M$ is the money supply, however defined (usually M1 or M2), $V$ is the income velocity of money, $P$ is the average level of prices of final goods and services, and $Q$ is the physical quantity of final goods and services produced in a given period (usually one year).

- $V$, the **velocity** of money, refers to the "turnover" rate, or the intensity with which money is used. $V$ represents the average number of times that a dollar is used in purchasing final goods or services in a one-year period. Thus, if individuals are hoarding their money, velocity will be low; if individuals are writing lots of checks on their checking accounts and spending currency as fast as they receive it, velocity will tend to be high.

- The expression $P\ Q$ represents the dollar value of all final goods and services sold in a country in a given year. But that is the definition of nominal gross domestic product (GDP). Thus, the average level of prices ($P$) times the physical quantity of final goods and services ($Y$) equals nominal GDP.

- The quantity equation of money could also be expressed as: $M\ V$ = Nominal GDP, or $V$ = Nominal GDP/$M$. That, in fact, is the definition of velocity: The total output of goods divided by the amount of money is the same thing as the average number of times a dollar is used in final goods transactions in a year.

- The magnitude of $V$ will depend on the definition of money that is used. The average dollar of money turns over a few times in the course of a year, with the precise number depending on the definition of money.

- The equation of exchange is a useful tool when we try to assess the impact in a change in the money supply (M) on the aggregate economy. If $M$ increases, then one of the following must happen:

  1) $V$ must decline by the same magnitude, so that $M\ V$ remains constant, leaving $P\ Q$ unchanged;

  2) $P$ must rise;

  3) $Y$ must rise; or

  4) $P$ and $Q$ must each rise some, so that the product of $P$ and $Q$ remains equal to $M\ V$.

  In other words, if the money supply increases and the velocity of money does not change, there will be either higher prices (inflation), greater real output of goods and services, or a combination of both.

- If one considers a macroeconomic policy to be successful when real output is increased but unsuccessful when the only effect of the policy is inflation, an increase in $M$ is a good policy if $Q$ increases but a bad policy if $P$ increases. Likewise, dampening the rate of increase in $M$ or even causing it to decline will cause nominal GDP to fall, unless the change in $M$ is counteracted by a rising velocity of money. Intentionally decreasing $M$ can also either be good or bad, depending on whether the declining money GDP is reflected mainly in falling prices ($P$) or in falling real output ($Y$).

- Expanding the money supply, unless counteracted by increased hoarding of currency (leading to a decline in V), will have the same type of impact on aggregate demand as an expansionary fiscal policy—increasing government purchases, reducing taxes, or increases in transfer payments. Likewise, policies designed to reduce the money supply will have a contractionary impact (unless offset by a rising velocity of money) on aggregate demand. This is similar to the impact obtained from increasing taxes, decreasing transfer payments, or decreasing government purchases.

# Chapter 16: The Federal Reserve System and Monetary Policy

- What the quantity equation of exchange relationship illustrates is that monetary policy can be used to obtain the same objectives as fiscal policy. Some economists, often called monetarists, believe that monetary policy is the most powerful determinant of macroeconomic results.

- Economists once considered the velocity of money a given. We now know that it is not constant, but it often moves in a fairly predictable pattern. Thus, the connection between money supply and GDP is still fairly predictable. Historically, the velocity of money has been quite stable over a long period of time, particularly using the M2 definition. However, velocity is less stable when measured using the M1 definition and over shorter periods of time.

- For example, an increase in velocity can occur with anticipated inflation. When individuals expect inflation, they will spend their money more quickly. They don't want to be caught with money that is going to be worth less in the future. Also, an increase in the interest rates will cause people to hold less money because people want to hold less money when the opportunity cost of holding money increases. This, in turn, means that the velocity of money increases.

- There is international support for the fact that the inflation rate tends to rise more in periods of rapid monetary expansion. The relationship is particularly strong with hyperinflation, as illustrated by the hyperinflation in Germany in the 1920s. The cause of hyperinflation is simply excessive money growth.

## I    REVIEW

A useful relationship that helps us understand the role that money plays in the national economy is called the quantity equation of _____.

In the equation, $M$ stands for the _____ supply, $V$ is the _____ of money, $P$ is the average level of _____, and $Q$ represents the _____ of goods and services produced in a given time period.

Velocity represents the average number of times that a _____ is used in purchasing final goods or services in a one-year period.

The quantity equation of _____ is a useful tool when we try to assess the impact of a change in the supply of _____ on the aggregate economy.

The inflation rate tends to _____ more in periods of monetary expansion than in periods of slower monetary growth.

## II    TRUE/FALSE

____T____ 1. An increase in the money supply, unless counteracted by decrease in the velocity of money, will have the same type of impact on aggregate demand as an expansionary fiscal policy.

____T____ 2. If the money supply increases, $P$ will rise, so long as $V$ and $Q$ remain constant.

____T____ 3. Historical evidence shows that in the United States, the price level tends to rise more in periods of rapid monetary expansion than in periods of slower monetary growth.

## III    MULTIPLE CHOICE

1.  The velocity of money is
    A)  established by the Federal Reserve Board of Governors.
    B)  the average number of times that a dollar is used in purchasing final goods and services.
    C)  inversely related to the rate of inflation.
    D)  the rate at which the Consumer Price Index rises.

2.  The quantity equation of money states that
    A)  government spending = taxes plus the federal budget deficit.
    B)  the reciprocal of the reserve requirement = the deposit expansion multiplier.
    C)  the money supply times the velocity of money = the price level times the quantity of goods and services produced.
    D)  the price level times the velocity of money = the money supply times the quantity of goods and services produced.

## IV    APPLICATION AND DISCUSSION

During the sixteenth century, Spanish Conquistadors like Hernán Cortes overwhelmed the Aztecs and other indigenous peoples in America by pillaging their cities and taking their gold and silver.

The gold and silver was sent back to Spain, causing her money supply to increase tenfold. Assuming that $V$ remained stable and $Q$ increased only slightly, what do you think happened to prices in Spain during this period?

# SECTION 16.3

# IMPLEMENTING MONETARY POLICY: TOOLS OF THE FED

## KEY POINTS

- The Board of Governors of the Fed and the Federal Open Market Committee are the prime decision makers for monetary policy in the United States. They decide whether to change policies to expand the supply of money and, hopefully, the real level of economic activity, or to contract the money supply, hoping to cool inflationary pressures.

- The Fed controls the supply of money, even though privately owned commercial banks actually create and destroy money by making loans.

- The Fed has three major methods that it can use to control the supply of money: It can engage in open market operations, change reserve requirements, or change its discount rate. Of these three tools, the Fed uses open market operations the most. It is by far the most important device used by the Fed to influence the money supply.

- **Open market operations** involve the purchase and sale of government securities by the Federal Reserve System. Decisions regarding whether to buy or sell government bonds are made by the Federal Open Market Committee at its regular meetings.

- Open market operations are the most important method the Fed uses to change the supply of money.

  It can be implemented quickly and cheaply—the Fed merely calls an agent who buys or sells bonds.

  It can be done quietly, without a lot of political debate or a public announcement.

It is also a rather powerful tool, as any given purchase or sale of securities usually has an ultimate impact on the money supply of several times the amount of the initial transaction.

- When the Fed buys bonds, it pays the seller of the bonds with a check written from one of the Federal Reserve banks. The person receiving the check will likely deposit it in her bank account, increasing the money supply in the form of added transactions deposits. More importantly, the commercial bank, in return for crediting the account of the bond seller with a new deposit, gets cash reserves or a higher balance in its reserve account at the Federal Reserve Bank in its district.

- Generally, in a growing economy where the real value of goods and services is increasing over time, an increase in the supply of money is needed even to maintain stable prices. If the velocity of money ($V$) in the equation of exchange is fairly constant and real GDP (denoted by $Q$ in the equation of exchange) is rising between three and four percent a year (as it has over the period since 1840), then a three or four percent increase in $M$ is consistent with stable prices. In periods of rising prices (meaning $M\ V$ would be rising considerably), if $V$ is fairly constant, the growth of $M$ likely will exceed the 3 to 4 percent annual growth seemingly consistent with long-term price stability.

- While open market operations are the most important and widely utilized tool that the Fed has to achieve its monetary objectives, it is not its potentially most powerful tool. The Fed possesses the power to change the **reserve requirements** of member banks by altering the reserve ratio. This can have an immediate impact on the ability of member banks to create money. Suppose the Fed lowers reserve requirements. That will create excess reserves in the banking system. The banking system as a whole can then expand deposits and the money stock by a multiple of this amount (equal to 1/10 the required reserve ratio).

- Relatively small reserve requirement changes can have a big impact on the potential supply of money by changing the money multiplier. The tool is so potent, in fact, that it is seldom used. The Fed changes reserve requirements rather infrequently, and when it does make changes, it is by very small amounts. For example, between 1970 and 1980, the Fed changed the reserve requirement twice, and less than one percent on each occasion. The Fed did make an out-of-the-ordinary move in 1992 when it lowered the reserve requirement from 12 to 10 percent.

- Banks having trouble meeting their reserve requirement can borrow funds directly from the Fed. The interest rate the Fed charges on these borrowed reserves is called the **discount rate.** If the Fed raises the discount rate, it makes it more costly for banks to borrow funds from it to meet their reserve requirements. The higher the interest rate banks have to pay on the borrowed funds, the lower the potential profits from any new loans made from borrowed reserves, and fewer new loans will be made and less money created.

- If the Fed wants to contract the money supply, it will raise the discount rate, making it more costly for banks to borrow reserves; if the Fed is promoting an expansion of money and credit, it will lower the discount rate, making it cheaper for banks to borrow reserves. The discount rate changes fairly frequently, often several times a year. Sometimes the rate will be moved several times in the same direction within a single year, which has a substantial cumulative effect.

- The discount rate is a relatively unimportant tool, mainly because member banks do not rely heavily on the Fed for borrowed funds. There seems to be some stigma among bankers about borrowing from the Fed; borrowing from the Fed is something most bankers believe should be reserved for real emergencies. When banks have short-term needs for cash to meet reserve requirements, they are more likely to take a very short-term (often overnight) loan from other banks in the **federal funds market.** For that reason, many people pay a lot of attention to the interest rate on federal funds. The discount rate's main significance is that changes in the rate signal the Fed's intentions with respect to monetary policy.

- The Fed can do three things if it wants to reduce the money supply.

  1) sell bonds,

  2) raise reserve requirements, or

  3) raise the discount rate.

  Of course, the Fed could also opt to use some combination of these three tools in its approach. These moves would tend to reduce nominal GDP, hopefully through a decrease in $P$ rather than $Y$. These actions would be the monetary policy equivalent of a fiscal policy of raising taxes, lowering transfer payments, and/or lowering government purchases.

- If the Fed is concerned about underutilization of resources (e.g., unemployment), it would engage in precisely the opposite policies:

  1) buy bonds,

  2) lower reserve requirements, or

  3) lower the discount rate.

  The government could use some combination of these three approaches. These moves would tend to raise nominal GDP, hopefully through an increase in $Y$ (in the context of the quantity equation of exchange) rather than $P$. Equivalent expansionary fiscal policy actions would be to lower taxes, increase transfer payments, and/or increase government purchases.

- The Fed's control of the money supply is largely exercised through the three methods outlined above, but it can influence the level and direction of economic activity in numerous less important ways as well.

- The Fed can attempt to influence banks to follow a particular course of action by the use of **moral suasion**. For example, if the Fed thinks the money supply and credit is growing too fast, it might write a letter to bank presidents urging them to be more selective in making loans, and suggesting that good banking practices mandate that banks maintain some excess reserves. During business contractions, the Fed may urge bankers to lend more freely, hoping to promote an increase in the supply of money.

- The Fed also has at its command some selective regulatory authority over specific types of economic activity. For example, the Federal Reserve Board of Governors establishes margin requirements for the purchase of common stock. This means that the Fed specifies the proportion of the purchase price of stock that a purchaser must pay in cash. By allowing the Fed to control limits on borrowing for stock purchases, Congress believes that the Fed can limit speculative
  market dealings in securities and reduce instability in securities markets (although whether the margin requirement rule has in fact helped achieve such stability is open to question).

- In the last few decades, the Federal Reserve regulatory authority has been extended into new areas. Beginning in 1969, the Fed began enforcing provisions of the Truth in Lending Act, which requires lenders to state actual interest rate charges when making loans. Similarly, in the mid-1970s, the Fed assumed the authority of enforcing provisions of the Equal Lending Opportunity Act, designed to eliminate discrimination against loan applicants.

## I    REVIEW

In the United States, monetary policy is the responsibility of the Federal Reserve Board of _____ and the Federal Open Market _____.

The Fed has three major tools that it can use to control the supply of money: open _____ operations, changes in _____ requirements, and changes in the _____ rate.

When the Fed wants to increase the money supply, it can _____ bonds. When it wants to decrease the money supply, it can _____ bonds.

If the Fed lowers reserve requirements, the money supply will _____. When it raises reserve requirements, the money supply will _____.

The interest rate that the Fed charges banks for borrowing funds is called the _____ rate. Commercial banks borrow from each other in the _____ funds market.

If the Fed wants to increase the money supply, it _____ the discount rate. When it wants to decrease the money supply, it _____ the discount rate.

## II       TRUE/FALSE

T   1. Open market operations are the most important method the Fed uses to change the stock of money.

F   2. The federal funds rate is the interest rate the Fed charges when it makes loans to banks.

## III      MULTIPLE CHOICE

1. In order to increase the rate of growth of the money supply, the Fed can
   A)  raise the discount rate.
   B)  raise the reserve requirement.
   C)  buy government securities on the open market.
   D)  sell government securities in the open market.

2. Which of the following actions of the Fed is likely to lead to a decrease in the money supply?
   A)  a decrease in the discount rate
   B)  an increase in reserve requirements
   C)  a decrease in reserve requirements
   D)  a purchase of government securities by the Fed in the open market

3. Which of the following would constitute *contractionary* monetary policy by the Fed?
   A)  an increase in income tax rates, a cut in government spending, and an elimination of the investment tax credit
   B)  an increase in tariffs on imported goods and a decrease in foreign aid
   C)  open market purchases of government securities, a cut in the discount rate, and a decrease in reserve requirements
   D)  open market sales of government securities, an increase in the discount rate, and an increase in reserve requirements

## IV       APPLICATION AND DISCUSSION

Imagine that you were to become Chairman of the Fed during a period of persistent high inflation. What could you do to restore stable prices?

SECTION 16.4

# MONEY, INTEREST RATES, AND AGGREGATE DEMAND

## KEY POINTS

- The Federal Reserve's policies with respect to the supply of money has a direct impact on short-run real interest rates, and accordingly, on the components of aggregate demand.

# Chapter 16: The Federal Reserve System and Monetary Policy

- The money market is the market where money demand and money supply determine the equilibrium nominal interest rate. When the Fed acts to change the money supply by changing one of its policy variables, it alters the money market equilibrium.

- People have three basic motives for holding money instead of other assets: for transactions purposes, precautionary reasons, and asset purposes.

- The quantity of money demanded varies inversely with the rate of interest. When interest rates are higher, the opportunity cost—in terms of the interest income on alternative assets forgone—of holding monetary assets is higher, and persons will want to hold less money for each of these reasons. At the same time, the demand for money, particularly for transactions purposes, is highly dependent on income levels because the transactions volume varies directly with income. And lastly, the demand for money depends on the price level. If the price level increases, buyers will need more money to purchase their goods and services. Or if the price level falls, buyers will need less money to purchase their goods and services.

- At lower interest rates, the quantity of money demanded, but not the demand for money, is greater. An increase in income will lead to an increase in the demand for money, depicted by a rightward shift in the money demand curve.

- The supply of money is largely governed by the regulatory policies of the central bank. Whether interest rates are 4 percent or 14 percent, banks seeking to maximize profits will increase lending as long as they have reserves above their desired level because even a 4 percent return on loans provides more profit than maintaining those assets in noninterest-bearing cash or reserve accounts at the Fed. Given this fact, the supply of money is effectively almost perfectly inelastic with respect to interest rates over their plausible range, controlled by Federal Reserve policies that determine the level of bank reserves (through open market purchases or sales of government bonds and changes in the discount rate) and the money multiplier (through changes in reserve requirements). Therefore, we draw the money supply curve as vertical, other things equal, with changes in Federal Reserve policies acting to shift the money supply curve.

- Combining the money demand and money supply curves, money market equilibrium occurs at that nominal interest rate where the quantity of money demanded equals the quantity of money supplied.

- Rising national income will increase the amount of money that people want to hold at any given interest rate; therefore shifting the demand for money to the right, leading to a new higher equilibrium nominal interest rate. An increase in the money supply lowers the equilibrium nominal interest rate .

- Say the Fed wants to pursue an expansionary monetary policy. It will buy bonds on the open market, increasing the price of bonds. Bond sellers will deposit their checks from the Fed, increasing the money supply. The immediate impact of expansionary monetary policy is to decrease interest rates. The lower interest rate, or the fall in the cost of borrowing money, then leads to an increase in aggregate demand for goods and services at each and every price level. The lower interest rate will increase home sales, car sales, business investments, and so on. That is, an increase in the money supply will lead to lower interest rates and an increase in aggregate demand.

- Suppose the Fed wants to pursue a contractionary monetary policy. It will sell bonds on the open market, lowering the price of bonds. The purchasers of bonds take the money out of their checking account to pay for the bond, and bank reserves are reduced by the amount of the check. This reduction in reserves leads to a reduction in the supply of money, which leads to an increase in the interest rate in the money market. The higher interest rate then leads to a reduction in aggregate demand for goods and services. In sum, when the Fed sells bonds, it lowers the price of bonds, raises interest rates, and reduces aggregate demand, at least in the short run.

- There is an inverse correlation between the interest rate and the price of bonds. When the price of bonds falls, the interest rate rises. When the price of bonds rises, the interest rate falls.

- Some economists believe the Fed should try to control the money supply; others believe the Fed should try to control the interest rate. Unfortunately, the Fed cannot do both—it must pick one or the other.

- Suppose the demand for money increases. If the Fed doesn't allow the money supply to increase, interest rates will rise and aggregate demand will fall. If the Fed wants to keep the interest rate stable, it will have to increase the money supply.

- The problem with targeting the money supply is that the demand for money fluctuates considerably in the short run. Focusing on the growth in the money supply when the demand for money is changing unpredictably will lead to large fluctuations in the interest rate, which can seriously disrupt the investment climate.

- Keeping interest rates in check would also create problems. When the economy grows, the demand for money also grows, so the Fed would have to increase the money supply to keep interest rates from rising. And if the economy was in a recession, the Fed would have to contract the money supply. This would lead to the wrong policy prescription—expanding the money supply during a boom would eventually lead to inflation and contracting the money supply during a recession would make the recession even worse.

- The federal funds rate is the interest rate the Fed has targeted since about 1965. At the close of the meetings of the Federal Open Market Committee (FOMC), the Fed will usually announce whether the federal funds rate will be increased, decreased, or left alone.

- Monetary policy actions can be conveyed through either the money supply or the interest rate. A contractionary policy can be thought of as a decrease in the money supply or an increase in the interest rate. An expansionary policy can be thought of as an increase in the money supply or a decrease in the interest rate.

- The interest rate is used for monetary policy because

  1) Many economists believe the primary effects of monetary policy are felt through the interest rate;

  2) the money supply is difficult to accurately measure;

  3) changes in the demand for money can complicate money supply targets; and

  4) people are more familiar with changes in interest rates than changes in the money supply.

- The real interest rate is determined by investment demand and saving supply. The nominal interest rate is determined by the demand and supply of money. Many economists believe that in the short run, the Fed can control the nominal interest rate and the real interest rate.

- The real interest rate is equal to the nominal interest rate minus the expected inflation rate. So a change in the nominal interest rate tends to change the real interest rate by the same amount because the expected inflation rate is slow to change in the short run. However, in the long run, after the inflation rate has adjusted, the real interest rate is determined by the intersection of the saving supply and investment demand curves.

## I    REVIEW

The _____ market is where money demand and supply determine the equilibrium nominal interest rate.

The three motives for holding money as an asset are: to make _____, to be prepared for _____ expenses, and to maintain a stock of _____ assets.

The quantity of money demanded varies inversely with the _____ rate, but the supply of money is almost perfectly _____ with respect to interest rates.

Thus, when drawn on a graph, the demand curve for money slopes _____ while the supply curve for money is _____.

When we combine the money demand and supply curves, money market equilibrium occurs at that nominal _____ rate where the quantity of money demanded equals the quantity of money _____.

Rising national income _____ the demand for money and shifts the money demand curve to the right.

An increase in the money supply is shown as a shift in the money supply curve to the _____, which causes the equilibrium interest rate to _____.

A reduction in the money supply is shown as a shift in the money supply curve to the _____, which causes the equilibrium interest rate to _____.

If the Fed pursues an expansionary monetary policy, it will _____ bonds, resulting in _____ interest rates and an _____ in aggregate demand.

If the Fed pursues a contractionary monetary policy, it will sell _____, resulting in _____ interest rates and a _____ in aggregate demand.

The Fed cannot completely control the growth in the _____ supply and the _____ rate at the same time.

## II     TRUE/FALSE

_T_ 1. When interest rates fall, the quantity of money demanded increases.

_T_ 2. When the Fed increases the money supply, the money supply curve will shift to the right.

_F_ 3. In the United States, the supply of money is controlled by the U.S. Treasury Department.

## III     MULTIPLE CHOICE

1. When Ramesh keeps money in his checking account just in case he may have to pay an unexpected medical bill or other expense, he is holding money for
   A)  transaction purposes.
   B)  precautionary purposes.
   C)  asset purposes.
   D)  nondenominational purposes.

2. Ten-year-old Sadako carries $2.00 to school in order to pay for a $2.00 lunch at the cafeteria. She is holding money for
   A)  transactions purposes.
   B)  precautionary purposes.
   C)  asset purposes.
   D)  nondenominational purposes.

3. The money demand curve shows the
   A)  various amounts of money that individuals will hold at different price levels.
   B)  various amounts of money that individuals will spend at different levels of GDP.
   C)  various amounts of money that individuals will hold at different interest rates.
   D)  quantity of bonds that the Fed will buy at different price levels.

4. If the central bank persistently increases the money supply faster than the rate of real output, the result will be
   A)  unemployment.
   B)  inflation.
   C)  stagflation.
   D)  recession.

## IV    APPLICATION AND DISCUSSION

There are several motives for holding assets in the form of money. Analyze your own motives for holding money. How much money do you usually carry in your wallet or purse? Is it all for making transactions? What is the balance in your checking account? Do you keep something in the account for precautionary reasons or "just in case"?

SECTION 16.5

# EXPANSIONARY AND CONTRACTIONARY MONETARY POLICY

## KEY POINTS

- An increase in A*D* through monetary policy can lead to an increase in real GDP if the economy is initially operating at less than full employment.

- An increase in *AD* through monetary policy can lead to only a temporary, short-run increase in real GDP, if the economy is initially operating at or above full employment, with no long-run effect on output or employment.

- A contractionary monetary policy would reduce aggregate demand. When the economy is temporarily beyond full employment, an appropriate countercyclical monetary policy would shift the aggregate demand curve leftward, to combat a potential inflationary boom.

- If the Fed pursues a contractionary monetary policy when the economy is at full employment, the Fed could cause a recession by shifting the aggregate demand curve leftward, resulting in higher unemployment and a lower price level. At a lower than expected price level, owners of inputs will then revise their expectations downward, causing a rightward shift in the *SRAS* curve, leading to a new long-run equilibrium back at full employment.

- For simplicity, we have assumed that the global economy does not impact domestic monetary policy. This is incorrect. Suppose the Fed buys bonds on the open market, leading to an increase in the money supply and a fall in interest rates. Some domestic investors will seek to invest funds in foreign markets, exchanging dollars for foreign currency, leading to a depreciation of the dollar. This increases exports and decreases imports, and the increase in net exports increases RGDP in the short run. Suppose the Fed sells bonds on the open market, leading to a decrease in the money supply and a rise in interest rates. Some foreign investors will seek to invest funds in the U.S. market, exchanging foreign currency for dollars, leading to an appreciation of the dollar. This decreases exports and increases imports, and the decrease in net exports decreases RGDP in the short run.

- The shape of the aggregate supply curve is a source of debate among economists, and it has important policy implications.

- If the aggregate supply curve is relatively inelastic, expansionary monetary and fiscal policy are less effective at increasing RGDP in the short run, but have larger effects on the price level in the short run. If the aggregate supply curve is relatively elastic, expansionary monetary and fiscal policy are more effective at increasing RGDP in the short run, and have smaller effects on the price level in the short run.

- If the aggregate supply curve is relatively inelastic, contractionary monetary and fiscal policy are less effective at changing RGDP in the short run, but have larger effects on the price level in the short run. If the aggregate supply curve is relatively elastic, contractionary monetary and fiscal policy are more effective at changing RGDP in the short run, and have smaller effects on the price level in the short run.

# Chapter 16: The Federal Reserve System and Monetary Policy

## I   REVIEW

An increase in the money supply when the economy is operating at _____ than full employment can lead to an _____ in real GDP and the price level.  An increase in the money supply at _____ employment, however, can temporarily increase real _____, but in the long run, only the _____ level will rise.

When the economy is operating beyond full employment, the Fed can combat inflation through _____ monetary policy.  If the Fed pursues contractionary monetary policy when the economy is at full employment it may cause a _____.

In an open economy, expansionary monetary policy will lead to a(n) _____ in the foreign exchange value of the dollar.  Contractionary monetary policy will lead to a(n) _____ in the foreign exchange value of the dollar.

## II   TRUE/FALSE

__F__ 1. If the economy is operating at full employment, an increase in the money supply will result in a decrease in the overall price level.

__T__ 2. Expansionary monetary policy will tend to make U.S. products more attractive to foreign buyers.

__F__ 3. When the Fed cut the federal funds rate by 2 percentage points in early 2001, it was trying to reduce aggregate demand and keep inflation in check.

## III   MULTIPLE CHOICE

1. The economy is in a recession.  The unemployment rate is high and businesses are pessimistic about the future.  Which of the following would constitute appropriate monetary policy?
   A) a tax increase
   B) a tax cut
   C) an increase in the rate of growth of the money supply
   D) a decrease in the rate of growth of the money supply

2. The economy is growing at a very rapid rate and prices are rising at a rapid rate of 8 percent per year.  The unemployment rate is extremely low.  Which of the following would constitute appropriate monetary policy?
   A) an increase in government expenditures
   B) a tax cut
   C) an increase in the rate of growth of the money supply
   D) a decrease in the rate of growth of the money supply

**IV    APPLICATION AND DISCUSSION**

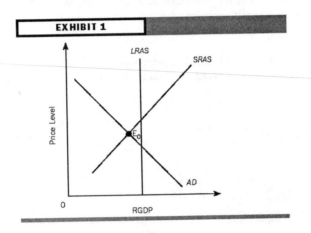

A)  If the economy is operating at less than full employment, as shown in Exhibit 1, what effect will expansionary monetary policy have on the *AD, SRAS,* and *LRAS* curves? Show what happens on the graph.

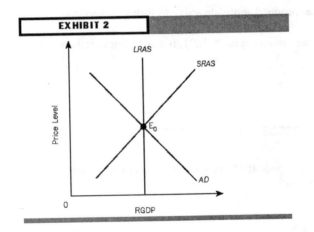

B)  If the economy is operating at full employment, as shown in Exhibit 2, what effect will expansionary monetary policy have on the *AD, SRAS,* and *LRAS* curves? Show what happens on the graph.

SECTION 16.6

# PROBLEMS IN IMPLEMENTING MONETARY AND FISCAL POLICY

## KEY POINTS

- The lag problem inherent in adopting fiscal policy changes are much less acute for monetary policy, largely because the decisions are not slowed by the same budgetary process. The FOMC of the Federal Reserve, for example, can act quickly (in emergencies, almost instantly, by conference call) and even secretly to buy or sell government bonds, the key day-to-day operating tool of monetary policy. However the length and variability of the impact lag before its effects on output and employment are felt is still significant and the time before the full price level effects are felt is even longer and more variable. According to the Federal Reserve Bank of San Francisco, the major effects of a change in policy on growth in the overall production of goods and services usually are felt within three months to two years, and the effects on inflation tend to involve even longer lags, perhaps one to three years or more.

- One limitation of monetary policy is that it ultimately must be carried out through the commercial banking system. The Central Bank (Federal Reserve System in the United States) can change the environment in which banks act, but the banks themselves must take the steps necessary to increase or decrease the supply of money.

- Usually, when the Fed is trying to constrain monetary expansion, there is no difficulty in getting banks to make appropriate responses. Banks must meet their reserve requirements, and if the Fed raises bank reserve requirements, sells bonds, and/or raises the discount rate, banks must obtain the necessary cash or reserve deposits at the Fed to meet their reserve requirements. In response, they will call in loans that are due for collection, sell secondary reserves, and so on, to obtain the necessary reserves, and in the process of contracting loans, they lower the supply of money.

- When the Federal Reserve wants to induce monetary expansion, however, it can provide banks with excess reserves (e.g., by lowering reserve requirements or buying government bonds), but it cannot force the banks to make loans, thereby creating new money. Ordinarily, of course, banks want to convert their excess reserves to work earning interest income by making loans. But in a deep recession or depression, banks might be hesitant to make enough loans to put all those reserves to work, fearing that they will not be repaid. Their pessimism might lead them to perceive that the risks of making loans to many normally creditworthy borrowers outweigh any potential interest earnings. Banks maintaining excess reserves rather than loaning them out was, in fact, one of the monetary policy problems that arose in the Great Depression.

- A second problem with monetary policy relates to the fact that the Fed can control deposit expansion at member banks, but it has no control over global and nonbank institutions that also issue credit (loan money) but are not subject to reserve requirement limitations, like pension funds and insurance companies. Therefore, while the Fed may be able to predict the impact of its monetary policies on member bank loans, the actions of global and nonbanking institutions can serve to partially offset the impact of monetary policies adopted by the Fed on the money and loanable funds markets. Hence, there is a real question of how precisely the Fed can control the short-run real interest rates through its monetary policy instruments.

- Another possible problem that arises out of existing institutional policy making arrangements is the coordination of fiscal and monetary policy. Decision making with respect to fiscal policy is made by Congress and the president, while monetary policy decision making is in the hands of the Federal Reserve System. A macroeconomic problem arises if the federal government's fiscal decision makers differ on policy objectives or targets with the Fed's monetary decision makers.

- In recognition of potential macroeconomic policy coordination problems, the Chairman of the Federal Reserve Board has participated for several years in meetings with top economic advisers of the president. An attempt is made in those meetings to reach a consensus on the appropriate policy responses, both monetary and fiscal. Still, there is often some disagreement, and the Fed occasionally works to partly offset or even neutralize the effects of fiscal policies that it views as inappropriate.

# Chapter 16: The Federal Reserve System and Monetary Policy

- Some people believe that monetary policy should be more directly controlled by the president and Congress, so that all macroeconomic policy will be determined more directly by the political process. Also, it is argued that such a move would enhance coordination considerably. Others, however, argue that it is dangerous to turn over control of the nation's money stock to politicians, rather than allowing decisions to be made by technically competent administrators who are focused more on price stability and more insulated from political pressures from the public and from special interest groups.

- Much of macroeconomic policy in this country is driven by the idea that the federal government can counteract economic fluctuations: stimulating the economy (with increased government purchases, tax cuts, transfer payment increases, and easy money) when it is weak, and restraining it when it is overheating. But policy makers must adopt the right policies in the right amounts at the right time for such "stabilization" to do more good than harm. And for government policy makers to do more good than harm, they need far more accurate and timely information than experts can give them.

- First, economists must know not only which way the economy is heading, but also how rapidly. And no one knows exactly what the economy will do, no matter how sophisticated the econometric models used.

- Second, even if economists could provide completely accurate economic forecasts of what will happen if macroeconomic policies are unchanged, they could not be certain of how to best promote stable economic growth. If economists knew, for example, that the economy was going to dip into another recession in six months, they would then need to know exactly how much each possible policy would spur activity in order to keep the economy stable. But such precision is unattainable given the complex forecasting problems faced. Further, economists aren't always sure what effect a policy will have on the economy. Will an increase in government purchases quicken economic growth? It is widely assumed so. But how much? And increasing government purchases increases the budget deficit, which could send a frightening signal to the bond markets. The result can be to drive up interest rates and choke off economic activity. So even when policy makers know which direction to nudge the economy, they can't be sure which policy levers to pull, or how hard to pull them, to fine tune the economy to stable economic growth.

- A third crucial consideration is how long it will take a policy before it has its effect on the economy. Even when increased government purchases or expansionary monetary policy does give the economy a boost, no one knows precisely how long it will take to do so. The boost may come very quickly, or many months (or even years) in the future, when it may add inflationary pressures to an economy that is already overheating, rather than helping the economy recover from a recession.

- Macroeconomic policy making is like driving down a twisting road in a car with an unpredictable lag and degree of response in the steering mechanism. If you turn the wheel to the right, the car will eventually veer to the right, but you don't know exactly when or how much. In short, there are severe practical difficulties in trying to fine-tune the economy. Even the best forecasting models and methods are far from perfect. Economists are not exactly sure where the economy is or where or how fast it is going, making it very difficult to prescribe an effective policy. Even if we do know where the economy is headed, we cannot be sure how large a policy's effect will be or when it will take effect.

- The Fed must take into account the influences of many different factors that can either offset or reinforce monetary policy. This isn't easy because sometimes these developments occur unexpectedly, and because the size and timing of their effects are difficult to estimate. The 1997–98 currency crisis in East Asia is an example.

- In addition, the "new" economy may increase productivity, allowing for greater economic growth without creating inflationary pressures. The Fed must estimate how much faster productivity is increasing and whether those increases are temporary or permanent, which is not an easy task.

- The shape of the aggregate supply curve also has some interesting implications for the unsustainable area of output beyond full employment. With steeper (more inelastic) aggregate supply curve, output expands only slightly at a much higher price level. With a flatter (more elastic) aggregate supply curve, output expands considerably with only a small increase in the price level. If the SRAS is relatively flat, perhaps it can help explain the U.S. macroeconomy in the late 1990s—low rates of unemployment coupled with low rates of inflation.

# Chapter 16: The Federal Reserve System and Monetary Policy

## I    REVIEW

The problem of time lags in making policy changes is _____ acute for monetary policy than it is for fiscal policy.

One limitation of monetary policy is that it must be carried out through the _____ banking system. This is not a big problem when the Fed initiates _____ monetary policy, because banks must take actions that _____ the money supply when the Fed sells bonds, increases the discount rate, or raises the reserve requirement. It is a problem, however, when the Fed initiates _____ monetary policy because it cannot force banks to make the loans that create new _____.

A second limitation of monetary policy is the fact that the Fed has no control over _____ and nonbank institutions that loan money.

A third problem is the fact that monetary policy is conducted by the Fed while _____ policy is made by Congress and the president. A macroeconomic problem arises if Congress and the president have _____ objectives than those of the Fed.

Economists _____ forecast the future course of the economy with precision. In addition, economists _____ always sure what effects specific policies will have on the economy, nor are they sure about how long it will take before a policy _____ the economy.

## II    TRUE/FALSE

F ___1. In the United States, monetary and fiscal policy are the responsibilities of the Fed.

F ___2. Economists have perfected their forecasting models to the point where they are usually able to predict future rates of inflation, output, and employment with precision.

T ___3. The East Asian currency crisis of 1997–98 created a problem for the Fed, since it led to a reduction in the demand for U.S. exports.

## III    MULTIPLE CHOICE

1. Compared to fiscal policy, which of the following is an advantage of using monetary policy to attain macroeconomic goals?
    A) The economists who help conduct monetary policy are smarter than those who help with fiscal policy.
    B) The implementation of monetary policy is not slowed down by the same budgetary process as fiscal policy.
    C) The effects of monetary policy are certain and predictable while the effects of fiscal policy are not.
    D) It takes a long time for fiscal policy to have an effect on the economy but the effects of monetary policy are immediate.

2. An important limitation of monetary policy is that
    A) it is conducted by people in Congress who are under pressure to get re-elected every two years.
    B) when the Fed tries to buy bonds, it is often unable to find a seller.
    C) when the Fed tries to sell bonds, it is often unable to find a buyer.
    D) it must be conducted through the commercial banking system and the Fed cannot always make banks do what it wants them to do.

## IV    APPLICATION AND DISCUSSION

In 1910 the basic plan for the Federal Reserve System was drawn up at a secret meeting of a small group of men at the private resort of J. P. Morgan on Jekyll Island off the coast of Georgia. The Fed was created three years later and since that time it has faced frequent criticism.

One criticism is that the Fed is undemocratic and that monetary policy should be controlled by our elected representatives in Congress. What do you think? Should Congress conduct monetary policy? What are the pros and cons of this suggestion?

### Questions

1.  What are the "Tools of the Fed?"

2.  How would you use these tools to combat a recession? How would you use them to fight inflation?

# CHAPTER 17
# ISSUES IN MACROECONOMIC THEORY AND POLICY

# SECTION 17.1
# THE PHILLIPS CURVE

## KEY POINTS

- Despite legislation committing the federal government to the goal of full employment and the development of macroeconomic theory purporting to show that full employment can be achieved by manipulating aggregate demand, periods of high unemployment still occur.

- Similarly, price stability, which had been achieved for long periods before the 1930s, has not been consistently observed since that time. In every year in the lifetimes of most readers of this book, the general level of prices has risen.

- We usually think of inflation as an evil. But some economists believe that inflation could actually help eliminate unemployment. If output prices rise but money wages do not go up as quickly or as much, real wages fall. At the lower real wage, unemployment is less because the lower wage makes it profitable to hire more, now cheaper, employees than before. The result is real wages that are closer to the full employment equilibrium wage that clears the labor market. Hence, with increased inflation, one might expect lower unemployment.

# Chapter 17: Issues in Macroeconomic Theory and Policy

- An inverse relationship between the rate of unemployment and the changing level of prices has been observed in many periods and places in history. Credit for identifying this relationship generally goes to British economist A. H. Phillips, who in the late 1950s published a paper setting forth what has since been called the Phillips curve. Phillips, and many others since, have suggested that at higher rates of inflation, the rate of unemployment is lower, while during periods of relatively or falling stable prices, there is substantial unemployment. In short, the cost of lower unemployment appears to be greater inflation, and the cost of greater price stability appears to be higher unemployment.

- The **Phillips curve** illustrates an inverse relationship between the rate of unemployment and the rate of inflation. The Phillips curve is steeper at higher rates of inflation and lower levels of unemployment. This suggests that once the economy has relatively low unemployment rates, further reductions in the unemployment rate can occur only by accepting larger increases in the inflation rate. Once unemployment is low, it takes larger and larger doses of inflation to eliminate a given quantity of unemployment. Presumably, at lower unemployment rates, an increased part of the economy is already operating at or near full capacity, and further fiscal or monetary stimulus primarily triggers inflationary pressures in sectors already at capacity, while eliminating decreasing amounts of unemployment in those sectors where some excess capacity and unemployment still exist.

## I    REVIEW

The inverse relationship between the rate of unemployment and the rate of inflation is called the _____ curve.

Some economists believe that inflation can help reduce unemployment by causing a _____ in real wages. When the real wage goes down, unemployment goes _____ because a lower real wage makes it profitable for employers to hire _____ labor than before.

## II    TRUE/FALSE

_____1. The Phillips curve shows the relationship between changes in the money supply and changes in the price level.

_____2. In the 1960s there was a positive relationship between inflation and unemployment.

## III    MULTIPLE CHOICE

1. If output prices rise faster than money wages, the real wage will
   A) rise and the unemployment rate will fall.
   B) rise, as will the unemployment rate.
   C) fall and the unemployment rate will rise.
   D) fall, as will the unemployment rate.

2. If the Phillips curve is steeper at higher rates of inflation, it suggests that
   A) once the economy has relatively low unemployment rates, further reductions in the unemployment rate can occur only be accepting larger increases in the inflation rate.
   B) once the economy has relatively low unemployment rates, further reductions in the unemployment rate can occur only by reducing the rate of inflation.
   C) when the economy is experiencing high inflation rates, the unemployment rate can be reduced only by reducing the rate of inflation.
   D) when the economy is experiencing low inflation rates, the unemployment rate can be reduced only by accepting lower rates of inflation.

**IV    APPLICATION AND DISCUSSION**

Consider the Phillips curve shown in Exhibit 1.

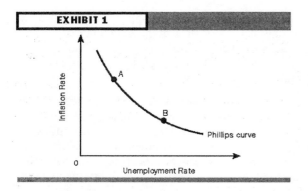

A)   What actions can the Fed take to cause movement from point A to point B on the curve?

B)   What actions can the Fed take to cause a movement from point B to point A on the curve?

S E C T I O N   1 7 . 2

# THE PHILLIPS CURVE OVER TIME

## KEY POINTS

- It became widely accepted in the 1960s that policy makers merely had to decide on the combination of unemployment and inflation they wanted from the Phillips curve and then simply pursue the appropriate economic policies. A reduction in the rate of unemployment came at a cost (more inflation) as did a reduction in the amount of inflation (more unemployment). Nonetheless, policy makers believed they could influence economic activity in a manner in which some goal could be met, though with a trade-off in terms of other macroeconomic goals. The empirical evidence on prices and unemployment fits the Phillips curve approach so beautifully at first that it is not surprising that it was embraced so rapidly and completely.

- Economists like Milton Friedman and Edmund Phelps, who questioned the long-term validity of the Phillips curve, were largely ignored in the 1960s. These economists believed there might be a short-term trade-off between unemployment and inflation, but not a permanent trade-off. According to Friedman, the short-run trade-off comes from *unanticipated* inflation.

- In the 1970s (and 1980s and 1990s), economists recognized that macroeconomic decision making was not as simple as picking a point on the Phillips curve. The data from the 1970s showed the Phillips curve started to break down. From 1970–96, every data point was to the right of the 1960s Phillips curve, meaning a worsening trade-off between inflation and unemployment. The 1970s experienced more of both inflation and unemployment than existed in the 1960s. However, in the 1980s, the Fed followed a very tight monetary policy to combat high inflation rates. People altered their expectations of inflation downward. In the mid-1990s, when lower inflation was achieved and expected, the Phillips curve shifted inward, back to the level of the 1960s.

- The **long-run Phillips curve** shows the relationship between the inflation rate and the unemployment rate when the actual and expected inflation rates are the same. The long-run Phillips curve is vertical at the natural rate of unemployment. This is equivalent to the vertical long-run aggregate supply curve. Along the long-run Phillips curve we see that the natural rate of unemployment can occur at any rate of inflation. That is, regardless of fiscal and monetary stimulus, output and employment will be at their natural rate in the long run.

- Suppose that, starting from the natural rate of unemployment, the growth rate of the money supply increases. If it is unanticipated, it will stimulate aggregate demand. In the short-run, the increase in aggregate demand will increase output and decrease unemployment below the natural rate as the economy moves up along the short-run Phillips curve, increasing the actual inflation rate. However, over time, people adjust to the new inflation rate and the short-run Phillips curve shifts up. If the now higher inflation rate continues, the adjustment of expectations will move the economy to where the expected and actual inflation rates are equal at the natural level of output and the natural rate of unemployment. This reveals that there is no trade-off between the inflation rate and the unemployment rate in the long run. The policy implication is that the use of fiscal or monetary policy to alter real output from the natural level of real output or unemployment from the natural rate of unemployment is ineffective in the long run.

- Alternatively, say there was a decrease in the rate of growth in the money supply. If unanticipated, it would reduce aggregate demand. In the short run, the decrease in aggregate demand moves the economy down along the short-run Phillips curve, where the actual inflation rate has decreased and the unemployment rate has risen above the natural rate. The decrease in aggregate demand has led to lower production and to a fall in employment. When people recognize that prices are not rising as rapidly as before, they adjust their expectations to reflect that fact, and the short-run Phillips curve shifts downward. The inflation rate is now lower and unemployment and output have returned to their natural rates. In this scenario, the economy's road to lower inflation rates has come at the expense of higher unemployment in the short run, until people's expectations adapt to the new lower inflation rate in the long run.

- Changes in the expected inflation rate can shift the short-run Phillips curve. But so can supply shocks. An adverse supply shock, such as higher energy prices, causes a leftward shift in the *SRAS* curve, with a higher price level and lower RGDP—stagflation. But the higher inflation rate and higher unemployment rate that result shift the short-run Phillips curve to the right.

- A favorable supply shock, such as lower energy prices, causes a rightward shift in the *SRAS* curve, with a lower price level and higher RGDP. But the lower inflation rate and lower unemployment rate that result shift the short-run Phillips curve to the left.

- The impact of adverse or favorable shocks depend on expectations. If people expect the changes to be permanent, then the shifted Phillips curve will stay in the new position until something else happens. If the shock is expected to be temporary, the Phillips curve will soon shift back to its original position.

- If economic fluctuations are expected to be permanent and are caused primarily by supply-side shifts, then there may be a positive relationship between the inflation rate and the unemployment rate—a shifting Phillips curve. Higher rates of inflation will be coupled with higher rates of unemployment and lower rates of inflation will be coupled with lower rates of unemployment.

## I   REVIEW

In the 1960s, economic policy makers believed the Phillips curve described the _____ between two macroeconomic goals, inflation and unemployment. A reduction in unemployment could be achieved at the cost of _____ inflation, and inflation could be reduced at the cost of _____ unemployment.

Other economists, such as Milton _____ and Edmund _____, thought the Phillips curve represented only a _____-term trade-off between inflation and unemployment. This trade-off was the result of _____ inflation.

Starting in the 1970s, the Phillips curve relationship broke down. Points since 1969 show a _____ tradeoff between inflation and unemployment.

The long-run Phillips curve shows the relation between unemployment rates and the inflation rate when actual and _____ inflation rates are the same. It is vertical at the _____ rate of unemployment, so in the long run the _____ rate of unemployment holds at any rate of inflation. Regardless of monetary or fiscal stimulus, output and employment will be at the natural rate in the _____ run.

In the _____ run, a trade-off between inflation and unemployment exists. An increase in aggregate demand caused by expansionary monetary or fiscal policy will result in _____ prices. If the resulting inflation was _____, real wages and other input prices will fall. As real wages fall, firms will _____ output and hire more workers, so unemployment falls.

Eventually, workers negotiate for _____ wages. In response to the increase in wages, firms _____ output and employment, so unemployment increases. The short-run Phillips curve will shift to the _____ and _____ rates of inflation will be required to achieve any level of unemployment.

There is no trade-off between the inflation rate and the unemployment rate in the _____ run. Neither fiscal nor monetary policy is _____ at reducing unemployment below the natural rate in the long run.

An adverse supply shock leads to a _____ price level and _____ output. A favorable supply shock leads to a _____ price level and a _____ rate of unemployment.

## II      TRUE/FALSE

_____1. In the short run, as the rate of inflation increases, the natural unemployment rate declines.

_____2. The long-run Phillips curve shows the rate of unemployment that occurs when people correctly anticipate the rate of inflation.

_____3. The long-run and short-run Phillips curve relationships suggest that macroeconomic policy can reduce the unemployment rate below the natural rate but only in the long run because it takes a long time.

_____4. An adverse supply shock is shown as a leftward shift in the *SRAS*.

## III      MULTIPLE CHOICE

1.   Which of the following is *not* a correct statement about the Phillips curve?
   A)  In the short run, it shows a positive relationship between the inflation rate and the unemployment rate.
   B)  In the 1960s, it showed a stable trade-off between unemployment and inflation.
   C)  In the 1970s, a higher rate of inflation was associated with any given unemployment rate than in the 1960s.
   D)  The long-run Phillips curve is a vertical line.

2. Edward Ott is the chief economist for the Nation of Balaban. Edward is able to use fiscal and monetary policy to keep the unemployment rate below the natural rate. Which of the following is the best explanation for Edward's macroeconomic wizardry?
   A) Edward uses only monetary policy to achieve his macroeconomic goals.
   B) The residents of the Nation of Balaban have a really high natural rate of unemployment.
   C) The residents of the Nation of Balaban always underestimate the actual rate of inflation.
   D) Edward produces the statistics on the Balabanish economy, so he simply cheats and estimates the natural rate is higher than the actual rate.

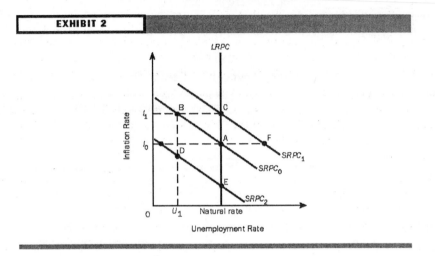

EXHIBIT 2

3. Which of the following pairs of points in Exhibit 2 have different anticipated rates of inflation?
   A) A, B
   B) B, C
   C) C, F
   D) D, E

## IV    APPLICATION AND DISCUSSION

Throughout history many governments have financed government operations "with the printing press," paying government bills by increasing the money supply. The United States followed this path during the Civil War, approximately doubling the U.S. money supply between 1860 and 1865 using paper fiat money called "Greenbacks."

1. What do you think this rapid increase in the money supply did to inflation and inflationary expectations?

2. Suppose the economy was in long-run equilibrium by the end of the war and the government began to remove the "Greenbacks" and reduce the money supply. Use your understanding of the Phillips curve relationship to explain the effect on the economy.

SECTION 17.3
# RATIONAL EXPECTATIONS

## KEY POINTS

- Is it possible that people can anticipate the plans of policy makers and alter their behavior quickly, to neutralize the intended impact of government action? For example, if workers see that the government is allowing the money supply to expand rapidly, they may quickly demand higher money wages in order to offset the anticipated inflation. In the extreme form, if people could instantly recognize and respond to government policy changes, it might be impossible to alter real output or unemployment levels through policy actions unless consumers and businesses could be surprised. An increasing number of economists believe that there is at least some truth to this point of view.

- At a minimum, most economists accept the notion that real output and the unemployment rate cannot be altered with the ease that was earlier believed; some believe that the unemployment rate can seldom be influenced by fiscal and monetary policies. The relatively new extension of economic theory that leads to this rather pessimistic conclusion regarding macroeconomic policy's ability to achieve our economic goals is called **the theory of rational expectations.**

- The notion that expectations or anticipations of future events are relevant to economic theory is not new; for decades economists have incorporated expectations into models analyzing many forms of economic behavior. Only in the recent past, however, has a theory evolved that tries to incorporate expectations as a central factor in the analysis of the entire economy.

- Rational expectation economists believe that wages and prices are flexible, and that workers and consumers incorporate the likely consequences of government policy changes quickly into their expectations. In addition, rational expectation economists believe that the economy is inherently stable after macroeconomic shocks, and that tinkering with fiscal and monetary policy cannot have the desired effect unless consumers and workers are caught off guard (and catching them off guard gets harder the more you try to do it).

- Rational expectations theory suggests that government economic policies designed to alter aggregate demand to meet macroeconomic goals are of very limited effectiveness. When policy targets become public, it is argued, people will alter their own behavior from what it would otherwise have been, and, in so doing, they largely negate the intended impact of policy changes. If government policy seems tilted towards permitting more inflation in order to try to reduce unemployment, people start spending their money faster than before, become more adamant in their wage and other input price demands, and so on. In the process of quickly altering their behavior to reflect the likely consequences of policy changes, they make it more difficult (costly) for government authorities to meet their macroeconomic objectives.

- Rather than fooling people into changing real wages, and therefore unemployment, with inflation "surprises," changes in inflation are quickly reflected into expectations with little or no effect on unemployment or real output even in the short run. As a consequence, policies intended to reduce unemployment through stimulating aggregate demand will often fail to have the intended effect. Fiscal and monetary policy, according to this view, will work only if the people are caught off guard or fooled by policies so that they do not modify their behavior in a way that reduces policy effectiveness.

- In the case of an expansionary monetary policy, *AD* will shift to the right. As a result of anticipating the predictable inflationary consequences of that expansionary policy, the price level will immediately adjust to a new higher price level. Consumers, producers, workers, and lenders who have anticipated the effects of the expansionary policy simply built the higher inflation rates into their product prices, wages, and interest rates because they realize that expansionary monetary policy can cause inflation if the economy is working close to capacity. Consequently, in an effort to protect themselves from the higher anticipated inflation, workers ask for higher wages, suppliers increase input prices, and producers raise their product prices. Because wages, prices and interest rates are assumed to be flexible, the adjustments take place immediately. This increase in input costs for wages, interest, and raw materials causes the aggregate supply curve to also shift up or leftward. So the desired policy effect of greater real output and reduced unemployment from a shift in the aggregate demand curve is offset by an upward or leftward shift in the aggregate supply curve caused by an increase in input costs.

- An *unanticipated* increase in *AD* as a result of an expansionary monetary policy stimulates output and employment in the short run. The output is beyond the full-employment level, and so is not sustainable in the long run. The price level ends up higher than workers and other input owners expected. However, when they eventually realize that the price level has changed, they will require higher input prices, shifting *SRAS* left to a new long-run equilibrium at full employment and a higher price level. In the short run, the policy expands output and employment, but only increases the price level—inflation—in the long run.

- A correctly anticipated increase in *AD* from expansionary monetary or fiscal policy will not change real output, employment or unemployment even in the short run. The only effect is an immediate change in the price level. The only way that monetary or fiscal policy can change output in the rational expectations model is with a surprise—an unanticipated change.

- In the rational expectations model, when people expect a larger increase in *AD* than actually results from a policy change (say, from a smaller increase in the money supply than expected), it leads to a higher price level and a lower level of RGDP—a recession. That is, a policy designed to increase output may actually reduce output if prices and wages are flexible and the expansionary effect is less than people anticipated.

- Rational expectations theory does have its critics. Critics want to know if consumers and producers are completely informed about the impact that an increase in money supply will have on the economy. In general, not all citizens will be completely informed, but key players like corporations, financial institutions, and labor organizations may well be informed about the impact of these policy changes. But there are other problems, too. For example, are wages and other input prices really that flexible? That is, even if decision makers could anticipate the eventual effect of policy changes on prices, those prices may still be slow to adapt (e.g., what if you had just signed a three-year labor or supply contract when the new policy is implemented?).

- Many economists reject the extreme rational expectations model of complete wage and price flexibility. In fact, most still believe there is a short-run trade-off between inflation and unemployment. The reason is that some input prices are slow to adjust to changes in the price level. However, in the long run, the expected inflation rate adjusts to changes in the actual inflation rate at the natural rate of unemployment.

# I    REVIEW

An increasing number of economists believe that people can _____ the moves of policy makers and alter their behavior to _____ the intended impact of government action.

Rational _____ economists believe that wages and prices are _____, and that workers and consumers incorporate the likely consequences of government policy changes quickly into their expectations.

Rational expectations theory suggests that government economic policies have _____ effectiveness. According to this view, monetary and fiscal policy will affect output and employment only if people are _____ by policy moves so that they do not modify their behavior in ways that reduce policy effectiveness.

An unanticipated increase in the money supply will result in an _____ in both output and employment in the _____ run. An increase in the money supply that is fully anticipated will result in a higher _____ level, but will have no effect on _____.

# II    TRUE/FALSE

_____1. Rational expectations economists believe that people anticipate government policy moves.

_____2. Rational expectations economists believe that wages and prices are relatively rigid.

## III    MULTIPLE CHOICE

Use Exhibit 3 to answer questions 1 and 2.

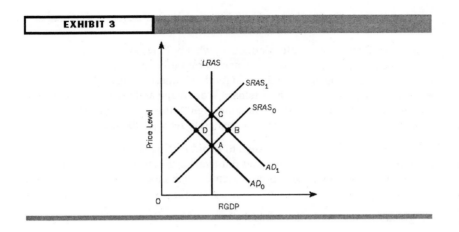

**EXHIBIT 3**

1.  If an increase in aggregate demand from $AD_0$ to $AD_1$ is unanticipated, the economy will move from point A to point _____ in the short run.
    A)  A
    B)  B
    C)  C
    D)  D

2.  If an increase in aggregate demand from $AD_0$ to $AD_1$ is fully anticipated, the economy will move from point A to point _____.
    A)  A
    B)  B
    C)  C
    D)  D

## IV    APPLICATION AND DISCUSSION

How do you think each of the following would affect the unemployment rate?

A)  The Fed increases the money supply and engineers an unexpected increase in the rate of inflation from 2 percent to 5 percent.

B)  The rate of inflation remains stable at 2 percent over a five-year period, as expected.

C)  There is an unexpected decrease in the rate of inflation from 10 percent to 3 percent.

SECTION 17.4

# WAGE AND PRICE CONTROLS AND INDEXING

## KEY POINTS

- If monetary and fiscal policy are ineffective or counterproductive, what policies are left to control inflation? It is possible that the federal government could set up a comprehensive program over wages and prices—often called **incomes policy.** We have imposed such controls three times in modern American history, during World War II, during the Korean War, and in 1971 near the end of the Vietnam War. Wage and price controls involve either a complete freeze on wages and prices at pre-control levels or some rigid limits as to the increases in wages and prices that will be permitted. One or more government agencies are created to monitor the program.

- Sometimes voluntary guidelines or guideposts are established to avoid forcing companies and unions to limit their price and wage levels. This approach avoids the expense and political acrimony associated with establishing a control bureaucracy. Sometimes the "jawboning" gets pretty intense. Such guidelines can come close to being mandatory controls.

- There are two justifications given for wage and price controls.

  First, by limiting price increases by law, the government directly reduces the rate of inflation legally allowed.

  Second, especially with respect to wage controls, it is argued that wage and price controls lower the inflationary expectations of workers and their unions, reducing the "inflation psychology" that contributes to cost-push inflation.

- Wage and price controls have several major disadvantages, which are very likely to be viewed as greater than the advantages, except possibly during wartime situations when aggregate demand is growing very rapidly. There is the problem of enforcing the controls. Black markets (illegal sales) often develop. These problems are often very hard to solve. Another even more fundamental problem with wage and price controls is that they lead to shortages of goods, services, and workers; inflationary pressures are not eradicated but rather disguised, manifesting themselves not in price increases but in the lack of desired goods or human resources. Severe and prolonged controls can lead to a very serious misallocation of resources as a result.

- Straightforward supply and demand analysis indicates the misallocation of resources due to wage and price controls. At the legal price ceiling, the quantity demanded exceeds the quantity supplied and shortages arise.

- Problems with price controls are illustrated by the 1973 Arab oil boycott, when the federal government imposed price ceilings on gasoline that prevented gas prices from rising as they normally would have in response to reduced supply. At the ceiling price, quantity demanded exceeded quantity supplied; gas stations ran out of gas, were often closed, or placed a limit on the amount of gas they would sell. When drivers were able to buy gas, they often not only filled their tanks but also several containers they carried along to reduce the risk of being unable to buy gas when they needed it. In the former Soviet Union, where price-control-related shortages were commonplace, citizens typically carried briefcases or even suitcases and large quantities of cash, in case they were able to purchase a normally unavailable good. Rather than just buy the product for themselves, they would buy several items for their friends and relatives as well, to keep them from having to stand in line for hours, often in vain, trying to buy it.

- In the case of prolonged wage controls, shortages of personnel can occur. Wages serve as market signals. Rising wages in an occupation increases an occupation's attractiveness, leading to new entrants of workers. If, however, the government had decreed that salaries in that field could not rise enough, the increase in the quantity of new workers supplied would not have occurred and a shortage would arise.

- Whether the gains from wage and price controls in the form of reduced inflation outweigh the costs in the form of shortages and inefficient resource allocation is debatable. This is a normative issue where honest, informed persons can differ in their perceptions of costs and benefits. (An example was the debate over the removal of price controls on natural gas, with one side arguing that controls should be removed to end shortages and enhance long-term supply, while the other side argued that removing controls would lead to inflated prices for gas and inflated profits for gas producers, while causing hardships to lower income users of gas.)

- The attempt to control prices politically can take another form. The presence of monopolistic elements in an industry can lead to higher prices for that industry's products than would be the case for a more competitive industry. By stimulating price competition among private firms, the government may be able to help in reducing inflationary pressures. However, there has been relatively little actual use of antitrust laws to try to reduce inflation pressures. Moreover, monopoly power can also be artificially created by government regulations.

- Another approach to some of the problems posed by inflation is **indexing.** Inflation poses substantial equity and distributional problems only when it is unanticipated or unexpected. One means of protecting parties against unanticipated price increases is to write contracts that automatically change prices of goods or services whenever the overall price level changes, effectively rewriting agreements in terms of dollars of constant purchasing power. By making as many contracts as possible payable in dollars of constant purchasing power, those involved can protect themselves against unanticipated changes in inflation.

- Indexing seems to eliminate most of the wealth transfers associated with unexpected inflation. Why then is it not more commonly used? One main argument against indexing is that it could well worsen inflation. As prices go up, wages and certain other contractual obligations (e.g., rents) would also automatically increase. This immediate and comprehensive reaction to price increases will lead to greater inflationary pressures.

- If inflation gets bad enough, it may become almost impossible administratively to maintain the indexing scheme. There are other inefficiencies, as well. During the German hyperinflation of the early 1920s, prices at one point rose so rapidly that workers demanded to be paid twice a day, at noon and at the end of work. During their lunch hour, workers would rush money home to their wives, who would then run out and buy real goods before price increases further eroded purchasing power.

- Indexing also reduces the ability for relative price changes to allocate resources where they are more valuable. Further, not everything can be indexed, so indexing would cause wealth redistributions plus the cost of negotiating cost of living (COLA) clauses.

- Excessive inflation leads to great inefficiency, as well as a loss of confidence in the issuer of money, namely the government.

## I      REVIEW

The government uses _____ policy when it imposes controls on wages and prices to manage inflation. These policies set _____ to the permitted increase in wages and prices.

There are two arguments in support of wage and price controls. First, price and wage controls _____ reduce the rate of inflation. Second, they also lower inflationary _____ and the psychology that leads to _____ -push inflation.

Wage and price controls have many disadvantages. They are difficult and costly to _____. They result in _____ of goods, services, and labor. Price controls result in the _____ of resources.

Because prices are higher in monopolistic industries, stimulating _____ in monopolistic industries may reduce inflationary pressure.

_____ is another way to control the problems posed by inflation. It protects people from _____ price increases by writing contracts that automatically change prices of goods or services whenever the _____ price level changes. Agreements are effectively written in terms of dollars of _____ purchasing power.

Indexing seems to eliminate most of the wealth _____ associated with unexpected inflation, but it would probably _____ inflation because one price increase will automatically lead to another.

# Chapter 17: Issues in Macroeconomic Theory and Policy

In periods of rapid inflation the _____ costs of indexing will be high because prices may have to be changed frequently. Indexing also reduces the ability of _____ prices to reallocate resources to where they are more valuable. Indexing also has high costs associated with _____ contracts.

Because not every price can be indexed, inflation results in some _____ redistribution even with indexing.

---

## II    TRUE/FALSE

_____1. Indexing eliminates the wealth redistribution effects of inflation by eliminating rapid price increases.

_____2. Jawboning occurs when governments pass laws that control prices and wages.

_____3. Wage and price controls may control inflation but at the cost of misallocating resources.

---

## III    MULTIPLE CHOICE

1.  Which of the following is a cost of wage and price controls?
    A)  Wage and price controls lower inflationary expectations.
    B)  Wage and price controls have high enforcement costs.
    C)  Wage and price controls increase competition.
    D)  Wage and price controls increase the price of jawbones.

Answer questions 2 and 3 by referring to Exhibit 4, which shows the market for skateboards. The market starts out in equilibrium at point A where quantity supplied equals quantity demanded at the price $P_0$. The government has imposed a price guideline that prevents increases in the price of skateboards, so the price will remain $P_0$.

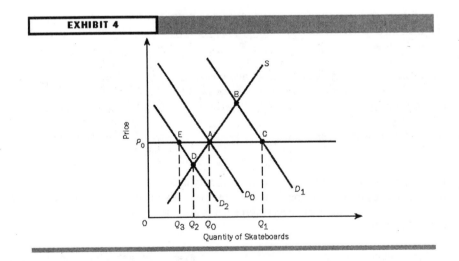

2.  Movies about skateboarding increase its popularity, so demand increases to $D_1$. How many skateboards will be sold?
    A)  $Q_0$
    B)  $Q_1$

C) $Q_2$

D) $Q_3$

3. If the demand for skateboards falls to $D_2$ because people's incomes decline, the new equilibrium will be

A) A.

B) B.

C) C.

D) D.

## IV    APPLICATION AND DISCUSSION

In 1971, President Nixon tried to control inflation by using wage and price controls. This resulted in a misallocation of resources and prevented the economy from operating in the most efficient way.

1. Explain why each of the following possible effects of wage and price controls prevents the economy from operating in its most efficient way.

A) A shortage is created in the market for furniture.

B) People stand in line to buy furniture.

C) Government officials take furniture makers to court to force them to stick to the price guidelines.

2. How does inflation result in inefficiency in the market?

3. In your opinion, should governments use wage and price controls during periods of rapid inflation?

## Questions

1. In macroeconomics, what is the Phillips curve?

2. What is the difference between the short-run and long-run Phillips curve?

# CHAPTER 18
# INTERNATIONAL TRADE

## SECTION 18.1
# THE GROWTH IN WORLD TRADE

### KEY POINTS

- In a typical year, about 15 percent of the world's output is traded in international markets.

- While the importance of the international sector varies enormously from place to place, the volume of international trade has increased substantially.

### I    REVIEW

Although it varies from country to country, in a typical year about _____ percent of the world's output is traded in international markets.  In 1998, about _____ percent of U.S. output was _____, and imports amounted to over _____ percent of GDP.

The United States has important trading relations with many countries, but our three most important partners are _____, _____, and Japan.

## II     TRUE/FALSE

_____1. In 1998, U.S. imports of goods from Canada were over twice as large as our imports of goods from China.

_____2. Over time, trade with other countries has remained insignificant to the United States.

## III     MULTIPLE CHOICE

1. The Canadian politician Terry F. Razer wants to limit trade in goods with the United States to preserve Canadian culture. Why would this action be more important to the U.S. economy than the same type of policy in Italy?
   A) Canadians speak English so U.S. citizens are more interested in what they do.
   B) Canada ranks behind only the United Kingdom as our second most important trade partner.
   C) Canada accounts for approximately one-fifth of all U.S. exports and imports of goods.
   D) Canada exports most of the hockey players who play for the National Hockey League.

2. Dr. Mary K. Furst uses her 1940 dissertation research to justify her isolationist view that the U.S. economy would be affected only slightly if it were isolated from the rest of the world. Why might her conclusion be more correct in 1940 than it is today?
   A) The last 50 years have seen a dramatic increase in the importance of international trade to the U.S. economy.
   B) Technological changes over the last 50 years have reduced the importance of international trade throughout the world.
   C) The last 50 years have seen a dramatic reduction in the importance of international trade to the U.S. economy.
   D) Over the last 50 years, international trade has increased in importance in the world but not for the United States.

## IV    APPLICATION AND DISCUSSION

In 1999, the countries of the world *exported* a total of $6.7 trillion dollars worth of goods and service. From this information, can you tell how many total dollars worth of goods and services they *imported* in 1999?

# SECTION 18.2

# COMPARATIVE ADVANTAGE AND GAINS FROM TRADE

## KEY POINTS

- The very existence of trade suggests that trade is economically beneficial. Because almost all trade is voluntary, it would seem that trade occurs because the participants feel that they are better off because of the trade. Both participants of an exchange of goods and services anticipate an improvement in their economic welfare.

# Chapter 18: International Trade

- The classical economist David Ricardo's theory that explains how trade can be beneficial to both parties centers on the concept of comparative advantage. A person, a region, or a country can gain from trade if it produces a good or service at a lower opportunity cost than others. That is, an area should specialize in producing and selling those items where it has a **comparative advantage.**

- What is important for mutually beneficial specialization and trade is comparative advantage, not **absolute advantage**.

- The gains from comparative advantage—specialization where one has a lower opportunity cost—can be illustrated with a production possibility curve. The differences in opportunity costs provide an incentive to gain from specialization and trade.

## I    REVIEW

We know trade is economically _____ because it exists. Since trade is
_____ and people _____ utility, participants must expect trade to
make them better off.

David Ricardo developed the explanation of the mutual _____ of trade. His theory is the
Principle of _____ Advantage.

The Principle of Comparative Advantage states that a nation can gain from trade by _____ in
the production of those goods it can produce at a _____ opportunity cost than other countries.
This principle also applies to regions and individuals.

A country has a(n) _____ advantage in producing a good when it uses fewer resources to
produce a given level of output.  A country may have a comparative advantage in a good without having an absolute
advantage when the production of the good has _____ opportunity costs than its trading partner.

By specializing in the production of goods and services for which they have the lowest opportunity cost, trading partners can
produce _____ of all of the goods they trade. _____ in
opportunity costs between trading partners provide the _____ to gain from specialization and
trade.

## II    TRUE/FALSE

_____1. People and nations trade because trade makes them better off.

_____2. History has shown that specialization and trade are often in conflict with economic growth.

_____3. In the United States, one person working for 8 hours can produce 20 shirts, while in Malawi it would take one person 16 hours to produce 20 shirts.  In trade with Malawi, the United States will always have a comparative advantage in the production of shirts.

# Chapter 18: International Trade

## III    MULTIPLE CHOICE

1. In France it takes one worker one year to produce either 500 bottles of wine or 1,000 bottles of sparkling water. If resources in France are fully employed, what is the opportunity cost of a bottle of French wine?
   A) 1,000 bottles of water
   B) one-half a bottle of water
   C) $3.25
   D) two bottles of water

2. In Bangladesh, one person can produce 330 pounds of rice or 110 shirts in one year. In Singapore, one person can produce 400 pounds of rice or 200 shirts in one year. Which of the following statements is true?
   A) Bangladesh has an absolute advantage in the production of rice.
   B) Bangladesh has a comparative advantage in the production of rice.
   C) Singapore has both an absolute and comparative advantage in the production of rice.
   D) Singapore has a comparative advantage in the production of rice.

## IV    APPLICATION AND DISCUSSION

1. Bud and Larry have been shipwrecked on a deserted island. Their economic activity consists of either gathering berries or fishing. We know that Bud can catch four fish in one hour or harvest two buckets of berries. In the same time Larry can catch two fish or harvest two buckets of berries.

   A) Fill in the following table assuming that they *each* spend four hours a day fishing and four hours a day harvesting berries.

   |       | Fish per day | Buckets of Berries per day |
   |-------|--------------|-----------------------------|
   | Bud   | _____  | _____                 |
   | Larry | _____  | _____                 |
   | Total | _____  | _____                 |

   B) If Bud and Larry don't trade with each other, who is better off? Why?

   C) Assume that Larry and Bud operate on straight-line production possibility curves.

   Fill in the following table.

   |       | Opportunity Cost of a Bucket of Berries | Opportunity Cost of a Fish |
   |-------|------------------------------------------|-----------------------------|
   | Bud   | _____                              | _____                 |
   | Larry | _____                              | _____                 |

   D) If they traded, who has the comparative advantage in fish? In berries?

   E) If Larry and Bud specialize in and trade the good in which they have a comparative advantage, how much of each good will be produced in an eight hour day? What are the gains from trade?

SECTION 18.3

# SUPPLY AND DEMAND IN INTERNATIONAL TRADE

## KEY POINTS

- The difference between the most a consumer would be willing and able to pay for a quantity of a good and what a consumer actually has to pay is called **consumer surplus.** The difference between the least amount for which a supplier is willing and able to supply a quantity of a good or service and the revenues a supplier actually received for selling it is called **producer surplus**. With the tools of consumer and producer surplus, we can better analyze the impact of trade.

- The demand curve represents a collection of maximum prices that consumers are willing and able to pay for different quantities of a good or service while the supply curve represents a collection of minimum prices that suppliers require to be willing to supply different quantities of that good or service. Trading at the market equilibrium price generates both consumer surplus and producer surplus.

- Once the equilibrium output is reached at the equilibrium price, all of the mutually beneficial opportunities from trade between suppliers and demanders will have taken place; the sum of consumer surplus and producer surplus is maximized.

- The total gains to the economy from trade is the sum of consumer and producer surplus. That is, consumers benefit from additional amounts of consumer surplus and producers benefit from additional amounts of producer surplus.

- When the domestic economy has a comparative advantage in a good because it can produce it at a lower relative price than the rest of the world, international trade raises the domestic market price to the world price, benefitting domestic producers but harming domestic consumers. However, while this redistributes income from consumers to producers, there are net benefits from allowing free trade because producer surplus increases more than consumer surplus decreases. While domestic consumers lose from the free trade, those negative effects are more than offset by the positive gains captured by producers. In net, export trade increases domestic wealth.

- When a country does not produce a good relatively as well as other countries, international trade will lower the domestic price to the world price, with the difference between what is domestically supplied and what is domestically demanded supplied by imports. Domestic consumers benefit from paying a lower price for the good, increasing their consumer surplus. But domestic producers lose because they are now selling at the lower world price. However, while this redistributes income from producers to consumers, there is a net increase in domestic wealth from free trade and imports because the consumer surplus increases more than producer surplus decreases.

## I    REVIEW

The difference between what a consumer is willing to pay for a given amount of a good and what they have to pay is called consumer _____. Consumers benefit from paying less than they would be willing to pay.

Producer _____ is the difference between the revenue the producer receives for selling a given amount of the good and the amount the producer is willing to accept. Producers benefit from receiving more than they would be willing to accept.

The demand curve represents the _____ prices consumers are willing and able to pay for different quantities of a good or service. The supply curve represents the _____ prices at which suppliers are willing to offer different quantities of the good or service.

As long as the maximum price the consumer is willing to pay _____ the minimum price the supplier requires for one more unit of a good or service, there are mutually _____ opportunities for trade.

When markets reach the _____ price, all the opportunities for mutually beneficial trade have taken place and the sum of consumer and producer surplus is _____.

When a country trades with the rest of the world, the price of the exported good is _____ after trade than before. Domestic consumers _____ from free trade because their consumer surplus is _____. However, these losses are offset by the positive gains captured by domestic _____. On net, export trade _____ domestic wealth.

When an economy trades with the rest of the world, the price of the imported good is _____ after trade than before. Domestic consumers _____ from free trade because their consumer surplus is _____. However, domestic producers lose because their producer surplus is _____. On net, import trade _____ domestic wealth since the gain to consumers _____ the loss to producers.

## II    TRUE/FALSE

_____1. Trade between producers and consumers will occur as long as consumers benefit.

_____2. If the farming industry vigorously supports free trade while the cement industry opposes free trade, we could assume our country's comparative advantage is in farm products and not cement.

_____3. The price of bananas in Greece is higher than the world price. Ms. Margaret Stake is correct to assert that Greece has a comparative advantage in banana production.

## III    MULTIPLE CHOICE

1.  The difference between the price the seller receives for a good or service and the minimum price he would be willing to accept is called
    A)  the market price.
    B)  the producer surplus.
    C)  the consumer surplus.
    D)  the equilibrium difference.

Answer questions 2 through 4 by referring to Exhibit 1. This shows the domestic supply and demand curves for a good for which the country has a comparative advantage. Without trade the country produces $Q_{BT}$ at a price of $P_{BT}$. Trade takes place at the world price of $P_{AT}$.

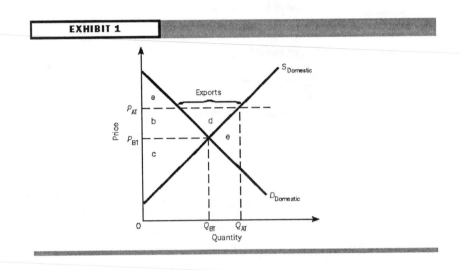

**EXHIBIT 1**

2.  Trade reduces consumer surplus by an amount equal to the area
    A)  a.
    B)  b.
    C)  c.
    D)  d.

3.  With trade, producer surplus increases by an amount equal to
    A)  d.
    B)  d + e.
    C)  b + c + d.
    D)  b + d.

4.  Export trade will increase this country's domestic wealth because
    A)  consumer surplus increases by more than producer surplus by an amount equal to e.
    B)  consumer surplus increases by more than producer surplus by an amount equal to d.
    C)  producer surplus increases by more than consumer surplus by an amount equal to e.
    D)  producer surplus increases by more than consumer surplus by an amount equal to d.

## IV     APPLICATION AND DISCUSSION

1.  To protect its domestic apple industry, Botswana has for many years prevented international trade in apples. Exhibit 2 represents the Botswana domestic market for apples. $P_{BT}$ is the current price and $P_{AT}$ is the world price.

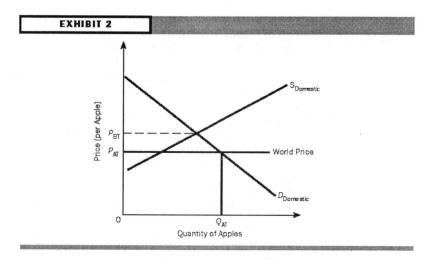

**EXHIBIT 2**

A) If the government allows world trade in apples, what will happen to the price of apples in Botswana? Why?

B) Indicate the amount of apples domestic producers produce after there is trade in apples as $Q_{DT}$. How many apples are imported?

C) Trade in imports causes producer surplus to be reduced by the amount b. Show b on the graph.

D) The gains from trade equal the amount increased consumer surplus exceeds the loss in producer surplus. Show this gain, g, on the graph.

E) Explain why consumers in Botswana would still be better off if they were required to compensate producers for their lost producer surplus.

# SECTION 18.4
# TARIFFS, IMPORT QUOTAS, AND SUBSIDIES

## KEY POINTS

- A **tariff** is a tax on imported goods. Tariffs are usually relatively small revenue producers that retard the expansion of trade. They bring about higher prices and revenues to domestic producers, lower sales and revenues to foreign producers, and higher prices to domestic consumers. The gains to producers are more than offset by the losses to consumers.

- With import tariffs, the domestic price of goods is greater than the world price. At the new price, the domestic quantity demanded is lower and the quantity supplied domestically is greater, reducing the quantity of imported goods. While domestic producers do gain more sales and producer surplus at the expense of foreign producers, and the government gains from tariff revenue, consumers lose more in consumer surplus than producers and the government gain from the tariff.

# Chapter 18: International Trade

- One argument for tariffs is that tariff protection is necessary temporarily to allow a new industry to more quickly reach a scale of operation at which economies of scale and production efficiencies can be realized. This argument has many problems. How do you identify "infant industries" that genuinely have potential economies of scale and will become quickly efficient with protection? Moreover, would it not be wise to make massive loans to the industry in such a case, allowing it to instantly begin large-scale production rather than slowly and at the expense of consumers with a protective tariff? Finally, the history of infant industry tariffs suggests that the tariffs often linger long after the industry is mature and no longer in "need" of protection.

- Tariffs can lead to increased output and employment and reduced unemployment in domestic industries where tariffs were imposed. Yet the overall employment effects of a tariff imposition are not likely to be positive. Not only might the imposition of a tariff lead to retaliatory tariffs by other countries, but domestic employment would likely suffer outside the industry gaining the tariff protection. If new tariffs lead to restrictions on imports, fewer dollars will be flowing overseas in payment for imports, which means that foreigners will have fewer dollars available to buy our exports. Other things equal, this will tend to reduce our exports, thus creating unemployment in the export industries.

- Sometimes it is argued that tariffs are a means of preventing a nation from becoming too dependent on foreign suppliers of goods vital to national security, but the national security argument is usually not valid. If a nation's own resources are depletable, tariff-imposed reliance on domestic supplies will hasten depletion of domestic reserves. From a defense standpoint, it makes more sense to use foreign supplies in peacetime and perhaps stockpile "insurance" supplies so that large domestic supplies would be available during wars.

- An **import quota** gives producers from another country a maximum number of units of the good in question that can be imported within any given time span.

- The case for quotas is probably even weaker than the case for tariffs. Like tariffs, quotas directly restrict imports, leading to reductions in trade and thus preventing nations from fully realizing their comparative advantage. But tariffs at least use the price system as the basis of restricting trade, while quotas do not. Further, unlike with a tariff, the U.S. government does not collect any revenue as a result of the import quota.

- Nations have also devised still other, more subtle means to restrict international trade. Examples include product standards ostensibly designed to protect consumers against inferior, unsafe, dangerous, or polluting merchandise, which, in effect, are sometimes a means to restrict foreign competition.

- Except in rather unusual circumstances, the arguments for tariffs and import quotas are rather suspect. They exist because of producers' lobbying efforts to gain profits from government protection called **rent seeking.** Because these resources could have produced something instead of being spent on lobbying efforts, the measured deadweight loss from tariffs and quotas will likely understate the true deadweight loss to society.

- Working in the opposite direction, governments sometimes try to encourage exports by subsidizing producers. With a subsidy, revenue is given to producers for each exported unit of output, stimulating exports. While not a barrier to trade like tariffs and quotas, subsidies can also distort trade patterns, leading to ones that are inefficient.

- With subsidies, producers export goods not because their costs are lower than that of a foreign competitor, but because their costs have been artificially reduced by government action transferring income from taxpayers to the exporter. The actual costs of production are not reduced by the subsidy—society has the same opportunity costs as before. A nation's taxpayers end up subsidizing the output of producers who, relative to producers in other countries, are inefficient. The nation, then, exports products in which it does not have a comparative advantage. Gains from trade in terms of world output are eliminated or reduced by such subsidies.

---

## I    REVIEW

A tariff is a(n) _____ on imported goods.

Tariffs are used today to _____ domestic industry from foreign competition.

# Chapter 18: International Trade

A tariff is a(n) _____ on imported goods.  Tariffs result in
_____ prices to domestic producers and _____ sales and
revenues to foreign producers.

Domestic producers gain from tariff protection, but domestic consumers lose _____ than
producers gain.

The _____ industry argument in support of tariffs argues that tariff protection helps new
industries reach the scale of operation at which they can be efficient.

Because tariffs increase domestic production they are often supported as a mechanism for reducing _____
in protected industries.

However, employment in other industries may suffer if exports are reduced because of _____
by other countries. Export industries may also suffer because with a reduction in foreign imports, other countries will have
_____ dollars to purchase our exports.

Tariffs are also supported for national security reasons. They can be used to limit our _____
on foreign producers for those goods vital to our national security.

A tariff on a good will create _____ for producers and
_____ for consumers. Even when losses exceed the benefits, a tariff may be adopted,
because producers are a more effective _____ group for a tariff than consumer groups who
lobby against tariffs.

An import _____ limits international trade by defining a maximum number of units of a good that can
be imported in a time period. Unlike tariffs, governments do not collect any _____ with a quota.

Import quotas make domestic producers _____ off, but make domestic consumers
_____ off.

Governments may also try to encourage exports by _____ producers. With subsidies, producers
export goods, not because their costs are relatively _____ than other countries, but because
their costs have been _____ lowered by transferring income from
_____ to exporters.


## II     TRUE/FALSE

_____1. Import quotas generate more government revenue than a tariff that is designed to realize the same level of imports.

_____2. Export subsidies can be used to change a country's comparative advantage.

_____3. If it can be shown that a tariff on steel imports will increase employment in the steel industry, we can be sure the
effect of the tariff on U.S. employment will be positive.

## III    MULTIPLE CHOICE

1. Which of the following is *not* a result we would expect from a tariff on leather shoes?
   A) The price of leather shoes in the United States would increase.
   B) The amount of shoes imported into the United States would decline.
   C) Fewer pairs of shoes would be sold in the United States.
   D) Domestic producers would sell fewer shoes at the higher prices.

2. Tariffs result in a decrease in consumer surplus because
   A) the price and quantity consumed of the protected good increase.
   B) the price and quantity consumed of the protected good decrease.
   C) the price of the protected good increases and quantity consumed decreases.
   D) the price of the protected good decreases and quantity consumed increases.

Answer questions 3 through 5 by referring to Exhibit 3. This graph shows the domestic market for sweaters for which this country has a comparative disadvantage. With the adoption of a tariff, the price of purchasing imports increases by the amount of the tariff. $P_0$ is the original domestic price.

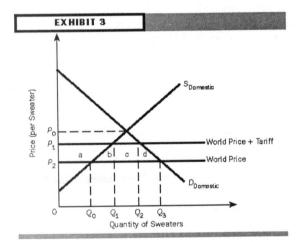

3. After the tariff on sweaters in imposed, the domestic price of sweaters will be
   A) $P_0$.
   B) $P_1$.
   C) $P_2$.
   D) zero because sweaters will no longer be imported.

4. The tariff on sweaters reduces consumer surplus by an amount equal to the area
   A) a.
   B) a + b.
   C) a + b + c.
   D) a + b + c + d.

5. The net loss in welfare caused by imposing the tariff is an amount equal to what area in the exhibit?
   A) a + c
   B) b + c
   C) b + d
   D) b + c + d

## IV   APPLICATION AND DISCUSSION

1. When the United States, Canada, and Mexico created the North American Free Trade Agreement (NAFTA) in 1993, they began to lower tariffs and other trade barriers. Suppose tariffs had protected the U.S. maple syrup industry from lower cost Canadian producers.

   A) What would you expect to happen in the U.S. maple syrup market after the tariffs are removed?

   B) What would you say to critics that argue NAFTA is bad because it costs jobs in the maple syrup industry?

### Questions

1. According to Jerry Lee, who has an absolute advantage in window washing and vacuuming?

2. How could you use the principle of comparative advantage to decide who does which household chores in the Lowell household?

# CHAPTER 19
# INTERNATIONAL FINANCE

SECTION 19.1 THE BALANCE OF PAYMENTS

SECTION 19.2 EXCHANGE RATES

SECTION 19.3 EQUILIBRIUM CHANGES IN THE FOREIGN EXCHANGE MARKET

SECTION 19.4 FLEXIBLE EXCHANGE RATES

# SECTION 19.1
# THE BALANCE OF PAYMENTS

## KEY POINTS

- The record of all of the international financial transactions of a nation over a year is called the **balance of payments**. It records all the exchanges those in a nation engaged in that required an outflow of funds to other nations or an inflow of funds from other nations, and provides information about a nation's world trade position.

- The balance of payments is divided into three main sections: the current account, the capital account, and "statistical discrepancy."

- The **current account** is a record of a country's current imports and exports of goods and services.

- Because the United States gains claims over foreign buyers by obtaining foreign currency in exchange for the dollars needed to buy U.S. exports, all exports of U.S. goods abroad are considered a credit or plus item in the U.S. balance of payments. When a U.S. consumer buys an imported item, the reverse is true. U.S. imports are considered a debit item in the balance of payment because the dollars sold to buy the necessary foreign currency add to foreign claims against U.S. buyers.

- Imports and exports of goods are the largest component of the balance of payments. Nations also import and export services.

- Private and government grants and gifts to foreigners also count as a debit item in a country's balance of payments, and grants and gifts from foreigners count as a credit item.

- The balance on current account is the net amount of debits or credits after adding up all transactions of goods, services, and fund transfers. If the sum of credits exceeds the sum of debits, a nation is said to have a balance of payments surplus on current account. If debits exceed credits, it is running a balance of payments deficit on current account.

- The import/export goods relationship is often called the **balance of trade,** which is different from the balance on current account.

- A deficit on current account is settled by movements of financial, or capital, assets. A current account deficit is financed by a **capital account** surplus. The capital account records foreign purchases of assets in the U.S. and U.S. purchases of assets abroad.

- Due to the reciprocal aspect of trade, the balance of payments must balance so that credits and debits are equal; however, errors and omissions mean the official measures do not come out equal. The **statistical discrepancy** is included so that the official balance of payments do balance.


## I      REVIEW

The record of all the international transactions of a nation over a year is called the balance of _____. The balance of payments is divided into three main sections: the _____ account, the _____ account, and the _____ _____.

The current account is made up of imports and _____ of goods and services. When a foreign buyer buys a good from a U.S. producer, the foreigner usually pays for the good in U.S. _____.

All exports of U.S. goods are considered _____ items in the U.S. balance of payments.

When a U.S. buyer buys an imported good the buyer usually pays in _____ currency. All imports of foreign goods are considered _____ items in the U.S. balance of payments.

When the United States gives foreign aid to another country or when private individuals send money to relatives in foreign countries, it is recorded as a _____ in the U.S. balance of payments.

The balance on current account is the net amount of credits and _____ after adding up all transactions of goods, services, investment income, and fund transfers.

Countries finance deficits in their current accounts by running _____ in their capital accounts.


## II      TRUE/FALSE

_____1. In recent years, the United States has run persistent deficits in its balance on current account.

_____2. Another term for the balance on current account is "balance of trade."

_____3. If a country has a deficit in its current account, it must necessarily have a surplus in its capital account.

## III    MULTIPLE CHOICE

1. Which of the following is a credit in the U.S. current account?
   A) A U.S. consumer buys a TV made in Malaysia.
   B) Singapore Airlines buys a jumbo jet made in the United States.
   C) British investors purchase U.S. government bonds.
   D) An American citizen flies to Lithuania on Lithuanian Airlines.

2. If consumers in Europe and Asia develop strong preferences for American goods, America's current account will
   A) not be affected because purchases of American goods by foreigners are recorded in the capital account.
   B) not be affected because purchases of American goods based on mere preferences are recorded under "statistical discrepancy."
   C) move toward surplus because purchases of American goods are recorded as credits on our current account.
   D) move toward deficit because purchases of American goods by foreigners are counted as debits in our current account.

## IV    APPLICATION AND DISCUSSION

How are each of the following classified, as debits or credits, in the U.S. balance of payments accounts?

[insert 27.1]

|  | Credit | Debit |
|---|---|---|
| 1. Americans buy autos from Japan. | | |
| 2. American tourists travel to Japan. | | |
| 3. Japanese consumers buy rice grown in the U.S. | | |
| 4. United States gives foreign aid to Rwanda. | | |
| 5. General Motors, a U.S. company, earns profits in France. | | |
| 6. Royal Dutch Shell earns profits from its U.S. operations. | | |
| 7. General Motors builds a new plant in Vietnam. | | |
| 8. Japanese investors purchase U.S. government bonds. | | |

SECTION 19.2
# EXCHANGE RATES

## KEY POINTS

- U.S. consumers must first exchange U.S. dollars for the seller's currency in order to pay for imported goods. Similarly, foreigners buying U.S. goods must sell their currencies to obtain U.S. dollars in order to pay for exported goods.

- The price of a unit of one foreign currency in terms of another is called the **exchange rate,** which can be expressed either as the number of units of currency A per unit of currency B or its reciprocal, the number of units of currency B per unit of currency A.

- Prices of goods in their own currencies combine with exchange rates to determine the domestic price of foreign goods. For instance, an increase in the euro–dollar exchange rate from $1 per euro to $2 per euro would increase the U.S. price of German goods, reducing the number of German goods that would be demanded in the United States.

- The demand for foreign currencies is a **derived demand** because it derives directly from the demand for foreign goods and services or for foreign capital. An increased demand for a currency will push up the exchange value of that currency relative to other currencies.

- Similarly, the supply of foreign currency is provided by foreigners who want to buy the exports of a particular nation. The more foreigners demand U.S. products, the more of their currencies they will supply in exchange for U.S. dollars.

- Just as in the product market, the supply of and demand for a foreign currency determine the equilibrium price (exchange rate) of that currency.

- The demand for a foreign currency is downward sloping because, as the price of the foreign currency falls relative to the dollar, foreign products become relatively more inexpensive to U.S. consumers, who therefore buy more foreign goods. To do so, the quantity of foreign currency demanded by U.S. consumers will increase to buy more goods.

- The supply curve of a foreign currency is upward sloping. In trade with Europe, as the price, or value, of the euro increases relative to the dollar, American products become relatively more inexpensive to European buyers and the quantity of dollars they will demand will increase. Europeans will, therefore, increase the quantity of euros supplied to the U.S. by buying more U.S. products.

- Equilibrium in the foreign exchange market is reached where the demand and supply curves for a given currency intersect.


## I     REVIEW

When U.S. consumers buy goods from foreigners, the sellers of those goods want to be paid in their _____ currency. As a result, U.S. importers must _____ foreign currency with dollars in order to finance their purchases. Similarly, people in other countries buying goods made in America must _____ their currencies to obtain U.S. dollars in order to pay for those goods.

The price of a unit of one foreign currency in terms of another is called the _____ rate.

The demand for foreign currencies is what economists call _____ demand. The more foreign goods are demanded, the _____ of that foreign currency that will be needed to pay for those goods. Increased demand for a currency will cause the exchange value of that currency to _____.

Foreign currency is supplied by foreigners who want to buy _____ of a particular nation. For example, the more U.S. goods that foreigners demand, the _____ of their currency they will supply.

The equilibrium exchange rate for a currency is determined by the supply and _____ for that currency in the foreign exchange market.

## II    TRUE/FALSE

_____1. The exchange value of the dollar, in terms of foreign currency, is established by the U.S. government.

_____2. If the euro becomes relatively more expensive in terms of dollars, Americans will buy fewer European goods.

## III    MULTIPLE CHOICE

1. If the exchange rate between the dollar and the euro changes from $1 = 1 euro to $2 = 1 euro, European goods will become
   A) less expensive for Americans and imports of European goods to the United States will rise.
   B) less expensive for Americans and imports of European goods to the United States will fall.
   C) more expensive for Americans and imports of European goods to the United States will rise.
   D) more expensive for Americans and imports of European goods to the United States will fall.

2. Which of the following would result in an increase in the dollar price of a Japanese Yen?
   A) An increase in the Japanese supply of Yen.
   B) An increase in the Japanese demand for dollars.
   C) A decrease in the U.S. demand for Japanese Yen.
   D) A decrease in the Japanese supply of Yen.

## IV    APPLICATION AND DISCUSSION

1. Which of the following parties would be pleased by an *increase* in the value of the U.S. dollar in relation to the euro?
   A) American farmers
   B) Americans planning to take trips to Europe
   C) American producers of manufactured exports like airplanes and tractors
   D) Europeans who consume lots of American products
   E) Americans who enjoy French cheese

2. Which of the following parties would be pleased by a *decrease* in the value of the dollar in relation to the Japanese yen?
   A) American farmers
   B) Americans planning to visit Tokyo
   C) General Motors stockholders
   D) Japanese students planning to attend American colleges and universities
   E) Japanese hotel owners

SECTION 19.3

# EQUILIBRIUM CHANGES IN THE FOREIGN EXCHANGE MARKET

## KEY POINTS

- Any force that shifts either the demand for or supply of a currency will shift the equilibrium in the foreign exchange market, leading to a new exchange rate. An increased demand for euros will result in a higher equilibrium price (exchange value) for euros, while a decreased demand for euros will result in a lower equilibrium price (exchange value) for euros.

- Changes in a currency's exchange rate can be caused by changes in tastes for goods, changes in income, changes in relative real interest rates, changes in relative inflation rates, and speculation.

- Because the demand for foreign currencies is derived from the demand for foreign goods, any change in the demand for foreign goods will shift the demand curve for foreign currency in the same direction. For instance, an increase in tastes for European goods in the United States would increase the demand for Euros, increasing the equilibrium price (exchange value) of Euros; a decrease in tastes for European goods in the United States would decrease the demand for Euros, decreasing the equilibrium price (exchange value) of Euros.

- An increase in incomes in the United States would increase the amount of European imports purchased by Americans, which would increase the demand for euros, resulting in a higher exchange rate for euros. A decrease in incomes in the U.S. would decrease the amount of European imports purchased by Americans, which would decrease the demand for euros, resulting in a lower exchange rate for euros.

- A decrease in U.S. tariffs on European goods would tend to have the same effect as an increase in U.S. incomes, by making imports more affordable, increasing the U.S. demand for European goods and increasing the exchange rate for euros.

- If interest rates in the United States were to increase relative to European interest rates, other things equal, the rate of return on U.S. investments would increase relative to that on European investments, increasing European's demand for U.S. investments. Therefore, it would increase the supply of euros to obtain the added dollars to buy added U.S. investments. At the same time, U.S. investors would also shift their investments away from Europe, decreasing their demand for euros. The combination of the increased supply of euros and the decreased demand for euros will lead to a new lower exchange rate for euros.

- If Europe experienced a higher inflation rate than the United States, European products would become more expensive to U.S. consumers, decreasing the quantity of European goods demanded by Americans and, therefore, decreasing the demand for euros. U.S. products would become less expensive to European consumers, increasing the quantity of U.S. goods demanded by Europeans and, therefore, increasing the supply of euros. The combination of the increased supply of euros and the decreased demand for euros will lead to a new lower exchange rate for euros.

- If currency speculators believe that the United States was going to experience more rapid inflation in the future than Japan, they will believe that the value of the dollar will soon be falling as a result. That will increase the demand for yen, so the yen will appreciate relative to the dollar. The opposite will occur if speculators expect less rapid inflation in the United States.

## I ___ REVIEW

Any force that shifts either the demand for or supply of a currency will shift the _____ in the foreign exchange market, leading to a new _____ rate.

# Chapter 19: International Finance

Factors that shift the demand for and supply of a currency include changes in _____ for goods and services, changes in _____, changes in real _____ rates, and changes in relative _____ rates.

If incomes increase in the United States, Americans will buy _____ goods, including European goods. This increase in demand for foreign goods will cause an _____ in the demand for euros.

If incomes decrease in the United States, Americans will buy _____ goods, including European goods. This decrease in demand for foreign goods will cause a _____ in the demand for euros.

If interest rates in the United States increase relative to those in Europe, other things equal, the rate of return on U.S. investments will _____ relative to that on European investments. European investors seeking higher rates of return will _____ dollars with euros.

If interest rates in the United States decrease relative to those in Europe, investors will _____ dollars and _____ euros in order to make European investments.

If the rate of inflation is higher in Europe than in the United States, European products will become _____ expensive to U.S. consumers. Americans will _____ the quantity of European goods they demand and their demand for euros will _____. At the same time, the higher rate of European inflation will make U.S. goods relatively _____ expensive to Europeans. This will lead Europeans to _____ the quantity of U.S. goods demanded and lead to an _____ in the supply of euros.

Overall, the result of the higher rate of European inflation will be a new, _____ equilibrium price for the euro.

If speculators believe that the price of a country's currency is going to rise they will buy _____ of that currency.

## II     TRUE/FALSE

_____1. The equilibrium exchange rate of the dollar seldom changes.

_____2. If interest rates rise in the United States, relative to those in the rest of the world, the exchange value of the dollar will tend to appreciate.

_____3. Janelle, who lives in Dallas, has been saving for years in order to take a trip to Japan this summer. She should be happy if the dollar suddenly appreciates in value against the yen.

## III     MULTIPLE CHOICE

1. An economic boom in the United States, which increases the incomes of Americans, will result in
   A) a decrease in the U.S. demand for goods, including foreign goods, and a decrease in the supply of dollars on the foreign exchange market.
   B) an increase in the U.S. demand for goods, including foreign goods, and an increase in the supply of dollars on the foreign exchange market.
   C) a decrease in the U.S. demand for goods, including foreign goods, and an increase in the supply of dollars on the foreign exchange market.
   D) an increase in the U.S. demand for goods, including foreign goods, and a decrease in the supply of dollars on the foreign exchange market.

2. If the exchange rate changes from 100 yen per dollar to 120 yen per dollar,
   A) the dollar has depreciated.
   B) the dollar has appreciated
   C) the yen has appreciated.
   D) None of the above will occur.

## IV    APPLICATION AND DISCUSSION

What will happen to the supply of dollars, the demand for dollars, and the equilibrium exchange rate of the dollar in each of the following cases?

| | Supply of Dollars | Demand for Dollars | Equilibrium Exchange Rate |
|---|---|---|---|
| 1. Americans buy more European goods. | _____ | _____ | |
| 2. Europeans invest in U.S. stock market. | _____ | _____ | |
| 3. European tourists flock to the United States. | _____ | _____ | |
| 4. Europeans buy U.S. government bonds. | _____ | _____ | |
| 5. American tourists flock to Europe. | _____ | _____ | |

# SECTION 19.4
# FLEXIBLE EXCHANGE RATES

## KEY POINTS

- Since 1973, the world has essentially operated on a system of flexible exchange rates under which currency prices are allowed to fluctuate with changes in supply and demand, without governments stepping in to prevent those changes.

- Before 1973, governments operated under what was called the Bretton Woods **fixed exchange rate system,** in which they would maintain a stable currency exchange rate by buying or selling currencies or reserves to bring demand and supply for their currencies together at the fixed exchange rate.

- Governments are still sensitive to sharp changes in the exchange value of their currencies, and they do intervene from time to time to prop up exchange values considered to be too low or falling too rapidly or depress exchange values considered too high or rising too rapidly. Therefore, economists sometimes say the current exchange rate system is a "dirty float" system, where fluctuations in currency values are partly determined by market forces and partly determined by government intervention.

- When exchange rates change, they effect not only the currency market, but product markets as well. If the exchange value of the dollar relative to the yen or pound fell, it would increase the cost, and therefore decrease the volume of U.S. imports. It would also decrease the cost and lead to an increase in the volume of Japanese and British imports from the United States.

- Since the advent of flexible exchange rates, world trade has expanded.

- The most important advantage of the flexible rate system is that the recurrent crises that led to speculative rampages and major currency revaluations under the fixed Bretton Woods system, have significantly diminished. Today, exchange rates change almost constantly, but each change is much smaller in magnitude, with major changes typically occurring only over periods of months or years.

- Perhaps the most significant problem with fixed exchange rates is that they can result in currency shortages, just as domestic wage and price controls can lead to shortages.

- Under flexible exchange rates, an imbalance between debits and credits arising from shifts in currency demand and/or supply is accommodated by changes in currency prices rather than through the special financial borrowings or reserve movements necessary with fixed rates. In a pure flexible exchange-rate system, balance of payments deficits and surpluses tend to disappear.

- Flexible exchange rates also alleviate the need to use restrictive monetary and/or fiscal policy to end a currency imbalance, while maintaining fixed exchange rates, imposing less of a constraint on countries' internal macroeconomic policies.

- Flexible exchange rates have not been universally endorsed. Traditionally, the major objection to flexible exchange rates was that the resulting currency fluctuations introduce considerable uncertainty into international trade, potentially reducing the volume of trade and reducing the gains from international specialization.

- Flexible rate proponents have given three answers:

   1) the empirical evidence points to faster growth of international trade after the adoption of flexible exchange rates;

   2) one can, in effect, buy insurance against exchange rate risk through the forward or futures market in currencies; and

   3) the alleged certainty of currency prices under Bretton Woods was fictitious because countries could, at a whim, drastically revalue their currencies.

- A second, more valid, criticism of flexible exchange rates is that they can contribute to inflationary pressures by reducing the discipline the fixed-rate approach provided governments to constrain their domestic prices because lower domestic prices increase the attractiveness of their exported goods. Yet this criticism is not so clear given the inflationary potential in sudden substantial currency devaluations under the Bretton Woods system. Flexible exchange rate advocates argue that flexible exchange rates do not cause inflation; rather, it is caused by the expansionary macroeconomic policies of governments and central banks.

## I  REVIEW

Since 1973 the world has essentially operated on a system of _____ exchange rates. Governments, however, sometimes _____ in foreign exchange markets in order to prop up an exchange rate that they consider too _____ or to depress an exchange rate they consider to be too _____.

Prior to 1973, the world operated on a system of _____ exchange rates called the Bretton Woods system.

When exchange rates change they affect not only the currency market but the _____ markets as well. For example, if the dollar increases in value relative to other currencies, the relative prices of foreign goods for Americans will _____. Foreigners will find that the stronger dollar makes U.S. products _____ expensive for them.

Since the advent of flexible exchange rates, world trade has not only continued, but _____.

Changes in exchange rates occur _____ often under a flexible-rate system than they do under a fixed-rate system, but the changes are much _____ than the drastic, overnight revaluations of currencies under the fixed-rate system.

Under a fixed-rate system, as the supply and demand for currencies _____, currency prices are not allowed to shift to a new equilibrium, leading to surpluses and _____ of currencies.

One major argument against flexible exchange rates is that they cause _____ and may lead to a decrease in the level of world trade.

Another argument against flexible rates is that they may allow governments to pursue expansionary fiscal and monetary policies that may lead to _____.

## II    TRUE/FALSE

_____1. The world economy currently operates under a system in which the exchange values of nations' currencies are fixed by an international organization.

_____2. Under the current exchange rate system, governments sometimes intervene in the foreign exchange market in order to alter the exchange value of currencies.

## III    MULTIPLE CHOICE

1. Under a system of flexible exchange rates, a decrease in the demand for a country's currency on the foreign exchange market will
   A)  cause the country's currency to depreciate in value.
   B)  cause the country's currency to appreciate in value.
   C)  make the country's goods more expensive to foreigners.
   D)  make foreign goods less expensive to the country's citizens.

2. Critics of flexible exchange rates argue that flexible rates
   A)  reduce uncertainty in international trade.
   B)  automatically create an equilibrium price for each currency in the foreign exchange market.
   C)  make nations more constrained in carrying out internal macroeconomic policies.
   D)  increase uncertainty in international trade.

3. Critics of fixed exchange rates argue that fixed rates
   A)  reduce uncertainty in international trade.
   B)  result in currency shortages just as wage and price controls lead to shortages in markets for goods and services.
   C)  make nations less constrained in carrying out internal macroeconomic policies.
   D)  lead to constant, day-to-day changes in the exchange values of currencies.

## IV    APPLICATION AND DISCUSSION

What affect would a sudden shift by the Fed to a more expansionary monetary policy have on the exchange value of the dollar and on America's balance on current account?

**Questions**

1.  Why is the value of the yen important to the Lowells?

2.  What kinds of things could have happened to have caused the dollar to double in value against the yen?

# ANSWER KEY

## CHAPTER 1 THE ROLE AND METHOD OF ECONOMICS

Section 1.1 Economics: A Brief Introduction

### I     Review

A student of economics learns that much of life involves making a <u>choice</u> between conflicting wants in a world of scarcity. Students develop an economic way of <u>thinking</u> about their options, which is a valuable problem-solving tool.

<u>Economics</u> is defined, as the study of the allocation of our <u>limited</u> resources to satisfy our unlimited wants.

The factors like machinery, labor, water, and land, that are used to make goods and services are called <u>resources</u>.

The problem of <u>scarcity</u> results because our wants are greater than the goods and services our resources can produce.

We are forced to make <u>choices</u> about the best use of our limited resources. The cost of choosing to use a resource one way is the lost <u>opportunity</u> to use the resource in another way.

Making costly choices about the use of scarce resources is known as the <u>economic</u> problem.

### II     True/False

1. True. City budget decisions are choices about the use of scarce resources.

2. False. Resources are those things used to make goods and services; they include factories, machinery, and tools that are man-made.

3. True. Scarcity means we can think of many uses for our limited resources, so we have to choose the best use.

4. False. The cost of using a resource, like a truck, is the lost opportunity to produce other goods and services we value. For example, the trucks could be used to haul bats and balls.

5. False. Economics can help us understand a wide variety of problems involving scarce resources, such as the use of time, family decisions, and the allocation of government funds.

6. True. Time is a scarce resource and you have made a decision to use it in a particular way.

### III    Multiple Choice

1. The answer is C. Resources are things used to produce goods and services. Toys are consumed. Rubber trees, paint sprayers, and hammers are used to produce other goods and services.

2. The answer is C. Resources are scarce, so we must choose how to use them. The cost of our choice is the loss of the opportunity to use the resource in other ways.

3. The answer is B. An economic problem exists whenever we make choices about the use of scarce resources. We have only a limited amount of time.

4. The answer is D. Every choice we make involves a trade-off. When we use resources one way, we can't use them in any other way. We trade off one use for the other. Answer D is the only answer that does not involve a choice. Winning the lottery may reflect past choices and require future choices about the use of your money. When you win you make no choice, you have been chosen.

# ANSWER KEY

1. One of the most important resources used raising children has historically been the mother's time. As opportunities for women to hold jobs, start businesses, and participate in political life increase, the cost of using women's time for raising children increases. As the cost rises, fewer children are born.

2. A problem is an economic problem when scarce resources force people to make a costly choice. The decision to go on a date is an economic decision because you give up the time to do other things when you choose to go on a date. The cost of going on a date with one person also involves giving up the opportunity to go with someone else. Basketball coaches have a limited number of scholarships to award. To use this scarce resource on a point guard has a cost, the lost opportunity to offer the scholarship to a center or forward. Finally, the decision to admit one student usually means that some other student will be denied admission to the university. Universities have limited capacity in classrooms and dorms, and admissions policy are the rules schools use to allocate these scarce resources. Admissions policy is usually set to ensure that the students who get into the university are the ones most likely to succeed.

3. The definition must recognize the central parts of the economist's point of view: resources are scarce; scarcity forces us to make choices; and the cost of these choices is the lost opportunities.

## Section 1.2 Economics as a Science

I   Review

Like other social sciences, the central concern of economics is <u>human behavior</u>. It is the social science that studies people's <u>choices.</u>

Of the two main branches of economics, <u>macroeconomics</u> examines the effects of human behavior on the total economy, while <u>microeconomics</u> deals with human behavior in smaller units like the household or the firm. Economic problems affecting the whole of society such as inflation and unemployment are topics of <u>macroeconomics</u>. Microeconomics examines the choice making behavior of firms and households and their interaction in <u>markets</u>.

II   True/False

1. False. All social sciences are interested in human behavior, so they often examine the same questions from their particular perspectives.

2. True. Microeconomics is the branch of economics that attempts to understand the decision-making behavior of small units like firms and households within the economy. Economists try to understand the factors that determine the number of avocados that farmers choose to produce and the amount consumers choose to buy.

3. False. The analysis of the small units of the economy helps us to understand the behavior of the aggregate economy, and macroeconomic events like recessions affect households and firms. Both branches are concerned with the determinants and results of human interaction.

4. False. Inflation is an increase in the general price level. It affects the total or aggregate economy. It is a subject of macroeconomics.

III   Multiple Choice

1. The answer is D. Social science examines human behavior. While some biologists study the human body, their interest is in the way the body works, not the way humans behave and interact with others.

2. The answer is C. Microeconomics is the study of individual decision making units such as firms and households. Studies A, B, and D focus on macroeconomic problems.

3. The answer is C. The Archer's choice of vacation spots is based on tradition. Economics teaches us to think about the alternatives in terms of the costs and benefits associated with each. In each of the other answers the decision is made only after considering the costs and benefits.

# ANSWER KEY

4. The answer is A. Economics is concerned with reaching eneralizations about human behavior. Economists are attempting to identify and describe the factors that affect most of the people most of the time. Economics attempts to understand and to predict the average behavior of groups of individuals.

5. The answer is C. Unemployment and its consequences are the topics of study of many different sciences. Unemployment can be study by macroeconomics, microeconomics, as well as other social sciences, like anthropology. The consequences of unemployment can also be studies by physical sciences, like biology and health sciences. While these physical sciences may share a subject with economics and the other social sciences, they are not social sciences since they do not study human behavior.

## IV    Application and Discussion

1. Identify which of the following headlines represents a microeconomic topic and which is a macroeconomic topic.

| Topic | Micro | Macro |
|---|---|---|
| A. "U.S. Unemployment Rate Reaches Historic Lows" | | X |
| B. "General Motors Closes Auto Plant in St. Louis" | X | |
| C. "OPEC Action Results in a General Increase in Prices" | | X |
| D. "Companies Cut the Cost of Health Care for Employees" | X | |
| E. "Lawmakers Worry about the Possibility of a US Recession" | | X |
| F. "Colorado Rockies Make Outfielder Highest Paid Ballplayer" | X | |

Macroeconomics examines economic problems that influence the whole economy. The focus is on aggregate or total economic activity. Headlines A, C, and E reflect the overall health of the economy. Microeconomics explains the actions of smaller units. The focus is on the decision-making behavior of firms and households. Headlines B, D, and F reflect the actions of firms.

## Section 1.3 Economic Behavior

### I    Review

Economists assume that people act as if they were motivated by self-interest. Since people are also assumed to respond to changes in predictable ways, self-interest is a good predictor of behavior.
Self-interest motivates people to produce more and may also encourage benevolence. Pursuing self-interest is not the same as being selfish.
Choices will have both positive and negative consequences. Economists believe that it is rational for people to consider the consequences of their actions before they make a decision.

### II    True/False

1. False. Economists assume that people act out of self-interest and that they consider the consequences of their actions. If someone commits a crime, economists assume that the criminal decided that the expected benefits exceed the expected costs.
2. False. Economists are famous for their assumption that people are motivated by self-interest. A person's self-interest, however, may include concern for his family, community, and others.
3. False. Economists assume that individuals try to anticipate the likely consequences of their behavior or actions. This does not mean that individuals will always make right choices, but they at least thought about the possible consequences.
4. False. Economists assume that individuals act as if they are motivated by self-interest and respond in predictable ways to changing circumstances.

5. False. Self-interest can include benevolence. Self-interest is not the same as selfishness. Most people consider providing for their family part of their self-interest. If the health and welfare of other pople is important for our own happiness, self-interested actions may be those that allow us to do the most for others.

6. True. Economists believe that it is rational for a person to anticipate the likely consequences of their actions. We may not know the outcome of any action with certainty, but we consider the likely benefits and cost when making decisions. Chandler certainly doesn't behave in this rational way.

## III    Multiple Choice

1. The answer is D. Economists observe the behavior of large groups of people, like consumers in the United States, and make predictions about how they will respond to certain events, especially changes in economic incentives like prices.

2. The answer is C. Anyone who invites a bull into his china shop certainly seems oblivious to the consequences, although it is possible that Mr. Haviland either knows that "Tornado" is a pussycat or he wants to collect insurance. Economists, who assume that behavior is rational, would expect an unseen motive on Mr. Haviland's part.

3. The answer is D. As Adam Smith, the "father" of economics has stated, "It is not from the benevolence of the butcher, the baker, or the brewer that we expect our dinner, but from their regard to their own interest."

4. The answer is D. The new contract changes the rewards of Bobby's actions. His rewards are greater for completions, so he will change his behavior to increase the number of completions he makes by throwing short passes. He will continue to train because being in shape will help his performance. But the change in the circumstances of his contract will give him the incentive to choose short passes more often than either the run or long passes.

## IV    Application and Discussion

1. Of course, it is up to you to decide on this one. Economists, however, believe that their predictions gain accuracy if they assume that people act out of self-interest and usually don't use the terms "self-interest" and "selfishness" interchangeably. While some self-interested people cheat, self-interest can also lead to honesty. Most successful businesses find it to be in their interest to treat customers fairly. Businesses that have reputations as cheaters don't find many customers.

## Section 1.4 Economic Theory

## I    Review

A theory is an explanation that is supported by the facts of the real world. Economic theories are propositions used to explain and predict human behavior in different circumstances.

Economic theories cannot account for every event; to be useful theories must abstract or focus on only the essential factors.

A hypothesis is a prediction about how people will behave in certain economic circumstances and can be tested to see how well the prediction fits the facts.

Economists engage in empirical analysis to test hypotheses by seeing if they are consistent with the real world observations.

## II    True/False

1. False. An economic theory abstracts from the complexities of the real world to better understand economic behavior. We expect a good theory to explain and predict well, not provide a complete description of the world.

2. True. Economic theories are statements about patterns of human behavior that are expected to take place under certain circumstances. Good theories should explain and predict well. In a situation, the idea that incentives matter can be used to predict what will happen when incentives change in a certain way.

3. False. A hypothesis is a testable proposal that makes a prediction about behavior in response to certain changed conditions. While this statement predicts behavior, it is not testable since we can't live on Mars.

4.  True. A hypothesis is a testable proposal about behavior. A hypothesis can only be stated as a theory if it has been tested against the facts of the real world and shown to be a good predictor of behavior. A hypothesis that is not supported by the facts sends the economist "back to the drawing board" to find a new explanation.

5.  False. Hypotheses are testable proposals that make a prediction about behavior. A hypothesis is not a theory; a hypothesis must be tested by comparing its predictions to the real behavior. Following an untested story about stock market behavior is a risky strategy.

III    Multiple Choice

1.  The answer is B. Making a hypothesis about behavior is the first step in developing a theory. A hypothesis is a testable proposal that makes a prediction about behavior in response to changes. Once a hypothesis can be shown to predict what actually happened, it can be restated as an economic theory.

2.  The answer is C. A good theory should help us explain and predict human behavior. Marion's proposition is a good theory if it can be shown to explain the facts of the real world and is useful in predicting the way people behave under different circumstances.

3.  The answer is D. Economic theories cannot realistically include every event that has ever occurred. To learn anything about the real world we have to abstract from its complexities. We often decide to set aside information and isolate only the important relationships to learn more about the world. Trying to incorporate too much information will simply confuse us.

4.  The answer is D. The scientific method starts with a hypothesis, a testable proposal that makes a prediction about behavior. This hypothesis is tested against the facts; economists ask whether the prediction of the hypothesis fit the historic facts. If the facts support the hypothesis, the hypothesis can be restated as a theory. If they facts don't support the hypothesis, the economist needs to develop a new hypothesis.

IV    Application and Discussion

1.  A hypothesis should be simple because we need to abstract from the real world's complexity. It should be a proposal that makes some type of prediction. Finally, a hypothesis should be testable. Your hypothesis might be generated from a number of sources such as your reading, your observations of the world, or your explorations of similar or related issues. Examples of hypotheses include "Women's wages are lower because they work fewer hours per week" or "Women have lower wages because they have on average less education that men."

2.  The data support the second hypothesis better than the first. The number of days with polluted air generally increases with the population. The five cities with the most days "with polluted air" are large places. The first hypothesis does not seem to be supported by the data. El Paso, Texas, was the hottest place on our list and had relatively few polluted days. The causes of air pollution are complex and many things affect the level of pollution in a city. In our limited world of seven cities, the second hypothesis is supported by the facts, and we could make a theoretical statement that air pollution will increase in general as population increases.

Section 1.5 Problems to Avoid in Scientific Thinking

I    Review

The Latin expression for "let everything else be equal" is _ceteris paribus_.

Without a theory of causation, scientists cannot understand the complexity that occurs in the real world.

In seeking to find causes for events, people sometimes mistake correlation for causation.

If someone observes that new car sales and auto accidents rise at the same time and concludes that new car sales cause auto accidents, they are mistaking correlation for causation.

When someone assumes that what is true of an individual is also true of a group, they are committing the fallacy of <u>composition</u>.

## II    True/False

1.  False. This phrase, often-used by economists, means "holding other things equal" or "let everything else be equal."

2.  True. Scientists in laboratories do this all the time. For economists dealing with human behavior in a dynamic world where many variables change all the time, this is a big problem.

3.  False. Two things may occur together, without one necessarily causing the other. Just because MTV was introduced in 1982 doesn't mean it caused the 1982 recession or vice versa.

4.  True. An individual may be able to attract attention by painting their house with black and pink stripes, but if everyone in the subdivision does it, no one attracts special attention.

## III    Multiple Choice

1.  The answer is B. The scientist would hold all the variables except alcohol consumption constant in order to isolate the effect of the alcohol on longevity.

2.  The answer is C. Just because tall people play basketball doesn't mean that playing basketball causes people to become taller.

3.  The answer is A. Just because these two phenomena are associated there is no reason to expect a causal relationship

4.  The answer is D. What is true for one team is not necessarily good for the group. One team can gain a competitive advantage b y p aying m ore a nd h iring b etter p layers; m aybe t hey can win the World Series. But if all other teams expand their payrolls to compete, they all simply end up with higher labor costs. The only parties who are better off are the players!

## IV    Application and Discussion

1.  This is a case of mistaking correlation for causality. People in Wisconsin tended to live long lives and since cancer is a disease of middle and old age, it was a more frequent cause of death in Wisconsin than in other states. An area low in cancer deaths is likely to be an area of poor health where inhabitants die young. (Cited in Martin Gardner, *Fads and Fallacies in the Name of Science,* Dover Publications, 1957, p. 341.)

Section 1.6 Positive and Normative Analysis

I    Review

When economists study h uman b ehavior t hey e mphasize h ow p eople b ehave n ot h ow t hey s hould b ehave. T his o bjective approach is called <u>positive</u> analysis.

When economists comment on the desirability of particular actions they are making <u>normative</u> statements. Normative statements involve judgements about what <u>ought</u> to happen.

It is especially important to be able to <u>distinguish</u> between normative and positive analysis when policy considerations contain both. The majority of <u>disagreements</u> among economists involve normative issues.

A second important reason economists disagree is disagreement on the <u>validity</u> of the economic <u>theories</u> in a particular policy application.

# ANSWER KEY

1.  False. This is a positive statement. It is a proposition about how people will behave and it can be tested. A normative statement might be "The tax on cigarettes should be increased because people should smoke less." This describes an opinion about how people ought to behave.

2.  True. Economists have opinions and make judgments. Normative statements reflect their opinions about economic policy.

3.  False. As in all sciences, economists often disagree about economic policy matters. There are two main reasons for this disagreement. Differences may be a matter of opinion or values, economists may disagree about what ought to happen. Economists may also disagree about the legitimacy of specific theoretical explanations of behavior that are important for a policy question.

4.  True. The first statement is a positive statement while the second is a normative statement. We expect more disagreement over matters of opinion or normative statements.

5.  False. Economists are scientists seeking the truth about the way people behave. As scientists, economists try to promote an objective, value-free approach to the study of economic behavior. When an econ professor states her opinions, she is not teaching economics.

## III    Multiple Choice

1.  The answer is A. The value of preserving small farms is a matter of opinion, a normative statement. The other statements are propositions about how the world works that can be tested, positive statements.

2.  The answer is B. You could test this hypothesis against the facts of the world by comparing the IQs of people who watch different amounts of television.

3.  The answer is C. Positive analysis of proposed policy change will provide decision makers with an understanding of the effects associated with a policy change. Normative statements reflect the weights and values the speaker gives to these changes. These values reflect one person's opinions and will differ across people.

4.  The answer is D. Economists, like all scientists, disagree over policy issues and theories. The text offers two general reasons economists disagree. Difference in values or beliefs (normative issues) is the most important reason for disagreement. Disagreement over the validity of particular theories is also important.

## IV    Application and Discussion

1.  This is a normative statement because it is a matter of opinion. Unless you held this opinion or respected the speaker, this normative statement would not cause you to support a zero tolerance standard for air pollution. To add to the debate positive statements about the effect of such standards could be tested; these statements should most importantly reflect the changes in the costs and benefits of adopting the more extreme standards. For example, "imposing zero pollution standards will significantly reduce the industrial output of the U.S. economy" and "the reduction in health problems resulting from the imposition of zero pollution standards will provide the benefits of significant reduction in health care costs."

# CHAPTER 2 THE ECONOMIC WAY OF THINKING

Section 2.1 Idea 1: Scarcity

I        Review

Scarcity is the problem that exists because we have limited resources and unlimited wants for goods and services.

The physical and mental labor expended by people in the production of goods and services is called labor.

Natural resources like trees, water and minerals, that are used in production are classified as land resources.

Resources like tools, office buildings, and factories are called capital, while people who make the risky decisions about what goods to produce and how to produce them are called entrepreneurs.

Items that we value or desire are called goods, while intangible acts for which people are willing to pay are called services.

Because no one can have all the goods and services they desire, everyone, even the very rich, faces the common problem of scarcity.

Overtime the resources available to individuals and societies may increase, but scarcity will not be eliminated because our wants will continue to increase.

II       True/False

1.  False. A nation's wealth increases as its resources increase but new goods and services are also introduced. As a nation grows richer, both wants and resources increase leaving us with the problem of scarcity.

2.  False. Just like nations, individuals find that as their resources increase so do their wants. Wealth provides no cure for the condition of scarcity.

3.  True. The problem of rising expectations means that people can always think of more and more ways to use any increase in resources produced by new technology.

4.  False. Harriet must choose among many worthy charities when she gives away her riches. She faces a scarcity problem because there are many more deserving activities than she could support.

III      Multiple Choice

1.  The answer is D. Whenever a person has to make a choice about the use of resources, they face the problem of scarcity.

2.  The answer is C. Invention and innovation would reduce the problem of scarcity if it only increased the goods and services our resources could produce, but it also increases our wants by introducing new goods and services. As long as wants exceed the resources available to satisfy them, the problem of scarcity exists.

3.  The answer is A. The reduction in travel cost caused by the jet introduced the possibility of worldwide travel to visit interesting and beautiful places.

4.  The answer is A. As societies get more resources, they find more wants. Historically, solving pollution problems and preserving the environment become more important as country's income rises. This is another example of wants staying ahead of resources.

5.  The answer is C. Tangible goods are things we can see, hold, taste, or smell. Automobiles, bouquets of flowers and bags of potato chips are tangible goods. A haircut is a service like medical care and legal services.

IV      Application and Discussion

# ANSWER KEY

1. Being poor means that you have access to few resources, which limits the goods and services you consume. Scarcity means you don't have enough resources to do everything you want to do, so you have to make choices. Everyone experiences scarcity because we can always think of more things that we want than we can produce with our resources.

2. The car freed Americans to travel and helped to create the tourism business. New wants included motels, resorts, and theme parks. The increased importance of auto and truck transportation also created the desire for more and better roads and highways. Finally the car allowed people to live farther from where they worked; people wanted more land and newer houses.

Section 2.2 Idea 2: Opportunity Cost

I    Review

Economics is the study of the <u>choices</u> we make among our <u>unlimited</u> wants and desires and our <u>limited</u> resources.

The highest, or best, foregone opportunity resulting from a decision is called the <u>opportunity</u> cost of that decision. The expression "There's no such thing as a free <u>lunch</u>," is often used to express the relationship between scarcity and opportunity cost.

II    True/False

1. True. The problem of scarcity requires us to choose which wants we should satisfy with our limited resources.

2. True. The opportunity cost of attending college includes foregone income plus other things like the cost of books and tuition.

3. False. The opportunity cost of an action includes the time, money, and other things that are given up because of that action.

4. False. Because taxpayers give up money they could have used to buy other goods and services in order to pay for teachers salaries, books, and school construction, public education is not free. The resources used to provide public education have opportunity costs.

5. True. Even though the price is the same, one person may have to give up more than the other in order to eat the dinner. For example, one person's time may be worth more than the other's, or one person may value the things she has to give up in order to buy the dinner more highly than the other.

III    Multiple Choice

1. The answer is A. Economics is the study of how people and societies choose to allocate scarce resources to satisfy unlimited wants.

2. The answer is B. The opportunity cost of an action is the value of the highest valued alternative that is foregone.

3. The answer is C. The opportunity cost includes everything you give up to train—not just the cost of equipment, but the value of everything else sacrificed for the training like going to the movies, sleeping, etc.

4. The answer is D. In other words, scarcity necessitates giving up one thing to have another.

IV    Application and Discussion

1. Since Sarah's time is probably worth more during school (it would cost part of her salary), the opportunity cost of the trip is higher in February than in July.

2. No. First of all, McDonald's uses scarce resources to produce the burger, so it's not "free" to them. Secondly, if people value their time at all, ten minutes standing in line to get the burger carries an opportunity cost equal to whatever else they could have done with the ten minutes. Also included is the opportunity cost of driving to McDonald's to get the "free" Big Mac.

269

# ANSWER KEY

## Section 2.3 Idea 3: Marginal Thinking

### I    Review

People rarely make "all or nothing" choices. Most choices involve changes from the status quo or <u>marginal</u> changes.

The positive results of these additional changes are called marginal <u>benefits</u> and the negative results are marginal <u>costs</u>.

When people make choices for which the expected marginal benefits exceed the marginal costs of the change, they are following the rule of <u>rational</u> choice.

The benefits and costs of many choices occur in the future. We can't know future outcomes for certain because the world is <u>uncertain</u>. People make choices they can only compare what they think is likely to happen, so they compare the <u>expected</u> marginal benefits and costs.

### II    True/False

1.  False. Marginal choices concern decisions that focus on additional changes. The marginal choice would be whether to go to Tuscaloosa one more time.

2.  True. The rule of rational choice states that people act rationally when they make decisions for which the marginal benefits are greater than the marginal costs.

3.  True. The expected cost of robbery depends on the penalty and the chance of being caught. By increasing the police patrols the city will increase the chance robbers will be caught.

4.  False. Increasing wilderness areas has real benefits but it also has costs. The costs include loss of land for housing and farms. At some point the marginal benefits of additional wilderness will be less than the marginal costs.

### III    Multiple Choice

1.  The answer is C. Following the rule of rational choice, you compare the marginal benefits and costs of increasing your study time. The high benefits associated with doing well on this exam increase the likelihood of studying more for this exam. The low marginal benefits in A probably don't encourage increased study time; marginal costs increase in B; and the information in D doesn't effect either benefits or costs on the margin.

2.  The answer is D. Marginal thinking deals with making relatively small changes to the status quo. Becoming a vegetarian is an all or nothing type of choice. Increasing the amount of vegetables you eat or reducing the amount of meat are marginal decisions.

3.  The answer is A. Your friend will make jaywalking decisions by comparing the expected benefits and costs each time she has the opportunity. As her time becomes more valuable, the benefits of saving time crossing the street will increase, causing her to jaywalk more often. Answers B, C, and D increase the expected marginal costs of jaywalking.

4.  The answer is C. The price of Bill's airline ticket is certain. Bill is uncertain about the weather, hotel neighbors, and his health. All of these will affect the benefits he receives from his trip.

5.  The answer is D.  We should do something to make the air cleaner only if the expected marginal benefits of doing so are greater than the expected marginal costs.

### IV    Application and Discussion

1.  The benefits of going to the movie include the happiness you receive from being entertained and the social interaction with friends. These are uncertain because they depend on the quality of the move and your companionship. Costs include the price of the movie ticket and the value of the time you give up to go to the movie. Uncertainty also affects your costs since you do not know for certain what you would get out of your alternative use of your time.

2. As long as a person follows the rule of rational choice, they will always make decisions were they expect to gain more in benefits than they have to give up in costs. They will always be better off in this case. If a person's expectations about benefits or costs are wrong, their decisions may make them worse off.

## Section 2.4 Idea 4: Incentives Matter

### I        Review

According to economists, rational people react to changes in expected marginal <u>costs</u> and expected marginal <u>benefits</u>. If a rational person engages in criminal activity the perceived benefits of criminal activity must be greater than the perceived <u>costs</u>.

Economics expect that harsher penalties for criminal activity will <u>reduce</u> the amount of crime.

Positive incentives are things that either <u>increase</u> benefits or reduce costs.

Negative incentives are things that <u>reduce</u> benefits or increase costs.

Since economists believe that people respond to incentives they would predict that couples would choose to have <u>fewer</u> children if the government imposed a tax on each baby born.

Economics would predict a(n) <u>decrease</u> in the amount of cheating that takes place in schools if penalties on cheating were harsher.

### II       True/False

1. True. That people respond in predictable ways to changes in incentives is one of the basic postulates of economics.

2. False. Economists believe that people commit crimes because they view the benefits of criminal activity to be greater than the costs.

3. False. A tax on bicycles would be an example of a negative incentive, since it would increase the costs of owning a bike.

4. False. A tax deduction increases the benefit of having a child and is thus a positive incentive.

5. True. Since people respond to incentives, and the death penalty increases the likely costs of drug trafficking, the frequency of this activity is reduced by the harsh penalty.

6. False. According to the survey cited in the text, 94 percent of students who cheat never get caught.

7. True. The level at which a driver is legally drunk in the United States is at 0.08 percent alcohol, while in Norway the limit is 0.05 percent.

### III      Multiple Choice

1. The answer is C. More generous unemployment benefits reduce the cost of remaining unemployed and are therefore a positive incentive for people to remain unemployed longer.

2. The answer is C. The offer of a free laptop is a positive incentive since it increases the benefits of doing well on the exam. All the other examples are negative incentives.

3. The answer is B. A fine is negative incentive since it increases the cost of a certain behavior. The other examples are positive incentives.

4. The answer is D. The tax probably provides more anti-smoking incentive than the other alternatives. Studies by economists support the notion that taxes that make cigarettes more expensive result in less teen smoking.

# ANSWER KEY

1. An organ market that provided cash rewards would likely increase the supply of available organs, especially if people from poor countries were allowed to participate. It would also allow people in dire need of a particular organ to go into the market and purchase it rather than put their name on a waiting list. Many people, however, feel that a person's body parts have a special status and should not be offered for sale. Some people worry that only the rich would get organs in a market while others fear that a market would result in people being murdered for their valuable organs. They prefer the current system where only donated organs are accepted, and are allocated by physicians according to need.

## Section 2.5 Idea 5: Specialization and Trade

### I    Review

When people <u>specialize</u> they dedicate their resources to one primary activity.

Specialization allows people to make the most out of their limited resources by lowering the <u>opportunity</u> cost of producing goods and services. When a person, region, or country can produce a good at a lower opportunity costs they have a <u>comparative</u> advantage in the production of it.

When we specialize we rely on others to produce most of the goods and services we consume, so <u>trade</u> is important for specialization to succeed.

Trade allows people, regions, and countries to increase their <u>wealth</u> by concentrating on the production of goods and services at which they are relatively better.

### II    True/False

1. False. In a trading situation, the country with the lowest opportunity costs has the comparative advantage.

2. False. While Stan can paint the house in less time than the average painter can, the value of his time is high. Stan's opportunity cost of painting the house is higher than painters who take longer, because he could earn more using the time in medicine.

3. False. We all specialize to some extent. Teachers, mechanics, farmers, and lawyers all concentrate on one job and rely on others to provide the goods and services we want.

4. True. Labor can be trained on very specific jobs. Capital equipment can be design for specialized functions. Productivity is increased because both labor and capital is better at performing these specialized tasks.

5. True. Trade allows countries to specialize in the goods and services they are relatively best at producing. If countries specialize and produce the goods and services for which they have they lowest opportunity cost, more goods and services can be produced from the countries' resources.

6. False. It is relatively more costly to grow coffee in the United States than in Brazil. We would use more resources to produce coffee. We are better off using United States resources in more productive activities and trading with Brazil.

### III    Multiple Choice

1. The answer is C. Individuals, regions, and countries choose to specialize in that activity they have the lowest opportunity cost in. The Candlestick maker gives up less or has the lowest cost by giving up careers as a Butcher or Baker than she would not being a Candlestick maker.

2. The answer is B. Axel has a comparative advantage in auto mechanics. Axel's opportunity cost of cutting the lawn is higher than it is for the person he hires.

3. The answer is D. Firms gain through the specialization of jobs because the cost of producing falls when workers learn their jobs better, spend less time starting and stopping to change tasks, and work in jobs they are best at. Specialization does not allow workers to learn all of the jobs in the factory.

4. The answer is A. Trade allows countries to specialize in the production of the goods and services in which they have a comparative advantage. When all countries shift production to the goods for which they have the lowest opportunity cost, the same resources will produce more goods and services.

5. The answer is D. Specialization is decided by opportunity costs, not the absolute cost of the materials used to produce the good. While the South might have used fewer resources to grow food than the West, the real cost would have been the valuable lost cotton production.

6. The answer is B. Sergei has a comparative advantage in playing hockey. While he might take less time to sew clothes, the value of his time is great. The cost to Sergei is greater than if he were to buy his clothes from someone else.

## IV    Application and Discussion

1. Of course answers to this question will vary. If you live in Nebraska, your answer might be corn; in Alaska, it might be oil and fish; in Hawaii, it might be tourism or macadamia nuts.

2. Denying trade possibilities also eliminates the possibility of specialization. In autarky, a country must produce everything it consumes. Scarce resources will be wasted producing goods with a higher opportunity costs. Trading would allow the country to produce more with the same resources.

3. The opportunity cost of growing soybeans is the lost value because Fran can't grow corn for $60. The opportunity cost of growing corn is the lost opportunity to grow and sell soybeans, which equals $75. Fran should specialize in soybeans, which is the crop with the lowest opportunity cost. For each acre of corn Fran converts to soybeans, she will gain $15.

## Section 2.6 Idea 6: Market Prices Coordinate Economic Activity

### I    Review

In a market economy most of the resources are owned by <u>private</u> individuals and firms.

The <u>market</u> system provides a way for millions of producers and consumers to allocate <u>scarce</u> resources. Individuals indicate their wants and desires through their <u>actions</u> and inactions in the marketplace. Market <u>prices</u> serve as the language of the market.

Market prices communicate important <u>information</u> to buyers and sellers. This communication results in a shifting of resources from uses that are less valued to those that are <u>more</u> valued.

Government policies that set prices above or below what they would be in a free market are called price <u>controls</u>.

When the market mechanism fails to allocate resources efficiently it is called market <u>failure</u>. For example, lack of competition in a market can lead to <u>higher</u> prices and <u>reduced</u> product quality.

A question of special concern is whether or not the market economy provides a <u>fair</u> distribution of income.

### II    True/False

1. False. In a market economy most of the resources are owned by private parties.

2. False. Physical violence has been used since the beginning of time to gain control of scarce resources.

3. True. Since the collapse of the Soviet Union, which relied on government control to allocate resources, the market has emerged as the predominant form of economic organization.

# ANSWER KEY

4. False. Market prices communicate information about the relative value of products to both buyers and sellers.

5. False. Price controls interrupt communication between buyer and sellers.

6. True. Since minimum wage laws raise wages above market levels, they discourage employers from hiring unskilled teens, while at the same time increasing the number of teens looking for work.

7. True. Pollution and lack of competition are examples of market failure.

## III    Multiple Choice

1. The answer is D. Sexton and other economists liken the signals that prices send to consumers and suppliers to language.

2. The answer is C. An increase in prices means that oranges have become more scarce and therefore more valuable than before.

3. The answer is A. As the book says, price controls strip the market price of its meaning for consumers and suppliers. Using the language metaphor, market prices tell the truth, while price controls lie.

4. The answer is C. As the book says, minimum wage laws have two effects on teenage employment. The higher wage (1) makes teens want to work more, but (2) discourages employers from hiring.

5. The answer is D. Air pollution, which imposes costs on others not connected with producing or consuming a particular good, is a symptom of market failure.

## IV    Application and Discussion

1. A)  People who see an energetic and loveable Jack Russell Terrier in a popular TV series want Jack Russell Terriers as pets.

   Price of Jack Russell Terriers __X__ Rises _____ Falls

   B)       Aging retirees flock to Tampa, Florida to live.

   Price of housing in Tampa    __X__ Rises _____ Falls

   C)  Weather-related crop failures in Colombia and Costa Rica reduce coffee supplies.

   Price of Coffee              __X__ Rises _____ Falls

   D)  Sugar cane fields in Hawaii and Louisiana are replaced with housing.

   Price of sugar              __X__ Rises _____ Falls

   E)  More and more students graduate from U.S. medical schools.

   Wages of U.S. doctors        _____ Rises __X__ Falls

   F)  Americans are driving more and they are driving bigger, gas-guzzling cars like sports utility vehicles.

   Price of gasoline           __X__ Rises _____ Falls

2. A, B, and C would cause increases in the value and prices of potatoes. A reduction in the prices of potato substitutes would make them more attractive and reduce the value and price of potatoes.

# CHAPTER 3 SCARCITY, TRADE-OFFS, AND ECONOMIC GROWTH

Section 3.1 The Three Economic Questions Every Society Faces

I    Review

Scarcity forces all societies from the richest to the poorest to answer three fundamental questions.

1) <u>What</u> do we produce?

2) <u>How</u> do we produce these goods and services?

3) For <u>whom</u> do we produce the goods and services?

In market economies, individuals control the production decisions by "voting" with their <u>dollars</u> for the goods and services they want. This consumer control is called consumer <u>sovereignty</u>.

Societies organize in two major ways to answer these economic questions. Economies are called <u>command</u> economies when government officials make decisions in a highly centralized system.

When many individual producers and consumers make economic decisions in a decentralized manner the economy is a <u>market</u> economy.

Since there are several ways to produce any good or service, all economies must decide <u>how</u> to produce the goods and services they want. If an economy uses lots of labor to produce goods and services, economists would say production is <u>labor</u> intensive.

Countries tend to use production processes that conserve its relatively <u>scarce</u> resources and use more of their relatively <u>abundant</u> resources.

"Who gets what?" is an economic questions that <u>scarcity</u> forces all societies to answer. This question is about the <u>distribution</u> of output.

In a market economy, the amount of output any one person can secure depends on their <u>income</u>, which depends on the amount and quality of scarce <u>resources</u> they control.

II    True/False

1.  False. The decision our society makes about what goods and services to produce is difficult to make because we have to choose among a wide variety of known wants. We have to choose because our resources are scarce.

2.  False. In a market economy, consumers decide what goods and services are produced by voting with their dollars. If a manufacturer produces a good that no one wants, they will not be rewarded for producing it, and so will stop its production. The power of consumers to decide what is produced in a market economy is called consumer sovereignty.

3.  True. In high wage countries, capital-intensive production methods tend to be used in order to economize on relatively expensive labor resources.

4.  False. Because of scarcity there will not be enough goods and services to go around, so societies need to find a way to decide who gets the goods and services that are produced.

5.  False. LeBron James has a very high income. The typical college student has a low income. James can consume more because his higher income allows him to buy more of the goods and services produced each year.

---

### III    Multiple Choice

1. The answer is A. Economic decisions in a command economy are made by government officials in a central planning organization. Individual consumers and producers make economic decisions in a market economy. As economies go through the transition from command to market, we would expect the decisions of individual consumers and producers to replace those made by officials of central government organizations.

2. The answer is A. In a market economy, production decisions are controlled by the consumer. Consumer sovereignty is the concept that consumers' decisions about how to spend their money determine what goods and services are produced. Consumers are already getting what they think is best for them. Barry's list would impose a command economy on consumers.

3. The answer is C. A fishing boat is an example of a man-made resource that is used to produce final goods.

4. The answer is B. For every good and service we produce, there is more than one method of production. We can use capital intensive or labor-intensive production techniques. For example, we can build houses out of wood or brick with lots of labor or lots of machines. We can build sprawling homes on large plots of land or three story homes on less land.

5. The answer is D. In a market economy, a person's claim on the economy's goods and services depends on their income. The greater a person's income, the more goods and services they can consume.

### IV    Application and Discussion

1. Hollywood will probably make more movies like *Titanic* because of consumer sovereignty. Consumers, "voting" with their dollars have shown they want movies like *Titanic*. Since movie studios are in the business to make money, not simply movies, they will produce what the consumers want, not what the critics like.

2. The relevant question here is how to produce household goods and services like meals and laundry services. Since in most homes women do most of the housework, an increase in their earnings and job opportunities outside the home raises the opportunity cost of their time. Such an increase in the cost of labor would likely cause households to economize on labor and substitute capital, in the form of household appliances.

Section 3.2 The Circular Flow Model

---

### I     REVIEW

Households make payments to firms for goods and services in the product market. Money flows to the firms in exchange for the goods and services that flow to households.

Firms buy inputs from households in the factor market. Firms use households' labor, land, capital, and entrepreneurship to produce goods and services.

Money flows from the firms to the households as compensation for the use of these inputs. The households receive payments in the form of wages, rent, interest, and profit.

The simple circular flow model illustrates the continuous flow of payments, income, inputs, and goods and services between households and firms. This model shows how product and factor markets are interrelated.

## II TRUE/FALSE

1. False. Money moves in the opposite direction as the flow of goods and services. Money is a payment for these products. Money is exchanged for goods and services in the product market.

2. True. The factor market is where households sell the resources they own to firms for wages, interest, rent, and profits.

3. True. The money paid by firms in exchange for the use of the households' resources is the households' money income.

## III Multiple Choice

1. The answer is B. The money household receives as income from firms is used to buy the goods and services produced by the firms. In the circular flow model the money flows from firms to households to firms in the form of spending in the product and factor markets.

2. The answer is B. Households buy goods and services in the product market. Households spend their income in the product market. This spending becomes the revenue of the firms selling the products.

3. The answer is C. Wages, interest, rent, and profit are forms of payment households receive from firms for the use of their labor, land, capital and entrepreneurship.

## IV. APPLICATION AND DISCUSSION

Identify the appropriate market where each of the following transactions takes place by placing an X in the appropriate box.

| Transaction | Factor Market | Product Market |
|---|---|---|
| Billy buys a sofa from Home Time Furniture for his new home. | | X |
| Home Time Furniture pays its manager her weekly salary. | X | |
| The manager buys dinner at Billy's Café. | | X |
| After he pays all of his employees their wages and pays his other bills, the owner of Billy's Café takes his profit. | X | |

Furniture is a good purchased in the product market from firms. Labor is a resource that households sell to firms in the factor market. Restaurant food is a good purchased by consumers in the product market. Finally, Billy's entrepreneurial resource is paid a profit, which is the amount left over after all his other costs have been paid. This takes place in the factor market. These few transactions trace the circular flow of money between households and firms in the factor and product markets.

## Section 3.3 The Production Possibilities Curve

### I Review

The problem of making choices regarding what to produce and in what quantities can be illustrated with a production possibilities curve.

# ANSWER KEY

Most economies have resources that are <u>idle</u> for at least some period of time.

Efficiency requires society to use its resources to the fullest extent and get the <u>greatest</u> output from its scarce resources.

If an economy is operating at a point off and below its production possibilities curve, it means that resources are not being utilized <u>efficiently</u>.

When a production possibilities curve is bowed outward from the origin it is because of the law of <u>increasing</u> opportunity cost.

## II    True/False

1.  False. It represents the potential total output combinations of two goods for an economy with given amounts of land, labor, capital, and entrepreneurship.

2.  True. Since a production possibilities curve represents the total output combinations of two goods for an economy, using one to represent South Korea's total output combinations of rice and soybeans would be appropriate.

3.  True. All resources are not alike. A good fisherman may be a lousy boat builder.

4.  False. Factories are capital resources. Idle factories represent "unemployed" capital.

5.  True. Efficiency requires society to use its resources to the fullest extent possible.

## III    Multiple Choice

1.  The answer is A. Point A represents 500 million bushels of rice, as shown on the vertical axis, and 350 million bushels of soybeans, as shown on the horizontal axis.

2.  The answer is A. Point A represents an economy producing bananas but no coffee.

3.  The answer is D. At point E the economy is off its production possibilities curve and operating at less than full potential.

4.  The answer is C. As the economy moves from A to D, the quantity of bananas that must be given up in order to get another unit of coffee increases.

5.  The answer is B. When resources are unemployed they can't be used to produce goods and services.

6.  The answer is D. All of the concepts, except economic growth, are illustrated by the production possibilities curve. Scarcity requires that we choose how to allocate scarce resources between the production of two goods; opportunity cost is shown by the fact that we have to give up guns in order to have more butter, and increasing opportunity costs is shown as the economy gets less butter each time it gives up an equal number of guns. Economic growth, a long-term increase in total output, is not illustrated.

## IV    Application and Discussion

1.  Upon entry into the war, the United States would move from point A toward the production of military goods, as in the movement to point B. After the war the economy moves back to point A. [Exh0301ans]

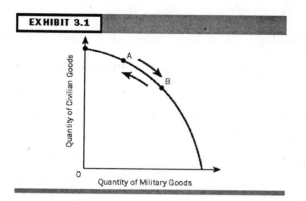

**EXHIBIT 3.1**

2.  A.  Unemployed Labor

    B.  Unemployed Capital

    C.  Unemployed Labor

    D.  Unemployed Land

3.  As you learned in Chapter 1, people respond to incentives. If government policies do not provide proper incentives to entrepreneurs so they can make profits and control their property, they may well sit on the sidelines and become idle.

## Section 3.4 Economic Growth and the Production Possibilities Curve

I    Review

A country's economic growth depends on the <u>sacrifices</u> made today. To grow we have to give up <u>consumer</u> goods and produce more <u>capital</u> goods.

An increase in an economy's capital stock will allow it to increase its future <u>productive</u> capacity and consume more in the future. The effect of the increase in a country's capital stock is represented by a(n) <u>outward</u> shift in its production possibilities curve.

Investment can be more than building new physical capital stock. Upgrading the <u>skills</u> and <u>knowledge</u> of a country's workforce has a similar effect on economic growth.

While today's sacrifices allow a country to produce more in the future, growth will not eliminate scarcity. Even with more resources countries must still make <u>choices</u> among the ways these resources will be used.

II    True/False

1.  False. Countries choose to grow. Economic growth requires that countries make sacrifices today to increase their future productive capacity. Economic growth requires that countries give up consumption goods today in order to increase their production of capital goods.

2.  False. While the expansion of a country's productive capacity provides benefits, economic growth has costs. The costs of economic growth are the current sacrifices necessary for growth. The essential question countries must ask is whether the increased consumption allowed by economic growth is worth the current sacrifices. Pursuit of economic growth is only good for a country if the benefits are greater than the costs.

# ANSWER KEY

3. False. While happy workers may be important to a country's economic performance, growth requires that sacrifices be made. A society must produce fewer consumer goods than possible in order to produce more capital goods. Capital goods are a resource used to produce other goods and services. To increase capital and its ability to produce more goods and services in the future, a country must sacrifice some consumption today.

4. True. The production possibilities curve represents the possible bundles of goods and services a country can produce with its available resources. As the resources available to the country increase or technological progress provides better ways of using these resources, the possible bundles of goods and services expands. This expansion is represented by a rightward shift in the production possibilities curve.

5. False. Scarcity is not a problem of poverty. Affluent societies also face the problem of scarcity. As long as there are a number of uses for any resource, people will have to make choices. Scarcity exists as long as you have to give up one thing to get more of something else.

## III    Multiple Choice

1. The answer is C. Investment in human capital includes all investments that improve the productivity of the population. Upgrading skills and knowledge through training and education are human capital investments. Investment in improving the health of the population can also be a human capital investment if it increases the average productivity of the population. Chile has invested in capital goods.

2. The answer is B. To expand its ability to produce goods and services, a country must increase the resources it has available. In order to increase a country's capital stock, the country must reduce its production of consumption goods unless it receives a gift of capital from another country. Many foreign aid programs of the United States and other rich nations transfer capital goods to less developed countries.

3. The answer is C. Growth occurs when the economy is able to produce more. Growth may result because the economy is more efficient (A to C) or because of new technologies or the addition of more resources (C to D and B to D). Movements along the production possibilities curve (C to B) represent a change in the way resources are used but not an expansion of productive capacity.

## IV    Application and Discussion

1.      Economic growth depends on a country's willingness to sacrifice current consumption and invest in capital goods or in human capital. Expanding the country's capital stock or improving the quality of its labor force allows it to produce more goods and services. Economic growth occurs when a country expands its productive capacity. A country will fail to grow if it chooses not to sacrifice because it cares a lot about current consumption (C) or if its sacrificed consumption is spent in other countries (A) and on goods other than capital goods (E). A country may also have such a low income that the sacrifices of giving up consumption are too great (B). Growth will also be limited if a country does not invest in human capital                                                                                                                                          (D).

# CHAPTER 4 SUPPLY AND DEMAND

## Section 4.1 Markets

### I    Review

A <u>market</u> is the process of buyers and sellers exchanging goods.

The term "market" is hard to define because an incredible variety of <u>exchange</u> arrangements exist in the world.

For some goods, like housing and cement, markets are numerous but <u>geographically</u> limited. For other goods, like gold and automobiles, markets are <u>global</u>.

The <u>buyers</u> determine the demand side of the market, while <u>sellers</u> determine the supply side.

A <u>competitive</u> market is one characterized by lots of buyers and sellers and in which no single buyer or seller can influence the market price.

### II    True/False

1. True. A bookstore, like any retail establishment, is a place where buyers and sellers come together to trade.

2. True. The doctor's office is a place where sellers of medical services (doctors and nurses) meet buyers of medical services (patients).

3. False.  A market, as stated in the book is "the process of buyers and sellers exchanging goods and services." eBay, for example, isn't a place, but it helps bring buyers and sellers together.

4. False. Fans are consumers of baseball services.  They are on the demand side of the market.  The sellers of baseball, the teams, players, and TV and radio stations, etc. are on the supply side of the market.

### III    Multiple Choice

1. The answer is C. A factory is a place where goods are produced, whereas a market is a place where buyers and sellers come together.

2. The answer is A. As the text says, when transportation costs are high relative to the selling price, as in the case of concrete, markets are numerous and geographically isolated. Goods will be produced close to the point of sale.

3. The answer is C. The market for autos is global. Cars made in the United States (or Japan or Germany or anywhere else for that matter) are sold all over the world.

### IV    Application and Discussion

1. The market is global. Manufacturers sell to dealers throughout the world. Transport costs are low relative to the costs of a laptop computer. Middlepeople make information about prices and quality easily available.

## Section 4.2 Demand

### I    Review

According to the law of demand, other things being equal, the quantity of a good or service demanded goes up when its price goes <u>down</u>.  The primary reason for the inverse relationship between price and quantity demanded is the substitution effect.

# ANSWER KEY

A(n) <u>individual</u> demand curve is a graphical representation of the relationship between the price of a good and the <u>quantity</u> demanded. The horizontal summing of the demand curves of all the buyers in the market is called the <u>market</u> demand curve.

## II    True/False

1. False. According to the law of demand, price and quantity demanded move in opposite directions.

2. True. The relationship described by the law of demand is an inverse, or negative, relationship. As price goes down, consumption goes up.

3. False. As the book points out, demand is an actual willingness to pay.

4. False. As the book points out, "need" is a fuzzy concept that is a poor guide to analyzing behavior.

5. False. An individual's demand schedule shows the amounts that a person will actually be willing to buy at various prices.

6. True. A demand curve shows graphically the various amounts that someone will buy at various prices.

7. True. As it says in the text, the market demand curve is created by summing horizontally the individual demand curves.

## III    Multiple Choice

1. The answer is B. The law of demand describes an inverse relationship between price and quantity demanded; as one goes up, the other goes down.

2. The answer is C. The relationship is inverse because price and quantity move in opposite directions.

3. The answer is C. The law of demand says that all other things constant, a decrease in the price of the product will result in an increase in the quantity purchased.

4. The answer is A. When economists use the term *ceteris paribus,* we recognize that although many things affect our consumption, we are focusing on the effect of price.

5. The answer is A. An individual demand schedule shows the different amounts of a product that a person would be willing to buy at various prices in a particular time interval.

6. The answer is C. The market demand curve is derived by adding the various amounts that all the demanders in the market will be willing to buy at various prices.

7. The answer is D. Because a demand curve describes a negative relationship between two variables, price and quantity demanded it slopes down and to the right.

## IV    Application and Discussion

1. Holding other variables such as incomes and tastes constant, land in rural Minnesota must be less expensive than land in New York. Sid's behavior is in accordance with the law of demand, which describes an inverse relationship between price and quantity demanded.

2. See Exhibit 4.1.

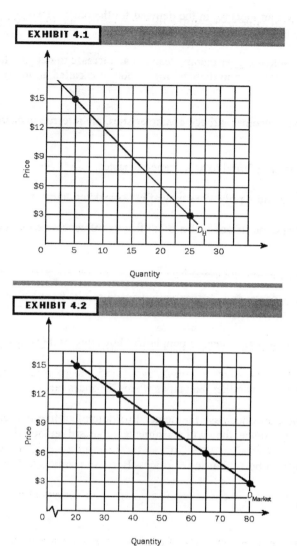

EXHIBIT 4.1

EXHIBIT 4.2

3.   See Exhibit 4.2.

| Price (dollars per ounce) | Quantity Demanded (ounces per week) | | | | | | | |
|---|---|---|---|---|---|---|---|---|
| | Hillary | Barbara | Nancy | Market | | | | |
| | | $15 | | | 5 | 0 | 15 | 20 |
| 12 | 10 | 5 | 20 | 35 | | | | |
| 9 | 15 | 10 | 25 | 50 | | | | |
| 6 | 20 | 15 | 30 | 65 | | | | |
| 3 | 25 | 20 | 35 | 80 | | | | |

## Section 4.3 Shifts in the Demand Curve

### I      Review

A change in a good's price leads to a change in <u>quantity</u> demanded, while a change in one of the <u>determinants</u> of demand will lead to a shift in the entire demand curve.

Determinants of demand are called demand <u>shifters</u> and they lead to a change in <u>demand</u>. Some possible demand shifters are: the prices of closely <u>related</u> goods; income; number of <u>buyers</u>; <u>tastes</u> of buyers; and <u>expectations</u> of buyers.

# ANSWER KEY

Two goods are substitutes if an increase in the price of one good causes an <u>increase</u> in the demand for the other. Two goods are complements if an increase in the price of one good causes a <u>decrease</u> in the demand for the other.

As their incomes rise, consumers generally buy <u>more</u> of most goods. When higher income leads to an increase in demand for a good the good is called a <u>normal</u> good. If higher income leads to a reduction in demand for a good, it is called an <u>inferior</u> good.

The vital statistics of the potential consumer population, including size, income, and age characteristics, are referred to as the <u>demographics</u> of a product.

When demand changes with changes in fashion, the cause of the change is referred to as a change in <u>tastes</u>.

<u>Expectations</u> about the future, such as fear of shortages or concern over future price rises may affect consumer <u>demand</u>.

If the price of a good changes it leads to a change in quantity <u>demanded</u>, but if one of the other factors influencing consumer behavior changes it leads to a change in <u>demand</u>.

## II     True/False

1.  False. A change in a good's price leads to a change in quantity demanded. A change in demand results from a change in one of the variables that shift the demand curve, such as consumers incomes or tastes.

2.  True. If the price of a good falls, it becomes cheaper relative to its substitutes, so people will buy more of it and less of the substitute goods.

3.  True. Because CDs and tapes are substitutes, consumers will buy CDs rather than tapes when CD prices fall.

4.  False. An increase in the price of a complement like hot dogs, will decrease the demand for a product like mustard. Higher hot dog prices mean that people will buy fewer hot dogs. Hence, they will consume less mustard on their dogs.

5.  True. According to the law of demand, more tennis racquets will be sold at lower prices. Because racquets and balls are complements, people will buy more tennis balls.

6.  False. As incomes rise, the demand for normal goods rises.

7.  True. Inferior goods are goods whose demand falls as income rises.

8.  False. Demographic changes, like changes in the average age of the population, do affect demand, but we would expect to see the demand for other products like orthopedic shoes and medical services to increase as the population ages.

## III     Multiple Choice

1.  The answer is A. A change in a good's price leads to a change in quantity demanded, or a movement along a given demand curve, while a change in one of the variables leads to a change in demand, or a shift in the demand curve.

2.  The answer is C. A change in the price of the product causes a change in quantity demanded but does not cause a change in demand.

3.  The answer is B. If people think that they can become better-looking by eating jelly beans, they will buy more at each and every price and the demand curve will shift to the right.

4.  The answer is D. If the demand for a good goes down when consumers' incomes increase, it is an inferior good.

5.  The answer is B. If higher incomes lead to an increase in the demand for a good, the good is a normal good.

# ANSWER KEY

6. The answer is C. An increase in the number of newborns will likely cause the demand for disposable diapers to go up. It is a change in demographics, or number of demanders.

7. The answer is D. An increase in the own-price of a good or service results in a decrease in quantity demanded, or a movement up along the demand curve.

8. The answer is B. Smokers in Alaska stocked up because of an expected increase in cigarette prices.

## IV   Discussion and Application

1.  A.   The price of chicken falls.
         Determinant: Price of substitute [Exh un0401ans]

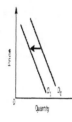

    B.   The price of hamburger buns doubles.
         Determinant variable: <u>Price of complement</u>

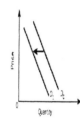

    C.   Scientists find that eating hamburger prolongs life.
         Determinant variable: <u>Tastes</u>

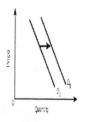

    D.   The population of Hilo doubles.
         Determinant variable: <u>Number of consumers</u>

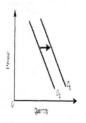

285

**ANSWER KEY**

2.  A.  The price of Fords plummets!
        Determinant variable: <u>Price of substitutes</u>

    B.  Consumers believe that the price of Chevrolets will rise next year.
        Determinants variable: <u>Expectations</u>

    C.  The incomes of Americans rise.
        Determinants variable: <u>Income</u>

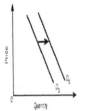

    D.  The price of gasoline falls dramatically.
        Determinants variable: <u>Price of complements</u>

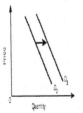

3.  A.  Point B represents an increase in quantity demanded.

    B.  Point E represents an increase in demand.

    C.  Point F represents a decrease in demand.

    D.  Point C represents a decrease in quantity demanded.

Section 4.4 Supply

I       Review

The answer to the questions, "What do we produce and in what quantities?" depends on the interaction of both <u>buyers</u> and <u>sellers</u>.

The law of supply states that, other things being equal, quantity supplied varies <u>directly</u> with price.

A producer requires a higher price to produce additional units of the good because of the law of <u>increasing</u> opportunity costs.

The individual supply curve is <u>upward</u> sloping as you move from left to right.

Adding the amount each individual producer would supply at each price will give us the <u>market</u> supply curve.

II      True/False

1.   False. Market outcomes depend on understanding both the demand and supply sides of the market.

2.   False. When two variables are directly related, like price and quantity supplied, they move in the same direction.

3.   True. Producers usually use the most efficient, lowest-opportunity-cost resources first when they produce a good.

4.   True. The supply curve shows how much a producer would produce at any price. The law of supply states that an increase in price is necessary for more to be produced.

5.   True. A change in the quantity supplied describes the response of producers to changes in the good's price. A change in one of the SPENT factors causes a change in supply.

III     Multiple Choice

1.   The answer is A. The result depends on the decisions of both buyers and sellers.

2.   The answer is C. The law of supply says that there is a direct relationship between price and quantity supplied.

3.   The answer is A. According to the law of supply, as prices fall, so does the amount any producer would produce.

4.   The answer is A. Because it is more costly to produce wheat in these fields, Jones would only do it if the price of wheat increased to cover his costs.

5.   The answer is B. The market supply curve is found by adding the amount produced at each price for every firm in the market.

IV      Application and Discussion

1.   The opportunity costs of production are higher at the second field. Felix would spend more time traveling to the second field, consume more gasoline, use extra time and energy to clear the rocks from the field, and probably use more fertilizer. Felix would have to give up more to produce from the second field.

2.   The market price of wheat would have to rise for Felix to have the incentive to produce from the second field. Because costs are higher in the second field, Felix must receive a higher price to compensate him for his higher costs.

3.   See Exhibit 4.3.

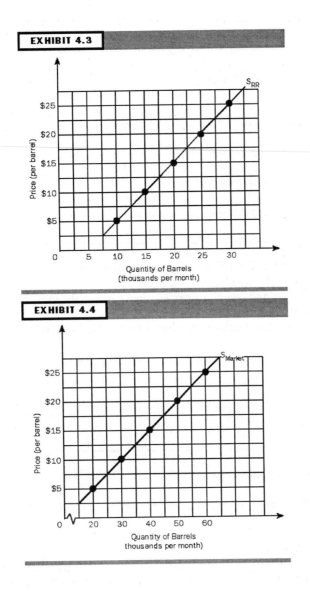

EXHIBIT 4.3

EXHIBIT 4.4

4.  See Exhibit 4.4.

Quantity Supplied (barrels per month)

| Price (dollars per barrel) | Rolling Rock | Armadillo | Pecos | Market |
|---|---|---|---|---|
| $ 5 | 10,000 | 8,000 | 2,000 | 20,000 |
| 10 | 15,000 | 10,000 | 5,000 | 30,000 |
| 15 | 20,000 | 12,000 | 8,000 | 40,000 |
| 20 | 25,000 | 14,000 | 11,000 | 50,000 |
| 25 | 30,000 | 16,000 | 14,000 | 60,000 |

## Section 4.5 Shifts In The Supply Curve

### I    Review

When other factors remain the same, price change results in a movement along the supply curve; this is called a change in quantity supplied. When the other important factors that affect supplier behavior change, the entire supply curve shifts; this is called a change in supply.

Labor, materials, and energy are examples of supplier <u>inputs</u>. Higher input prices increase the <u>costs</u> of production and shift the supply curve to the left. Lower input prices <u>lower</u> the costs of production and shift the supply curve to the <u>right</u>.

When two goods can be produced using the same resources they are called <u>substitutes</u> in production. Producers tend to substitute the production of <u>more</u> profitable goods for that of <u>less</u> profitable goods.

If suppliers expect the price of a good will be higher in the future, they will sell <u>less</u> now so that they will have <u>more</u> to sell in the future. If they expect prices to fall in the future they will supply <u>more</u> now rather than wait for their goods to be worth less.

An increase in the number of suppliers leads to an <u>increase</u> in supply, while a decrease in the number of suppliers will lead to a <u>decrease</u> in supply.

Improvements in <u>technology</u> lead to lower costs and increase in supply.

Government regulations that increase production costs cause <u>decreases</u> in the supply of goods.

Weather can also affect the supply of certain goods, especially <u>agricultural</u> products.

If the price of a good changes it will lead to a change in the <u>quantity</u> supplied. If one of the determinants of supply, such as supplier input prices or technology changes, it will lead to a change in <u>supply</u> and to a shift in the <u>supply</u> curve.

II    True/False

1. False. Timber is an input in lumber production. When the price of an input increases, production becomes more costly and the supply decreases.

2. True. When the price of a good falls, producers shift resources from producing it to producing more of its now relatively more profitable substitute in production.

3. False. If Midge expects future prices to be higher, she will sell less today and reduce current supply.

4. False. The relevant supply curve is the market supply curve; including more firms will increase the amount offered for sale at any given price and increase supply.

5. False. Improved technology lowers the cost of production, which increases supply.

6. True. Government actions such as taxes and tampering will make it more costly to produce the product and will shift the supply curve to the left.

III    Multiple Choice

1. The answer is C. This represents an increase in the number of firms in the market, which results in an increase in supply.

2. The answer is A. A change in the quantity supplied describes movement along the supply curve, while a change in supply represents a shift in the supply curve.

3. The answer is C. A change in the price of the product, *ceteris paribus,* will cause a movement along the supply curve, or a change in the quantity supplied.

4. The answer is B. El Niño is an example of one of the four Ts. Bad weather conditions reduce the supply of certain products.

# ANSWER KEY

5. The answer is C. Decreased taxes will lower the cost of production and cause supply to increase. All of the other changes will increase production costs and shift the supply curve to the left.

6. The answer is B. This represents a decrease in the number of sellers and results in a decrease in supply.

7. The answer is A. When the price of a supplier's inputs falls, supply will increase.

## IV  Application and Discussion

1. A.  Tomato prices skyrocket!
       Determinant: <u>Supplier input prices</u>

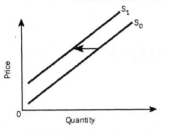

   B.  Congress places a 20 percent tax on salsa.
       Determinant: <u>Taxes and subsidies</u>

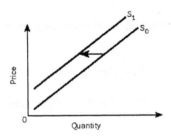

   C.  Ed Scissorhands introduces a new, faster vegetable chopper.
       Determinant: <u>Technology</u>

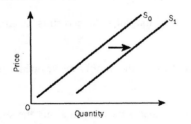

D. Elton John, Madonna, and Paul Newman each introduce new brands of salsa.
   Determinant: <u>Number of suppliers</u>

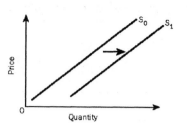

2. A. Freezing temperatures wipe out half of Brazil's coffee crop.
      Determinant: <u>Weather</u>

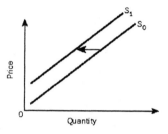

   B. Wages of coffee workers in Latin America rise as unionization efforts succeed.
      Determinant: <u>Supplier input prices</u>

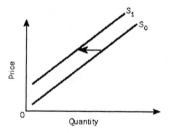

   C. Indonesia offers big subsidies to its coffee producers.
      Determinant: <u>Taxes and subsidies</u>

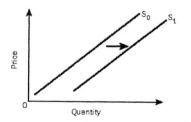

   D. Genetic engineering produces a super coffee bean that grows faster and needs less care.
      Determinant: <u>Technology</u>

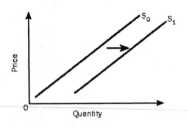

E. Coffee suppliers expect prices to be higher in the future.
   Determinant: <u>Expectations</u>

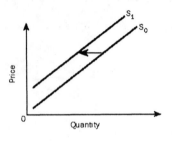

3. A. Point B represents an increase in quantity supplied.

   B. Point C represents an increase in supply.

   C. Point D represents a decrease in quantity supplied.

   D. Point E represents a decrease in supply.

ANSWER KEY

# CHAPTER 5 BRINGING SUPPLY AND DEMAND TOGETHER

Section 5.1 Market Equilibrium Price and Quantity

I       Review

The price at the intersection of the market demand curve and the market supply curve is call the <u>equilibrium</u> price.

If the price of a good or service is below the equilibrium price, a <u>shortage</u> will result.

If the price is above equilibrium, a <u>surplus</u> will result.

If there is a shortage of a good, the price of that good will <u>rise.</u>  If there is a surplus of a good, the price will <u>fall</u>.

II      True/False

1.  False.  Although prices tend toward equilibrium, the actual price may be higher or lower than the equilibrium price.  If so, the result will be a shortage or a surplus.

2.  True.  When a market is in equilibrium, the quantity demanded is equal to the quantity supplied.

3.  True.  Shortages cause prices to go up.

4.  False.  It's just the opposite.  A surplus exists when quantity demanded is less than quantity supplied.

5.  False.  The surplus, like any surplus, will put downward pressure on prices.

III     Multiple Choice

EXHIBIT 4.5

| Price | Quantity Demanded | Quantity Supplied |
|---|---|---|
| $6 | 700 cans | 100 cans |
| 7 | 600 | 200 |
| 8 | 500 | 300 |
| 9 | 400 | 400 |
| 10 | 300 | 500 |

1.  The answer is D.  The equilibrium price is $9.00, where the quantity demanded equals quantity supplied at 400 cans.

2.  The answer is B.  At $7.00 the quantity demanded is 600 cans but the quantity supplied is only 200.  Hence there is a shortage of 400 cans.

3.  The answer is B. At a price of $10.00, the quantity supplied exceeds the quantity demanded by 200 cans.

4.  The answer is A.  At $5.00 the quantity supplied will exceed the quantity demanded, which means a surplus exists.

5.  The answer is C. The market is in equilibrium where the demand and supply curves intersect, which is where quantity demanded equals quantity supplied.

6.  The answer is C.  At $2.00 the quantity demanded exceeds the quantity supplied, which means a shortage would occur.  The shortage would tend to drive donut prices up.

## IV    Application and Discussion

The Deputy Commissioner may be correct. Fewer young people may want to be lifeguards now than in the past. An economist, however, knows that shortages are caused by prices that are below equilibrium. Since the quantity of lifeguards demanded in New York exceeds the supply, it would seem that wages are too low. An economist would advise the city to raise lifeguards' wages in order to eliminate the shortage.

## Section 5.2 Changes in Equilibrium Price and Quantity

## I    Review

A shift in either the supply or demand curves for a good will result in a change in its <u>equilibrium</u> price and quantity.

An increase in the demand for a good or service is represented by a shift of the demand curve to the <u>right</u> and results in an <u>increase</u> in the equilibrium price and quantity.

If the supply curve does not change, an increase in demand causes a <u>movement</u> along the supply curve and an increase in the <u>quantity</u> of the good supplied.

A(n) <u>decrease</u> in the supply of a good or service is represented by a shift in the supply curve to the left. If demand does not change, the decrease in supply will cause a decrease in the quantity <u>demanded</u> of the good and an <u>increase</u> in the equilibrium price.

If supply increases at the same time that demand decreases, equilibrium price will <u>fall</u> while the change in quantity will be <u>indeterminant</u>.

If both supply and demand increase, the equilibrium quantity will <u>rise</u>, while the change in equilibrium price will be <u>indeterminant</u>.

An increase in either demand or supply is shown by shifting the curve to the <u>right</u>. A decrease in either demand or supply is shown by shifting the curve to the <u>left</u>.

## II    True/False

1.  True. With an increase in demand for bing cherries, people will want to buy more cherries at every price, including the original equilibrium price. The quantity people want to buy at $1 will now be greater than the quantity people want to sell at this price. This excess quantity demanded is a shortage.

2.  False. Compact disc players and compact discs are complementary goods. As the price of a complement falls the demand for the related good increases. An increase in demand, *ceteris paribus,* causing an increase in the equilibrium price and quantity of the good.

3.  False. An increase in the number of chicken farmers represents an increase in the number of suppliers. An increase in the number of suppliers causes an increase in supply and shifts the supply curve to the right. When supply increases, *ceteris paribus,* the equilibrium price of the product will decrease, not increase.

4.  True. At the equilibrium price, the quantity of the good people want to buy equals the quantity people want to sell. Either a decrease in demand or an increase in supply will result in the quantity of the good people want to buy falling below the quantity people want to sell creating a surplus.

5.  True. This new information will give people one more reason to appreciate chocolate and will result in a change in their taste for chocolate. At all prices people will want to buy more chocolate so demand will increase. An increase in demand results in an increase in the quantity supplied and more chocolate will be consumed.

6.  False. Both an increase in demand and a decrease in supply would tend to raise the price of apples. When they occur together, the equilibrium price will rise.

# ANSWER KEY

7. True. The population decrease means less demand for housing, while the additional construction means an increase in supply. These two factors would result in a excess supply of housing and falling prices.

8. False. When there are simultaneous shifts in both curves we can only determine which way one of the variables will go. The direction of the other, either price or quantity, will be indeterminate.

## III    Multiple Choice

1. The answer is A. Troy changes peoples' tastes, a determinant of demand. The increased demand results in an excess quantity demanded at the original equilibrium price. In order to secure ostrich meat consumers will raise the price. The increased price will encourage producers to increase the quantity supplied and consumers to reduce the quantity demanded until a new equilibrium price is reached. The new equilibrium will be at a higher price and a larger quantity.

2. The answer is B. The wage increase increases the price of inputs used to produce Broadway shows. This results in a shift to the left of the supply curve. A decline in the quantity supplied at each price will cause prices to rise and the quantity of shows produced to decline.

3. The answer is B. The medical news will change consumers' taste for chickens so they like it more. This will cause an increase in the amount of chicken consumers want to buy at every price or a shift to the right of the demand curve. This shift will result in a shortage at the original price and an increase in the price consumers offer. The increased price will encourage farmers to increase the quantity of chicken supplied. Farmers will move along their supply curve in response to the price increase.

4. The answer is A. Technological change is one of the determinants of supply. New technology causes the supply curve to shift to the right. The new equilibrium will be at a lower price and a greater quantity of beef sold.

5. The answer is C. There is no reason that a shift to the right of the gasoline demand curve will cause a similar shift to the right of the supply curve. The increase in demand will cause a shortage at $1.19 and an increase in the price consumers are willing to pay for gasoline. The increased price will result in producers increasing the quantity of gasoline they produce or moving along their supply curve.

6. The answer is B. The increase in the demand for plywood resulting from the hurricane means that at every price consumers want to buy more plywood. At the pre-hurricane equilibrium price, the quantity demanded would exceed the quantity supplied. There would be a shortage of plywood.

7. The answer is B. Of the possibilities listed, only an increase in the demand for wheat, represented by a rightward shift in the demand curve, would cause the price to increase.

8. The answer is D. Of the choices listed only a simultaneous decrease in demand and increase in supply would cause the price to drop.

9. The answer is D. We can only predict that the quantity bought and sold (the equilibrium quantity) will rise. In order to predict which way price would go, we would have to have information about how much demand and supply actually changed.

10. The answer is A. For a simultaneous increase in supply and demand to lower price, the supply curve would have to shift to the right more than the demand curve. It's just like the example of VCRs in the textbook.

## IV    Application and Discussion

1. Show the effects of the changes listed below on the relevant supply and demand curves.

Label the new equilibrium price, $P1$, and the new equilibrium quantity, $Q1$.

A. An increase in the price of hot dogs on the hamburger market.

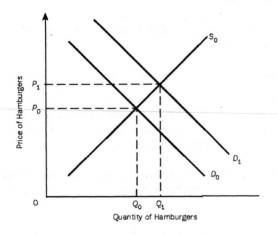

B. A decrease in the number of taxicab companies in New York City on cab trips.

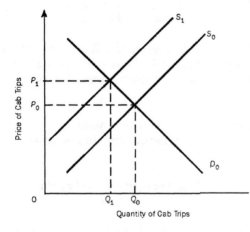

C. El Niño rain storms destroy the broccoli crop in two California counties.

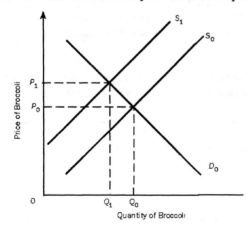

# ANSWER KEY

2.  A.   simultaneous increases in supply and demand, with a large increase in supply and a small increase in demand.

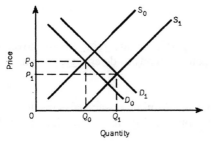

B.   simultaneous increases in supply and demand, with a small increase in supply and a large increase in demand.

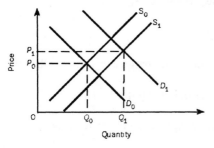

C.   simultaneous decreases in supply and demand, with a large decrease in supply and a small decrease in demand.

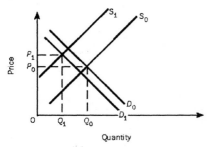

D.   simultaneous decrease in supply and demand, with a small decrease in supply and a large decrease in demand.

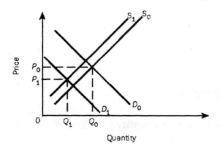

## Section 5.3 Price Controls

I     Review

Price controls involve the use of government power to impose <u>nonequilibrium</u> prices.

# ANSWER KEY

A maximum price imposed by government is called a <u>ceiling</u> price. A minimum price is called a price <u>floor</u>.

Rent controls are laws that set rental prices <u>below</u> the equilibrium price.

Rent controls have several effects. First, people living in rent-controlled apartments are <u>reluctant</u> to move; second, the incentive to build new rental housing is <u>reduced</u>; third, the stock of rental housing tends to <u>deteriorate</u> over time; and fourth, rent control promotes <u>discrimination</u> against people that landlords deem undesirable.

Minimum wage laws set wages for unskilled workers <u>above</u> the equilibrium wage. Minimum wage laws result in a(n) <u>decrease</u> in the quantity of labor demanded and a(n) <u>increase</u> in the quantity of labor supplied. Minimum wage laws may also result in a <u>reduction</u> of fringe benefits to employees.

## II    True/False

1.  False. Price controls are used to establish prices that are either above or below equilibrium.

2.  False. Price ceilings are prices that are set below equilibrium by law.

3.  True. Price floors are minimum prices, set above equilibrium. It is illegal to charge a price lower than the floor price.

4.  True. Rent controls, like those in Berkeley, set maximum rental prices below equilibrium.

5.  True. Price floors fix prices above equilibrium, where the quantity supplied is greater than the quantity demanded, which means a surplus.

## III    Multiple Choice

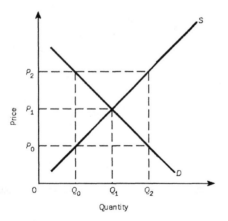

1.  The answer is B. The equilibrium price is $P1$, where the demand and supply curves intersect.

2.  The answer is C. A price ceiling at $P0$ will result in a quantity demanded of $Q2$ and a quantity supplied of $Q0$. Hence there will be a shortage in the amount $Q2 - Q0$.

3.  The answer is A. A price floor at $P2$ will mean quantity supplied of $Q2$ but a quantity demanded of only $Q0$. Hence a surplus of $Q2 - Q0$ will result.

4.  The answer is D. Rent controls don't increase tenant turnover. In fact tenants move less often because they want to hang onto their rent-controlled units.

# ANSWER KEY

5. The answer is C. An increase in the federal minimum wage is likely to increase the quantity of labor supplied, decrease the quantity demanded and result in an increase in teen unemployment. It is *not* likely to reduce teen unemployment.

## IV    Application and Discussion

The $2.00 price ceiling will likely result in a shortage of movie tickets. At the new, lower price, quantity demanded will rise. People will want more tickets at $2.00 then they did at $10.00. Assuming that the equilibrium price is somewhere around $10.00, the ceiling will cause the quantity of tickets sold to decline. Some theaters may reduce their hours of operation and some may even go out of business. Some theaters may stop showing first-run movies. Theater owners will certainly suffer. While some movie-goers may benefit from lower prices, they may also have to stand in long lines to buy tickets. They may also see a reduction in the quality of movies offered by theaters.

# CHAPTER 6 ELASTICITIES

Section 6.1 Price Elasticity of Demand

## I    Review

The price elasticity of demand measures the <u>responsiveness</u> of quantity demanded to changes in the price.

Price elasticity of demand is defined as the <u>percentage</u> change in quantity demanded divided by the <u>percentage</u> change in price.

Demand is <u>elastic</u> when the quantity demanded is very responsive to changes in price. In this case the price elasticity is <u>greater</u> than one and the percentage change in quantity is <u>greater</u> than the percentage change in price.

When demand is inelastic, the price elasticity is <u>less</u> than one and the quantity demanded is <u>not</u> very responsive to price changes.

If the demand is perfectly <u>inelastic,</u> consumers will buy the same amount regardless of the price.

Demand for a good will be more elastic the greater is the number of close <u>substitutes</u> available for the good. Elasticity of demand will also be greater for goods that take up a <u>larger</u> proportion of a household's budget.

The price elasticity of demand will be greater the <u>longer</u> the time period consumers have to adjust to price changes.

## II    True/False

1.  False. The price elasticity of demand does measures the responsiveness of changes in quantity demanded to changes in price or movement along a demand curve. Elasticity is measured as the percentage change in quantity divided by the percentage change in price. Using percentage eliminates problems caused by different units of measurement and allows us to compare elasticity of demand across goods and services.

2.  True. E-mail is a substitute for regular postal service; a person can send a letter or an email message. With the widespread use of this good substitute the demand for postal services has become more elastic.

3.  True. The price elasticity of demand is the percentage change in quantity, six percent, divided by the percentage change in price, ten percent. The demand is inelastic since the price elasticity (.6) is less than one. For inelastic demand the percentage change in quantity is less than the percentage change in price.

4.  False. Cars are expensive goods and car payments are likely to be a relatively large part of a household's budget. Auto wax is an insignificant component of most households' budgets. The impact of a change in the price of auto wax on a consumer's budget is likely to be much smaller than the impact of the same percentage change in the price of a car. Consumers will respond less to price changes for auto wax than for automobiles, so the demand will be relatively less elastic for auto wax than for automobiles.

## III    Multiple Choice

1   The answer is A. The percentage change in the quantity of steel demanded is much greater than the percentage change in the price. The price elasticity of demand is greater than one. The demand facing Marge and Al is elastic.

2.  The answer is C. The price elasticity of demand is calculated by dividing the percentage change in quantity demanded by the percentage change in price. For the Up and Down Co. this is 3, 15 divided by 5.

3.  The answer is B. The demand is inelastic. A change in price produces very little change in the quantity demanded. This is most likely because there are few good substitutes for heroin once someone is addicted.

# ANSWER KEY

4. The answer is A. The demand over a longer period of time is more elastic than over the shorter period because consumers have more time to adjust to the price change. When demand is relatively more elastic the change in quantity demanded will be relatively larger for a given percentage change in price.

## IV    Application and Discussion

|  | More Substitutes | Greater Share of Budget | More Time |
|---|---|---|---|
| 1. Cars or <u>Chevrolets</u> | X |  |  |
| 2. Salt or <u>Housing</u> |  | X |  |
| 3. <u>New York Mets</u> or Cleveland Indians | X |  |  |
| 4. Natural Gas this month or <u>over the year</u> |  |  | X |

The price elasticity of demand for a product will increase the more and better substitutes are available. Chevrolets have more substitutes than cars in general since any other brand is a good substitute. There are more, good substitutes for the Mets than the Indians because the Mets share a market with the Yankees. Natural gas has a more price elastic demand in the long run since this gives consumers time to adjust their habits and complementary capital to any change. Finally, the price elasticity of demand for housing will be greater than for salt because of the large role housing plays in the household budget.

## Section 6.2 Total Revenue and Price Elasticity of Demand

### I    Review

Total revenue is equal to the price of a good times the <u>quantity</u> of the good sold.

If the demand for a good is elastic, total revenues will <u>rise</u> as price declines. On the other hand, if the demand for a good is inelastic, total revenues will <u>fall</u> as the price declines.

If the demand for wheat is inelastic, farmers will become <u>better</u> off as a result of a reduction in the supply of wheat.

The steeper one demand curve is relative to another, the more <u>inelastic</u> it is relative to the other, although the elasticity of demand <u>varies</u> along a linear demand curve.

As you move along a linear demand curve from a high price to a low price, the demand changes from relatively <u>elastic</u> at high prices to relatively <u>inelastic</u> at low prices.

### II    True/False

1.  True. total revenue is equal to price times quantity sold, in this case $3.6031005$360.

2.  True. When price and total revenue move in opposite directions, demand is elastic.

3.  False. When demand is elastic price and total revenue vary inversely. For example when price goes up, total revenue goes down.

### III    Multiple Choice

1.  The answer is A. Total revenue goes up because you gain revenue by selling *lots* more units as price declines. The percentage increase in quantity demanded is large while the percentage decrease in price is relatively small.

2.  The answer is C. Total revenues rise as price goes up because the seller gains more from the price increase than she does from the relatively small decrease in quantity demanded.

3.  The answer is A. At $4 their total revenue is $200 ($4 x 50 videos = $200). When they lower the price to $3, total revenue is $300 ($3 x 100 videos = $300). So as price falls from $4 to $3, total revenue goes from $200 to $300 per week.

301

4. The answer is B. Between $2 and $1, price and total revenue move in <u>opposite</u> directions. Therefore demand is inelastic. At $2, for example, they rent 150 videos and total revenue is $300. As you can see, if they lower the price to $1, they rent 200 videos and total revenue goes down to $200.

## IV    Application and Discussion

1. Lastic actually gave Wayne good advice. If the demand facing the Gotham City hotel is inelastic, then raising prices will increase total revenue, even if it reduces the number of guests. Lastic assumed that the demand facing the Gotham City Hotel was inelastic. There are three reasons for this assessment. First, since there are no other first class hotels in Gotham, there are few good substitutes for the services provided by the hotel. The fewer the available substitutes the more inelastic the demand elasticity. Second, hotel expenditures are probably a small part of budgets of people who stay in first class hotels, and the elasticity of demand will be less the less important an item in a household's budget. Finally, it takes time for people to adjust their behavior, especially if they are traveling to Gotham City. In the short run, demand will be relatively inelastic.

## Section 6.3 Price Elasticity of Supply

## I    Review

The price elasticity of <u>supply</u> is defined as the percentage change in the quantity supplied divided by the percentage change in the price. It measures how <u>responsive</u> the quantity sellers are willing to sell is to changes in price.

When supply is perfectly <u>inelastic</u>, a change in the price will not change the amount supplied. When supply is perfectly <u>elastic</u>, no goods will be sold below a certain price, but at higher prices, as much as buyers want will be supplied.

Supply is more elastic in the <u>long</u> run than in the <u>short</u> run.

The relative supply and demand elasticities determine the <u>distribution</u> of the burden of a tax imposed on a good or service. If the demand is relatively <u>more</u> elastic than supply, the producer pays the greater proportion of the tax. If demand is relatively <u>less</u> elastic than supply, the consumer pays the greater proportion of the tax.

## II    True/False

1. False. The price elasticity of supply is usually greater in the long run. It takes producers time to adjust to price changes just like consumers. In the short run expanding output may require expensive changes. Given time firms can adjust production schedules and add machinery which allows them to produce more at lower prices.

2. The answer is false. The price in the two markets depends on the interaction of demand and supply. The Price elasticity of supply only describes how the amount sellers are willing to sell responds to price changes. All we know is that California electricity suppliers are less responsive than suppliers in New York; with a given increase in price California will see a smaller percentage increase in quantity supply than New York.

3. The answer is true. When supply is perfectly inelastic, the same amount will be supplied no matter what the price.

## III    Multiple Choice

1. The answer is B. The price elasticity of supply measures the responsiveness of the quantity supplied to a change in price. An increase in the price elasticity of supply will result in a greater percentage increase in supply from any given percentage increase in price.

2. The answer is C. The two extremes of the range of price elasticity of supply are perfectly elastic supply and perfectly inelastic supply. When supply is perfectly inelastic there is no change in quantity supplied in response to the price.

3. The answer is B. The price elasticity of supply equals the percent change in the quantity supplied divided by the percent change in the price. In this case the percent change in quantity is 23 and the percent change in price in 10, so the price elasticity is 23/10 or 2.3.

# ANSWER KEY

4. The answer is B. The elasticity of demand and supply will affect the share of a sales tax paid by consumers in the form of higher price and producers in the form of lower revenue per unit. The distribution of this burden will depend on the relative elasticity of supply and demand. If demand is relatively more elastic than supply, the producer will pay the largest portion of the tax. In this case the demand becomes more elastic relative to supply and the proportion of the tax paid by producers will increase.

## IV    Application and Discussion

When demand is less elastic than supply, the tax burden falls primarily on consumers. When demand is more elastic than supply, the tax burden falls primarily on producers.

The tax burden of a tax on food would fall primarily on consumers while the tax burden of a tax on basketball tickets would fall primarily on producers.

## Section 6.4 Other Types of Elasticities

### I    Review

The cross elasticity of demand measures the effect on the quantity demanded of one good of a change in the price of <u>another</u> good. It is equal to the percentage change in the quantity demanded of one good at a given <u>price</u> divided by the percentage change in the price of a second good.

The <u>direction</u> as well as the magnitude of the change is measured by the cross elasticity.

In general, a positive cross elasticity means the two goods are <u>substitutes</u> and a negative cross price elasticity means the two goods are <u>complements.</u>

An elasticity that measures the percentage change in the quantity demanded of a good, ceteris paribus, given a one-percent change in income is called the <u>income</u> elasticity of demand.

The good is a normal good when demand and income move in the <u>same</u> direction and it will have a positive income elasticity. If the income elasticity of demand is negative, the good is an <u>inferior</u> good.

### II    True/False

1. False. Cars made by Ford and Toyota are substitutes. The cross elasticity of demand between substitute goods will be positive. As the price of Fords rises people will, at a given price, increase their demand for Toyotas.

2. False. Inferior goods have a negative income elasticity. Income and quantity demanded for inferior goods move in the opposite direction. Per capita bus travel should decline as incomes increase. Of course, this assumes that other important determinants of demand and supply remain constant.

3. False. The income elasticity of demand measures the responsiveness of quantity demanded to a change in income, *ceteris paribus*. The elasticity is estimated by dividing the percentage change in quantity demanded by the percentage change in income. In the melon case the income elasticity equals one.

4. The answer is true. An income elasticity of less than one means that the percentage increase in expenditure on food will be less than the percentage increase in income. As a result, the share of income spent on food will decline as a country's income increases.

### III    Multiple Choice

1. The answer is D. The income elasticity of demand is calculated by dividing the percentage change in quantity by the percentage change in income. The calculation assumes that price and the other factors that affect demand do not change.

2. The answer is A. When the quantity demanded of one good and the price of another good move in opposite direction the cross elasticity will be negative and the goods are substitutes.

# ANSWER KEY

3. The answer is C. When the income elasticity of demand is negative the good is inferior. In Anchorage the probability of owning a mobile home declines as a household's income rises.

4. The answer is B. The cross price elasticity of demand can be used to identify substitutes and complements when they may not be obvious. When the cross price elasticity of demand is positive the goods are substitutes. In this case, they are substitutes because an increase in the price of gasoline causes a consumer to substitute frozen food for trips to the store to buy fresh food.

## IV   Application and Discussion

1. The income elasticity of demand equals (the percentage change in the quantity demanded)/ (the percentage change in incomes). The percentage change in quantity demanded over the period equals $(19.5-20)/[20+19.5]/2) = -.025$. The income elasticity of demand for rail travel equals $(-.025)/(.13) = -.19$

2. The cross price elasticity equals (percentage change in quantity demanded)/ (percentage change in the price of air travel). The percentage change in quantity demanded equals $(19-17.5)/([19 +17.5]/2) = .082$. The cross price elasticity of demand for rail travel equals $(.082)/(.075) = 1.09$.

3. The positive cross price elasticity shows us that air travel and rail travel are substitute goods. The negative income elasticity shows us that rail travel is a inferior good.

# CHAPTER 7 MARKET EFFICIENCY AND WELFARE

Section 7.1 Consumer Surplus and Producer Surplus

## I     Review

The difference between what a consumer *actually* pays for a good and what they are *willing* to pay is called consumer <u>surplus</u>.

A consumer's willingness to pay <u>declines</u> for each additional unit of the good he consumes. Earlier units purchased add <u>more</u> to consumer surplus than later ones.

When price falls, consumer surplus increases because you buy <u>more</u> of the good and because you get <u>more</u> consumer surplus from those units you would have purchased at the original price.

As the price of a product falls, the consumer surplus derived from consumption of the product <u>increases</u>.

The difference between the price a seller is paid for a good and her cost of providing it is <u>producer</u> surplus.

The welfare gain from trade of a product equals the <u>sum</u> of the consumer surplus and the producer surplus created by each unit traded.  Both buyer and seller are <u>better</u> <u>off</u> from each of the units traded than they would have been without trade.

Once the equilibrium output is reached, all <u>mutually</u> <u>beneficial</u> trade opportunities between suppliers and demanders will have taken place.

A deadweight loss is a reduction in total surplus that results from the <u>misallocation</u> of resources.

## II     True/False

1.   False. The prices consumers *actually* pay are often less than they would be *willing* to pay, yielding them a consumer surplus.

2.   True. The consumer surplus is the monetary difference between what a consumer is willing to pay and what he is actually required to pay. In this case, it's the difference between the $30 Choon is willing to pay and the $20 he actually pays, or $10.

3.   True. Producer surplus is the difference between the price the producer receives for a unit of his product and the cost of producing it. When the cost of electricity production increases, utility producer surplus may fall for two potential reasons. First, producers may sell fewer units of electricity and lose the producer surplus on those units. Second, the high costs reduce the producer surplus on the units they continue to produce.

## III     Multiple Choice

1.   The answer is B. Because of the law of diminishing marginal utility, the marginal willingness to pay for the extra apple is less than that of previous apples. Since the price that Roy actually has to pay for apples has fallen, however, his consumer surplus is larger.

2.   The answer is C. His consumer surplus, if the price is P0, is equal to the area above the price and below the demand curve or the area, a.

3.   The answer is B. As the price falls from P0 to P1, Carmine's consumer surplus is the area above P1, but below the demand curve. Thus he *gains* an amount equal to (b + c).

4.   The answer is C. The mutually beneficial gains from trade equal the sum of producer and consumer surplus. While trade might create greater surplus from one group or the other, both producers and consumers will gain as long as they receive positive surplus.

## IV    Application and Discussion

A)    Steve is willing to pay $4.50 for one bag of potato chips.

B)    Steve is willing to pay $4.00 for a second bag of potato chips.

C)    Steve's consumer surplus is $5.00 when he buys five bags. He gets a $2.00 surplus on the first bag, $1.50 on the second, $1.00 on the third, and $.50 on the fourth. At $2.50 per bag he gets no consumer surplus on the fifth bag.

D)    Steve's total willingness to pay when he buys 5 bags is $17.50. He is willing to pay $4.50 for the first bag, $4.00 for the second, $3.50 for the third, $3.00 from the fourth, and $2.50 for the fifth bag.

## Section 7.2 The Welfare Effects of Taxes and Subsidies

### I    Review

The efficient output occurs at the market-clearing price, which is where the sum of consumer and producer surplus is <u>maximized</u>. Economists refer to the gains and losses associated with government intervention in the economy as <u>welfare</u> effects.

The net loss in consumer and producer surplus from government intervention in the economy is called a <u>deadweight</u> loss. This loss results because government intervention distorts market <u>incentives</u>, like price.

Taxes result in consumers buying <u>less</u> because they pay a higher price and suppliers selling less because they receive a <u>lower</u> price. The net loss results because the <u>efficient</u> output is not produced.

The size of the deadweight loss from a tax on a good depends on the <u>price</u> <u>elasticities</u> of supply and demand.

The deadweight loss from a price ceiling results from production that is <u>less</u> than the efficient output. The loss from a price floor results from consumers buying <u>less</u> than the efficient output and producers producing <u>more</u>.

### II    True/False

1.    False. The lower the elasticity of either supply or demand, the smaller will be the deadweight loss from a tax. The deadweight loss results from the tax-induced changed in the amount of the good produced. The less elastic either supply or demand the smaller is the change in output from the efficient amount.

2.    False. The visitor tax will be partly paid by the producers of tourist services, like tour operators, fishing guides, and waitresses. The distribution of the loss will depend on the elasticities of supply and demand. If the supply curves is less than perfectly elastic, any reduction in output will result in a loss of producer as well as consumer surplus.

3.    True. Price celings prevent the price from rising to the market clearing level. There would still be mutually beneficial gains from increasing the amount of housing provided. There is a loss of consumer and producer surplus from producing "too little" housing.

4.    False. Deadweight loss imposes real cost on society. We give up the welfare measured by lost consumer and producer surplus. We also use our scarce resources inefficiently. It is a deadweight loss because we give something up and receive nothing in return.

### III    Multiple Choice

1    The answer is B. The deadweight loss from a tax increase results because output falls below its efficient level. When demand is perfectly inelastic, the change in price will not result in a change in the amount consumed or produced. The price consumers pay will increase and consumer surplus will fall by the amount of the tax revenue, but there will be no deadweight loss.

2.  The answer is B. The deadweight loss that results from taxes designed to raise the same revenue will be greater the more elastic the demand for the product. We might expect the demand for used cars would be relatively elastic since new cars are very good substitutes. The demand for cigarettes would be inelastic for smokers since there are few god substitutes for those with the smoking habit. Since salt and matches are a small part of most households' budgets, the demand for each of these products is also relatively inelastic.

3.  The answer is C. With this scheme, the consumer is doubly affected suffering both a reduction in consumer surplus and paying increased taxes to buy the surplus cheese. Producers gain because they receive a higher price then they would without government interference and they produce more.

## IV    APPLICATION AND DISCUSSION

A.  The consumers lose consumer surplus equal to area B, since they consume less electricity. They gain surplus equal to C.

B.  The producers lose producer surplus equal to areas C + D. Since they produce less and receive a lower price for electricity.

C.  California's total loss is the sum of the producer and consumer loss or the area B + D since the amount produced is less than the competitive equilibrium $E_0$.

D.  California's brownouts are another way of saying that there were shortages that arose from the price being below $P_0$. The brownouts reflect the shortage, $E_D$ minus $E_S$.

E.  Allowing the market to set the price $P_0$ would increase the total surplus by B + D. However, consumer surplus may actually fall if area B was less than area C. With market set prices producers would receive the surplus C and consumers would gain surplus B.

# CHAPTER 8 MARKET FAILURE AND PUBLIC CHOICE

Section 8.1 Market Failure and Externalities

I     Review

When the costs or benefits of an activity impact people outside the market mechanism, economists say an <u>externality</u> exists.

If production or exchange harms outside parties it is called a(n) <u>negative</u> externality. If production or exchange benefits outside parties it is called a(n) <u>positive</u> externality.

Air pollution is an example of a(n) <u>negative</u> externality.

If the education of a person benefits not only that person, but others as well, economists say that education generates <u>positive</u> externalities.

When producers are unable to collect payments from all those who benefit from a good, the market has a tendency to produce too <u>little</u> of the good.

When producers shift the costs of producing a good onto others who are not involved in production or consumption of the good, the market tends to produce too <u>much</u> of the good.

II     True/False

1.  False. Litter, like other forms of pollution, is an example of a negative externality.

2.  False. Negative externalities like pollution are created by people responding to certain incentives. Economists believe that if you reduce the incentive to pollute you will reduce pollution.

3.  True. Few people consistently enjoy the smell of smoke from other peoples' cigarettes. Cigarette smoke imposes costs on people not directly involved in the production or consumption of that good.

4.  True. Pleasant aromas from plants in neighbors' yards are positive externalities. They are benefits that you don't have to pay for.

5.  False. If producers can lower their own costs by shifting some onto others, they are likely to produce *too much* fertilizer.

6.  True. Markets by themselves, tend to underproduce goods that yield positive externalities. Hence, a subsidy that results in more production can improve efficiency.

III     Multiple Choice

1.  The answer is C. Vinnie is shifting some of the costs of his drum-playing onto Mae. Noise pollution is a negative externality.

2.  The answer is B. When firms can shift some of their costs to others who are not directly involved in production or consumption of the good output will be *higher* than it would be if producers paid all the costs.

3.  The answer is B. Carl is providing neighbors with a positive externality. They can enjoy looking at his new, beautified yard and the value of their own property may rise as well since property in a nice neighborhood is worth more than property in a run-down neighborhood.

4.  The answer is B. If the Mayor thinks education merits more public money he must believe that taxpayers in general, not only those whose children are in school, benefit from education. In economic parlance, he probably believes that education yields positive externalities.

# ANSWER KEY

5. The answer is D. Taxes, prohibitions against pollution, and mandatory cleanup would help correct a negative externality like pollution. Subsidies would result in more pollution rather than less.

6. The answer is A. If government wants to promote any activity it should <u>not</u> tax it.

## IV    Application and Discussion

Since honey bees pollinate apple trees and help increase apple production, the apiaries would provide a positive externality to apple growers and strengthen the local economy. Thus, the Mayor's proposal might have some merit. Since land has many uses, however, there is an opportunity cost involved in giving the land to beekeepers. to fully evaluate the proposal all of the benefits of the proposal have to be weighed against all of the costs.

## Section 8.2 Public Goods

## I    Review

A good that is yours and yours alone is called a <u>private</u> good. Goods, that are both not rival and not excludable are called <u>public</u> goods.

Someone who receives benefits that they don't pay for is called a <u>free</u> rider.

Because non-payers can't be excluded from consumption and because of the free rider problem, the market tends to produce too <u>few</u> public goods.

## II    True/False

1. True. Since consumption of national defense is nonrivalrous and since it is difficult to exclude those who don't pay for it, national defense is a good example of a public good.

2. False. Any vehicle is a private good. Nonpayers can be excluded from owning one and one person's use of the vehicle precludes another's use.

3. False. The status of the owner has nothing to do with whether a good is private or public.

4. False. The market actually tends to underproduce public goods and governments often try to do things that encourage additional production.

## III    Multiple Choice

1. The answer is A. Crystal is a free rider. She gets the benefit of the show without paying.

2. The answer is B. Radio programs are not excludable because anyone who owns a radio and is within the broadcast range of the radio station can listen. It is impossible to charge listeners and exclude those who don't pay.

3. The answer is C. A public good is both nonrival in consumption (everyone can consume it simultaneously) and nonexclusive (it is hard to exclude people who don't pay for it).

4. The answer is A. Where free-riding is possible producers can't collect fees from consumers. Hence goods are underproduced and overconsumed.

## IV    Application and Discussion

| GOOD | NONRIVAL CONSUMPTION | NONEX-CLUSIVE | PRIVATE GOOD | PUBLIC GOOD |
|---|---|---|---|---|
| 1. Hot Dogs | NO | NO | X | |
| 2. Cable TV | YES | NO | X | |
| 3. Broadcast TV | YES | YES | | X |
| 4. Automobiles | NO | NO | X | |
| 5. National Defense | YES | YES | | X |

# ANSWER KEY

| | | | | |
|---|---|---|---|---|
| 6. Pollution Control | YES | YES | | X |
| 7. Parking in a<br>Parking Structure | NO | NO | X | |
| 8. A Sunset | YES | YES | | X |
| 9. Admission to<br>a Theme Park | NO | NO | X | |

## Section 8.3 Imperfect Information

### I    Review

Since information is scarce like other goods, people will stop searching for it when the <u>costs</u> of obtaining additional information outweighs the <u>benefits</u> they expect to gain from it.

Government often acts to reduce <u>information</u> costs for consumers.

Occupational <u>licensing</u> laws are intended to insure consumers that certain standards will be met by providers of goods and services.

Occupational licensing laws often restrict the <u>supply</u> of services and lead to <u>higher</u> prices to consumers.

Governmental information policies can actually reduce efficiency when the costs of providing the information exceed the <u>benefits</u> of the information.

Asymmetric <u>information</u> exists when one party to a trade has better information than the other. In the used car market this may result in "<u>bad</u> cars driving good cars from the market."

Obtaining a college degree may be considered a form of <u>signaling</u> behavior that indicates intelligence and perseverance.

<u>Moral</u> hazard is an information problem in the insurance market that results from the high cost of monitoring the insured. Insurance against risks changes a person's <u>incentive</u> to take precautions against risk.

### II    True/False

1.  False. A rational person will gather information only as long as the extra benefit of gathering the information is greater than the extra costs.

2.  True. The government supplies lots of information about the characteristics of a wide variety of goods and services. The more information consumers have the better their decisions will be.

3.  True. The federal government requires those warnings that contain some information about the effects of smoking.

4.  True. This is an example of moral hazard. The Park Service guarantee is like an insurance policy. Climbers know they will be rescued, so this changes their incentives. The expected cost of being less cautious is reduced by the Park Service policy.

5.  False. Signaling behavior, like a college degree, neat appearance, and punctuality when arriving for a job interview, can be indicators of future productivity and job performance.

### III    Multiple Choice

1.  The answer is D. Elimination of the licensing requirement will increase the supply of taxis and lower fares.

2.  The answer is C. You can have too much information. If people go to great time and expense to gather information that has little value they will make themselves worse off.

3.  The answer is C. There is little, if any, criticism regarding the governments role in warning consumers about possible dangers involved in using certain products like insecticides or flammable materials.

4. The answer is C. Economist think that "one bad apple spoils the bunch" is a saying about the problems of asymmetric information. Consumers are not willing to pay more for an apple than they expect it to be worth. If there were a good chance they would get a bad apple, they would offer no more than what they would pay for a bad apple. If the amount they would pay for a bad apple were less than the cost of producing a good apple, good apple growers would be driven from the business.

## IV    Application and Discussion

The exam, its cost, and the waiting period likely decreases the supply of veterinarians. The time and expense of the exam may discourage some foreigners from even applying. The rationale for the exam is that it improves quality and informs consumers that veterinarians, wherever they are trained, are competent. Another motive for the exam may be that is protects existing veterinarians from competition.

### Section 8.4 Public Choice

#### I    Review

The application of economic principles to politics is called public <u>choice</u> theory.

Economists assume that people are influenced by self-<u>interest</u> in both the private and public arenas.

In the public sector the presence of <u>scarcity</u> forces politicians and voters to make choices.

Unlike the private sector, choices made in the public sector by majority rule break the individual-consumption- <u>payment</u> link. When the majority decides what to purchase, individuals pay for goods through higher <u>taxes</u>, independent of the value they attach to the goods.

#### II    TRUE/FALSE

1. False. Public choice theory is the study of how people make decisions in the public or political arena.

2. False. They assume that politicians and voters are motivated by self-interest, just like individuals in the private market.

3. True. Individual consumers make private sector decisions. The only information required is how the individual values the good. If he values it more than the cost he will make an efficient purchase, since benefits outweigh costs. In the public sector decisions often affect many people. Efficient decisions would require that information from everyone affecting be collected in a way that would result in their telling the truth about how they value the good. The more people involved the greater is the collection costs.

#### III    Multiple Choice

1. The answer is C. Both public choice theorists and economists who study market behavior assume that people are motivated by self-interest.

2. The answer is A. The new approach forces consumers to pay a given amount for goods they may not like. Consumers no longer are able to make decisions that reflect their comparison of the value they attach to the goods with the price they have to pay. Consumers no longer make the choice based on comparing the cost to them and the benefits they receive. As with public sector decisions, this approach breaks the link between consumption and payment for the consumer.

3. The answer is A. According to Roger G. Noll an economist at the Brookings Institution they provide no significant benefits. Any small benefits they may generate are swamped by their costs.

4. The answer is D. For most people, the costs of becoming politically informed are substantial, while the personal benefits are negligible.

**ANSWER KEY**

## IV    Application and Discussion

| Individual | Incentive |
|---|---|
| 1) Grocery Shopper | c) low food prices |
| 2) U.S. Senator | a) re-election |
| 3) Business Owner | d) high profits |
| 4) U.S. Federal Agency Director | e) a bigger budget |
| 5) Factory Worker | b) a higher salary |
| 6) Voter | f) more government services |

# CHAPTER 9 MACROECONOMIC GOALS

Section 9.1 Macroeconomic Goals

## I     Review

The three major macroeconomic goals of the United States are: (1) maintaining employment of human resources at relatively <u>high</u> levels; (2) maintaining prices at relatively <u>stable</u> levels; and (3) achieving a <u>high</u> rate of economic growth.

Other economic goals that the United States has pursued include concern for the <u>quality</u> of life, <u>fairness</u> in the distribution of income, and becoming self-<u>sufficient</u> in the production of certain goods and services.

With the Employment Act of 1946, the U.S. government committed itself to reduce <u>unemployment</u> in a manner consistent with price <u>stability</u>.

## II     True/False

1. True. It was pursuing the goal of becoming self-sufficient in the production of certain goods and services, in this case, oil. Whether or not self-sufficiency is a wise goal or not is a hotly-debated topic, but the fact remains that it is a goal often pursued by many countries.

2. True. Most societies want lots of jobs, stable prices, and growth in output. They also want other things like clean air and water, and a fair distribution of income.

## III    Multiple Choice

1. The answer is B. When the President decries inflation (a sustained increase in the price level) and deflation (a sustained decrease), he is expressing support for a stable level of prices.

2. The answer is B. The price freeze was an attempt to keep inflation at bay without resorting to policies that would increase unemployment and diminish Nixon's chances in the 1972 election.

## IV    Application and Discussion

Read the following quotations and indicate which of our major macroeconomic goals they refer to by checking the appropriate box.

See Exhibit 17.1

| EXHIBIT 17.1 | High Rate of Employment | Stable Level of Prices | High Economic Growth |
|---|---|---|---|
| A study of economics usually reveals that the best time to buy anything was last year.—Marty Allen | ☐ | X | ☐ |
| Inflation is the one form of taxation that can be imposed without legislation. —Milton Friedman | ☐ | X | ☐ |
| A lot of fellows nowadays have a B.A., M.D., and Ph.D. Unfortunately, they don't have a J.O.B.—Fats Domino | X | ☐ | ☐ |
| In practice, growth creates winners and losers. It spurs the expansion of some industries and regions—and the decline of others. It confers and revokes status. It undermines tradition. It empowers some nations and imperils others. It disrupts settled ways and compels people (and institutions) to alter comfortable habits. It generates insecurity.—Robert Samuelson, in The Good Life and Its Discontents | ☐ | ☐ | X |
| We should offer help and hope to those Americans temporarily left behind by the global marketplace or by the march of technology. That's why we have more than doubled funding for training dislocated workers since 1993—and if my new budget is adopted, we will triple funding.—President Bill Clinton in his 1998 State of the Union Address | X | ☐ | ☐ |

## Section 9.2 Employment and Unemployment

### I    Review

High rates of <u>unemployment</u> cause society to suffer losses in the potential output of goods and services because some of its productive resources are idle. High unemployment results in a loss of <u>efficiency</u>.

The <u>labor</u> force is the number of people over the age of 16 who are willing and able to work. This includes people who are employed and <u>unemployed</u>.

The unemployment rate is the <u>percent</u> of the labor force who are unemployed or unable to find a job. To calculate the unemployment rate, we <u>divide</u> the number of unemployed by the number of people in the labor force.

When people think the chances of finding a job are so bleak they quit looking they are called <u>discouraged</u> workers. They are <u>not</u> counted as unemployed because they are not in the labor force.

The incidence of unemployment varies widely among the population. Unemployment rates are <u>greater</u> than average for the very young, minorities, and less skilled workers. Unemployment rates are also significantly <u>lower</u> for college educated people than for those without a high school diploma.

It is a common misconception that most of the unemployed have lost their jobs. In reality there are four categories of unemployed workers: job <u>losers</u>, job <u>leavers</u>, re-entrants, and <u>new</u> entrants to the labor force.

Government policies to reduce unemployment may result in inflation and inefficiencies resulting from the <u>mismatch</u> of worker skills and job requirements. <u>Underemployment</u> occurs when the skills an employee has are greater than those required by the job.

The duration of unemployment is as important as the amount of unemployment at any time. The duration of unemployment tends to be <u>greater</u> when the amount of unemployment is high.

### II    True/False

1.  False. When any resource is unemployed, society suffers a loss in the production of goods and services. Society is operating inefficiently and producing less than its potential.

# ANSWER KEY

2. True. When unemployment is low, there are many good job opportunities and workers are more likely to quit their jobs to look for better ones. When the economy is good, fewer people are likely to lose their jobs, so the proportion of unemployed who quit their jobs is likely to be greater.

3. False. There are four categories of unemployed. Workers who have been in the labor force may become unemployed if they lose their jobs or quit to find better jobs. People are also counted as unemployed if the enter or re-enter the labor force and are unable to find work.

## III    Multiple Choice

1. The answer is C. The unemployment rate is found by dividing the number of unemployed by the number of people in the labor force. In Iuka there are 250 people unemployed and the labor force is 500. The unemployment rate equals 250/500 or 50 percent.

2. The answer is B. The incidence of unemployment varies among the U.S. population. Unemployment rates tend to relatively low for college graduates and higher than average for these other groups.

3. The answer is D. Once Wendy gets a job she is no longer considered unemployed. Wendy would prefer to be employed full-time instead of only part-time. However, you will recall that the definition of the unemployment rate will ignore her partially unemployed time.

## IV    Application and Discussion

1. The unemployment rate is calculated by dividing the number of unemployed by the number of people in the labor force. It will be affected by changes in the number of people who are unemployed or the number who are in the labor force.
   A) The unemployment rate is 10 percent; 1,000 unemployed divided by 10,000 in the labor force.
   B) The unemployment rate is 5.3 percent; 500 unemployed divided by 9,500 in the labor force (discouraged workers are not counted in either the labor force or unemployment statistics).
   C) The unemployment rate is 5.1 percent; 500 unemployed divided by 9,750 in the labor force (when they work, the discouraged workers are part of the labor force).
   D) The unemployment rate is 12.8 percent; 1,250 unemployed divided by 9,750 in the labor force.
   E) The unemployment rate is 12.5 percent; 1,250 unemployed divided by 10,000 in the labor (the new entrants with jobs are added to the labor force).

## Section 9.3 Types of Unemployment

### I    Review

Unemployment that results from persons being temporarily between jobs is called <u>frictional</u> unemployment, while unemployment that reflects a mismatch between the skills that people have and the skills they need to find employment is called <u>structural</u> employment.

Unemployment that results from insufficient overall demand for labor is called <u>cyclical</u> unemployment.

Unemployment that occurs because certain types of jobs are seasonal in nature is called <u>seasonal</u> unemployment.

Unemployment compensation <u>lowers</u> the opportunity cost of being unemployed and <u>raises</u> the unemployment rate.

New inventions generally <u>lower</u> production costs, generate <u>higher</u> incomes for producers, and <u>reduce</u> prices for consumers.

Economists refer to the median or "typical" rate of unemployment as the <u>natural</u> rate of unemployment.

### II    True/False

1. True. Labor turnover is normal in a healthy economy. People quit jobs they don't like, change jobs as they move from one place to another, or become temporarily unemployed for other reasons.

2. False. Because it reduces the opportunity cost of being unemployed, it contributes to a higher unemployment rate.

3. False. The natural rate of unemployment changes over time. In the 1960s it was considered to be around 4 percent, in the 1970s it was around 5 percent, and in the 1980s economists thought that it might be as high as 6 or 7 percent.

## III    Multiple Choice

1. The answer is D. A ski instructor who loses his job during the summer is seasonally unemployed, as is the lifeguard who loses her job in the winter.

2. The answer is B. When unemployment results from a lack of necessary skills for jobs that are available it reflects structural unemployment.

3. The answer is C. The natural rate of unemployment roughly equals the sum of frictional and structural unemployment. Thus, when unemployment rises above the natural rate it reflects the existence of cyclical unemployment

## IV    Application and Discussion

Although technological advances destroy certain jobs, they create others. The example of the computer industry in the textbook is a good one. Although computers may have eliminated the jobs of typists, file clerks, and typewriter repair people, they created a growth industry that created even more jobs. Economist Joseph Schumpeter referred to this process as a "gale of creative destruction."

## Section 9.4  Reasons for Unemployment

### I    Review

When wages are above the equilibrium wage rate, the quantity of labor supplied is greater than the quantity of labor demanded.

Economists have cited three reasons for the failure of wages to balance labor demand and supply. They are (1) minimum wages; (2) unions; and (3) efficiency wages.

Unemployment insurance lowers the opportunity cost of being unemployed and raises the rate of unemployment.

New technologies usually reduce production costs and generate higher incomes for producers and result in lower prices and better products for consumers.

### II    True/False

1. False. The main effect of minimum wage laws is on the market for unskilled workers with little experience.

2. True. This hypothesis holds that union members are concerned primarily for themselves when bargaining with employers.

### III    Multiple Choice

1. The answer is B. Following the law of demand, if the price of unskilled workers goes up due to the minimum wage, the quantity demanded (hired) will go down.

2. The answer is D. Employers pay efficiency wages in the belief that they improve worker productivity and reduce turnover and training costs.

3. The answer is B. Although new technology may replace some workers, it raises incomes and creates jobs for others.

## IV    Application and Discussion

If the unemployed could receive larger benefits for a longer period of time economists would expect the unemployment rate to rise and the average duration of unemployment to increase. Unemployment insurance reduces the cost of unemployment and gives the unemployed less incentive to seek employment.

### Section 9.5 Inflation

## I    Review

Most prices in the United States tend to <u>rise</u> over time.

When the price level is rising, we have <u>inflation</u>. When the price level is <u>falling</u>, we have deflation. The standard measure of the price level in the United States is the Consumer Price <u>Index</u>.

Without price stability it is difficult to <u>coordinate</u> plans and decisions. Most people consider <u>unanticipated</u> sharp price changes a bad thing.

Inflation <u>lowers</u> the real incomes of people who live on fixed incomes such as retirees. Workers and suppliers who operate on <u>long</u>-term contracts that set prices will also see their real incomes decline as a result of inflation.

Creditors may be hurt by inflation since it reduces the real value of the <u>principal</u> loaned by the time it is paid back. <u>Debtors</u> gain from inflation since the dollars they are paying back have less purchasing power.

Inflation imposes other costs on society. <u>Menu</u> costs are the costs incurred when firms have to change posted prices frequently. <u>Shoe</u>-leather costs are the costs associated with managing your assets to minimize the loss from inflation.

The real interest rate is corrected for <u>inflation</u>. The nominal interest rate is the real interest rate plus the <u>anticipated</u> rate of inflation. We can calculate actual real interest rates by <u>subtracting</u> the inflation rate from the nominal interest rate.

Nominal interest rates are determined by the intersection of the <u>demand</u> and <u>supply</u> for loanable funds. Expected inflation will shift the demand curve for loanable funds to the <u>right</u> and the supply curve to the <u>left</u>, which increases the <u>nominal</u> interest rate.

If people correctly <u>anticipate</u> inflation, they will behave in a way that will protect them from loss. When creditors expect inflation they will be <u>less</u> willing to lend funds at any given nominal interest rate, which results in nominal rates <u>rising</u> to account for the effects of inflation. Groups, such as labor unions, may also use <u>cost</u> of living clauses in contracts to protect themselves from inflation.

## II    True/False

1. False. Price instability imposes costs on society. Without a good idea of the future of prices, people have problems making decisions and coordinating plans. There are also additional costs from instability, such as menu and shoe leather costs. Finally, price instability may redistribute income that results in social disruptions.

2. False. When wage earners are covered by long-term contracts, their wages will be set for a number of years. Inflation over this period will reduce the real value of their contracted wages. To be protected from inflation, workers include cost of living clauses in their contracts that insure negotiated wages increase with the price level.

3. True. The nominal rate of interest can be thought of as the real rate of interest adjusted for the anticipated inflation. When there is an increase in the real rate of interest, the nominal rate of interest will also increase.

## III    Multiple Choice

1. The answer is C. While the prices of farmers' crops would most likely increase with an increase in the general price level, the nominal value of their loans would stay constant. Inflation would reduce the real value of the farmers' loan amount.

# ANSWER KEY

2. The answer is A. When creditors correctly anticipate inflation, they can protect themselves from its consequences by raising nominal interest rates. Inflation imposes a cost on creditors because the real value of the loan is less when it is paid back than when the loan was made. By raising his nominal interest rate, Nathan can offset the effects of inflation on the real value of the principal. This is certainly advice that Nathan can't refuse.

3. The answer is D. Expected inflation will cause a shift to the left in the supply curve of loanable funds, which, *ceteris paribus*, will result in an increase in the nominal interest rate. Expected deflation will cause a shift to the left in the demand curve for loanable funds, which, *ceteris paribus*, will result in a decrease in the nominal interest rate. When lenders and borrowers have different expectations about future inflation, the resulting effect on nominal interest rates are indeterminate. Because both the supply and demand curves shift to the left, we will be able to determine that the amount of funds that will be borrowed will decrease.

## IV    Application and Discussion

See Exhibit 17.2.

**EXHIBIT 17.2**

| Historical Period | Inflation Rate for Previous Year | Nominal Interest Rate | Inflation Rate for Loan Year | Real Interest Rate |
|---|---|---|---|---|
| 1946–1947 | 18.1% | 18.1% | 8.8% | 9.3% |
| 1978–1979 | 9.0 | 9.0 | 13.3 | –4.3 |
| 1993–1994 | 2.7 | 2.7 | 2.7 | 0 |
| 1920–1921 | 2.6 | 2.6 | –10.8 | 13.4 |

The banker will only be worse off when the real interest rate is less than zero. This occurs whenever the nominal interest rate is less than the rate of inflation. Only in the period 1978–1979 would the banker lose by incorrectly anticipating inflation.

## Section 9.6 Economic Fluctuations

## I    REVIEW

Short-term fluctuations in the level of economic activity are called business <u>cycles</u>.

A business cycle usually has four phases. During the <u>expansion</u> output is increasing and unemployment is falling. Output reaches its highest level at the <u>peak</u>. Unemployment rises and output falls during the <u>contraction</u>. The <u>trough</u> occurs when output reaches its lowest level. There is <u>no</u> uniform length to a business cycle.

Recessions occur during the <u>contraction</u> phase of the business cycle. When contractions are severe, they are called <u>depressions</u>.

Business cycles are of interest to politicians. There is strong positive correlation between the performance of the <u>economy</u> and the fate of an incumbent president's re-election.

Economists use historical relationships between things like consumer expenditures, the supply of money, and tax revenues and fluctuations in the overall level of economic activity to formulate <u>econometric</u> models.

## II    True/False

False. Output and unemployment move in opposite directions over the business cycle. As output increases in the expansion phase of a business cycle, companies hire more workers to increase production and unemployment will fall. In the contraction phase as companies produce less output they lay off workers and unemployment increases.

# ANSWER KEY

2. False. Business cycles are the short-term fluctuations in the amount of economic activity in a country relative to the long-term trend in the growth of output. Business cycles occur even though an economy generally expands the level of economic activity in the long run.

3. True. The contraction phase of a business cycle is called a recession. When a recession is especially severe and lasts for a long time, it is called a depression.

## III    Multiple Choice

1. The answer is A. The 1990–1991 recession and the slow recovery from this contraction became Clinton's top campaign issue in 1992. There is a historical correlation between the performance of the economy and an incumbent President's chances of being re-elected. Clinton felt his chances of winning were greater because the economy had recently experienced a contraction.

2. The answer is C. Output is rising and unemployment falling in the expansion phase of the business cycle. The opposite occurs in the contraction phase. Investment is most likely to increase in the expansion phase. The peak is when output is the highest in the business cycle and the trough occurs when output is the lowest.

## IV    Application and Discussion

1. A)  The peak occurred in 1984 and the trough occurred in 1989.
   B)  The expansion was four years long, from 1981 to 1984. The contraction lasted five years, from 1984 to 1989.
   C)  The business cycle went from 1981 to 1989. It lasted nine years.

# CHAPTER 10 MEASURING ECONOMIC PERFORMANCE

Section 10.1 National Income Accounting

I    Review
_____

National income accounting provides a <u>uniform</u> means of accounting for a country's economic performance. The development of this methodology was so important that one of its earlier developers, Simon <u>Kuznets</u>, won a Nobel Prize for his work.

The most widely used measure of aggregate national output is the Gross <u>Domestic</u> Product. This is defined as the value of all <u>final</u> goods and services <u>produced</u> within a country during a given period of <u>time</u>.

The value of a good or service is determined by its market <u>price</u>.

Final goods are goods that are purchased for their <u>ultimate</u> use. Goods and services used to produce other goods and services are called <u>intermediate</u> goods and services.

Only the value of <u>final</u> goods is counted in the Gross Domestic Product (GDP), because the value of intermediate goods and services is included in the value of the goods they are used to produce. Counting the value of intermediate goods in the GDP would be <u>double</u> counting.

Two methods can be used to calculate national economic output—the <u>expenditure</u> and the <u>income</u> approaches. These two methods produce similar estimates of <u>GDP</u>.

II    True/False
_____

1.  False. There are two primary ways to calculate Gross Domestic Product, the income approach and the expenditure approach. Although these methods differ, except for minor statistical differences the results are the same.

2.  False. In the calculation of GDP, the value of a good or service is determined by its market price. The price and the value assigned in the GDP calculation is the same for everyone.

3.  False. The GDP includes the value of all final goods and services produced in a year. The hamburger, buns, and coleslaw are intermediate goods whose value is included in the value of the final product. Counting these purchases in the GDP would be double counting.

III    Multiple Choice
_____

1.  The answer is C. Intermediate goods and services are goods and services that are used to produce other goods and services.

2.  The answer is B. GDP measures production not consumption. A good may be consumed in the United States this year but be produced in another country in a prior year. The Gross Domestic Product is the *value* of all *final* goods and services *produced within* a country during a given period.

IV    Application and Discussion
_____

The only purchases included in the calculation of GDP are those final goods and services produce within the United States during 2000.

# ANSWER KEY

**EXHIBIT 18.1**

| Expenditure | Yes | No | |
|---|---|---|---|
| 1. I buy a new Ford F-150 pickup truck. | ☒ | ☐ | Final good |
| 2. Tina's construction company buys lumber to build 50 new homes. | ☐ | ☒ | Intermediate good |
| 3. Ted and Janet buy dinner at the Weinershack. | ☒ | ☐ | Final good |
| 4. Emil buys Jenny's 1965 Corvette. | ☐ | ☒ | Produced in 1965 |
| 5. Jarett buys a nesting doll from Russia. | ☐ | ☒ | Produced in another country |

## Section 10.2 The Expenditure Approach to Measuring GDP

### I    Review

Using the expenditure approach, GDP is equal to the sum of all expenditures on final goods and services by consumers, business, government, and foreigners over a period of time.

The purchase of goods like food, clothing, and home appliances by households is called consumption.

Consumer goods like food and clothing, that are used up in a relatively short period of time are referred to by economists as nondurable goods, while goods that last longer, like appliances and automobiles, are referred to as durable goods.

Intangible items like healthcare, legal help, and haircuts are called services.

The creation of capital goods like machines and tools is called investment by economists.

Also included as investment expenditure in the calculation of GDP is the value of all unsold business inventories.

In calculating GDP, the "government spending" category includes governments' purchases of goods and services and payments of salaries to its employees, but does not include transfer payments like welfare.

Net exports are calculated as exports minus imports.

### II    True/False

1.  False. It is counted as consumption. More specifically, it is categorized as a durable good.

2.  False. Over the past 50 years, service expenditures have been growing faster than spending on goods.

3.  False. Investment spending is the most volatile category of GDP and fluctuates considerably with changing business conditions.

### III    Multiple Choice

1.  The answer is A. Consumption is by far the largest component of GDP, comprising 68 percent of GDP in 1997.

2.  The answer is B. Residential housing, because it provides benefits over many years, is counted as investment. It is the only part of investment that is directly tied to household expenditure decisions.

3.  The answer is D. The purchase of stocks is not counted in GDP. It represents a transfer of an ownership share in a corporation but is not an expenditure related to the production of goods or services.

4. The answer is D. Her purchase is an import; when she buys French wine, our net exports, $(X - M)$, go down.

## IV    Application and Discussion

| EXHIBIT 18.2 | Amount (billions of dollars) |
|---|---|
| Consumption | $4,500 |
| Consumption of Durable Goods | 500 |
| Consumption of Non-Durable Goods | 1,500 |
| Consumption of Services | 2,500 |
| Investment | 1,000 |
| Fixed Investment | 1,000 |
| Government Expenditures on Goods and Services | 1,300 |
| Government Transfer Payments | 300 |
| Exports | 750 |
| Imports | 850 |
| **GPD Equals** | $6,700 |

Given these numbers GDP equals $6,700 billion, or $6.7 trillion. Remember, GDP equals consumption, plus investment, plus government expenditures on goods and services, plus net exports (exports *minus* imports). In this list of numbers you don't count consumption of durable goods, consumption of nondurable goods, or consumption of services, since they are *already* included in the $4,500 million consumption figure. Fixed investment isn't counted either since it is already in the $1,000 million investment figure. Transfer payments are not part of GDP.

If you got this one on the first try, you're good. It's a tricky question.

## Section 10.3 The Income Approach to Measuring GDP

### I    Review

When someone buys a good or service, their spending creates <u>income</u> for someone else. The <u>income</u> approach to calculating Gross Domestic Product involves summing the incomes received by those producing the goods and services.

<u>Factor</u> payments are the incomes received by persons who own the resources used to produce goods and services. These include <u>wages</u> for labor services, <u>rents</u> for the services of natural resources, <u>interest</u> for capital services, and <u>profits</u> earned by business.

The difference between Gross Domestic Product and the net income of foreigners is called Gross <u>National</u> Product.

Sales taxes are an example of <u>indirect</u> business taxes.

National Income is a measure of the income earned by the owners of productive <u>resources</u>, while Disposable Personal Income is personal income available to individuals after <u>taxes</u>.

### II    True/False

1. True. The income approach adds two non-income payments to the sum of incomes earned by productive factors to arrive at GDP. These non-income expenses are indirect business taxes and depreciation.

2. False. Profits in this case are a payment to the entrepreneur. The entrepreneur is the factor of production that organizes production.

III     Multiple Choice

1. The answer is B. National income is less than Gross Domestic Product since it excludes indirect business taxes, depreciation, and income earned by foreigners in the United States.

2. The answer is A. In Balonia, DDP can be calculated by adding profits and depreciation to wages, rent, and interest. The difference between GDP and the income items listed is $1,481.75, which equals the sum of profits and depreciation, so profits are less than $1,481.75.

IV     Application and Discussion

The simple circular flow model in Concept A illustrates the relationship between the income and expenditure approaches to calculating GDP. In the factor market, households sell or rent their resources to businesses in exchange for income. Resources flow to firms, and income flows to households. In the product market, households exchange the money they have earned for the goods and services firms are producing. Goods and services flow to household, and spending flows from households to firms. Since these flows are equal, total spending has to equal total income. It is helpful to remember that profits are a residual income (the difference between the firms earning and its payment to all other factors) earned by entrepreneurial households; the residual nature of profits ensures these flows will be equal.

Section 10.4 Problems in Calculating an Accurate GDP

I       Review

The primary problem in calculating U.S. GDP over time is the problem of a changing price level.

Economists attempt to adjust for the changing purchasing power of the dollar by using price indexes.

Our attempts to construct price indexes are complicated by several factors, including changes in the quality of goods and services over time, the introduction of new products, and the disappearance of old, outmoded products.

Price indexes are used to adjust nominal GDP in order to get real GDP.

The measure of economic welfare most often cited by economists is real per capita GDP.

II      True/False

1. False. The increase in nominal GDP can be due to inflation. The economy can produce the same amount, or even less, of real goods and services, but if prices go up enough nominal GDP will rise.

2. False. Most economists who have studied this problem, including Michael Boskin of Stanford University, think that the Consumer Price Index (CPI) tends to overstate the rate of inflation by anywhere from 0.2 percentage points to 1.5 percentage points. Thus, when the CPI indicates a 3.5 percent rate of inflation, the actual rate may only be 3.3 or even 2.0 percent.

3. False. Nominal GDP exceeds real GDP only during periods of inflation. When the price level falls, as it did in the United States during the later part of the nineteenth century and during the 1920s, nominal GDP will be less than real GDP.

III     MULTIPLE CHOICE

1. The answer is C. The CPI measures changes in the prices of a bundle of specific goods purchased for consumption—things like hamburger, haircuts, and clothing.

2. The answer is B. To get real GDP from nominal GDP, use the formula in the book:

Real GDP = Nominal GDP ($7,254)/Price Level index (107.6) 3100

= $6,742

3. The answer is B. Since 1992 is the base year for the index (i.e. the index number is 100) nominal GDP and real GDP are identical.

## IV    Application and Discussion

Real GDP goes down. Nominal GDP has gone up by 10 percent, but prices have gone up by 25 percent. Using the formula from the book to convert nominal GDP to real GDP, the real GDP in year 2 is only $4,400.

Real GDP = 3100 = $4,400

## Section 18.5 Problems with GDP as a Measure of Economic Welfare

### I    Review

Although real GDP is often used as a measure of a nation's economic welfare it is a questionable measure. GDP does not include the value of nonmarket transactions, transactions in the underground economy, leisure, or externalities. GDP also ignores the distribution of income.

Nonmarket activities provide goods and services outside the market. Money is not exchanged for these goods and services. Housework is an important nonmarket activity in the United States.

The underground economy includes all legal and illegal unreported income. Underground activity is omitted, not because it is illegal, but because there is no reporting of the payments.

Leisure has a positive value that is omitted in calculating the GDP. When the amount of leisure consumed varies either over time or between countries, GDP is an imperfect tool for making welfare comparisons.

When positive or negative externalities are present market prices will not reflect the true value of goods and services to society. Since market prices are used to value output in national income accounts, externalities mean that GDP will misrepresent the true value of output to society.

In order to correct for the failure of GDP to account for things like negative externalities and the value of leisure, economists have developed an indicator called the Measure of Economic Welfare.

Although GDP is not a perfect measure of welfare for society, no widely accepted alternative has won acceptance. GDP can be used to make comparisons of market values over time and across countries. In general, increases in GDP are associated with increased consumption and economic welfare, while decreases in GDP are associated with lower consumption and reduced economic welfare.

### II    True/False

1. True. The average MBA consumes more goods and services than the average surfer does. However, the average MBA also consume less leisure than the average surfer does. Leisure has value that is not included in GDP. Comparison of welfare would depend on the value citizens in each country place on leisure.

2. False. These transactions are not part of the calculation of GDP because information about the value of these transactions is difficult to obtain.

3. False. GDP does not decrease to reflect the damage from pollution.

### III    Multiple Choice

1. The answer is B. Hunting, fishing, and gathering are nonmarket activities. Because it is difficult to assign a value to the output of these activities they are not included in the estimates of GDP. The existence of nonmarket production will mean that GDP will underestimate the true value of the nation's output.

2. The answer is A. The production of liquor and beer became activities in the underground economy after 1920. Even if the value of production did not change, GDP would have fallen. Production in the underground economy is not included in GDP because it is difficult or impossible to track.

## IV     Application and Discussion

1. A) Dr. Pool and her chef change cooking at home from a market transaction to a nonmarket transaction. GDP falls but output and welfare do not change.

   B) The government action moves pizza production to the underground economy. GDP goes down but output and welfare are unchanged.

   C) GDP and output do not change, but the change in the production method causes welfare to decline because it produces negative externalities.

   D) GDP declines but output doesn't because Karen has changed a market transaction to a nonmarket transaction.

   E) GDP and output fall when Bob stops working his second job, but welfare has probably increased. Leisure has value and by quitting the second job Bob is saying he values leisure more than the wages he gives up.

# CHAPTER 11 ECONOMIC GROWTH IN THE GLOBAL ECONOMY

Section 11.1 Economic Growth

I Review

Economic growth is measured by the annual percentage change in the per capita real output of a country's goods and services. In the long run, economic growth is a crucial determinant of the well-being of a nation's population.

A country's production possibilities curve defines the economy's potential output. Growth results in a(n) outward shift in a country's production possibilities curve.

Increases in the quantity and quality of an economy's resources, improved technology, and increased entrepreneurial activity will result in an increase in its potential output.

Small differences in countries' rates of economic growth will result in large disparities in those countries' standards of living in the long run.

There are significant differences in income, output, and wealth among countries of the world.

Productivity is the amount of goods and services a worker can produce per hour.

II True/False

1. False. If population increases faster than the growth in real output, the welfare of the population may not improve. In this case the per capita amount of goods and services will decline. Economic growth is usually measured as annual increases in the real per capita output of goods and services.

2. True. Improvements in the quantity and quality of resources will shift a country's production possibilities curve to the right and increase its potential output. By investing in themselves college students increase the human capital in a country. Output in the short run may suffer because students are not in the labor force, but this investment results in long-run increases in output.

III Multiple Choice

1. The answer is D. Economic growth results from an increase in a country's natural resources (as in A), improvements in technology (as in B), and increases in human capital (as in C). The Union Army reduced the South's capital stock, which resulted in a reduction in the potential output, not economic growth.

2. The answer is B. Differences in GDP and the standard of living among countries have existed for a long time. The text suggests these differences between the United States and European Union countries and the poorer countries existed in 1800.

IV Application and Discussion

The grasshopper would point out that their approach would give the society higher consumption today. The ants would say that by saving and investing they are providing for higher consumption in the future. As the ant economy increases its capital stock, its production possibilities curve will shift out allowing more to be produced in the future. The ants may be more concerned about the welfare of future generations than the grasshoppers; they may live longer or have a better developed social conscience. If consumption in the future were of no concern then there would be no reason to invest. Their views may also depend on the current GDP. If the grasshoppers lived in an economy with very low output they may not be able to sacrifice current consumption without serious hardship; the cost of economic growth may be too high.

Section 11.2 Determinants of Economic Growth

## I    REVIEW

There are <u>many</u> theories on the causes of economic growth.

Economic growth is a <u>complex</u> process created by many different factors. Nearly everyone would agree that four important factors resulting in economic growth have been:

    1. Growth in the quantity and <u>quality</u> of labor resources.

    2. Increased use of <u>natural</u> resources.

    3. <u>Increased</u> physical capital.

    4. <u>Technological</u> knowledge.

Increasing population will not necessarily increase per <u>capita</u> output. However, per capita output will increase if <u>more</u> of the population works or works <u>longer</u> hours or if the population's "<u>human</u> capital" is improved.

The abundance of <u>natural</u> resources has been cited as a major contributor to U.S. economic growth. If each worker has more natural resources to work with, *ceteris paribus,* they will produce <u>more</u> goods and services.

There is almost universal agreement that <u>capital</u> formation plays a significant role in economic growth.

Technological change reflects people's creativity in finding new ways to <u>combine</u> factors of production. Technological advance permits us to economize on <u>inputs</u> used in production. <u>Innovation</u> is the adoption of technological advances to produce goods and services. Innovation is an important role of the <u>entrepreneur</u>.

## II    True/False

1. False. Nearly all economists believe that economic growth is a complex process with no single dominant factor. The text provides eight factors that most economists believe are important determinants of economic growth.

2. True. Technological advance requires scientific and inventive talents to provide new ideas, but it also requires the talent to put these ideas to use in producing goods and services. The entrepreneur provides the talents necessary to identify good ideas and put them to work in the marketplace.

3. True. Increased population will increase the labor force in a country; however, there is no guarantee that output will increase faster than population. If population increases faster than output, per capita output will fall. Improving human capital or expanding the amount of labor a given population provides are more likely to result in economic growth.

## III    Multiple Choice

1. The answer is C. If a smaller proportion of the population works, output will decline.

2. The answer is C. If faster labor force growth in Country A is due to an increase in population, per capita growth may actually decline.

## IV    Application and Discussion

See Exhibit 19.1.

| EXHIBIT 19.1 | | | |
|---|---|---|---|

| Action | + | – | 0 | |
|---|---|---|---|---|
| 1. The government expands the capacity of the nation's universities and increases the number of college graduates. | X | ☐ | ☐ | This action increases the quality of the nation's labor input. |
| 2. Falling incomes reduce the amount that the average Russian is willing to save. | ☐ | X | ☐ | Reducing savings will reduce the amount of capital created. |
| 3. The Russian economy shifts from producing military equipment to producing consumer goods. | ☐ | ☐ | X | This is a movement along the production possibilities curve, not economic growth. |
| 4. High taxes discourage businesses from making new capital investments. | ☐ | X | ☐ | The action will reduce the stock of physical capital. |

## Section 11.3  Raising the Level of Economic Growth

### I  Review

Individuals can either consume or <u>save</u> their income. Generally speaking, higher levels of saving lead to higher levels of <u>capital</u> formation and economic <u>growth</u>. Some scholars believe that <u>research</u> and development activities work hand-in-hand with investment to spur economic <u>growth</u>.

Economic growth rates tend to be higher in countries that enforce <u>property</u> rights. Free <u>trade</u> can also lead to greater output because of the principle of <u>comparative</u> advantage.

Education, sometimes known as investment in <u>human</u> capital may be just as important as improvements in physical capital.

### II  True/False

1. False. Increased saving provides the funds that are used for investment and capital formation.

2. True. High rates of adult literacy in countries like the U.S. and Japan are associated with high output per person. Low literacy rates are associated with low output per person.

### III  Multiple Choice

1. The answer is C. Miners were developing a system to define and enforce property rights to the gold claims. They knew that without such rules they would spend all of their time protecting their own claims and the cost of mining would be increased. Without these rules, fewer resources would have been devoted to mining and the region would have experienced less economic growth.

2. The answer is D. the argument for government subsidies for education is based on the notion that education can lead to things that benefit all, or at least most, members of society.

### IV  Application and Discussion

According to Plymouth Governor William Bradford, the colony was "afflicted by an unwillingness to work, by confusion and discontent" when property was held in common. Since the industrious got no more than the slackers, there was no incentive for individuals to produce. The pilgrims had encountered the classic "free rider" problem.

With privatization, people had an incentive to work and colonists became responsible for their own actions. If they worked hard they benefited and if they didn't, they went without.

## Section 11.4 Population and Economic Growth

### I    Review

If population growth increases faster than output, per capita output will <u>fall</u>.

A greater population generally results in a <u>greater</u> labor force.

A larger population can result in economic benefits because larger markets associated with large populations can lead to <u>economies</u> of large-scale production.

Rapid population growth, however, can threaten sustained economic growth if it leads to <u>diminishing</u> returns in production.

### II    True/False

1.  False. U.S. economic growth was among the highest in the world over this period. Both the population *and* the economy grew rapidly.

2.  True. Per capita output is equal to output divided by the number of people in the population. If output increases faster than population, per capita output will rise.

### III    Multiple Choice

1.  The answer is C. The population of the world was 5.8 billion in 1997.

2.  The answer is A. Malthus predicted declining growth as population increased faster than production.

3.  The answer is C. Malthus believed that per capita output would decline because the supply of land was fixed, technological growth was not a real possibility, and that unchecked sexual desire would cause population to increase.

### IV    Application and Discussion

Early in life when he consumes without producing, a child imposes costs on his family and on society as a whole. The family must feed, clothe, and entertain the child, and siblings may be forced to share their parents attention, toys and bedrooms with the interloper. Taxpayers provide extra money for schools and other services, and neighbors may be bothered by extra noise.

When the new child grows up, however, he provides labor, energy, and ideas that promote his own and others' well-being. He produces goods and services in the marketplace, works on projects that benefit the community, and provides new, innovative ideas that improve efficiency and make others better off. The problem is not so much the addition of another person, but that of providing for that person until they become productive.

Malthus, of course, may have seen things differently. With him additional people not only represent a burden on society as consumers, but as producers they represent a variable (labor) input which, when added to fixed inputs, results in diminishing returns. Simon stresses the ability of people's knowledge and ideas to bring about new ways of doing things that overcome the impact of diminishing returns.

Of course your view may differ from either Simon or Malthus.

# CHAPTER 12 INVESTMENT AND SAVING

Section 12.1 Financial Markets

---

I     Review

---

Stockholders are the owners of corporations. They own shares of stock in the company and their voting rights and dividend income are proportionate to the proportion of total stocks that they own.

Holders of preferred stock receive a regular, fixed dividend, which is the same regardless of the company's profits. Dividends are paid to preferred stockholders before the holders of common stock. Common stock owners are the residual claimants on the resources of the corporation.

Companies issue bonds when they borrow. The bondholder is a creditor, not an owner of the company.

The random walk theory of the stock market holds that it is very difficult to consistently pick winning stocks without illegal inside information.

The price-earnings ratio is the current price of the stock divided by last year's earnings per share.

---

II    True/False

---

1. False. Votes in corporations are allocated on the basis of shares owned. If Jerry only owns on share, he will only have one vote. Chandra with her thousand shares will have one thousand votes.

2. True. Owners of preferred stock are paid a fixed yearly dividend independent of the corporation's profits. The dividend owners of common stock are paid depends on how well the company does. Common stock owners run the risk of receiving no dividend but they also might expect larger dividends if the company does well.

3. True. A stock's price will reflect people's expectations about the firm's future earnings. If government policy or the economic environment changes and convinces investors the firms earnings will decline, the stock's price will reflect that expectation.

---

III   Multiple Choice

---

1. The answer is B. Bondholders as creditors are paid off first. Preferred stock is paid off before common stock.

2. The answer is D. One way corporations raise funds for investment is by borrowing. When they borrow, they issue a promise to pay the creditor back. These promises to pay are bonds.

3. The answer is D. In an efficient market, prices quickly take into account all of the information about the firm and the economic environment. Consistent, extraordinary profit opportunities will not exist. The benefit of a hot tip does not last long. If prices quickly account for any information, a random portfolio is likely to do as well as one subject to expert analysis.

4. The answer is A. The price-earnings ratio is the ratio of the current price to last year's earnings per share. If the price rises, it means investors expect the earning per share to rise in the future.

---

IV   Application and Discussion

---

A) Hewlett Packard's stock price has changed most, 23.2 percent.

B)   The highest dividend per share was paid by Hershey, $1.58 per share.  The lowest is Hewlett Packard at 32¢ per share.

C)   Hewlett Packard has the highest PE ratio at 44, and General Mills has the lowest at 18.

Section 12.2 Investment Demand and Saving Supply

I      Review

The investment demand curve is <u>downward</u> sloping, reflecting the fact that investment spending varies <u>inversely</u> with the real interest rate.

If firms expect higher rates of return on their investments, for a given interest rate, the <u>investment</u> demand curve will shift to the <u>right</u>.  If firms expect lower rates of return, the investment <u>demand</u> curve will shift to the <u>left</u>.

The supply of national saving is composed of both private and <u>public</u> saving.

In equilibrium, desired <u>investment</u> equals desired national <u>saving</u> at the intersection of the investment <u>demand</u> and saving <u>supply</u> curves.  The intersection of these curves determines the real equilibrium <u>interest</u> rate.

People would rather have money now than in the future.  They are willing to pay <u>interest</u> to have money today.  The present value of $1000 in the future depends on the <u>years</u> you have to wait and the market <u>interest</u> rate.

If the present value of the benefits of an investment <u>exceeds</u> the cost, it is a profitable investment.  If the cost exceeds the present value of the benefits of an investment, it is an <u>unprofitable</u> investment.

From our knowledge of the circular flow in a closed economy, we know that the total income of households must equal the total <u>output</u> of the economy.

Private saving is the amount of income that households have left over after <u>consumption</u> and net taxes, while public saving is the amount of income that government has left over after paying its <u>spending</u>.

If the government collects more in taxes than it spends it will run a budget <u>surplus</u>.  If it spends more than it collects in tax revenue it will run a budget <u>deficit</u>.

Budget surpluses on the part of government cause interest rates to <u>fall</u>, while budget deficits cause interest rates to <u>rise</u>.

II     True/False

1.   True.  *Ceteris paribus*, as interest rates rise, investment falls; as interest rates fall, investment rises.

2.   False.  Lower interest rates stimulate the quantity of investment demanded.  To combat recessions, the government often tries to lower interest rates.

3.   False. The sum of the benefits ($12,000=10 years x $1,200 per year) is greater than the cost of the oven, but simply looking at the totals ignores the fact that you have to wait for the benefits. The present value of the earnings over the ten years is less than $12,000; how much less depends on the market interest rate. This will only be a good investment if the interest rate is low enough to make the present value of these earnings greater than $10,000.

4.   True. While both deals pay you the same, you have to wait longer for Sigfrid to pay you back. The present value of Roy's offer is greater than the present value of Sigfrid's, since you get the money sooner.

# ANSWER KEY

5. False. A budget surplus will increase national saving and put downward pressure on interest rates.

---

III    Multiple Choice

1. The answer is D. A change in interest rates does not shift the investment demand curve. Lower interest rates would result in a rightward movement along the existing investment demand curve.

2. The answer is B. When disposable (after tax) incomes increase people save more.

3. The answer is B. Entrepreneurs buy additional capital as long as its marginal revenue product exceeds its marginal resource cost. In this case the years rental price of capital is $5,000 (50% * $10,000). Because they don't borrow the money to buy the machine, we know they don't expect the machines marginal revenue product to cover this cost.

4. The answer is C. Budget deficits reduce public saving and hence national saving falls. The saving supply curve shifts left and interest rates rise.

IV    Application and Discussion

1. Investment spending in Japan went down. Weak consumer spending and falling profits led businesses to forecast lower sales and profits, and firms with excess inventories have little incentive to invest in new capital. The investment demand curve would shift to the left.

2. The present value of Heather's promise to pay depends on both the timing of the payment and the interest rate. If the interest rate is 1 percent, the present value of the payment is greater than the $900 loan in either two or ten years. If the interest rate is 5 percent, the present value of the payment is greater than the $900 loan only if paid back in two years.

   At 5% interest rate:

   The present value of payment in two years = $1,000/(1 + .05)^2 = $907.03$.

   The present value of payment in ten years = $1,000/(1 + .05)^{10} = $613.91$.

   At 1% interest rate:

   The present value of payment in two years = $1,000/(1 + .01)^2 = $980.39$.
   The present value of payment in ten years = $1,000/(1 + .01)^{10} = $905.31$.

# CHAPTER 13 AGGREGATE DEMAND AND AGGREGATE SUPPLY

Section 13.1 The Determinants of Aggregate Demand

I        Review

Aggregate demand is the sum of the demand for <u>all</u> goods and services in the economy. It describes the quantity of real GDP demanded at different <u>price</u> levels.

The four major components of aggregate demand are <u>consumption</u>, investment, <u>government</u> purchases and net <u>exports</u>.

Consumption is the largest component of aggregate demand. It accounts for almost <u>70</u> percent of GDP.

At the individual and national level, the greater our income the <u>greater</u> will be consumption spending. The level of our <u>disposable</u> or after-tax income will affect consumption.

The national level of consumption will also be affected by <u>interest</u> rates. Higher interest rates make saving <u>more</u> attractive and borrowing less attractive, so people consume <u>less.</u>

If people expect higher incomes in the future, they may consume <u>more</u> than their current incomes allow. When they consume more than their income, they <u>dissave</u>. College age and older people consume more than their <u>current</u> incomes allow; their spending decisions reflect their lifetime earnings expectations.

The fraction of their total income that households spend on consumption is called the average <u>propensity</u> to consume.

Marginal propensity to consume is a measure of the <u>additional</u> consumption that results from a one dollar increase in income. A household's marginal propensity to consume and its average propensity to consume are not necessarily <u>equal</u>.

<u>Investment</u> expenditures are the most unstable category of GDP. <u>Government</u> purchases is spending by federal, state, and local governments on new <u>goods</u> and services.

Goods and services that we sell to foreigners are called <u>exports</u>, while goods and services we buy from foreigners are called <u>imports</u>.

Exports minus imports $(X - M)$ is called <u>net</u> exports.

II       True/False

1.   False. The permanent income hypothesis suggests that college graduates have a relatively high average propensity to consume. Graduates will base their consumption on their expected lifetime income, which is likely to be higher than their starting income. They are likely to dissave or borrow to meet their desired consumption.

2.   True. Households make their consumption decisions based on their disposable income, which is their income after taxes. If their expectations are correct, Rose and Kareem will see their disposable income fall in 2002, because their taxes will increase by $50 more than their total income. They will probably reduce their consumption in 2002 because their disposable income will decrease.

III      Multiple Choice

1.   The answer is A. At a given price level, aggregate demand equals the sum of these four components. The largest component is consumption, which in the United States accounts for almost 70 percent of spending.

2.   The answer is D. Average propensity to consume equals the share of income the consumer spends on consumption. In 2001, Marcus' APC is 75 percent and in 2000 it is 59 percent ($1,187,500/$2,000,000). Marcus' Marginal Propensity to Consume equals the change in consumption per dollar change in income or .57 ($1,000,000/$1,750,000).

3. The answer is B. Income and consumption are positively related. As income increases, households spend more on consumption. Because consumption is the major component of aggregate demand, aggregate demand will increase.

## IV    Application and Discussion

| | | AD | | Component(s) |
|---|---|---|---|---|
| 1. Congress passes a reduction in personal income tax rates. | + | | C | |
| 2. Interest rates rise. | | – | | C, I |
| 3. U.S. runs a trade deficit. | | – | | (X-M) |
| 4. Government education spending rises. | + | | G | |

## Section 13.2 The Aggregate Demand Curve

### I    Review

The <u>aggregate</u> demand curve shows the quantities of real gross domestic product that people wish to purchase at different price levels. It shows the relationship between the total quantity of goods and services people demand in a given time period and the <u>price</u> level.

There is an <u>inverse</u> relationship between the price level and the quantity of goods and services demanded.

The aggregate demand curve is <u>different</u> from the demand curve for a particular good. The quantity of a particular good demanded is inversely related to the good's <u>relative</u> price, while aggregate demand describes the relation between the total output demanded and the average level of <u>all</u> prices.

The real <u>wealth</u> effect is one explanation of the negative slope of the aggregate demand curve. Changes in the price level will reduce the <u>real</u> value of consumers' money assets, which decreases their real <u>wealth</u>. A reduction in real wealth causes consumers to buy <u>fewer</u> goods and services which leads to a reduction in real GDP demanded.

The <u>interest</u> rate effect is another way to explain the relation between the average price level and the total output demanded. If the price level increases, consumers will need <u>more</u> money to buy the same amount of the more expensive goods and services. An increase in the <u>demand</u> for money without an <u>increase</u> in supply will cause money's price, the <u>interest</u> rate, to increase. Higher interest rates will <u>discourage</u> investment and cause a reduction in the quantity of goods and demanded.

If U.S. price levels increase, domestic goods will be relatively <u>more</u> expensive than foreign goods. Consumers will <u>import</u> more and <u>reduce</u> the quantity of domestic goods and services they buy. This <u>open</u> economy effect provides another explanation for the <u>negative</u> relation between the average price level and the quantity of output demanded described by the aggregate demand curve.

### II    True/False

1. True. The interest rate effect is one explanation for the negative slope of the aggregate demand curve. As the average price of goods and services falls, consumers need less money to buy the same amount of goods and services. Their demand for money will fall, and cause a decrease in the interest rate. Lower interest rates will provide opportunities for investment and the purchase of durable goods that will increase the level of investment and the quantity of real GDP demanded.

2. False. The aggregate demand curve and the demand curve for pistachios may look the same but they represent different relationships. A change in the relative price of pistachios will affect the quantity of pistachios demanded but it will only reallocate total spending among all goods and services. Total real GDP demanded will not be affected by a change in the price of a single good, only by a change in the average price level.

III    Multiple Choice

1.  The answer is D. The open economy effect is one of three complementary explanations for the negative slope of the aggregate demand curve. It suggests that increases in the U.S. average price level will make imports relatively cheaper. U.S. households and firms will substitute foreign goods and services for the relatively more expensive domestic products.

2.  The answer is B. The real value of money assets are reduced by inflation. The real wealth effect suggests that a reduction in the real value of their assets will make households feel poorer and wish to consume less. This is one of the three complementary explanations of the negative slope of the aggregate demand curve.

3.  The answer is B. According to the interest rate effect, an increase in the price level makes goods and services more expensive and increases consumers' demand for money. This increased demand for money results in interest rates increasing and a reduction in the level of investment. Because investment is a component of aggregate demand, the quantity of goods and services people wish to purchase will decline.

IV    Application and Discussion

A(n) ☐ in the price level will result in a decrease in the demand for money, a(n) ☐ in the interest rate a(n) ☐ in investment, and a(n) ☐ in real GDP demanded.

A(n) increase in the price level will result in a(n) ☐ in imports and a(n) ☐ in real GDP demanded.

A(n) ☐ in the price level will result in a decrease in the real value of money assets, a(n) ☐ in purchasing power, and a(n) ☐ in real GDP demanded.

A(n) increase in the price level will result in a(n) ☐ in the demand for money, a(n) ☐ in the interest rate, a(n) ☐ in investment, and a(n) ☐ in real GDP demanded.

A(n) ☐ in the price level will result in a decrease in imports and a(n) ☐ in real GDP demanded.

A decrease in the price level will result in a(n) ☐ in the real value of money assets a(n) ☐ in purchasing power and a(n) ☐ in real GDP demanded.

Section 13.3 Shifts in the Aggregate Demand Curve

| I | Review |
|---|---|

If a non-price level determinant causes total spending to increase, the aggregate demand (AD) curve will shift to the <u>right</u>. If, on the other hand, a non-price determinant causes total spending to fall, the *AD* curve will shift to the <u>left</u>.

An increase in consumer confidence, an increase in wealth, or a tax cut can <u>increase</u> consumption and shift the *AD* curve to the <u>right</u>.

If consumers fear that the economy is headed for a recession, if the government raises taxes, or if wealth decreases, consumption will <u>fall</u> and the *AD* curve will shift <u>left</u>.

If business confidence increases, or if real interest rates fall, business investment will <u>rise</u> and the AD curve will shift to the <u>right</u>. If government raises taxes on business, or if interest rates rise, business investment will <u>fall</u> and the *AD* curve will shift to the <u>left</u>.

If government spending goes up, the *AD* curve will shift to the <u>right</u>. If government spending declines, the *AD* curve will shift to the <u>left</u>.

If net exports fall, the *AD* curve will shift to the <u>left</u>. If net exports increase the *AD* curve will shift to the <u>right</u>.

| II | True/False |
|---|---|

1. False. A change in the price level generates a movement *along* the AD curve. It is not one of the factors that causes the curve to shift.

2. True. A change in any component of total spending such as consumption, investment government expenditure, or net exports will cause the AD curve to shift.

| III | Multiple Choice |
|---|---|

1. The answer is B. A boom in China will lead to an increase in the incomes of the Chinese. As their incomes go up, Chinese consumers and businesses will buy more, including goods from the United States.

2. The answer is C. Because interest rates and investment are inversely related, an increase in the money supply that lowers interest rates will lead to an increase in investment.

| IV | Application and Discussion |
|---|---|

A) A tax cut will increase taxpayers' disposable incomes and lead to an increase in *consumption*.

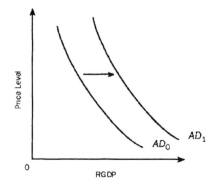

ANSWER KEY

B)   Higher consumer confidence will lead consumers to increase *consumption*.

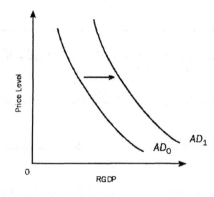

C)   A decrease in real interest rates will lead to an increase in *investment*.

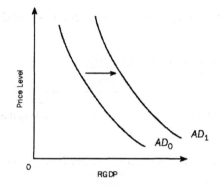

D)   A reduction in government spending will lead to a drop in the *government spending* component of AD.

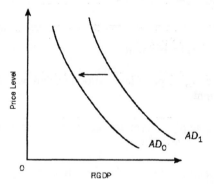

337

E)   Pessimism on the part of business will result in less *investment*.

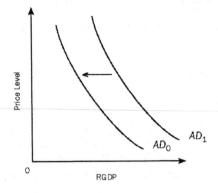

F)   An increase in exports will raise *net exports*.

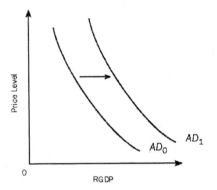

## Section 13.4 The Aggregate Supply Curve

### I    Review

The aggregate <u>supply</u> curve represents how much RGDP suppliers are willing to produce at different price levels.

In the short run, the aggregate supply curve is <u>upward</u> sloping, which means that at a higher price level, producers are willing to supply <u>more</u> real output and at lower prices they are willing to supply <u>less</u> real output.

There are two possible explanations for an upward sloping short-run aggregate supply curve: the <u>profit</u> effect and the <u>misperception</u> effect.

In the long run, the aggregate supply curve is drawn as a perfectly <u>vertical</u> line, indicating that output is insensitive to the <u>price</u> level.

The long-run aggregate supply curve is positioned at the <u>natural</u> rate of output, where all resources are fully employed.

### II    True/False

1.   False. According to this explanation, a high price level means higher prices for firms' output. Since input prices don't adjust as quickly, costs remain low and profit margins increase. Higher profit margins provide an incentive for producers to increase output.

2.   True. According to this explanation, producers are fooled into supplying more because they think that the price of their output has increased relative to other things—when in reality the prices of most other things have risen too.

III    Multiple Choice

1. The answer is C. In the short run, output prices can change, but input prices, many of which are fixed by contracts, cannot all change.

2. The answer is D. In the long run, *all* input and output prices have time to adjust.

IV    Application and Discussion

1. If the aggregate supply (AS) curve is upward-sloping, an increase in any component of aggregate demand, such as consumption or government spending will result in an increase in output, employment, and the price level. As shown in the graph, when the AS curve is upward-sloping an increase in AD raises equilibrium RGDP from RGDP0 to RGDP1. Although it is not shown on the graph an increase in output will lead to an increase in employment. The price level rises from PL0 to PL1.

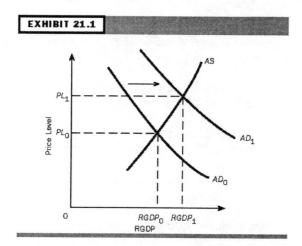

**EXHIBIT 21.1**

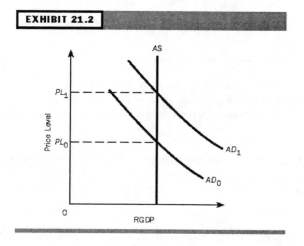

**EXHIBIT 21.2**

2. If the aggregate supply (AS) curve is vertical, the only thing that will change is the price level. A vertical AS curve means that output is fixed and will not change as the price level changes. An increase in aggregate demand shifts the AD curve right but the only thing that happens is that the price level rises from PL0 to PL1. Output and employment remain the same.

# ANSWER KEY

## Section 13.5 Shifts in the Aggregate Supply Curve

### I    Review

Change in the quantity of any factor of <u>production</u> can cause a shift in both the long and short-run aggregate supply curves.

The underlying determinant of shifts in short-run aggregate supply is production <u>costs</u>. Lower production costs will, *ceteris paribus,* result in <u>greater</u> production at every price level.

More and better quality capital will <u>lower</u> the costs of production in the short run and shift the short-run aggregate supply curve to the <u>right</u>. Investing in capital will also shift the long-run aggregate supply curve to the <u>right</u> and provide a <u>permanent</u> increase in potential output. Investment in <u>human</u> capital will have the same affect because it increases the <u>productivity</u> of labor.

Because they introduce new technology, <u>entrepreneurs</u> can increase both the short-run and long-run aggregate supply curves by <u>lowering</u> the cost of production and expanding real output <u>possibilities</u>. New technology allows <u>more</u> to be produced with the resources available to the economy.

An increase in natural resources will expand an economy's <u>sustainable</u> rate of output and lower its costs of production, shifting both short- and long-run aggregate supply curves to the <u>right</u>.

Additional workers will <u>depress</u> wages, *ceteris paribus,* and increase short-run aggregate supply. The economy's potential output and <u>long</u>-run aggregate supply will also increase with an increase in its labor force.

Increased government <u>regulation</u> can make it more costly to produce goods and services and <u>decrease</u> short-run aggregate supply. Regulations will also reduce society's potential output, which will shift the long-run aggregate supply curve to the <u>left</u>.

Changes in <u>input</u> prices and natural <u>disasters</u> affect the short-run aggregate supply curve but do not impact the long-run aggregate supply curve.

Changes in <u>input</u> prices will affect the short-run aggregate supply curve. <u>Increased</u> input prices will reduce short-run aggregate supply while a <u>decrease</u> in input prices will have the opposite effect. The economy's potential output and its <u>long</u>-run aggregate supply curve will not change unless the price changes reflect <u>permanent</u> changes in factor supplies.

Natural disasters, such as flooding, earthquakes, and droughts, cause <u>temporary</u> changes in an economy's productive capacity. Disasters will cause the short run aggregate supply curve to shift to the <u>left</u> but cause no change in the long run aggregate supply curve.

### II    True/False

1.  True. At every price level a decline in wage rates will result in an increase in the amount of real GDP producers choose to produce and aggregate supply curves will shift to the right. At each price level lower costs of production give firms the incentive to increase their production. If changes in wages do not reflect permanent changes in labor supply, they will affect only short-run aggregate supply.

2.  False. The floods were a natural disaster that produced only a temporary change in the U.S. productive potential. The floods caused the prices of agricultural goods to increase and the short-run aggregate supply curve to shift to the left. However, because permanent productive capacity was not changed, the long-run aggregate supply curve would, *ceteris paribus,* not change.

3.  False. Any increase in the quantity of any factor of production will cause both the long-run and the short-run curves to shift to the right. With more labor, the country could produce more output at any given level of prices.

# ANSWER KEY

1. The answer is C. Only the short-run aggregate supply curve will move in response to this change in the nominal wage rates. The employers' response to an exciting Super Bowl will not effect the amount of productive resources available to the U.S. economy or it potential output, so there will be no change in the long-run aggregate supply.

2. The answer is C. Increases in the amount of resources or access to resources will increase the US long run aggregate supply. New technology, which allows greater production, will have a similar effect. Increased government regulation will make it more costly to produce and result in both aggregate supply curves shifting to the left.

3. The answer is B. Entrepreneurs introduce new technology and new ways of doing things that lower the cost of production and expand the potential output from the resources available to the economy. Increased entrepreneurial activity will shift the LRAS and SRAS curves to the right.


## IV    APPLICATION AND DISCUSSION

See Exhibit 21.3.

**EXHIBIT 21.3**

| Consequence of a Major Hurricane | Long-Run Aggregate Supply | Short-Run Aggregate Supply | Explanation |
|---|---|---|---|
| 1. Hurricane kills 7,000 people. | – | – | Reduction in the amount of labor affects the country's productive capacity. |
| 2. Hurricane wipes out the country's cotton crop. | 0 | – | This year's production is reduced but the country maintains its productive capacity in cotton. |
| 3. Hurricane causes electric power to be interrupted for one month. | 0 | – | This is a temporary reduction in the supply of an input. |
| 4. Hurricane disrupts shipping and the importation of petroleum products. | 0 | – | This is a temporary reduction in the supply of an input. |
| 5. Hurricane destroys 75 percent of the country's coffee plants, a major export. | – | – | Coffee plants take time to mature. This has reduced the country's stock of natural resources and its productive capacity. |


## Section 13.6 Macroeconomic Equilibrium

### I    Review

The short-run equilibrium level of real output and the price level are determined by the intersection of the aggregate demand curve and the short-run aggregate supply curve.

Short-run equilibrium can change when either the aggregate demand curve or the short-run aggregate supply curve shifts, but the long-run level of RGDP changes only when the long-run aggregate supply curve shifts.

When equilibrium occurs at less than full-employment output, we call the gap between actual equilibrium and full-employment output a(n) recessionary gap. When equilibrium occurs beyond full-employment output we call the gap between full employment output and actual equilibrium a(n) inflationary gap.

When the price level rises as a result of an increase in aggregate demand, it is called demand-pull inflation.

When the price level rises as a result of a decrease in aggregate supply, it is called cost-push inflation.

# ANSWER KEY

In the 1970s and early 1980s, the United States experienced a phenomenon known as <u>stagflation</u>, where lower growth of RGDP and a higher price level occurred together.

When the economy is in a recession, it may <u>self</u>-correct through declining wages and <u>prices</u>.

When the economy is experiencing an inflationary gap the economy will self-correct through <u>higher</u> wages and prices.

## II    True/False

1. False. Higher oil prices can lead to cost-push inflation, as they did in the 1970s and early 1980s, but they don't cause demand-pull inflation.

2. True. Cost-push inflation, caused by increases in production costs, is shown graphically as a leftward shift in the SRAS curve.

3. False. When actual equilibrium is below potential RGDP a recessionary gap exists.

## III    Multiple Choice

1. The answer is D. Stagflation is a situation in which lower output and higher prices occur together.

2. The answer is B. A decrease in AD, caused by a decrease in any of the components of aggregate demand, could result in a recession.

3. The answer is D. The economy self corrects through a decrease in wages, which results in a decrease in the price level.

## IV    Application and Discussion

1. In the short run, an increase in aggregate demand is shown as a shift in the *AD* curve to the right. Output expands and the price level rises. A new, short-run equilibrium is established at point B.

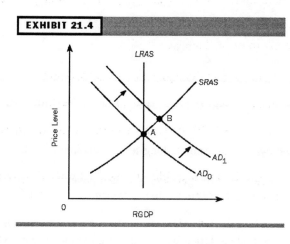

**EXHIBIT 21.4**

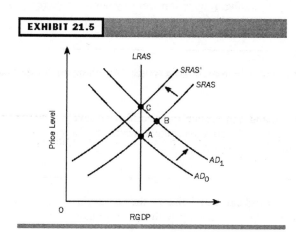

**EXHIBIT 21.5**

2.    In the long run, the increase in *AD* results in an increase in the price of inputs. Wages and other input prices rise, shifting    the    *SRAS*    curve    to    the    left.    A    new,    long-run    equilibrium    is    established    at    point    C.

# CHAPTER 14 FISCAL POLICY

Section 14.1 Fiscal Policy

### I Review

<u>Fiscal</u> policy is the use of the government's purchases, taxes, and transfer payments to alter the equilibrium level of real GDP and the price level.

In 2001 a large tax <u>cut</u> was implemented to combat an economic <u>slowdown</u> and to promote long-term economic growth.

When government spending exceeds government revenues there is a government budget <u>deficit</u>. When government revenues exceed government spending there is a budget <u>surplus</u>. A balanced budget occurs when government revenue <u>equals</u> government spending.

When the government wants to stimulate the economy it can <u>increase</u> the budget deficit by increasing government purchases, increasing transfer payments, or lowering taxes. <u>Expansionary</u> fiscal policy is associated with government budget deficits.

If the government wishes to dampen a booming economy it can <u>reduce</u> spending, <u>reduce</u> transfer payments, or <u>increase</u> taxes. <u>Contractionary</u> fiscal policy will tend to create budget surplus or reduce a budget deficit.

### II True/False

1. True. Expansionary fiscal policy consists of some combination of increased government spending or lower taxes. Either of these will push the budget toward deficit.

2. False. Contractionary fiscal policy will decrease aggregate demand and reduce the equilibrium level of output. In a recession, output levels are too low and unemployment is too high, so government wants to increase aggregate demand. Expansionary fiscal policy is the appropriate response to a recession.

### III Multiple Choice

1. The answer is C. Fiscal policy attempts to shift the aggregate demand curve and change the country's equilibrium level of real GDP and prices. Government's use fiscal policy when they are unhappy with the real GDP, price level, and unemployment in short-run equilibrium.

2. The answer is A. The government would like to use fiscal policy to increase aggregate demand. Expansionary fiscal policy increases government spending relative to revenues.

### IV Application and Discussion

See Exhibit 22.1

ANSWER KEY

**EXHIBIT 22.1**

| Situation | Taxes | Transfer Payments | Government Spending |
|---|---|---|---|
| 1. Government wishes to pull the economy out of a recession. | − | + | + |
| 2. Government wishes to slow down the growth of a booming economy. | + | − | − |
| 3. Government conducts expansionary fiscal policy. | − | + | + |
| 4. Government conducts contractionary fiscal policy. | + | − | − |

## Section 14.2 Government: Spending and Taxation

### I  Review

One way to gauge the degree of government involvement in the economy is to examine the ratio of government <u>spending</u> to total output.

Over the past 80 years government spending as a share of total output has <u>increased</u>.

In most years, the way the U.S. pays for government activity is through <u>taxation</u>.

Most tax revenues come to the U.S. government through personal and corporate <u>income</u> taxes.

The taxes that are used to fund Social Security and Medicare are called <u>payroll</u> taxes.

Some people consider <u>excise</u> taxes to be the least fair type of taxes since low-income families pay a greater proportion of their income on these taxes than do high <u>income</u> families.

Taxes that require those with higher incomes to pay a greater proportion of their income in taxes are called <u>progressive</u> taxes.

Taxes that take a greater proportion of the income of lower income groups than higher-income groups are called <u>regressive</u> taxes.

### II  True/False

1. False. The biggest growth has been in social insurance such as Social Security and other government pension programs.

2. False. The patterns of spending for state and local governments are very different than federal spending.

3. False. Income taxes provide the federal government with most of its money.

4. True. Excise taxes take more, as a percentage of income, from low-income people than from high-income people.

### III  Multiple Choice

1. The answer is B. From 1940 to 1945 the federal government dramatically increased spending on defense during World War II.

# ANSWER KEY

2. The answer is B. Social Security is the largest, comprising over 21 percent of total spending.

3. The answer is C. Education is by far the largest, comprising about 33 percent of state and local spending.

## IV    Application and Discussion

| Family | Total Income | Total Income Tax | Average Tax Rate |
|--------|--------------|------------------|------------------|
| 1 | $10,000 | $ 1,000 | 10% |
| 2 | $50,000 | $10,000 | 20% |
| 3 | $90,000 | $27,000 | 30% |
| 4 | $130,000 | $52,000 | 40% |

b)  The income tax is progressive.

## Section 14.3 The Multiplier Effect

### I    Review

A change in any one of the components of purchases of goods and services ($C, I, G,$ or $X - M$) can initiate changes in aggregate demand.

The multiplier effect is a chain reaction of additional income and purchases that results in an ultimate increase in total purchases that is greater than the initial increase in purchases.

The additional consumption made as a portion of additional income is measured by the marginal propensity to consume.

The larger the marginal propensity to consume, the larger the multiplier effect.

### II    True/False

1. False. A change in any of the components of spending ($C, I, G,$ or $X - M$) can generate the multiplier effect.

2. False. The full impact of the multiplier effect on GDP may not be felt for a year or more after the initial expenditure.

### III    Multiple Choice

1. The answer is C. The multiplier is 5.

   $\}1 - Ml \ PC\} = \}1 - 14/5\} = \}1/15\} = 5$

2. The answer is C. The multiplier is 10.

   $\}1 - Ml \ PC\} = \}1 - 91/10\} = \}1/110\} = 10$

### IV    Application and Discussion

See Exhibit 22.2.

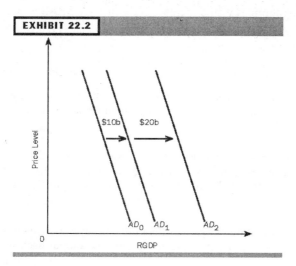

EXHIBIT 22.2

Section 14.4 Fiscal Policy and the AD/AS Model

I     Review

Budget deficits can be used to <u>stimulate</u> the economy when it is operating at less than full capacity.

Increasing g overnment s pending, r educing t axes, a nd e xpanding t ransfer p ayments i ncreases c onsumption, investment and government spending and causes the aggregate demand curve to shift to the <u>right</u>.

The effect of this increased aggregate demand depends on the position of the initial macroeconomic <u>equilibrium</u>. If policy change is of the right <u>magnitude</u> and timing, expansionary fiscal policy can move an economy out of <u>recession</u> to full employment.

When the economy is at full employment, expansionary fiscal policy will only result in an <u>increase</u> in the price level in the long run. Increases in aggregate demand cause output to rise above the <u>full</u> employment level in the short run. Pressure on input markets causes wages and other input prices to <u>increase,</u> which shifts the SRAS curve to the <u>left</u> until a new short-run equilibrium is reached at the <u>full</u> capacity level of output.

Contractionary fiscal policy has the potential to <u>dampen</u> the inflationary pressure of an overheated economy. Decreased government spending, increased taxes, or reductions in transfer payments will shift the aggregate demand curve to the <u>left</u>. If the initial short-run equilibrium is at a level of output <u>greater</u> than the economy's full productive capacity, such policies will move the economy back toward full employment real GDP and dampen the inflationary pressure.

If the initial equilibrium is at the full employment real GDP, contractionary fiscal policy will result in a short-run equilibrium at a <u>lower</u> level of output. The prices of labor and other inputs <u>fall</u>, which causes the SRAS curve to shift to the <u>right</u>. Input prices will continue to fall until new short-run equilibrium is reached at the <u>full</u> employment level of output. The only change in the long run will be a decrease in the <u>price</u> level.

II     True/False

1.  False. Tax cuts are a tool of expansionary fiscal policy. Tax cuts increase consumers' disposable income and increase the profits from investment opportunities, which increase aggregate demand and shift the aggregate demand curve to the right.

# ANSWER KEY

2. True. Expansionary fiscal policy will only increase real GDP in the short run. When the economy produces at a level of output greater than its full employment output, input prices would increase and cause the SRAS to decrease. A new stable equilibrium will only occur when the economy is producing at the full employment level of real GDP. The only long-run effect of this fiscal policy will be higher prices.

## III    Multiple Choice

1. The answer is B. Expansionary fiscal policy will increase aggregate demand. With input prices remaining unchanged, output will expand along the SRAS curve until E1 is reached. The new short-run equilibrium will have a higher price level and output greater than the full employment level.

2. The answer C. The short-run equilibrium is unstable because firms want to use more resources than are available in the long run. Competition for inputs will cause their prices to rise, which will decrease SRAS. The SRAS curve will shift left until a new long-run equilibrium is reached with *SRAS*1 at E2. The economy will produce the original full employment real GDP and the price level will be higher.

3. The answer is B. When the economy is producing a level of output greater than full employment real GDP in short-run equilibrium, upward pressure on input prices will move the SRAS curve to the left and output back to the long-run equilibrium.

4. The answer is B. To dampen the inflationary potential of the economy, the government should pursue contractionary fiscal policy and shift the aggregate demand curve to the left. Increasing government spending will expand the deficit and shift the aggregate demand curve to the right.

## IV    Application and Discussion

Going to war without equivalent tax increases is like pursuing expansionary fiscal policy. Increased government spending increases aggregate demand. Output increases in the short run as long as input prices remain constant. If the economy is producing at less than full employment, as in World War II, the expansion will not place much upward pressure on input prices. If the economy starts a war at full employment, as in the Vietnam War, increased aggregate demand will result in increased input prices and a shift in the SRAS to the left resulting in greater price level increases.

## Section 14.5 Automatic Stabilizers

## I    Review

Automatic <u>stabilizers</u> are changes in government transfer payments and tax collections that automatically counter business cycle fluctuations. They work <u>without</u> legislative or executive branch action.

The personal income <u>tax</u> is an automatic stabilizer. Income taxes vary <u>directly</u> with income. Taxes change by a <u>greater</u> percent than income when income increases or decreases, so changes in <u>disposable</u> income are not as great as changes in income.

Other income and profit-based taxes also <u>fall</u> during a recession partially offsetting the effects of declining income and profits on the economy.

The unemployment <u>compensation</u> program is another automatic stabilizer. During recessions as unemployment <u>rises</u>, unemployment compensation provides <u>income</u> to the unemployed. During boom times as unemployment <u>falls</u>, these government payments also decline.

The system of <u>public</u> assistance provides another example of an automatic stabilizer.

## II    True/False

1. True. Ophelia's disposable income would fall by less than her earnings because of automatic stabilizers. Her tax liability would fall by a greater proportion than her income because of the progressive nature of the income tax. She might also have been eligible for unemployment compensation or public assistance, which would prevent her disposable income from falling as much as her income.

# ANSWER KEY

2. False. The primary benefit of automatic stabilizers is that they require no legislative action, so there is no lag in the response of these tools to fluctuations in the business cycle.

## III   Multiple Choice

1. The answer is B. The automatic stabilizers will reduce the negative effects of the recession on aggregate demand. Disposable income and consumption will fall but not by as much as they would without the stabilizers. Aggregate demand will decrease but by less than it would without the automatic stabilizers.

2. The answer is D. Martha and George find their income falling by $25,000 but their disposable income only falls by $17,500. This happens because the fall in their income causes their tax rate to change. When their income was $50,000, they paid $10,000 in tax and had a disposable income of $40,000. When their income fell to $25,000 their tax payments fell to $2,500 and the disposable income was $22,500. The automatic stabilizer minimizes the effect of a recession by reducing the impact on consumption.

## IV   Application and Discussion

The tax would be automatic and would certainly fluctuate over the business cycle. But the balanced budget tax would be an automatic de-stabilizer. Currently, spending automatically rises during a recession and taxes automatically fall, creating an expansionary fiscal policy. The opposite happens in a boom time. The balanced budget tax would eliminate the effects of these automatic stabilizers. The balanced budget tax idea would increase taxes during a recession and reduce taxes during a boom. This would reduce aggregate demand even more in a recession and increase it during a boom period. The balance budget tax would eliminate the government's ability to carry out fiscal policy using either automatic stabilizers or legislative action.

## Section 14.6 Possible Obstacles to Effective Fiscal Policy

### I   Review

If government borrows to pay for deficit spending it increases the overall demand for loanable funds and drives interest rates up.

*Ceteris paribus,* higher interest rates will result in less private spending on goods and services.

When increased government spending drives up interest rates and chokes off private spending it is called crowding out.

In the open economy, budget deficits increase the demand for loanable funds, raise interest rates, and lead to an appreciation in the value of the dollar relative to other currencies.

The lag between the time that a fiscal response is desired and the time an appropriate policy is implemented and its effects felt is considerable.

### II   True/False

1. False. Higher interest rates increase the costs of borrowing and lead to less private spending. Higher interest rates mean that it is more costly to borrow in order to buy a car, a home, or other interest-sensitive goods. In addition, businesses must pay more to borrow in order to buy new capital equipment.

2. True. Higher interest rates attract foreign investors. To invest in the U.S., foreigners have to buy dollars with foreign currency. The increase in the demand for dollars causes the dollar to increase in value.

### III   Multiple Choice

1. The answer is C. Borrowing by the federal government represents an increase in the demand for loanable funds. Such an increase will lead to an increase in interest rates.

2. The answer is B. The time lags involved in implementing fiscal policy are considerable. Once a policy has been determined, it must be reviewed by both the president and congress. Significant delays exist in spending on public works projects due to the time needed to get bids from contractors, complete environmental impact studies, etc.

3. The answer is B. Higher U.S. interest rates will attract funds from abroad. In order to invest in the U.S. economy, foreigners will first have to convert their currencies into dollars. The increase in the demand for dollars will cause the dollar to appreciate, making foreign goods relatively cheaper in the United States and U.S. exports relatively more expensive in other countries. Americans will import more and foreigners will buy fewer U.S. exports. Thus U.S. net exports $(X - M)$ will decrease. In other words, budget deficits "crowd out" net exports via their effects on exchange rates.

## IV    Application and Discussion

The claim that the tax cut may lead to higher interest rates is plausible because a reduction in tax rates may lead to greater consumer spending and higher incomes through the multiplier effect. The higher incomes lead to a greater demand for money and higher interest rates.

## Section 14.7 Supply-Side Fiscal Policy

## I    Review

Supply-side economists encourage government to <u>reduce</u> taxes, deregulate, and increase spending on research and development because they think that these types of policies lead to <u>greater</u> economic growth.

Supply-siders believe that savings and investment could be improved through <u>lower</u> taxes.

Supply-siders believe that lower marginal tax rates will <u>raise</u> after-tax earnings and lead people to work <u>more</u> than they would otherwise.

According to supply-side economists, higher tax rates <u>discourage</u> investment and encourage investors to spend more time and effort seeking tax <u>shelters</u>.

According to the Laffer curve, an increase in tax rates when taxes are low will <u>increase</u> tax revenues. When tax rates are high, however, an increase in taxes will <u>reduce</u> tax revenue.

A tax cut can lead to increases in short-run aggregate <u>supply</u>, long-run aggregate <u>supply</u>, and to an increase in <u>aggregate</u> demand.

## II    True/False

1. False. Supply-siders believe that both aggregate supply *and* aggregate demand are affected by fiscal policy.

2. False. In order to combat high unemployment, Kennedy took the advice of his economic advisors and proposed a reduction in marginal tax rates and an increase in government spending in order to stimulate the economy.

## III    Multiple Choice

1. The answer is D. Supply-side proponents believe that people work and invest in order to earn after-tax income. Because lower tax rates mean more after-tax income, they believe that tax cuts will result in more work and more investment.

2. The answer is D. Supply-side policies such as reductions in tax rates and regulations, and investments in research and development, will create long-term effects on income, savings, and capital formation, shifting both the *SRAS* curve and the *LRAS* curve rightward. As income rises, it is spent, shifting the *AD* curve to the right.

3. The answer is C. Both Kennedy and Reagan advocated reductions in marginal tax rates in order to spur the economy. In both cases it appears that the rate reductions helped the economy grow.

## IV     Application and Discussion

Supply-siders would prefer an across-the-board tax cut because they believe it would stimulate aggregate supply *and* aggregate demand. According to supply-side proponents, tax cuts not only give workers more take-home pay but lower taxes give workers and investors greater incentive to work, save, and invest. These things shift the aggregate demand and the aggregate supply curves to the right. The other alternative gives taxpayers more disposable income, but it only serves to increase consumption. There's no supply-side effect with rebates and interest deductions. In fact, consumers are likely to save even less if they can deduct credit card interest.

## Section 14.8 The National Debt

## I     Review

Typically, the federal government funds deficit spending by issuing <u>bonds</u>, or IOUs. The sum total of the values of all outstanding bonds constitutes the federal <u>debt</u>.

From 1960 through 1997, the federal budget was in <u>deficit</u> every year except 1969, when the government ran a small <u>surplus</u>.

Historically, the largest budget deficits occur during <u>war</u> years. In the 1980s, however, deficits soared because tax <u>cuts</u> were not matched by reductions in government <u>spending</u>.

During the late 1990's the federal government ran <u>surpluses</u> in its budget. Recently, however, due to tax cuts, the war on terrorism, and the 2001 recession, the federal government has run budget <u>deficits</u>.

Although arguments can be made that the generation of <u>taxpayers</u> living at the time that the debt is issued shoulders the true cost of the debt, there is no denying that issuance of debt involves some <u>intergenerational</u> transfer of incomes. Long after the debt is issued a new generation of taxpayers must make <u>interest</u> payments on the debt.

Future generations, however, may also receive <u>benefits</u> from debt incurred by prior generations, especially if the debt is used to promote <u>expansion</u> of economic activity or provide vital <u>infrastructure</u> for the future.

## II     True/False

1. False. The debt is not a "life-threatening" problem. The size of the debt, in terms of GDP, is not as large now as it was in the 1940s and 1950s.

2. True. Future generations must make interest payments on the debt.

## III     Multiple Choice

1. The answer is C. In 2002 the national debt was equal to about 60 percent of GDP.

2. The answer is D. Budget surpluses add to national savings, and reduce interest rates. Lower interest rates stimulate private investment.

3. The answer is B. Since future generations must pay the interest on the national debt, they will have to pay higher taxes.

## IV     Application and Discussion

A large national debt can influence our balance of trade, $(X - M)$. A large national debt requires borrowing on the part of the federal government. Such borrowing increases the overall demand for loanable funds and causes interest rates to increase. Higher interest rates attract foreign investors who must buy dollars with foreign currencies. This increases the demand for dollars in the foreign exchange market and causes the dollar to appreciate in value making foreign imports relatively cheaper in the United States and U.S. exports relatively more expensive in other countries. This causes net exports $(X - M)$ to decrease. This, of course, means that America's balance of trade $(X - M)$ moves toward a deficit.

# ANSWER KEY

# CHAPTER 15 MONEY AND THE BANKING SYSTEM

Section 15.1 Money

## I    Review

Money is anything that is generally accepted in <u>exchange</u> for goods and services.

In colonial America, <u>commodities</u> such as tobacco and wampum were sometimes used as money. The main disadvantage of using commodities as money is that they tend to <u>deteriorate</u> after a few trades.

Coins made of precious metal such as gold and silver have been used as <u>money</u> for thousands of years due to their durability.

Currency consists of coins and <u>paper</u> that institutions or governments have created to be used as money. In the United States, the Federal Reserve System issues paper currency in various denominations called Federal Reserve <u>Notes</u>.

Currency that has been officially declared to be money is a form of <u>legal</u> tender.

Most of the money that Americans use for day-to-day transactions are assets in checking accounts called <u>demand</u> deposits.

In the United States, checking accounts have replaced paper and metallic currency as the major form of money used in large transactions for several reasons, including ease and <u>safety</u> of transactions, lower <u>transactions</u> costs, and transactions <u>records</u>.

Nontransaction deposits are fund accounts against which the depositor cannot directly write <u>checks</u>.

Money market mutual funds are interest-earning accounts provided by brokers who pool funds into <u>short</u>-term investments like <u>Treasury</u> bills.

Stocks and bonds are considered nonmonetary <u>assets</u>.

The ease with which one asset can be converted into another asset or into goods and services is referred to as <u>liquidity</u>. Money is a more <u>liquid</u> asset than stocks and bonds.

The narrow definition of money, called <u>M1</u>, consists of currency, checkable deposits, and travelers' checks, while a broader measure, called <u>M2</u> consists of M1 plus savings account, <u>time</u> deposits, and money market mutual funds.

## II    True/False

1. True. Time deposits, deposits that are made for a specific period of time like six months or a year, are also called "CDs."

2. False. Economists don't consider stocks and bonds to be money. They are assets, but their values fluctuate with market conditions and it takes days to convert stocks and bonds into cash.

3. False. The only thing "backing" the U.S. money supply is people's faith that it will continue to be accepted in exchange for goods and services.

## III    Multiple Choice

1. The answer is A. Checkable deposits are forms of transactions accounts that can easily be converted into currency or used to buy goods and services directly.

2. The answer is D. Credit cards are not money, but rather a convenient means of carrying out transactions. Credit card payments are guaranteed loans available on demand to users.

3. The answer is D. M1 is defined as currency, checkable deposits, and travelers' checks.

4. The answer is C. M1 consists of currency, checkable deposits, and travelers' checks while M2 includes all of the things in M1 *plus* savings accounts, small time deposits (less than $100,000), and money market mutual funds.

## IV Application and Discussion

In terms of liquidity the assets should be ranked as shown in Exhibit 23.1.

**EXHIBIT 23.1**

| Rank | Asset |
|------|-------|
| 1 | Currency |
| 4 | An Automobile |
| 2 | Checkable Deposit |
| 5 | A House |
| 3 | A Six-Month Certificate of Deposit |

Of course currency is the most liquid of all assets since it can be exchanged immediately and just about anywhere for goods or services. Checkable deposits aren't quite as liquid because checks are not universally accepted and you have to show some identification when you make the exchange. A six-month CD is probably next since you can withdraw your funds on any business day if you are willing to pay an interest penalty for early withdrawal. You might argue that an automobile is pretty liquid and maybe you can turn your car into cash pretty quickly. Over the weekend, if you can find a buyer, a car may be more liquid than a certificate of deposit.

A house is the least liquid, for sure, because it takes weeks or even months for a deal to become final, even after a buyer is found.

## Section 15.2 The Functions of Money

## I Review

The primary function of money is to serve as a medium of <u>exchange</u>. Money facilitates <u>transactions</u>, and lowers <u>transactions</u> costs.

In the absence of money, when individuals pay for goods and services by offering other goods and services in exchange, it is called <u>barter</u>.

Barter is <u>inefficient</u> because several trades may be necessary before individuals are able to get the goods or services they desire.

Besides serving as a medium of exchange, money is also both a <u>standard</u> of value and a <u>store</u> of value.

Because money makes it easier to borrow and repay loans, it also serves as a means of <u>deferred</u> payment.

## II True/False

1. False. She is using it as a store of value, as a means of storing her wealth.

2. True. He is using money in exchange for the coffee.

### III   Multiple Choice

1. The answer is D. Money serves as a medium of exchange, a store of value, a means of deferred payment, and as a unit of account. Its value fluctuates far less than the value of individual commodities.

2. The answer is C. In barter economies, money is not used as a medium of exchange, but rather goods and services are traded for other goods and services.

### IV   Application and Discussion

You could pay your tuition by offering goods you owned or by offering to provide specific services. If you were a good basketball player or a talented musician, maybe your university would make a deal and give you an education in return for your playing for the basketball team or performing in the band. Perhaps you could do clerical work in the administration building, take care of the grounds, or tutor.

If, on the other hand, you had things to offer that the university didn't want you'd be in a spot. You *could* try and find someone that had what the university wanted and, in turn, wanted what you had, and make a trade indirectly, but that could be very time-consuming. Makes you appreciate money!

## Section 15.3 How Banks Create Money

### I   Review

The biggest players in the banking industry are <u>commercial</u> banks. They are distinct from most other financial institutions in that they can create <u>demand</u> deposits.

Aside from commercial banks, the banking system includes two other types of financial institutions: Savings and <u>Loan</u> Associations, and <u>Credit</u> Unions.

Financial institutions serve as depositories for savings and liquid assets that are used by individuals and firms for <u>transaction</u> purposes. In making loans, financial institutions act as <u>intermediaries</u> between savers, who supply funds, and borrowers seeking to invest.

If someone borrows $1,000 from a bank, the bank usually will simply add $1,000 to their checking account, and in doing so will create new <u>money</u>.

Banks make profits by collecting higher interest payments on the <u>loans</u> they make than the interest they pay their depositors for those funds. The more loans a bank makes, the more <u>profit</u> it makes.

Reserve <u>requirements</u> require banks to keep on hand a quantity of cash or reserve accounts with the Federal Reserve equal to a prescribed proportion of their <u>checkable</u> deposits.

Our banking system is sometimes called a <u>fractional</u> reserve system because banks are required to maintain cash and other reserves equal to some specified fraction of their checkable deposits.

The <u>assets</u> of a bank are those things of value that the bank owns, including cash, bonds, buildings and outstanding loans. Financial obligations that banks have to others are called <u>liabilities</u>.

Banks create new <u>money</u> when they increase demand deposits through the process of creating loans.

### II   True/False

1. False. Reserve requirements exist primarily to control the amount of bank deposits, and thus the size of the money supply.

2. True. The money that people owe to banks for loans is an asset. For most banks, loans are their biggest asset item.

# ANSWER KEY

III   Multiple Choice

1.  The answer is D. A bank's capital is the difference between its assets, including cash, buildings, and loans, minus its liabilities, which include deposits.

2.  The answer is A. Required reserves are a specified percentage of their deposits. If, for example, the required reserve ratio is 10 percent, banks would have to keep $100 in reserves for every $1,000 in deposits.

3.  The answer is B. Banks create money when they increase checking accounts (demand deposits) through the process of creating loans.

IV   Application and Discussion

If you deposit $1,000 in a bank, calculate how much the bank must keep as required reserves and how much it can loan out under each of the following required reserve ratios.

**EXHIBIT 23.2**

| Required Reserve Ratio | Amount of Required Reserves | Amount of Loanable Funds |
|---|---|---|
| 1. 5% | $ 50 | $950 |
| 2. 10% | 100 | 900 |
| 3. 15% | 150 | 850 |
| 4. 20% | 200 | 800 |
| 5. 25% | 250 | 750 |

## Section 15.4 The Money Multiplier

I   Review

New loans create money directly, but they also create <u>excess</u> reserves in other banks, which leads to still further increases in both loans and the stock of <u>money</u>.

When borrowers get their loans, the borrowed money will likely be <u>spent</u> on something, such as new machinery, a new house, or greater store inventories.

The money <u>multiplier</u> is 1 divided by the reserve requirement. The larger the reserve requirement, the <u>smaller</u> the money multiplier.

In all, the potential impact of a new checkable deposit on the money supply is equal to the amount of the initial deposit times the <u>money</u> multiplier.

If borrowers do not spend all of their newly acquired checkable deposits, or if they wait a considerable period of time before doing so, the actual impact of an initial deposit is <u>less</u> than that indicated by the money multiplier.

When a person pays a loan back to a bank by writing a check for the amount due, demand deposits <u>decline</u> and the money stock is <u>reduced</u>.

II   True/False

1.  False. If banks maintained reserves of 100 percent, deposits would leave the money supply unaffected.

2.  True. The larger the reserve requirement, the smaller the money multiplier. With a 10 percent reserve requirement, for example, the multiplier is 10. With a 50 percent requirement, the multiplier is only 2.

III    Multiple Choice

1. The answer is C. To calculate the money multiplier, turn the reserve requirement into a fraction, in this case 1/5, and divide it into 1. Thus

   1/(1/5) = 5.

2. The answer is B. Because 25 percent is one-fourth, the money multiplier is 4 or

   1/(1/4).

IV    Application and Discussion

Without banks or checkable deposits, the creation of $10,000 in new currency simply adds $10,000 to the money supply. With a banking system the potential impact is equal to the $10,000 in new currency multiplied by the money multiplier, which in this case is 10. The $10,000 in new currency, if it finds its way into the banking system, has the potential of creating $100,000.

Section 15.5 The Collapse of America's Banking System, 1920–1933

I    Review

From the stock market crash of 1929 until 1933, the U.S. economy contracted and the entire banking system nearly collapsed, leading to an unprecedented <u>decline</u> in the money stock.

As depositors lost confidence in banks and converted their deposits to currency, bank reserves <u>fell</u>.

In early 1933, newly elected President Franklin Roosevelt declared a national bank <u>holiday</u>, closing every bank in the country for nearly two weeks. In mid-1933 passage of federal <u>deposit</u> insurance greatly strengthened depositor confidence in banks.

The combination of the Federal Deposit <u>Insurance</u> Corporation (FDIC) and the government's greater willingness to assist distressed banks has largely eliminated bank <u>runs</u>.

II    True/False

1. False. As people withdrew their money from the banking system, and as banks failed, the money supply decreased dramatically.

2. False. Deposit insurance and government's willingness to help distressed banks have virtually eliminated bank runs.

III    Multiple Choice

1. The answer is C. Actually, the industry consisted of thousands of separate, small banks in which depositors had no confidence.

2. The answer is C. In 1932, one-fourth of the labor force was out of work.

3. The answer is A. More than a thousand savings and loan or "thrift" institutions went bankrupt. Depositors were saved by federal deposit insurance, and taxpayers paid much of the bill.

IV    Application and Discussion

Because these loans are used to finance consumer purchases, and construction, bank deposits can be described as "out there working in the community, building businesses and providing jobs."

Of course, banks keep some cash on hand in order to meet the needs of customers who want to withdraw funds. If too many people show up at once, however, as they did during the Great Depression, the bank won't have the cash it needs to satisfy all its depositors.

# CHAPTER 16 THE FEDERAL RESERVE SYSTEM AND MONETARY POLICY

Section 16.1 The Federal Reserve System

I   Review

In most countries, the job of manipulating the supply of money belongs to the <u>central</u> bank. In the United States, this function is performed by the Federal <u>Reserve</u> System or "Fed."

The Fed is governed by a seven-member Board of <u>Governors</u>. Each member is appointed by the <u>President</u> of the United States.

An important aspect of the Fed's operation is that it has a considerable amount of <u>independence</u> from both the executive and legislative branches of government.

Many key policy decisions of the Federal Reserve are actually made by its Federal Open <u>Market</u> Committee.

II   True/False

1.  False. The Federal Reserve is our central bank. The Treasury Department is an entirely different entity that serves as the fiscal agent for the U.S. government.

2.  True. There are 12 district banks located in important cities like Boston, New York, Dallas, and San Francisco.

III   MULTIPLE CHOICE

1.  The answer is C. The Fed is not involved in collecting taxes.

2.  The answer is C. The Federal Reserve System was established with passage of the Federal Reserve Act in 1913.

IV   Application and Discussion

Person A is Jesse "The Body" Ventura, Governor of Minnesota. Person B is Christine Todd Whitman, former Governor of New Jersey and currently head of the Environmental Protection Agency. Person C is Alan Greenspan, current chairman of the Fed's Board of Governors.

Section 16.2 The Quantity Equation of Money

I   Review

A useful relationship that helps us understand the role that money plays in the national economy is called the quantity equation of <u>money</u>..

In the equation, $M$ stands for the <u>money</u> supply, $V$ is the <u>velocity</u> of money, $P$ is the average level of <u>prices</u>, and $Y$ represents the <u>quantity</u> of goods and services produced in a given time period.

Velocity represents the average number of times that a <u>dollar</u> is used in purchasing final goods or services in a one-year period.

The quantity equation of <u>money</u> is a useful tool when we try to assess the impact of a change in the stock of <u>money</u> on the aggregate economy.

The inflation rate tends to <u>rise</u> more in periods of monetary expansion than in periods of slower monetary growth.

# ANSWER KEY

## II    True/False

1.  True. In both cases, total spending will rise.

2.  True. In the equation of exchange, where $MV = PY$, an increase in the money supply, $M$, will require an increase in $P$, if $V$ and $Y$ are fixed.

3.  True. Historical evidence reveals a positive correlation between growth in the stock of money and inflation. This positive correlation exists in other countries too.

## III    Multiple Choice

1.  The answer is B. The velocity of money refers to the "turnover" rate, or the intensity with which money is used.

2.  The answer is C. $MV = PY$

## IV    Application and Discussion

According to the equation of exchange, if $M$ goes way up, while $V$ and $Y$ don't change very much, the price level ($P$) will rise. That's what happened. Spain experienced rapid inflation. In fact, prices rose all over Europe, especially near trading centers, as the new money was sent. It was the increase in the available currency (the new gold) relative to the available goods and services that fueled the increasing level of prices.

## Section 16.3 Implementing Monetary Policy: Tools of the Fed

### I    Review

In the United States, monetary policy is the responsibility of the Federal Reserve Board of <u>Governors</u> and the Federal Open Market <u>Committee</u>.

The Fed has three major tools that it can use to control the supply of money: open <u>market</u> operations, changes in <u>reserve</u> requirements, and changes in the <u>discount</u> rate.

When the Fed wants to increase the money supply, it can <u>buy</u> bonds. When it wants to decrease the money supply, it can <u>sell</u> bonds.

If the Fed lowers reserve requirements, the money supply will <u>increase</u>. When it raises reserve requirements, the money supply will <u>decrease</u>.

The interest rate that the Fed charges banks for borrowing funds is called the <u>discount</u> rate. Commercial banks borrow from each other in the <u>federal</u> funds market.

If the Fed wants to increase the money supply, it <u>lowers</u> the discount rate. When it wants to decrease the money supply, it <u>raises</u> the discount rate.

### II    True/False

1.  True. The purchase and sale of government securities in the open market is the most powerful and often-used tool of the Fed.

2.  False. The federal funds rate is the interest rate that banks charge one another to borrow reserves.

### III    Multiple Choice

1.  The answer is C. If the Fed wants to increase the rate of growth of the money supply, it will buy government securities. When the Fed buys the securities, it writes a check to the seller, which will likely be deposited in a bank account, thereby increasing the money stock in the form of added deposits. Each of the other alternatives will lead to a decrease in the rate of growth of the money supply.

2. The answer is B. By requiring banks to hold more money as reserves, the Fed reduces the amount of money that banks can loan out, and decreases the money supply.

3. The answer is D. Open market sales, a higher discount rate, and higher reserve requirements would all tend to reduce the size of the money stock. Option (A) is fiscal policy, which is not controlled by the Fed but by congress and the president. Option (B) is also controlled by congress and the president, not by the Fed. Of course, Option (C) is expansionary monetary policy.

## IV    Application and Discussion

In order to restore price stability (i.e., lower the rate of inflation) you could (1) sell government securities, (2) raise reserve requirements on bank deposits, and/or (3) raise the discount rate. You could also try to use moral persuasion and urge banks to be more selective in making loans. This is all *contractionary* monetary policy.

## Section 16.4 Money, Interest Rates, and Aggregate Demand

### I    Review

The <u>money</u> market is where money demand and supply determine the equilibrium nominal interest rate.

The three motives for holding money as an asset are: to make <u>transactions</u>, to be prepared for <u>unexpected</u> expenses, and to maintain a stock of <u>liquid</u> assets.

The quantity of money demanded varies inversely with the <u>interest</u> rate, but the supply of money is almost perfectly <u>inelastic</u> with respect to interest rates.

Thus, when drawn on a graph, the demand curve for money slopes <u>downward</u> while the supply curve for money is <u>vertical</u>.

When we combine the money demand and supply curves, money market equilibrium occurs at that nominal <u>interest</u> rate where the quantity of money demanded equals the quantity of money <u>supplied</u>.

Rising national income <u>increases</u> the demand for money and shifts the money demand curve to the right.

An increase in the money supply is shown as a shift in the money supply curve to the <u>right</u>, which causes the equilibrium interest rate to <u>decrease</u>.

A reduction in the money supply is shown as a shift in the money supply curve to the <u>left</u>, which causes the equilibrium interest rate to <u>increase</u>.

If the Fed pursues an expansionary monetary policy, it will <u>buy</u> bonds, resulting in <u>lower</u> interest rates and an <u>increase</u> in aggregate demand.

If the Fed pursues a contractionary monetary policy, it will sell <u>bonds</u>, resulting in <u>higher</u> interest rates and a <u>decrease</u> in aggregate demand.

The Fed cannot completely control the growth in the <u>money</u> supply and the <u>interest</u> rate at the same time.

### II    True/False

1. True. At lower interest rates people tend to hold more money because the opportunity cost of holding money, rather than other assets that earn more interest, is lower.

2. True. At each and every interest rate the quantity of money supplied will be greater.

3. False. The money supply is controlled by the Federal Reserve.

# ANSWER KEY

## III    Multiple Choice

1. The answer is B. If Ramesh holds money in order to be able to pay unexpected bills, he is holding it for precautionary purposes.

2. The answer is A. This is pure transactions demand. She carries $2.00 because she needs it to make a transaction—to buy lunch.

3. The answer is C. The demand curve for money shows how much money individuals will hold at different rates of interest. Because the opportunity cost of holding money is higher at higher interest rates, the quantity of money demanded is inversely related to the interest rate.

4. The answer is B. If the central bank increases the money supply faster than output and continues to do so, even at full employment, inflation will result.

## IV    Application and Discussion

You are the only one who can answer this. Most college students carry money for transaction purposes, although you may carry cab fare or phone money "just in case." If you analyze your checking account balance, you may find that you are carrying more than you need for transactions. If so, why do you keep more in your checking account than you need for transactions when those funds could be earning higher interest elsewhere?

## Section 16.5 Expansionary and Contractionary Monetary Policy

### I    Review

An increase in the money supply when the economy is operating at <u>less</u> than full employment can lead to an <u>increase</u> in real GDP and the price level. An increase in the money supply at <u>full</u> employment, however, can temporarily increase real <u>GDP</u>, but in the long run, only the <u>price</u> level will rise.

When the economy is operating beyond full employment, the Fed can combat inflation through <u>contractionary</u> monetary policy. If the Fed pursues contractionary monetary policy when the economy is at full employment it may cause a <u>recession</u>.

In an open economy, expansionary monetary policy will lead to a(n) <u>decrease</u> in the foreign exchange value of the dollar. Contractionary monetary policy will lead to a(n) <u>increase</u> in the foreign exchange value of the dollar.

### II    True/False

1. False. An increase in the money supply when the economy is at full employment will cause the price level to increase.

2. True. Expansionary monetary policy leads to depreciation in the value of the dollar, which makes U.S. products cheaper for foreigners.

3. False. The Fed cut the federal funds rate in order to help the economy avoid a recession.

### III    Multiple Choice

1. The answer is C. Since the economy is operating at less than full employment and since pessimistic businesses are unlikely to increase investment spending, at current interest rates an increase in the money supply, which stimulates aggregate demand, is appropriate (of course, a tax cut could stimulate aggregate demand, but that's fiscal policy).

2. The answer is D. The information given indicates that the economy is "overheated" and operating beyond full employment. Appropriate monetary policy would be a decrease in the rate of monetary growth, aimed at reducing aggregate demand.

## IV    Application and Discussion

A)  If the economy is operating at less than full employment, as at point $E0$, above, an increase in the money supply will cause total spending to increase, resulting in a rightward shift in the $AD$ curve. Output will expand, the price level will rise and, if the Fed does it right, full employment output will be attained.

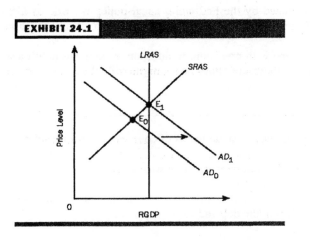

B)  If the economy is already at full employment at $E0$, an increase in the money supply will shift the $AD$ curve to the right to $AD1$, with the short-run equilibrium moving to $E1$, increasing the price level, increasing output temporarily, and putting upward pressure on wages and other input prices. As input prices rise, higher costs of production will shift the $SRAS$ curve to the left to $SRAS1$. The price level will continue to rise, output will fall back to the full employment level and a new long-run equilibrium will be established at $E2$.

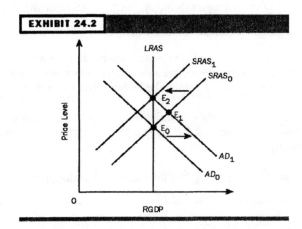

## Section 16.6 Problems in Implementing Monetary Policy and Fiscal Policy

### I    Review

The problem of time lags in making policy changes is <u>less</u> acute for monetary policy than it is for fiscal policy.

One limitation of monetary policy is that it must be carried out through the <u>commercial</u> banking system. This is not a big problem when the Fed initiates <u>contractionary</u> monetary policy, because banks must take actions that <u>reduce</u> the money supply when the Fed sells bonds, increases the discount rate, or raises the reserve requirement. It is a problem, however, when the Fed initiates <u>expansionary</u> monetary policy because it cannot force banks to make the loans that create new <u>money</u>.

A second limitation of monetary policy is the fact that the Fed has no control over <u>global</u> and non-bank institutions that loan money.

A third problem is the fact that monetary policy is conducted by the Fed while <u>fiscal</u> policy is made by Congress and the president. A macroeconomic problem arises if Congress and the president have <u>different</u> objectives than those of the Fed.

Economists <u>cannot</u> forecast the future course of the economy with precision. In addition, economists <u>aren't</u> always sure what effects specific policies will have on the economy, nor are they sure about how long it will take before a policy <u>impacts</u> the economy.

## II     True/False

1. False. The Fed implements monetary policy. Fiscal policy is in the hands of congress and the president.

2. False. Economists may be better at this than astrologers, but they are often wrong.

3. True. The currency crisis slowed growth in East Asia and led to a depreciation in the value of the currencies of some East Asian countries. Both of these led to a reduction in the demand for U.S. products.

## III     Multiple Choice

1. The answer is B. Although implementation of both types of policy have pitfalls, the budgetary process, which is necessary with fiscal policy, is not a problem with monetary policy. For example, if a tax cut is deemed necessary for good fiscal policy, a bill has to be introduced in the House of Representatives, debated, passed in both the House and Senate, etc. With monetary policy, the Fed can decide on a course of action and implement it immediately.

2. The answer is D. The Fed cannot force banks to take actions it may deem appropriate. This is especially true in the case of expansionary monetary policy. The Fed can provide banks with excess reserves, but it cannot force them to make the loans necessary for monetary expansion.

## IV     Application and Discussion

The main concern about having Congress conduct monetary policy is that our elected representatives might have an incentive to try and boost the money supply before an election in order to lower the unemployment rate and get more votes. Political control of the money supply was something Congress actually tried to avoid when it passed the Federal Reserve Act in 1913.

Economists and others worry that political control of the money supply would create an inflationary bias in monetary policy. This concern is supported by studies that show that inflation is lowest in countries that have relatively independent central banks like the Fed in the United States and the Bundesbank in Germany.

Of course, monetary policy is very important and perhaps voters should be able to register their approval or disapproval of the conduct of monetary policy at the ballot box.

# CHAPTER 17 ISSUES IN MACROECONOMIC THEORY AND POLICY

Section 17.1 The Phillips Curve

## I    REVIEW

The inverse relationship between the rate of unemployment and the rate of inflation is called the <u>Phillips</u> curve.

Some economists believe that inflation can help reduce unemployment by causing a <u>decrease</u> in real wages. When the real wage goes down, unemployment goes <u>down</u> because a lower real wage makes it profitable for employers to hire <u>more</u> labor than before.

## II    True/False

1.  False. It shows the relationship between the inflation rate and the unemployment rate.

2.  False. There was an inverse or negative relationship. Lower rates of unemployment corresponded to higher rates of inflation.

## III    Multiple Choice

1.  The answer is D. If output prices rise faster than money wages, workers' wages buy less and real wages fall. Lower real wages provide an incentive for employers to hire more labor and the unemployment rate will go down.

2.  The answer is A. If it is steeper at higher rates of inflation it means that you have to have higher rates of inflation in order to get unemployment down.

## IV    Application & Discussion

A)  In order to move from A to B, the Fed would have to use contractionary monetary policy in order to reduce the rate of inflation. T his w ould i nclude s elling b onds, r aising t he discount rate, and raising the reserve requirement. These policies would cause the money supply to contract, reducing the inflation rate, but increasing unemployment.

B)  In order to move from B to A, the Fed would use expansionary policy, including bond purchases, a reduction in the discount rate, and a reduction in the reserve requirement. These would cause the money supply to increase. The increase                          in                          the                          money supply would lead to a higher rate of inflation, but a lower rate of unemployment.

Section 17.2 The Phillips Curve Over Time

## I    Review

In the 1960s, economic policy makers believed the Phillips curve described the <u>tradeoff</u> between two macroeconomic goals, inflation and u nemployment. A r eduction i n u nemployment c ould b e a chieved a t t he c ost o f <u>m ore</u> i nflation, a nd i nflation could be reduced at the cost of <u>higher</u> unemployment.

Other economists, such as Milton <u>Friedman</u> and Edmund <u>Phelps</u>, thought the Phillips Curve represented only a <u>short</u>-term trade-off between inflation and unemployment. This trade-off was the result of <u>unanticipated</u> inflation.

Starting in the 1 970s, t he P hillips c urve r elationship b roke d own. P oints s ince 1 969 s how a <u>w orsening</u> t rade-off b etween inflation and unemployment.

The long-run Phillips Curve shows the relation between unemployment rates and the inflation rate when actual and <u>expected</u> inflation rates are the same. It is vertical at the <u>natural</u> rate of unemployment, so in the long run the <u>natural</u> rate of unemployment holds at any rate of inflation. Regardless of monetary or fiscal stimulus, output and employment will be at the natural rate in the <u>long</u> run.

# ANSWER KEY

In the <u>short</u> run, a trade-off between inflation and unemployment exists. An increase in aggregate demand caused by expansionary monetary or fiscal policy will result in <u>increased</u> prices. If the resulting inflation was <u>unanticipated</u>, real wages and other input prices will fall. As real wages fall, firms will <u>expand</u> output and hire more workers, so unemployment falls.

Eventually, workers negotiate for <u>higher</u> wages. In response to the increase in wages, firms <u>reduce</u> output and employment, so unemployment increases. The short-run Phillips curve will shift to the <u>right</u> and <u>higher</u> rates of inflation will be required to achieve <u>any</u> level of unemployment.

There is no trade-off between the inflation rate and the unemployment rate in the <u>long</u> run. Neither fiscal nor monetary policy is <u>effective</u> at reducing unemployment below the natural rate in the long run.

An adverse supply shock leads to a <u>higher</u> price level and less output. A favorable supply shock leads to a <u>lower</u> price level and a <u>lower</u> rate of unemployment.

## II    True/False

1.  False. The natural rate of unemployment is associated with the full employment of available labor and it is determined by supply and demand in the labor markets when everyone correctly anticipates the rate of inflation. The natural rate of unemployment will not be affected by inflation. In the short run, unanticipated rates of inflation result in changes in real wages and short-run changes in employment and unemployment rates.

2.  True. The long-run Phillips curve shows the unemployment rate that exists when the actual and expected inflation rates are the same.

3.  False. Macroeconomic policy can only reduce unemployment below the natural rate in the short run. The tradeoff between inflation and unemployment occurs only in the short run when the inflation rate differs from the anticipated rate. In the long run, the people will not be fooled by inflation and the unemployment rate will be at the natural rate independent of the inflation rate.

4.  True. An adverse supply shock results in higher production costs which cause a leftward shift in the *SRAS* curve.

## III    Multiple Choice

1.  The answer is A. In the short run, the Phillips curve shows a negative relationship between the inflation rate and the unemployment rate.

2.  The answer is C. As long as the Balabanish people underestimate the rate of inflation, macroeconomic policy will cause real wages to fall, firms to expand output and employment, and unemployment to fall. If workers don't realize their real wages have fallen, they will not renegotiate higher wage rates and unemployment will remain lower than the natural rate. In a normal place, the fall in real wages is only temporary. When labor realizes real wages have fallen they negotiate for higher wages causing real wages to increase and unemployment to rise to the natural rate.

3.  The answer is B. Along the short-run Phillips curve, the anticipated or expected rate of inflation is the same. Points B and C have the same actual inflation rate but the expected rate differs. The expected rate and the actual rate at C equals the actual rate of inflation at B.

## IV    Application and Discussion

1.  Increases in the money supply that are more rapid than the increase in productive capacity will cause inflation. The increased inflation will more than likely increase expected inflation rates and result in the short-run Phillips curve shifting to the right.

2.  Reducing the money supply after the Civil War is contractionary monetary policy. It would cause aggregate demand to decrease and the price level to fall. Real wages would increase and firms would reduce output and hire fewer workers. Unemployment would rise; the economy would move along the short-run Phillips curve to the right. Eventually wages would decline, real wages would fall, and firms would hire more workers until the natural rate of unemployment was achieved. People would probably also reduce their anticipated rate of inflation.

# ANSWER KEY

## Section 17.3 Rational Expectations

### I     Review

An increasing number of economists believe that people can <u>anticipate</u> the moves of policy makers and alter their behavior to <u>neutralize</u> the intended impact of government action.

Rational <u>expectations</u> economists believe that wages and prices are <u>flexible</u>, and that workers and consumers incorporate the likely consequences of government policy changes quickly into their expectations.

Rational expectations theory suggests that government economic policies have <u>limited</u> effectiveness. According to this view, monetary and fiscal policy will affect output and employment only if people are <u>fooled</u> by policy moves so that they do not modify their behavior in ways that reduce policy effectiveness.

An unanticipated increase in the money supply will result in an <u>increase</u> in both output and employment in the <u>short</u> run. An increase in the money supply that is fully anticipated will result in a higher <u>price</u> level, but will have no effect on <u>output</u>.

### II     True/False

1. True. They believe that people are quick to spot policy moves and that they modify their behavior accordingly.

2. False. They believe that wages and prices are flexible and change quickly with changes in supply and/or demand.

### III     Multiple Choice

1. The answer is B. If the change is unanticipated, the economy will move to point B, because the increase in aggregate demand will cause an unanticipated increase in the price level and lead to a reduction in real wages. Lower real wages will give employers an incentive to increase output and employment.

2. The answer is C. If the change in *AD* is anticipated, workers and others will build a higher expected rate of inflation into their expectations. As *AD* shifts right the *SRAS* curve will shift left as workers ask for wage increases and as other suppliers increase their prices. The economy will move from point A to point C.

### IV     Application and Discussion

A) An unanticipated increase in the rate of inflation should result in lower real wages and a lower unemployment rate in the short run.

B) Because the actual rate of inflation matches the expected rate, the unemployment rate won't change.

C) Unexpected deflation will raise real wages and cause the unemployment rate to rise in the short run.

## Section 17.4 Wage and Price Controls and Indexing

### I     Review

The government uses <u>incomes</u> policy when it imposes controls on wages and prices to manage inflation. These policies set <u>limits</u> to the permitted increase in wages and prices.

There are two arguments in support of wage and price controls. First, price and wage controls <u>directly</u> reduce the rate of inflation. Second, they also lower inflationary <u>expectations</u> and the psychology that leads to <u>cost</u>-push inflation.

Wage and price controls have many disadvantages. They are difficult and costly to <u>enforce</u>. They result in <u>shortages</u> of goods, services, and labor. Price controls result in the <u>misallocation</u> of resources.

Because prices are higher in monopolistic industries, stimulating <u>competition</u> in monopolistic industries may reduce inflationary pressure.

Indexing is another way to control the problems posed by inflation. It protects people from unanticipated price increases by writing contracts that automatically change prices of goods or services whenever the overall price level changes. Agreements are effectively written in terms of dollars of constant purchasing power.

Indexing seems to eliminate most of the wealth transfers associated with unexpected inflation, but it would probably worsen inflation because one price increase will automatically lead to another.

In periods of rapid inflation the administrative costs of indexing will be high because prices may have to be changed frequently. Indexing also reduces the ability of relative prices to reallocate resources to where they are more valuable. Indexing also has high costs associated with negotiating contracts.

Because not every price can be indexed, inflation results in some wealth redistribution even with indexing.

## II    True/False

1.  False. Indexing does not eliminate price increases; it may even result in greater inflation. Indexing eliminates the effects of unanticipated inflation by writing contracts that automatically change prices of goods, services, and factors whenever the overall price level changes. While indexing protects people from the effects of unanticipated inflation, it may actually worsen inflation because price increases will result in more price increases.

2.  False. Jawboning is a form of voluntary price controls. Governments use moral suasion to get businesses to stick to voluntary price increase guidelines.

3.  True. Wage and price controls reduce inflation and may lower inflationary expectations, but they distort the role of relative prices in the allocation of resources. Changes in relative prices cause resources to move to uses where they are most highly valued. Wage and price controls will limit price increases that are signals that particular goods and resources are more highly valued.

## III    Multiple Choice

1.  The answer is B. Wage and price control is government regulation of prices. Government officials have to spend resources reviewing price changes to make sure they are in line with the pricing guidelines. Government officials have to force firms and unions follow the price guidelines, which may require legal and police resources.

2.  The answer is A. With price controls holding the price to $P0$, suppliers have no incentive to bring more skateboards to the market. They will continue to sell $Q0$ and a shortage of skateboards will be created because consumers want to buy $Q1$ at the price $P0$.

3.  The answer is D. Price controls prevent firms from increasing prices but if demand falls, skateboarding companies will lower their price until the quantity supplied equals the quantity demanded. Equilibrium will be reached at point D. If firms believed the decrease in demand was only temporary, firms might not lower their prices if they believed their new, lower prices would become the new skateboard price guideline.

## IV    Application and Discussion

1.  A)  Wage and price controls keep furniture prices from rising to the market clearing level, which causes a shortage. The shortage means that buyers are willing to pay more for additional furniture than sellers would require, so increasing furniture production would be efficient. Resources that would be best used to produce furniture are being used to produce other less valuable things.
    B)  When people stand in line they are wasting resources. They could be using their human resources to produce other things of value or to consume leisure. Queuing wastes the economy's labor resources.
    C)  Government uses resources to find cases where firms are not following the guidelines and to take companies violating the guidelines to court. These resources do not produce any goods or services that people value. If they were used in enforcing wage and price controls they could be used to produce more goods and services.

2. Inflation results in the redistribution of income from people on fixed incomes, input suppliers with long-term contracts, and creditors. The redistribution effects make certain types of economic activity more risky. Excessive inflation makes it harder to plan for the future. Inflation also imposes menu costs on firms that must constantly readjust their prices. Inflation also imposes shoe leather costs on consumers and producers that results from having to take actions to protect your assets.

3. This is a normative question. Your answer would reflect which type of costs you feel are most important.

# CHAPTER 18 INTERNATIONAL TRADE

## Section 18.1 The Growth in World Trade

### I    Review

Although it varies from country to country, in a typical year about <u>15</u> percent of the world's output is traded in international markets. In 1998, about **12** percent of U.S. output was <u>exported</u>, and imports amounted to over <u>13</u> percent of GDP.

The United States has important trading relations with many countries, but our three most important partners are <u>Canada</u>, <u>Mexico</u>, and Japan.

### II    True/False

1.  True. As a percentage of our total imports, goods from Canada represented 19 percent of total goods imported. While goods from China constituted 8 percent.

2.  False. Over time the importance of international trade to the U.S. has increased dramatically.

### III    Multiple Choice

1.  The answer is C. Canada is our most important trading partner. Closeness and similar cultures may explain the extent of our trade. Canada accounts for almost twice the value of U.S. exports in goods as our second most important trading partner, Japan. The value of our imports from Canada exceeds the value of Japanese imports by almost 36 percent. Changes to the trade environment in Canada will affect our economy.

2.  The answer is A. Since 1940 international trade has become more important for the U.S. economy. Exports and imports have doubled as a percent of U.S. Gross Domestic Product. Both consumers and producers would be more aware of any reduction in their ability to trade with other countries.

### IV    Application and Discussion

For the world as a whole total exports have to equal total imports, since one country's exports are another country's imports, Consequently, if total exports are $6.7 trillion, total imports must also equal $6.7 trillion.

## Section 18.2 Comparative Advantage and Gains from Trade

### I    Review

We know trade is economically <u>beneficial</u> because it exists. Since trade is <u>voluntary</u> and people <u>maximize</u> utility, participants must expect trade to make them better off.

David Ricardo developed the explanation of the mutual <u>benefits</u> of trade. His theory is the Principle of <u>Comparative</u> Advantage.

The Principle of Comparative Advantage states that a nation can gain from trade by <u>specializing</u> in the production of those goods it can produce at a <u>lower</u> opportunity cost than other countries. This principle also applies to regions and individuals.

A country has a(n) <u>absolute</u> advantage in producing a good when it uses fewer resources to produce a given level of output. A country may have a comparative advantage in a good without having an absolute advantage when the production of the good has <u>lower</u> opportunity costs than its trading partner.

By specializing in the production of goods and services for which they have the lowest opportunity cost, trading partners can produce <u>more</u> of all of the goods they trade. <u>Differences</u> in opportunity costs between trading partners provide the <u>incentive</u> to gain from specialization and trade.

1.  True. We know voluntary trade makes people better because individuals are utility maximizers. Trade allows people and nations to specialize in the production of the goods and services they are relatively best at producing. This allows trading partners to produce more of the traded goods.

2.  False. History has shown that as the economy of a country grows, self-sufficiency declines and specialization increases. Trade between individuals and countries is necessary once specialization occurs in production.

3.  False. The United States has an absolute advantage in the production of shirts. If the United States also has an absolute advantage in the production of potatoes, Malawi may have a comparative advantage in shirt production. Comparative advantage is based on a country's relative opportunity costs. The United States may have to give up more potatoes to produce one more shirt than Malawi does.

## III    MULTIPLE CHOICE

1.  The answer is D. The opportunity cost of a bottle of wine is the water you have to give up to produce the wine. In the time it takes a worker to produce one bottle of wine (1/500 of a person year) they could produce two bottles of sparkling water ([1/500]31000).

2.  The answer is B. Singapore has an absolute advantage in both the production of rice and shirts since one worker can produce more of each product in a year. Bangladesh has a comparative advantage in the production of rice, since the opportunity cost of rice production is lower. To produce six more pounds of rice would require the resources that could produce only two shirts in Bangladesh, while in Singapore it would use the resources that could produce three shirts.

## IV    Application and Discussion

A.  Fill in the following table assuming that they *each* spend four hours a day fishing and four hours a day harvesting berries.

|        | Fish per day | Buckets of Berries per day |
|--------|--------------|----------------------------|
| Bud    | 16 =<br>(4 fish per hour 3<br>4 hours) | 8 =<br>(2 buckets per hour 3<br>4 hours) |
| Larry  | 8 =<br>(2 fish per hour 3<br>4 hours) | 8 =<br>(2 bucket per hour 3<br>4 hours) |
| Total  | 24 fish      | 16 buckets of berries |

B.  Bud is better off because he has more of both fish and the same number of berries and works no more time than Larry. Bud has an absolute advantage in fish production.

C.  Assume that Larry and Bud operate on straight-line production possibility curves.

|        | Opportunity Cost<br>of a Bucket of Berries | Opportunity Cost<br>of a Fish |
|--------|--------------------------------------------|-------------------------------|
| Bud    | 2 fish                                     | 1/2 bucket<br>of berries      |
| Larry  | 1 fish                                     | 1 bucket of berries           |

D.  Larry has a comparative advantage in berry production since he has the relatively lowest opportunity cost. Bud has a comparative advantage in fish production since his opportunity cost is lower.

E. Larry can produce 16 buckets of berries in an eight hour day. Bud can produce 32 fish in an eight hour day. The gains from trade are the eight extra fish produced. Specialization in the activity in which Larry and Bud have the lowest opportunity cost allows them to increase the number of fish they produce with neither more time worked nor fewer berries consumed.

## Section 18.3 Supply and Demand in International Trade

### I    Review

The difference between what a consumer is willing to pay for a given amount of a good and what they have to pay is called consumer <u>surplus</u>. Consumers benefit from paying less than they would be willing to pay.

Producer <u>surplus</u> is the difference between the revenue the producer receives for selling a given amount of the good and the amount the producer is willing to accept. Producers benefit from receiving more than they would be willing to accept.

The demand curve represents the <u>maximum</u> prices consumers are willing and able to pay for different quantities of a good or service. The supply curve represents the <u>minimum</u> prices at which suppliers are willing to offer different quantities of the good or service.

As long as the maximum price the consumer is willing to pay <u>exceeds</u> the minimum price the supplier requires for one more unit of a good or service, there are mutually <u>beneficial</u> opportunities for trade.

When markets reach the <u>equilibrium</u> price, all the opportunities for mutually beneficial trade have taken place and the sum of consumer and producer surplus is <u>maximized</u>.

When a country trades with the rest of the world the price of the exported good is <u>higher</u> after trade than before. Domestic consumers <u>lose</u> from free trade because their consumer surplus is <u>reduced</u>. However, these losses are offset by the positive gains captured by domestic <u>producers</u>. On net, export trade <u>increases</u> domestic wealth.

When an economy trades with the rest of the world, the price of the imported good is <u>lower</u> after trade than before. Domestic consumers <u>gain</u> from free trade because their consumer surplus is <u>increased</u>. However, domestic producers lose because their producer surplus is <u>reduced</u>. On net, import trade <u>increases</u> domestic wealth since the gain to consumers <u>exceeds</u> the loss to producers.

### II    True/False

1. False. For voluntary trade to take place *both* consumers and producers must benefit. Consumer surplus will be positive as long as the price consumers pay is no greater than the maximum they would be willing to pay. However, producers will not trade if that price is less than the minimum price they would be willing to accept, and producer surplus is negative. Voluntary trade will increase both consumer and producer surplus.

2. True. If the United States has a comparative advantage in farm products, we would expect that farm prices would increase with world trade and the U.S. farm industry producer surplus would increase. If the United States has a comparative disadvantage in cement production, we would expect cement prices would decline with world trade and the producer surplus in the U.S. cement industry would decrease. The domestic industries would be supporting their own self-interest with these opposing views on free trade.

3. False. Greece would have a comparative advantage if it could produce bananas at a relatively lower cost than other countries. The fact that other countries can sell bananas at a lower price than Greece suggests that Greece does not have the relatively lowest opportunity cost for banana production.

### III    Multiple Choice

1. The answer is B. The producer surplus is the difference between the price the producer receives and the minimum price he would be willing to accept for a particular quantity of the product.

2. The answer is B. Consumer surplus is reduced because consumers pay a higher price, *PAT*, and consume a lower quantity of the good.

3. The answer is D. Producer surplus is increased because producers receive a higher price, *PAT*, after trade and produce a larger output, *QAT*, of the good. A portion of the increased producer surplus equal to the area b is a transfer from consumers.

4. The answer is D. Export trade increases the producer surplus and reduces the consumer surplus generated in the country by the good. Net wealth increases though because the gain to producers exceeds the loss to consumers. In Exhibit 1 the area d represents the gains from trade.

## IV    Application and Discussion

A) With international trade the Botswana price would fall to the world price. Once apples were available at the world price there would be no reason to pay more for apples.

B) Domestic production equals *QDT*. Apple imports equal an amount (*QAT – QDT*).

C) See the modified Exhibit 26.1.

D) See the modified Exhibit 26.1.

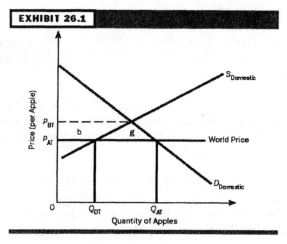

E) The increased consumer surplus equals a part, b, that is transferred from producers and a part, g, that results from the increased consumption. If consumers were required to compensate producers for their loss, they would give up b, but they would still receive increased consumer surplus equal to g.

## Section 18.4 Tariffs, Import Quotas, and Subsidies

### I    Review

A tariff is a(n) <u>tax</u> on imported goods.

Tariffs are used today to <u>protect</u> domestic industry from foreign competition.

A tariff is a <u>tax</u> on imported goods. Tariffs result in <u>higher</u> prices to domestic producers and <u>lower</u> sales and revenues to foreign producers.

# ANSWER KEY

Domestic producers gain from tariff protection, but domestic consumers lose <u>more</u> than producers gain.

The <u>infant</u> industry argument in support of tariffs argues that tariff protection helps new industries reach the scale of operation at which they can be efficient.

Because tariffs increase domestic production, they are often supported as a mechanism for reducing <u>unemployment</u> in protected industries.

However, employment in other industries may suffer if exports are reduced because of <u>retaliation</u> by other countries. Export industries may also suffer because with a reduction in foreign imports, other countries will have <u>fewer</u> dollars to purchase our exports.

Tariffs are also supported for national security reasons. They can be used to limit our <u>dependence</u> on foreign producers for those goods vital to our national security.

A tariff on a good will create <u>benefits</u> for producers and <u>losses</u> for consumers. Even when losses exceed the benefits a tariff may be adopted, because producers are a more effective <u>lobbying</u> group for a tariff than consumer groups who lobby against tariffs.

An import <u>quota</u> limits international trade by defining a maximum number of units of a good that can be imported in a time period. Unlike tariffs, governments do not collect any <u>revenue</u> with a quota.

Import quotas make domestic producers <u>better</u> off, but make domestic consumers <u>worse</u> off.

Governments may also try to encourage exports by <u>subsidizing</u> producers. With subsidies producers export goods, not because their costs are relatively <u>lower</u> than other countries, but because their costs have been <u>artificially</u> lowered by transferring income from <u>taxpayers</u> to exporters.

## II    True/False

1. False. A tariff is a tax, which increases the tax revenues of the country that imposes it. A quota limits the quantity of foreign goods entering a country but generates no tax revenue. Both tariffs and quotas result in higher domestic prices. The higher price paid for the import goes to the foreign producers under a quota.

2. False. Government subsidies can be used to lower the price at which a domestic producer can sell his product in other countries, but they do not change the cost of producing the good. Government subsidies shift part of the cost of producing export goods to taxpayers. Since export subsidies do not change the cost of production, they cannot change a country's comparative advantage. Such subsidies distort trade patterns and are inefficient.

3. False. Employment in other industries may suffer because of a tariff on steel. Jobs may be lost in the U.S. export sector because other countries may retaliate and impose tariffs on U.S. goods. Other countries may also import less because the U.S. tariff limits their ability to earn dollars. Finally, tariffs will raise the price of steel and make all goods for which steel is an input more expensive, which will result in reduced output and employment in these industries.

## III    Multiple Choice

1. The answer is D. Domestic producers are willing to supply more shoes to the market at the higher domestic price.

2. The answer is C. Consumer surplus is reduced by a tariff because consumers buy less of the protected good and pay a higher price for it.

3. The answer is B. The price of imports with the tariff, $P1$, is still lower than the no tariff price of $P0$. Consumers will pay no more than the lower import price for sweaters.

4. The answer is D. Consumer surplus is reduced by a tariff because consumers buy fewer sweaters and pay a higher price for them.

# ANSWER KEY

5.  The answer is C. The net loss in welfare equals the reduced consumer surplus (the area a + b + c + d) minus the gain in producer surplus (the area a) and government revenues (the area c).

## IV    Application and Discussion

A.  When the tariff is removed we would expect 1) domestic maple syrup prices would fall; 2) domestic maple syrup production would decline; 3) total maple syrup consumption in the United States would increase; and 4) the amount of imported maple syrup would increase.

B.  This is a sticky problem. If NAFTA did, in fact, result in a decrease in the U.S. production of maple syrup, U.S. jobs may be lost in that particular industry. However, with freer trade, it is likely that compensating increases in jobs in other industries will occur when Canada removes its tariff barriers, the United States will export more and this will create more jobs. Canadian maple syrup makers will also have more dollars to buy more U.S. goods. Even without the compensating job gains, removing the tariff on maple syrup is good policy because consumers would be able to compensate workers and producers from their increased consumer surplus and still be better off.

# CHAPTER 19 INTERNATIONAL FINANCE

Section 19.1 The Balance of Payments

I     Review

The record of all the international transactions of a nation over a year is called the balance of <u>payments</u>. The balance of payments is divided into three main sections: the <u>current</u> account, the <u>capital</u> account, and the <u>statistical</u> <u>discrepancy</u>.

The current account is made up of imports and <u>exports</u> of goods and services. When a foreign buyer buys a good from a U.S. producer, the foreigner usually pays for the good in U.S. <u>dollars</u>.

All exports of U.S. goods are considered <u>credit</u> items in the U.S. balance of payments.

When a U.S. buyer buys an imported good the buyer usually pays in <u>foreign</u> currency. All imports of foreign goods are considered <u>debit</u> items in the U.S. balance of payments.

When the United States gives foreign aid to another country or when private individuals send money to relatives in foreign countries, it is recorded as a <u>debit</u> in the U.S. balance of payments.

The balance on current account is the net amount of credits and <u>debits</u> after adding up all transactions of goods, services, investment income, and fund transfers.

Countries finance deficits in their current accounts by running <u>surpluses</u> in their capital accounts.

II     True/False

1.   True. We have run deficits in our balance on current account since the early 1980s.

2.   False. "balance of trade" records imports and exports of goods and services. The current account balance also includes trade in services and transfers.

3.   True. Overall the debits in the balance of payments equal the credits. If a nation buys more goods and services abroad than it sells, so that debits exceed credits on current account, it must settle its debts by borrowing abroad. When financial capital flows in, it is counted as an offsetting credit on the capital account.

III     Multiple Choice

1.   The answer is B. When Singapore Airlines buys an airplane made in the United States, its an export that counts as a credit to our current account. The British purchase of U.S. government bonds is also a credit, but it is a credit on our capital account.

2.   The answer is C. When foreigners' tastes move in favor of American goods, they buy more from us and because our exports count as credits on current account, our balance on current account moves toward surplus.

IV     Application and Discussion

See Exhibit 27.1.

**EXHIBIT 27.1**

| | Credit | Debit |
|---|---|---|
| 1. Americans buy autos from Japan. | ☐ | ☒ |
| 2. American tourists travel to Japan. | ☐ | ☒ |
| 3. Japanese consumers buy rice grown in the United States. | ☒ | ☐ |
| 4. United States gives foreign aid to Rwanda. | ☐ | ☒ |
| 5. General Motors, a U.S. company, earns profits in France. | ☒ | ☐ |
| 6. Royal Dutch Shell earns profits from its U.S. operations. | ☐ | ☒ |
| 7. General Motors builds a new plant in Vietnam. | ☐ | ☒ |
| 8. Japanese investors purchase U.S. government bonds. | ☒ | ☐ |

1. Imports of goods are debits in the current account.

2. When American tourists travel to Japan, they buy foreign-produced services, including the use of hotels, sightseeing tours, etc. They are "importing" services; it is classified as a debit.

3. When we export rice to Japan, it's a credit on our current account.

4. Foreign aid creates a debit in the U.S. balance of payments because it gives foreigners added claims against the United States in the form of dollars.

5. General Motor's profits can be viewed as compensation for the use of capital services. Thus, the United States obtains claims on foreign countries just as it does when it exports goods, only in this case, a U.S. corporation is exporting capital services.

6. When a Dutch company earns profits from U.S. operations, it obtains compensation for the use of its capital services and the transaction is classified as a debit on the U.S. balance of payments.

7. When General Motors builds a plant abroad it is a capital outflow and classified as a debit on our capital account.

8. When foreign investors buy U.S. bonds it is a capital inflow and classified as a credit on our capital account.

## Section 19.2 Exchange Rates

### I    Review

When U.S. consumers buy goods from foreigners, the sellers of those goods want to be paid in their <u>domestic</u> currency. As a result, U.S. importers must <u>buy</u> foreign currency with dollars in order to finance their purchases. Similarly, people in other countries buying goods made in America must <u>sell</u> their currencies to obtain U.S. dollars in order to pay for those goods.

The price of a unit of one foreign currency in terms of another is called the <u>exchange</u> rate.

The demand for foreign currencies is what economists call <u>derived</u> demand. The more foreign goods are demanded, the <u>more</u> of that foreign currency that will be needed to pay for those goods. Increased demand for a currency will cause the exchange value of that currency to <u>rise</u>.

Foreign currency is supplied by foreigners who want to buy <u>exports</u> of a particular nation. For example, the more U.S. goods that foreigners demand, the <u>more</u> of their currency they will supply.

# ANSWER KEY

The equilibrium exchange rate for a currency is determined by the supply and <u>demand</u> for that currency in the foreign exchange market.

## II    True/False

1. False. The exchange value of the dollar is determined by the supply and demand for dollars on the foreign exchange market.

2. True. If it costs more dollars to buy a euro, it will become more expensive for Americans to buy European goods and they will buy fewer of those goods.

## III    Multiple Choice

1. The answer is D. When Americans have to give up $2 to obtain a euro, rather than $1, it makes European goods more expensive. they will import fewer European goods.

2. The answer is D. The equilibrium dollar-yen exchange rate will increase when the supply of Yen decreases.

## IV    Application and Discussion

1. Those who would be pleased by an appreciation of the dollar include (B) Americans planning to take trips to Europe, and (E) Americans who enjoy French cheese. An appreciation in the value of the dollar will make it less expensive for American tourists to travel in Europe, and it will make imported French cheese cheaper. Because an appreciation in the value of the dollar makes American goods more expensive to foreigners, the others won't like it.

2. Those who would be pleased by a depreciation in the value of the dollar include (A) American farmers, (C) General Motors stockholders, and (D) Japanese students planning to study in America. A depreciation in the value of the dollar makes American goods less expensive to Japanese consumers, or anyone else who holds yen. On the other hand, a depreciation in the dollar makes Japanese goods more expensive to Americans. American farmers will be pleased because their oranges, rice, wheat, and other products will become less expensive for Japanese consumers and those consumers will buy more U.S. agricultural products. GM stockholders will like it because a weaker dollar makes Toyotas, Hondas, and other Japanese vehicles more expensive. Japanese students like it because their yen will go farther in terms of what they can buy.

## Section 19.3 Equilibrium Changes in the Foreign Exchange Market

## I    Review

Any force that shifts either the demand for or supply of a currency will shift the <u>equilibrium</u> in the foreign exchange market, leading to a new <u>exchange</u> rate.

Factors that shift the demand for and supply of a currency include changes in <u>tastes</u> for goods and services, changes in <u>income</u>, changes in real <u>interest</u> rates, and changes in relative <u>inflation</u> rates.

If incomes increase in the United States, Americans will buy <u>more</u> goods, including European goods. This increase in demand for foreign goods will cause an <u>increase</u> in the demand for euros.

If incomes decrease in the United States, Americans will buy <u>fewer</u> goods, including European goods. This decrease in demand for foreign goods will cause a <u>decrease</u> in the demand for euros.

If interest rates in the United States increase relative to those in Europe, other things equal, the rate of return on U.S. investments will <u>increase</u> relative to that on European investments. European investors seeking higher rates of return will <u>buy</u> dollars with euros.

If interest rates in the United States decrease relative to those in Europe, investors will <u>sell</u> dollars and <u>buy</u> euros in order to make European investments.

If the rate of inflation is higher in Europe than in the United States, European products will become <u>more</u> expensive to U.S. consumers. Americans will <u>decrease</u> the quantity of European goods they demand and their demand for euros will <u>decrease</u>. At the same time, the higher rate of European inflation will make U.S. goods relatively <u>less</u> expensive to Europeans. This will lead Europeans to <u>increase</u> the quantity of U.S. goods demanded and lead to an <u>increase</u> in the supply of euros.

Overall, the result of the higher rate of European inflation will be a new, <u>lower</u>, equilibrium price for the euro.

If speculators believe that the price of a country's currency is going to rise they will buy <u>more</u> of that currency.

## II    True/False

1. False. The equilibrium exchange rate of currencies like the dollar, the yen, and the euro, change constantly as factors such as tastes, incomes, relative interest rates, and relative inflation rates change. Changes in the exchange value of the dollar are followed daily in the business section of your newspaper.

2. True. Higher U.S. interest rates will attract investors who will have to buy dollars with foreign currency in order to earn interest in the United States. The increased demand for dollars will cause the dollar to appreciate in value.

3. True. If the dollar appreciates it will buy more yen. Janelle can buy more goods and services in Japan with the dollars she has saved. For example, if the dollar goes from $1 = ¥100 to $1 = ¥150 she can buy ¥150 worth of goods and services with each dollar, whereas before she could buy only ¥100 worth of goods and services with each dollar.

## III    Multiple Choice

1. The answer is B. If Americans' incomes rise, they will buy more goods, including those made in foreign countries. As they buy foreign goods, they supply dollars and demand foreign currencies, like yen and euros, on the foreign exchange market. The supply curve for dollars shifts to the right.

2. The answer is B. The dollar can now buy more yen and more Japanese goods. It has appreciated or become "stronger."

## IV    Application and Discussion

See Exhibit 27.2

**EXHIBIT 27.2**

|  | Supply of Dollars | Demand for Dollars | Equilibrium Exchange Rate |
|---|---|---|---|
| 1. Americans buy more European goods. | increase | same | decrease |
| 2. Europeans invest in U.S. stock market. | same | increase | increase |
| 3. European tourists flock to the United States. | same | increase | increase |
| 4. Europeans buy U.S. government bonds. | same | increase | increase |
| 5. American tourists flock to Europe. | increase | same | decrease |

1. When Americans buy European goods they supply dollars and demand Euros. The increases supply of dollars shifts the supply curve to the right and the equilibrium exchange rate for dollars decreases.

2.  When Europeans buy U.S. stocks, they must use their currency to buy dollars in order to make the investments. Europeans supply their currency and demand dollars. The increased demand for dollars causes the equilibrium exchange rate for dollars to rise.

3.  When European tourists visit America they must convert their currency to dollars. Thus, they supply their currency and demand dollars, causing the equilibrium exchange rate of the dollar to rise.

4.  When Europeans buy U.S. government bonds they must do so with dollars. To get the necessary dollars they supply their currency and demand dollars. The exchange value of the dollar rises.

5.  When Americans visit Europe they need euros, pounds, and other European currency. They supply dollars and demand those foreign currencies. The increase in the supply of dollars pushes the equilibrium exchange rate of the dollar down.

## Section 19.4 Flexible Exchange Rates

### I    Review

Since 1973 the world has essentially operated on a system of <u>flexible</u> exchange rates. Governments, however, sometimes <u>intervene</u> in foreign exchange markets in order to prop up an exchange rate that they consider too <u>low</u> or to depress an exchange rate they consider to be too <u>high</u>.

Prior to 1973, the world operated on a system of <u>fixed</u> exchange rates called the Bretton Woods system.

When exchange rates change they affect not only the currency market but the <u>product</u> markets as well. For example, if the dollar increases in value relative to other currencies, the relative prices of foreign goods for Americans will <u>decrease</u>. Foreigners will find that the stronger dollar makes U.S. products <u>more</u> expensive for them.

Since the advent of flexible exchange rates, world trade has not only continued, but <u>expanded</u>.

Changes in exchange rates occur <u>more</u> often under a flexible-rate system than they do under a fixed-rate system, but the changes are much <u>smaller</u> than the drastic, overnight revaluations of currencies under the fixed-rate system.

Under a fixed-rate system, as the supply and demand for currencies <u>change</u>, currency prices are not allowed to shift to a new equilibrium, leading to surpluses and <u>shortages</u> of currencies.

One major argument against flexible exchange rates is that they cause <u>uncertainty</u> and may lead to a decrease in the level of world trade.

Another argument against flexible rates is that they may allow governments to pursue expansionary fiscal and monetary policies that may lead to <u>inflation</u>.

### II    True/False

1.  False. Since 1973 the world has operated under a system of flexible exchange rates under which exchange values are determined by the forces of supply and demand.

2.  True. Governments intervene from time to time in order to prop up exchange rates that they consider to low, or to depress exchange rates that they consider to be too high.

### III    Multiple Choice

1.  The answer is A. A decrease in demand for the currency will cause the value of the currency to depreciate (i.e. one dollar will buy fewer Euros). The country's exports will become less expensive and foreign goods will become more expensive.

2.  The answer is D. A major argument against flexible rates is that they create uncertainty.

# ANSWER KEY

3. The answer is B. When currency rates are fixed, changes in supply and/or demand can lead to shortages or surpluses of currencies.

## IV    APPLICATION

A shift toward more expansionary monetary policy by the Fed would cause the exchange value of the dollar to decrease (depreciate) and would tend to move America's balance of trade toward surplus. Expansionary monetary policy would lower U.S. interest rates, boost incomes temporarily, and tend to cause inflation. All of these will result in a new, lower exchange value for the dollar. The weaker dollar will make U.S. exports cheaper to the rest of the world, so that our exports will increase. In turn, foreign goods will cost more imports will decrease.